D1391255

Romani in Britain

Romani in Britain

The Afterlife of a Language

YARON MATRAS

EDINBURGH UNIVERSITY PRESS

Edinburgh University Press Ltd
22 George Square, Edinburgh

www.euppublishing.com

Typeset in 10/12 Times New Roman
by Servis Filmsetting Ltd, Stockport, Cheshire, and
printed and bound in Great Britain by
CPI Antony Rowe, Chippenham and Eastbourne

A CIP record for this book is available from the British Library

ISBN 978 0 7486 3904 5 (hardback)

Contents

Figures, Tables and Maps

Figures

Tables

Maps

Abbreviations

abl.	ablative
adj.	adjective
adv.	adverb
AR	Angloromani
comp.	complementiser
conj.	conjunction
dat.	dative
dem.	demonstrative
ER	European Romani
excl.	exclamation
f.	feminine
gen.	genitive
id.	idiom
imp.	imperative
instr.	instrumental
inter.	interrogative
interj.	interjection
JGLS	*Journal of the Gypsy Lore Society*
loc.	locative
m.	masculine
MIA	Middle Indo-Aryan
n.	noun
nom.	nominative
num.	numeral
obl.	oblique
OIA	Old Indo-Aryan
past.	past tense marker
pl.	plural
pr.	pronoun
prep.	preposition
sg.	singular
v.	verb

{ }   translation of Romani words and phrases in transcripts; also
          graphemes
ital   Romani-derived words in longer transcripts
/   speaker self-repair

Preface

British Romanies are very much aware of a 'lost' form of language that was once used for a wide range of conversational functions within their community. Romani had been one of the minority languages of Britain for over four hundred years. It has even left a legacy within English in the form of Romani-origin colloquial words like *pal, chavvy, mush, minge* and *kushti* as well as regionalisms like *gaji, nash, peeve, ladj* and *yocks*. Its decline as the everyday language of the Romani community took place during the nineteenth century, when other languages of the British Isles were also being abandoned in favour of English. However, in a way Romani has actually survived the process of language death and now enjoys a kind of linguistic 'afterlife': Romanies in Britain continue to use a variety of speech which they refer to as *Rommanis, Romimus, Romani Jibb* 'the Romani language', or sometimes *Poggaddi Jibb* 'the broken language'. Researchers have labelled it 'Angloromani'. Broadly speaking, this form of speech consists of embedding a special lexical reservoir, largely derived from Romani, into English conversation. Along with this reservoir come certain word-formation techniques for enriching the lexicon as well as various stylistic and some structural particularities. Contemporary Angloromani thus remains the living speech variety of one of Britain's oldest and most established ethnic minorities.

Conservative or inflected dialects of Romani were spoken in Britain up to the second half of the nineteenth century and were closely related to the Romani varieties of continental Europe, especially those spoken in the North Sea area – in Germany and Scandinavia. Speaking 'Romani' today involves in the British context essentially speaking English with Romani word insertions. Speakers therefore often struggle to define their language: is it a form of English with Romani words, or is it a separate language? The question poses a challenge not just to the popular notion of where the boundaries of a particular 'language' are, but also to a theoretical understanding of how speakers compartmentalise their repertoire of linguistic structures and utilise its individual components for specialised functions. So far, the lack of contextual data on Angloromani has made it difficult to answer these questions. Discussions of Angloromani have been limited to lexical documentation, which in turn was based largely on secondary sources, like the well-cited word list compiled with the help of Manfri Wood in Acton and Kenrick (1984), or informal word compilations such as those by Robert Dawson (2002, 2006). To the extent that phrase examples were discussed, they have consisted largely of constructed, out-of-context examples, such as those presented by Hancock (1984). Nor has there been a systematic attempt to re-assess the rich corpus of older compilations dating as far back as the late eighteenth century, most of which were edited and published in the *Journal of the Gypsy Lore Society* in the early 1900s.

Very few monograph-length studies are devoted to so-called 'mixed languages' – speech varieties that are based on a combination of structures, e.g. lexicon and grammar from two separate source languages; among them are Bakker's (1997) study of Michif, the French–Cree mixed language spoken in Canada, Mous's (2003a) description of Ma'a, the parallel lexicon used by the Mbugu people of Tanzania, and Meakins' (2007) unpublished discussion of Gurindji Kriol, an Australian mixed language. The study of the special lexical reservoirs of minority peripatetic groups is, by contrast, relatively well developed (Ladstätter & Tietze 1994, Windolph 1998, Efing 2005, and more), but largely limited to the compilation of lexicon; an exception is Binchy (1993), who offers a sociolinguistic and discourse-oriented analysis of Shelta (also Cant, Gammon), the in-group lexicon used by Irish Travellers. The Romani-based lexicons of Romani–Gypsy minorities in other countries have also received rather extensive attention at the level of lexical documentation. Of particular relevance to our topic is the recent discussion of Swedish Romani by Lindell and Thorbjörnsson-Djerf (2008). It is clear therefore that our understanding of how such bilingual mixtures emerge, how they are composed structurally, and which conversational functions are assigned to them can be further enhanced through additional studies.

In 1998 I was approached for the first time by English Gypsies who enquired about published materials on their language and sought advice on how to learn the European dialects of Romani. Such enquiries continued over the next decade. They indicated a trend towards the emergence of yet another phase in the history of this extraordinary language, one that provoked a series of research questions: What shape did the conservative or inflected British Romani language have before its decline? How was the language abandoned? What has been retained from the language and what was the motivation to retain it? How is Angloromani used today and for which purposes? And finally, which direction is the interest in learning Romani and 'revitalising' it in the community taking?

These questions were pursued over a period of several years with the help of the research team and students on the Romani Project at the School of Languages, Linguistics and Cultures of the University of Manchester. The procedure involved a survey of language use and language competence among English and Welsh Gypsies who considered themselves to be users/

speakers of 'Romani', and documentation of the material in the form of digital recordings and transcriptions. The examples presented in this book, especially in the discussion in Chapters 4 and 5 and the lexicon presented in Appendix I, all derive from this corpus of recordings. Parallel to the material obtained from speaker consultants, all published material on British Romani was surveyed. Both sets of data were annotated in a shared database, parts of which are publicly accessible online in the form of a comprehensive electronic dictionary of English Romani (http://romani.humanities.manchester.ac.uk/angloromani).

The following chapters offer an analysis of this material. In Chapter 1 I examine the question of 'languageness' in connection with the Angloromani lexicon and survey various models that have so far offered historical and typological explanations for the emergence of Angloromani and other mixed varieties. In Chapter 2 I discuss the historical origins of Romani and its split into different dialects, laying the ground for Chapter 3, where, drawing on historical sources, I discuss the inflected form of Romani that was spoken in Britain until the nineteenth century and examine its position within the Romani dialectal landscape. On the basis of the corpus of recordings, I then provide a structural outline of present-day Angloromani, in Chapter 4, and an analysis of its conversational functions and ongoing efforts to extend them, in Chapter 5.

Chapter 6 contains a summary of the historical scenario which I propose as an explanation for the emergence of Angloromani: as English took over as the principal language of conversation in a growing number of domains, Romani underwent a turnover of functions. From a language of everyday conversation its relevance was reduced to an affectionate mode of discourse, one that triggers associations with the unique values of the Romani community but is no longer used for the default transmission of content information in most everyday settings. Gradually, Romani came to symbolise an emotive mode of speech, one that activates an exclusive presuppositional domain of attitudes, values and experiences and urges the listener to interpret the speech act against such background. This specialisation of Romani for specific conversational functions is inherently connected to the tight-knit structure of the community, to its mobility and individuals' dependency on close family relations, the organisation of work within the family, and the fundamental separation between group-insiders and group-outsiders. It also carries with it a reduction of the structural resources to merely those that are of relevance to the new functions – largely lexical material. The functional turnover in the use of Romani thus leads to a process of merely selective replication of structural material in the transmission of the language across generations, with the survival primarily of lexical material and strategies of lexical formation. These are the unique conditions that grant the language its so-called 'afterlife' following language death. We may be witnessing a further turning point in the history of the language today: as English Romani Gypsies are redefining the meaning of their identity as a minority group, a new intellectual and institutional interest in language and its symbolic and practical functions (as a means of communicating with Roms from other countries) is emerging. It remains to be seen whether this will lead to a genuine revitalisation of a form of inflected Romani in Britain.

For inspiration, insights and access to the English Romani community and its language, I am grateful to a number of people, in particular Shaun Lee, Davy Jones, Dai Lee and Tommy Thompson, as well as to several dozen speaker consultants, most of whom prefer to remain anonymous. Without their support and cooperation it would not have been possible to carry out this research. Our research team has made every effort to use the insights we gained to support a number of modest projects aimed at the community and individuals within it. These included the compilation of various audiovisual teaching and learning materials for Romani, the documentation of a selection of Angloromani words and their history on an audio CD called 'Romani Soundbites', publication of an online Angloromani dictionary, participation in numerous radio programmes and lectures to staff of the Traveller Education Services in order to raise awareness of Romani, and support in translation and codification of Romani and Angloromani in family-specific contexts. I sincerely hope that the findings presented in this study will equally be of interest and benefit to our consultants and their families and community.

I am especially grateful to Charlotte Jones, Hazel Gardner, Veronica Schulman and Ruth Hill for their help in collecting, processing, annotating and archiving the data, and to Christopher While and Christa Schubert for providing technical support. I also wish to thank Thomas Acton, Peter Bakker, Victor Friedman, Dieter Halwachs, Miriam Meyerhoff and Jonathan Starbrook (Research Development Manager at the School of Languages, Linguistics and Cultures) for supporting the project's work in various ways. Much of the work that led to the present monograph was supported by a Small Grant from the British Academy (2006), by a grant from the Economic and Social Research Council (ESRC) under the Standard Grants Scheme (2006–8), and by a grant from the Arts and Humanities Research Council (AHRC) under the Research Leave Scheme (in the second half of 2008).

Readers should note that different conventions are used throughout the book for different purposes: the international transliteration system for Romani, which is common in academic discussions of the language, is used in the book in the discussion of continental Romani dialects and Romani etymologies. Its most salient features are the use of wedge accents {č, š, ž}, the use of {x} for a velar or uvular fricative, the notation of aspiration through double graphemes {ph, th, kh}, and the use of bar accents to indicate vowel length, as in {ā, ē, ī}. The International Phonetic Alphabet is used for the notation of specific sound developments and the discussion of the phonetic and phonemic value of individual sounds, incorporating symbols such as [ʃ, ʒ, ə, χ, ʊ] and so on. In citing the presentation of Romani words in published sources, the original notation is usually replicated. Finally, for the notation of Angloromani forms from the corpus of recordings, an English-based orthography is used, designed for Angloromani by the Romani Project (see Matras et al. 2007).

1 Angloromani: A Different Kind of Language?

1.1 Gypsies and Travellers in Britain

Britain has at least three distinct ethnic minorities that are usually referred to as 'Travellers' or 'Gypsies': the English (and Welsh) Gypsies, the Irish Travellers and the Scottish Travellers. They are all best recognisable by their preference for living in caravans ('trailers') in either temporary or semi-permanent dwelling sites and by their traditional specialisation in itinerant service-providing occupations. Members of the first group usually refer to themselves in everyday conversation as 'Gypsies', or more specifically as 'English Gypsies' (or in some families 'Welsh Gypsies'). They have a special vocabulary that they use in interaction among themselves, which they call 'Romanes'. Some refer to various other aspects of their culture, values and lifestyle as 'Romany', and some refer to their community as 'Romanichal'. This book is about the speech form used by members of this community: the *Romani* speech of English and Welsh Gypsies, also called 'English Romanes', or in the scholarly literature 'Angloromani'.

The story of Angloromani begins with the arrival of Romani-speaking population groups – the Roms or 'Roma' – from continental Europe in Britain, from the early sixteenth or perhaps even from the late fifteenth century onwards. It is quite likely that England, and perhaps also Wales, had had indigenous Traveller populations prior to the arrival of the Roms. Like other indigenous European Traveller groups they specialised in providing itinerant services, maintained a tight-knit community structure based predominantly on kinship relations and valued marriage strictly within their own community, thereby constituting in practice an ethnic minority, albeit one whose boundaries may have been less hermetically sealed to outsiders than those of geographically settled ethnic or religious minorities. They also appear to have had their own group-internal speech form consisting primarily, as is the case with other indigenous European Traveller populations, of a special 'cryptolalic' vocabulary, i.e. a vocabulary that is used in order to exclude outsiders by disguising key words conveying sensitive information. There is evidence dating back to the seventeenth century of a form of English

'Cant' consisting of a lexical reservoir of dialectal and archaic English forms along with camouflaged ('cryptolalic') word formations based largely on figurative exploitation of English word meanings, e.g. *stocks* for 'feet' (cf. Gotti 1999). Nevertheless, it is impossible to identify an independent Traveller community in England today whose roots are exclusively in an indigenous Traveller population, and no group is known to have preserved a form of English Cant akin to the one documented in seventeenth-century sources, though some Cant words have made their way into the Romani vocabulary of English Gypsies. It appears quite likely that Romani immigrants and indigenous English Travellers mixed, at least in some regions, to form a single community.

The Irish Travellers of Britain are immigrants from Ireland, some of them recent. They too have preserved an itinerant economy and lifestyle for many generations, and they too have a speech form of their own, referred to in the scholarly literature as 'Shelta' or sometimes 'Gammon' but known within the community itself as 'Cant'. This form of Cant has no connection to the English Traveller Cant of the seventeenth century. The fact that both unrelated speech forms are referred to by the same label tells us in this case more about the similar functions that they had in their respective social contexts than about any similarities in their structural composition or origin. Like English Cant, Shelta or Irish Traveller Cant consists of a special lexical reservoir. There is general agreement among linguists that this lexicon originates in an Irish (Gaelic) vocabulary to which various strategies of lexical distortion ('cryptolalic' strategies), such as addition, reversal or substitution of phonemes and syllables had been applied (see Ó Baoill 1994, Binchy 1994). This suggests that it was formed during a period when the ancestors of today's Irish Travellers were still speakers of Irish and actively used lexical distortion strategies to camouflage their everyday vocabulary in certain situations. Once Irish was abandoned as an everyday language, the special lexical forms were preserved within a form of Hiberno-English, making the distorted words even less recognisable to outsiders.

Scottish Travellers constitute the main group of Travellers in Scotland. The in-group lexicon used by Scottish Travellers today contains a mixture of English Cant, Irish Traveller Cant (Shelta) and Romani words (cf. Douglas 2002, Dawson 2006: 39ff), quite possibly suggesting that all three populations mixed in the formation of the present-day groups of Scottish Travellers, or else that a group of indigenous Travellers in Scotland interacted with and absorbed influences from the other two groups. Members of the Travelling communities often portray a kind of symmetrical geographical partition between Irish Travellers, Scottish Travellers, and English (and Welsh) Gypsies. But both the contemporary relations among the various groups and their history appear to be much more complex. Close contacts and family ties can be seen today, embracing the communities of English Romani Gypsies and Irish and Scottish Travellers. Quite possibly, such bonds represent an interface that has existed for many generations among Traveller groups. On the one hand, sociocultural and kinship boundaries are maintained and individuals in contemporary communities are able to define their affiliation to a particular group clearly. These boundaries are based on a sense of descent, belonging, and loyalty to a group of related families. They also have practical manifestations, one of which is the use of distinct linguistic forms in each group. But boundaries can also be crossed. Individuals of Irish Traveller background may marry English Gypsies and adopt a Romani vocabulary as a token of their acquired allegiance to a new extended family and its values and practices.

It is for this reason that the speech form of English Gypsies, just like any other language, cannot be described either as static (in the sense that it is not affected by change), or as an absolutely unambiguous indicator of an individual's ethnic origin, descent or present-day kinship affiliation. None the less, it would not be inaccurate to describe Angloromani as the speech form of the community of English and Welsh Gypsies, and to describe this community in turn as comprising by and large the descendants of Romani speakers whose ancestors had arrived in Britain from the fifteenth century onwards from the European continent, and possibly of other population groups, families and individuals, some of them apparently Travellers of indigenous origin, who may have been absorbed into this community at some point in time and so have had a share in shaping it and lending it the character and composition that it has today. There are therefore boundaries that define what Angloromani is and who uses it, even though these boundaries may, at times, be crossed or interfered with: the shape of Angloromani may change over time, and it may take on different forms when used by different individuals; it may have been in use in a particular family for many generations, or it may have been acquired by individuals who have recently married into a Romani Gypsy family. In the following chapters we explore how best to define the 'speech form' referred to here as 'Angloromani'.

1.2 Language contact, language change and dialects

The notion of an absolutely 'pure' language – in the sense of a speech form that is 'clean' of external influence – is almost entirely alien to linguistic science. We accept as a proven fact that, since different population groups may interact with one another at some point in their history, this social interaction will also have an effect on the repertoire of linguistic structures that are used by these populations for communication. The most common effect is for a population to extend its linguistic repertoire by adopting some aspects of another group's speech form. The most frequently adopted linguistic structures are lexical content words, especially words for concepts and objects that were unknown to the population prior to contact. Together with adopted words, new sounds may also enter the recipient language in an attempt to replicate the original pronunciation. If bilingualism becomes widespread, speakers will have a rich and complex repertoire of linguistic structures and will acquire the skill to select those structures that are considered most appropriate and most effective for communication in various interaction settings. Over time, they may seek to simplify this selection task by generalising some structures across the entire repertoire. Sometimes, it is the syntactic features that undergo such generalisation, so that the organisation of sentences becomes uniform and consistent within the bilingual repertoire irrespective of the overt phonological word forms that are chosen. Uniformity within the repertoire may also affect the phonological system, especially prosody and syllable structure, as well as lexical semantics and the inventory of grammatical function words, especially discourse markers, greetings and conjunctions (cf. Matras 2009). The effect of such processes is that the two languages gradually converge or become similar to one another in certain aspects of their structure. We thus accept in linguistics that the borderlines between one language and another are not static, but subject to dynamic change, especially in situations of cultural contacts among two or more populations.

How, then, do we define a speech form as belonging to one language rather than another? We will see in the course of this chapter that the answer is not always straightforward. However, most cases are not considered problematic. While we accept that words and other linguistic structures such as sounds, grammatical morphemes, form–meaning patterns and syntactic organisation rules can all be adopted from one language into another, we also realise that in most cases such processes require gradual development, usually spanning several generations of speakers. During this process, every generation of speakers will pass on to the next generation the bulk of linguistic structures at its disposal, introducing only minor changes. A possible definition of what a language represents is therefore this: a speech form that is passed on as a single, coherent 'package' from a parent generation to the next generation of speakers (cf. also Thomason & Kaufman 1988). Since the parent generation transmits a wholesale linguistic inventory, cross-generational change will be rather minor and parents and children will communicate with one another using structures that are on the whole very similar or even nearly identical. This continuity is what gives every language its identifiable shape and its particular features. Over time, some changes will accumulate. Different structural innovations may be adopted by different sectors of the population, or in different locations, giving rise to 'dialects'. But the slow pace of language change will dictate that varieties or dialects of a single language tend to remain quite similar to one another and that more often than not they will also be mutually intelligible.

Linguistic science is unable to offer a clear-cut distinction between related languages and related dialects of the same language. It is widely accepted that a *language* is a form of speech that enjoys some degree of institutionalisation, for example an accepted form of writing and spelling conventions and a degree of uniformity that is maintained in institutional communication, whereas a *dialect* lacks such overt regulation. Two closely related and by and large mutually intelligible speech varieties may be considered separate languages if they are subjected to separate institutionalisation contexts, e.g. as official speech forms of different states and state institutions, or of different religious-ethnic communities. This institutional separation might be manifested in different spelling conventions, in differences in grammar and style, or in the adoption of different writing systems. Examples of such language pairs are Norwegian and Swedish, Hindi and Urdu, Arabic and Maltese, Turkish and Azeri, Bulgarian and Macedonian, and more. On the other hand, speech varieties that differ considerably in structure and are not always mutually intelligible, such as Moroccan Arabic, Yemeni Arabic and Lebanese Arabic, or Westphalian Low German and Bavarian German, may be considered dialects of the same language if their speakers have a common standard language to which these dialects are related and which acts as a common symbol of ethnic identity through its role as a language of writing and of institutions such as government, media or education.

Most of the world's languages, however, lack any form of institutional convention altogether. The usual test for separating *language* and *dialect* cannot be applied under such circumstances. Instead, we rely on speakers' perception of each other as belonging to a single nation or network of social organisation, as well as on the degree to which their speech forms are mutually intelligible, in order to define who shares their language. Both dimensions can be strongly subjective: the first is strongly dependent on ideology, the second on individuals' aptitude and flexibility in communicative interaction. We can therefore conclude this discussion by saying that the 'languageness' of a speech variety is conventionally determined by two principal factors. The first is the social context in which the speech variety is used and the social meaning that it has for speakers as a way of flagging their distinct identity, along with the status of that speech form in institutional communication. The second factor is the degree of similarity between the speech variety of one population and that of another. The English *language* is, by this definition, a speech variety that enjoys institutional support and whose institutionalised form(s) are accepted as an expression of individuals' identity and social and ethnic background; dialects of English are closely related speech forms that have evolved through gradual accumulation of a series of minor changes, so that their speakers are still able, and generally willing, to make the effort to understand one another.

The Romani *language*, by contrast, must be characterised in the absence of any centralised and accepted institutional norm as a cluster of speech varieties that are shared by population groups who feel a basic affinity with one another and recognise their speech forms as being similar to one another more than they are similar to the speech forms of non-Romani people. To some degree at least, Romani dialects are mutually comprehensible, but due to the geographical dispersion and isolation of the Romani-speaking populations and the strong effects of diverse contact languages on the structure and vocabulary of Romani dialects, inter-dialectal communication in Romani may require a high degree of skill and motivation. Still, we regard as Romani any variety that has been passed on as a coherent 'package' from a Romani-speaking parent generation to the next generation, accumulating no more than the usual subtle changes in the process. This means that we might have certain expectations of the structure of any given Romani variety: similarities in the lexicon, especially in everyday or basic vocabulary items, similarities in the sound system, similarities in the grammatical vocabulary that is less prone to the influence of contact languages (such as personal pronouns and lower numerals) and similarities in at least some of the grammatical inflections, their shape and their function. An in-depth discussion of dialectal change and variation within Romani will be presented in Chapter 2.

The following two examples are excerpts from recorded conversations with a member of an English (Romany) Gypsy community based in the Northeast of England. The speech form used here is described by the speaker community as *Romanes* or sometimes *Romimus* and is a fairly typical representation of what members of the English and Welsh Gypsy community would regard as their own Romani *language*. Romani word forms are italicised and are translated in the second version of the excerpt that follows the original:

(1)   Me dad used to say, ooh *dik* at that, that's for/ ooh loves *livvinda*.
        That would sell its *wudrus* to buy *livvinda*. You know, they don't
        kom these *fowkis*. You know what I mean? They didn't like that
        way of going on. And/ er/ me dad used to say, low life *fowkis*, oh,
        don't want *chichi*, never will have any *kuvva*. Be *waffadi* all their
        lives.

        Me dad used to say, ooh *look* at that, that's for/ ooh loves *beer*.
        That would sell its *bed* to buy *beer*. You know, they don't *like* these
        people. You know what I mean? They didn't like that way of going
        on. And/ er/ me dad used to say, low life *people*, oh, don't want
        nothing, never will have any *things*. Be *bad* all their lives.

(2)   And I was saying to our Jim: *Kushti, dordi, dordi, dik* at the *luvva*
        we've *lelled* today, our Jim. How *kushti*, I'll never *sutti torati* with
        excitement. You know [laughter], all this. (. . .) And me mam
        used to say: Mmm, my dear, *dik* at *lesti*, hmm, mm, *vater*, mmm,
        how ever did that come to *lel* such a *mush*. Oh what a *kushti chor*,
        dik, and it's got a *moi* like a *jukkel*. (. . .) And ooh he's a *chikla*
        mush he's a *luvni gaera*, mmm, and would/ mmm *dik* here, hmm,
        showbusiness, hmm, I know where that should be – *sterriben*. He

had more *monnishins* than what he had hot dinners, you know, me
mam's *penning* to/ mmm oh, more than I've had to *ol* he's had.

And I was saying to our Jim: *Good, my, my, look* at the *money*
we've *earned* today, our Jim. How *good*, I'll never *sleep tonight*
with excitement. You know [laughter], all this. (. . .) And me mam
used to say: Mmm, my dear, *look* at *him*, hmm, mm, *pay attention*,
mmm, how ever did that come to *get* such a *man*. Oh what a *good
boy*, *look*, and it's got a *mouth* like a *dog*. (. . .) And ooh he's a *dirty
man* he's a *whore's man*, mmm, and would/ mmm *look* here, hmm,
showbusiness, hmm, I know where that should be – *prison*. He had
more *women* than what he had hot dinners, you know, me mam's
saying to/ mmm oh, more than I've had to *eat* he's had.

This speaker's linguistic repertoire clearly contains structures that are not
represented in most everyday varieties of English. In fact, we can say with
certainty that this density of unique vocabulary for these particular concepts
does not occur in any variety of English apart from that spoken by English
and Welsh Gypsies (and their descendants in New World countries, especially North America and Australia). Moreover, although the uniqueness
in form is limited to just a handful of vocabulary items, these are important
key words in the content of the narrative which make the narrative incomprehensible to anyone who is not familiar with these words. An outsider
who is not a member of the speaker's community will therefore not be able
to understand these conversation excerpts. The structural uniqueness of this
speech form and the fact that it is not fully understandable to users of other
varieties of English – in other words the contrast between this speech variety
and everyday English – is represented from the speaker perspective by the
label *Romanes* or 'Romani', implying a separate 'language'.

In actual fact, the Romani-derived component in (1)–(2) is limited to just a
series of lexical content words. Not even most of the lexical vocabulary is of
Romani origin, and there are no Romani grammatical inflections. Moreover,
apart from a few lexical items, the bulk of the narrative is also incomprehensible to any speaker of Romani who does not have command of English as
well. Since English words outnumber Romani words, and since grammatical
function words, sentence structure and most other structural aspects are consistently English, the language of conversation in (1)–(2) appears more like
English with insertions from Romani. Indeed, the linguistic composition of
the narrative resembles to some extent the kind of conversational behaviour
often observed among bilinguals that is referred to as 'insertional codeswitching'. Unlike alternational codeswitching, where speakers switch languages at
the boundaries of phrases or utterances, insertional codeswitching is characterised by the occasional insertion of lexical content words from language B
into an utterance or discourse in language A (cf. Muysken 2000). Much like

fluent bilinguals, the speaker in (1)–(2) makes context-appropriate choices as to where to insert Romani words.

However, this choice is only applicable to a subset of their vocabulary, not to the overall structure of words, phrases or sentences. Codeswitching (and the related term 'codemixing') usually refers to a situation where speakers are able to communicate in monolingual forms of either language, A or B, if the situation requires monolingual communication. To be sure, two languages in contact may share a considerable amount of their vocabulary, in which case there will be structural similarities even between forms of monolingual discourse in each of them. Domari, for example, the Indo-Aryan language spoken by the tiny community of Dom in Jerusalem (Matras 1999c), has borrowed from Arabic, its principal contact language, not just numerous lexical content words, but also all conjunctions, most numerals, most prepositions, indefinite pronouns and more. For an Arabic–Domari bilingual, speaking Domari manifests itself in a particular choice of basic vocabulary items and inflections, but not in a distinct constituent order, choice of numerals or discourse markers, choice of prepositions and so on. Still, it is possible to converse in Domari drawing on a significant number of both lexical and grammatical structures that are unique to the language and not shared with Arabic. By contrast, Angloromani utterances that contain a minimum of English-based structure occur only in isolation:

(3)   *Pen chichi, muskra akai!*
        'Say nothing, [the] police [are] here!'

(4)   *Muk mandi rokker* the *mush.*
        'Let me speak [to] the man.'

Examples (3)–(4) confirm again that we are dealing with a speech variety that can be entirely inaccessible at the utterance level to speakers of English who have no knowledge of Romani. But such utterances are quite frequently isolated directives or otherwise emphasised statements that are singled out by the speaker for special conversational effect. A monolingual version of narration extracts as in (1)–(2) can be produced by the speaker in English, leaving out the Romani words, but not in Romani. The relation between the two component languages in the examples is thus asymmetrical. For users of Angloromani, speaking *Romanes* across a stretch of conversation relies intrinsically on being able to embed individual vocabulary items into English discourse. This rules out 'codeswitching' as an ad hoc strategy of language mixing at the conversation level. The only switching that users of Angloromani are able to conduct is a switch between English without Romani words, and an English-based discourse form that contains Romani words and is therefore unintelligible to outsiders.

Naturally, fluent speakers of other varieties of Romani, in central and eastern Europe, may also integrate elements of the majority or contact language into their monolingual Romani discourse – typically vocabulary relating to technical and institutional domains as well as certain classes of grammatical function words (cf. Matras 2009, Elšík & Matras 2006). But the density of non-Romani structural material will be nowhere near the impact of English in examples (1)–(2), or even of English grammar (word order, verb inflection and definite articles) in (3)–(4), while the density of Romani-derived vocabulary will almost always be significantly higher.

If the speech variety documented in (1)–(4) is a form of Romani, then it is substantially different from other varieties of Romani in that it lacks a mono-lingual mode, and instead requires full competence in English in order to follow and participate in 'Romani' interaction. If, by contrast, it is a variety of English, then it is one that similarly defies our common notion of what a variety of English is: it contains a significant amount of basic vocabulary that is not inherited from a parent variety of English, it is defined by its speakers as a separate language, and it is not entirely intelligible to speakers of other varieties of English. In the following sections we explore a number of scenarios that account for the mixed structural profile of Angloromani.

1.3 'Mixed' Romani dialects and Para-Romani

Angloromani is one of several speech varieties that are characterised by the insertion of Romani-derived (or largely Romani-derived) vocabulary into discourse in the indigenous, majority language. Other speech varieties of this type include the Spanish–Romani mixture known as *Caló*, which is widely documented in the form of lexical compilations (Bright 1818, A.R.S.A. 1888, Jiménez 1853, Quindalé 1867, Torrione 1987, Helzle-Drehwald 2004), includ-ing some recent attestations of its use by speakers (De Luna 1951, McLane 1977, Román 1995, Leigh 1998; see also Bakker 1995 for a discussion). A fair amount of documentation also exists on Scandinavian varieties that have Swedish and Norwegian as their respective base languages (Ehrenborg 1928, Etzler 1944, Iversen 1944, Johansson 1977, Lindell & Thorbjörnsson-Djerf 2008; for a discussion see Hancock 1992 and Ladefoged 1998). Significantly less material is available on the Basque–Romani mixture known as *errumantxela* (Baudrimont 1862, Ackerley 1929; see discussion in Bakker 1991), and on the use of Romani vocabulary in a Low German framework in Denmark, called *Romnisch* (Miskow & Brøndal 1923). Note that in all these cases, the name given to the mixed variety is akin to 'Romani', serving to high-light the contrast with the everyday indigenous language. The Scandinavian names are *romano*, *rommani* and *Romnisch*. The Basque name *errumantxela* is cognate with the self-appellation of English Gypsies, *romnichal*, and with that of Romani-speaking populations in France (*romanichel*), Finland (*romaseel*) and northwestern Greece (*romacil*). The term *Caló* used in Spain and Portugal is cognate with the self-appellation of the Welsh Gypsies, *Kååle* (Sampson 1926b), as well as with an earlier self-appellation used by German Gypsies, *Kaale* (Rüdiger 1782), and with the current self-designation of Finnish Gypsies, *Kaale* (all meaning 'black, dark-skinned').

All the above varieties have been recorded in the western fringe areas of Europe, where they have completely replaced inflected varieties of Romani. But there are further attestations of similar phenomena in southeastern Europe. Lewis (1950–5) describes the in-group or secret language of the population known as the Yürük nomads of Geygelli in Turkey, which appears to consist of a vocabulary of Romani origin (see also discussion in Bakker 2001). Sechidou (2000) describes a community in Greece where the intermarriage of local Romani speakers with descendants of Romani speakers from the Peloponnese who are only partly fluent in the language has resulted in the adoption of a mixed family code consisting of Romani lexicon embedded into Greek utterances.

Early authors writing on Romani dialectology, such as Miklosich (1872–80) and Pott (1844–5), had included descriptions of such varieties in their comparative corpus of Romani dialects, conscious of their value for the historical reconstruction of the language's early development. Subsequent scholarly discussions continued to label these varieties as forms of Romani: 'Anglo-Romani' (Sampson 1911), 'Basque Romani' (Ackerley 1929) and later 'Scandoromani' (Hancock 1992) or indeed just 'Romany/Rommani' (Iversen 1944, Johansson 1977). Following in these footsteps, a modern tradition has emerged in Romani linguistics that defines the employment of Romani-derived vocabulary in group-internal communication in indigenous languages as a special type of Romani. The most widely applied term is now 'Para-Romani', coined by Cortiade (1991) and applied to a number of case studies in a collection of essays edited by Bakker and Cortiade (1991) (see also contributions in Matras 1998b). The significance of the prefix *Para-* might be interpreted firstly as a means of diminishing the impression that these are fully fledged varieties of Romani, since they lack Romani morphosyntax (sentence and phrase organisation structure and grammatical inflection). A further reading of the term has diachronic implications: Para-Romani varieties develop out of inflected dialects of Romani and succeed them as community-internal speech varieties. 'Para-Romani' thus conveys the notion of coherent speech varieties that are historically related to Romani, and which are used as everyday means of communication by 'Gypsy' ethnic minority groups (see e.g. Bakker & Van der Voort 1991).

Boretzky and Igla (1994) therefore regard them as 'Romani mixed dialects'. As descendants of individual inflected dialects of Romani, the mixed dialects are seen as important sources of information on the dialectological position of their respective forerunner varieties. Thus Boretzky (1992, 1998) investigates the position of Iberian Romani in relation to the Romani dialects of western Europe (Britain and Germany), and Bakker (1999) postulates a

'Northern branch' relying partly on data from mixed dialects. Boretzky and Igla's (1994) model postulates a drift towards the abandonment of Romani as an everyday community language, countered by a motivation on the part of the younger generation to hold on to a distinct, Romani-based lexical reservoir for the purpose of group-internal communication. The contradictory process has been associated with a U-turn metaphor (cf. Boretzky 1985; see also Bakker 1998: 71, Grant 1998: 186): First the language is lost, then an effort is made to revive it, which, however, is only partially successful. The idea that language shift accounts for the mixture is also central in Kenrick's (1979) proposal to regard Angloromani as the result of gradual loss of competence in Romani morphosyntax among speakers in the nineteenth century, resulting in an abandonment of the grammatical framework of Romani. Romani lexicon continues to survive in an English framework, giving rise in effect to a Romani-flavoured variety of English ('Romani English').

Romani mixed dialects are viewed as fundamentally different from secret lexicons of indigenous travelling populations such as Bargoens in the Netherlands, Jenisch in the German-speaking regions, or Scottish Traveller Cant, all of which acquire some Romani-derived lexicon through a process of diffusion from a variety of different sources (cf. Bakker 1998). Both the notions of 'Para-Romani' and of 'Romani mixed dialects' imply more than just random usage of Romani-derived structures, suggesting instead some coherent and overarching structural type, which in turn has prompted interest in comparative investigations. Boretzky (1998) points out the extraordinary survival rate of Romani-derived lexemes in the three best-documented Romani mixed dialects – Angloromani, Caló and Scandoromani – and concludes that the Romani lexicon would have been able to serve as a basis for everyday conversation even after the loss of Romani morphosyntax.

A further interesting point for comparison is the survival of grammatical lexicon. Para-Romani varieties share a general pattern of restructuring of the paradigm of personal pronouns (see Matras 2002: 246–9). Firstly, non-nominative forms are selected and generalised for all syntactic functions: the historical locative *mande* etc. in English Para-Romani (Angloromani), the historical dative *mange* etc. or sociative *mansa* etc. in Spanish Para-Romani (Caló), and the historical genitive *miro* etc. in Scandinavian Para-Romani. Secondly, only singular forms are continued from Romani. No Para-Romani plural forms are attested at all for the second and third persons, and only Scandinavian Para-Romani has a unique form for the first plural pronoun, albeit one that is based on the Scandinavian possessive form *vår* 'our' (*vårsnus*). Finally, the possessive form of the pronoun is based on the inflection of the indigenous or 'host' language; thus English Para-Romani *mandi's* 'mine', *tuti's* 'yours', and even Scandinavian Para-Romani *miros* 'mine' (from Romani *miro* 'mine' with the Scandinavian possessive ending -*s*).

Such similarities in vocabulary composition and in the pathways of renewal and restructuring of grammatical lexicon suggest that similar mechanisms are involved in the emergence of Para-Romani varieties. The challenge is to describe these mechanisms adequately in a way that addresses the language-ecological setting and the pressure to abandon Romani morphosyntax, the sociolinguistic setting and motivation to retain a Romani lexicon, and the way that these motivations each map onto the content meaning and language processing functions that are associated with specific linguistic structures and expressions.

1.4 Creoles and pidgins

While we generally accept in linguistics a definition of 'language' as described above – in the sense of a coherent cross-generational transmission of an inventory of linguistic structures – there are, alongside Angloromani, also other types of speech forms that challenge this definition. The most widely discussed are pidgins and creoles, which have become known as a kind of prototype of linguistic mixtures or contact languages. The term 'creolisation' has even been taken over by other disciplines to denote a process of identity transformation through admixture of forms, customs and routines, brought about through colonial uprooting of peoples (cf. Hannerz 1992, Eriksen 2007). Both Hancock (1970) and later Boretzky (1985) addressed the relationship between the pidgin and creole model of language development, and mixed varieties with a Romani lexicon.

There are, in fact, several different points of potential resemblance between 'lexical' varieties of Romani, and pidgins and creoles. It is generally accepted that pidgins are characterised by the loss of grammatical inflections or even a more general loss of morphosyntax of the target or lexifier language (in the case of colonial pidgins, the European colonial languages such as Portuguese, English, French and Dutch), whereas the majority of structures that do survive are lexical content words and to a somewhat more limited extent grammatical function words (cf. Holm 2000). This can be compared with the loss of Romani morphosyntax and the survival of Romani lexicon and some grammatical lexicon in Para-Romani varieties. The comparison implies that what gave rise to Para-Romani varieties was, as in the case of pidgins, a process of only partial acquisition of a target language and the use of just selected, lexical items from the target language for makeshift communication. Moreover, in pidgins the acquisition process of a separate target language is understood as motivated by a need for inter-group communication in a multilingual setting. Hancock (1970, 1984) suggests that Angloromani emerged through a process of population admixture that took place as early as the sixteenth century, when Romani-speaking Gypsies absorbed a population of indigenous Travellers and outlaws (for a similar explanation for the emergence of Scandoromani see Hancock 1992). From this perspective,

Romani served, much like the colonial languages in the history of pidgins, as the target language and as the lexifier language for inter-ethnic communication. The obvious difference, however, is the availability in the English Romani context of English as a fully fledged, common language, which makes a makeshift vehicle for communication based on Romani rather redundant. Hancock (1984), however, regards the choice of Romani as a vital tool for flagging a new in-group identity shared by Travellers of Romani and indigenous origins. In this connection it is noteworthy that McWhorter (2000) interprets the emergence of plantation creoles as a conscious choice on the part of the enslaved population, who, rather than accommodate to the speech form of the colonists, reverted to a language that had served them as an inter-ethnic lingua franca in West Africa – namely the trade pidgins based on the same European colonial language. The use of what was perceived as an African language served to flag a common African heritage and a separate identity from the one represented by the colonists.

While Hancock's (1970) suggestion has attracted relatively little attention on the part of linguists in general and creolists in particular, it is given lengthy consideration in Coughlan's (2001: 6–51) discussion of the origins of present-day 'broken Romani' in Britain. Coughlan's preoccupation with Hancock's arguments is to a large extent textual, and concerns the interpretation of a number of sources which Hancock (1970) cites as evidence for the existence of a mixed population of Travellers, who are said to have created a mixed Traveller code based on Romani. Coughlan demonstrates quite convincingly that each of these sources is at the very least misinterpreted, if not indeed misrepresented, by Hancock, and that, while population admixture cannot possibly be ruled out, there is no evidence that Romani served as a contact variety between Traveller populations of Romani and non-Romani origin and so no historical evidence for the formation of a simplified, common language.

None the less, Hancock's (1970) ideas had been introduced into the context of non-linguistic discussion of Romani societies, where the ideas have been, to a considerable extent, misrepresented and, we may assume, misunderstood. Thus Okely (1983), in the introductory remarks to what is probably the most in-depth ethnographic discussion of an English Gypsy community, proposes to extend Hancock's suggestion "that Anglo-Romany is a creole" and to apply it to Romani in general, on the assumption that all Romani dialects "might be classified as creoles or pidgins which developed between merchants and other travelling groups along the trade routes [and] served as a means of communication between so-called Gypsy groups" (Okely 1983: 9). Okely's remarks remained largely unnoticed in the literature on Romani/Gypsy studies until they were echoed by social historian Willems (1997). Inspired by Okely, Willems dismisses the idea of an umbrella parent (Romani) language of Indian origin and proposes instead that Romani should be regarded plainly as a vocabulary that was adopted by indigenous

Gypsy (i.e. itinerant or Traveller) groups into the various languages that they spoke in order to camouflage the content of their speech, or even "as a kind of group ritual" (Willems 1997: 82–3). Both Okely and Willems make use of the linguistic argument in the first instance in order to dismiss the notion of a Romani immigration from India and the survival of Romani communities as 'diaspora' groups. A further supporter of this idea is Wexler (1997), who similarly claims that Romani generally constitutes no more than a vocabulary that is inserted into the morphosyntactic framework of a host language. In Wexler's case, the agenda is essentially to identify a parallel case for his controversial claims about the history of Yiddish, to which he similarly attributes Slavic and Turkic rather than Germanic origins, as well as about the history of Modern Hebrew, which he regards as a relexified form of Yiddish (and hence according to his model a Slavic or perhaps even a Turkic language).

Amidst all these different agendas that seek confirmation for a series of theories by drawing on bits and pieces of information about Romani and Para-Romani varieties, there remains a dilemma in comparing Para-Romani with creoles and pidgins: pidgins and creoles arise through simplification strategies that are part of the process of acquiring a target language (such as the colonial language) in a setting where there is no other common language of interaction among people of different linguistic-ethnic backgrounds. The population of learners succeeds in replicating content lexemes and their meanings, but not in replicating more abstract inflectional morphemes. As a result, they employ a makeshift grammar, which stabilises over time (the more traditional approach views pidgins as the makeshift medium and creoles as the more conventionalised variety that is acquired by a next generation as a native language). But in the case of Para-Romani, a means of communication exists in the form of the indigenous majority language, and its grammar is fully accessible to all speakers. Consider the following examples:

(5)   *Mandi pestered dusta luvva.*
        'I paid a lot of money.'

(6)   *Mandi pukkered the rakli.*
        'I told the woman.'

(7)   *Vater duvva's yoks!*
        'Look at this one's eyes!'

(8)   Don't *pukker* your *nav, mong* the *gaera* how much *luvva duvya* is.
        'Don't say your name, ask the man how much money this is.'

(9)   *Lesti's savv*ing
        'He's laughing'

(10)   The *mush jun*s the *rokkerpen*
        'The man knows the language/understands the conversation'

English is not rich in grammatical inflection, but its full inflectional potential is realised and exploited in these Angloromani utterances: We find past-tense inflection, definite articles, possessive suffixes, plural suffixes, gerundial suffixes and present-tense inflection, as well as a series of inflected function words such as negators, possessives, quantifiers and inflected copula forms. This contrasts sharply with creoles and pidgins, which are generally characterised by the absence of grammatical inflections. While this important difference cannot be dismissed, it is worth citing a further theory from the context of pidgin and creole studies. The substrate approach and the closely related relexification hypothesis view pidgins and creoles as more-or-less coherent continuations of the grammatical structures of the original languages of the speaker population, into which lexical shapes from the colonial languages are inserted. Keesing (1988) discusses this extensively for the Pacific creoles and their Oceanic substrate, and many authors, including Boretzky (1983), Holm (2000), Kouwenberg and LaCharité (2004), McWhorter (2005) and others have discussed individual morphosyntactic and lexico-semantic constructions and other structural domains that appear to survive from West African languages in Atlantic creoles. Some of the more radical ideas, such as those of Lefebvre (1998), attribute the emergence of creole to a wholesale relexification of the substrate languages, which replace their original vocabulary with lexemes from the colonial language but retain their original grammatical structure.

The analogy with the substrate and relexification model of creole genesis would be to regard English (and the other respective 'host' or majority languages) as the substrate language, and Romani as the lexifier language of Angloromani (and other Para-Romani varieties), analogous with the superstrate colonial languages that served as an acquisition target for speakers of creole. The problem with such an analogy is that it requires us to 'flip' the historical power relations among the two languages involved and, in the case of Angloromani, to regard the minority language that is in fact being abandoned by a generation of fluent speakers as the superimposed idiom that speakers struggle to learn (the superstrate), and to view the majority language to which the community is shifting as an underlying blueprint (a substrate) for the acquisition of a 'new' lexifier language. Can such a flipping of the sociolinguistic roles make any sense in the case of Angloromani?

There are at least two scenarios within which this idea might be contemplated. The first is Boretzky's (1985) so-called 'U-turn hypothesis'. Here it is claimed that the younger generation of Roms was in the process of losing competence in the community language of their parental generation, and had in practice shifted to the majority language while still being exposed to Romani in interactions with the older generation. The comparison puts this young generation in a similar position to the creator generation of pidgins: they are exposed to a target language which they wish to acquire for all-purpose communication, but since immersion in the target language is only partial, and perhaps motivation for immersion isn't quite strong enough, their mode of acquisition is to replicate just the content lexemes of the target language and to employ them within the more familiar grammatical framework of their own everyday language (i.e. English, or the respective majority language, in the case of other Para-Romani varieties).

The second scenario option is that suggested by Hancock (1970), which assumes that the replication of Romani lexicon in a non-Romani grammatical framework was due to the impact of Travellers of non-Romani origin who joined the Romani community and made an only partially successful effort to acquire the language as a symbol of their belonging to the new community. To some extent, both positions are reconcilable with McWhorter's (2005) model of creole genesis. The model regards the first generation of speakers of pidgins/creoles as creative language users. In order to communicate effectively, they will make use of a range of structures that are accessible to them in the particular social setting, and if necessary improvise a form of speech with which a majority of them is able to identify. Angloromani appears to contradict the creole stereotype of a complete absence of grammatical inflection, showing English inflection wherever it is required. But in line with the substrate model in creole genesis, this might be regarded as a coincidence of a substrate language which, unlike the West African languages, relies more heavily on grammatical inflection. Here, too, we can find an explanation in McWhorter's prediction that the degree of inflectional retention from the substrate language will vary in pidgins and creoles depending among other things on language attitudes and the size of the groups of speakers in the colonial diaspora, as well as on the availability and prominence of inflection in the substrate language itself.

1.5 Mixed languages

Contrasting with the ideas formulated by Hancock (1970), Kenrick (1979), Boretzky (1985), and later Boretzky and Igla (1994), Thomason and Kaufman (1988: 103–4) discuss Angloromani not as an example of language shift, but rather as a case of language maintenance, where over time and due to very intense contact "borrowing [has been] so extensive as to constitute complete grammatical replacement at least in one subsystem". Without further specifying, they hypothesise that the retention of Romani lexicon, avoiding complete assimilation and language shift, was motivated by certain communicative functions that the language continued to possess. The result is a language that inherited its lexicon from one source and its grammar from another and must therefore be classified as a genetically 'mixed language'. In subsequent work, Thomason (1997a, 2001) refers to mixed languages as 'bilingual mixtures', setting a clear-cut demarcation between those contact languages that emerge out of a situation of community bilingualism and language maintenance, such as Angloromani, and those that are the outcome of a process of language acquisition, namely pidgins and creoles.

Thomason and Kaufman's (1988) discussion of genetically mixed languages set in motion an attempt to extend both the documentation and the analysis of candidate languages that fall into this category. The collection by Bakker and Mous (1994b) documented several case studies. Along with Bakker's (1997) monograph-length discussion of Michif, a Cree–French mixture of the Canadian Plains, this collection became influential in putting forward a new theoretical position on the emergence of mixed languages as a unique and distinctive language type. Bakker (1997) (see also Bakker & Mous 1994b, Bakker & Muysken 1995) regards the emergence of mixed languages as a process that is structurally and typologically pre-determined, given the appropriate sociolinguistic circumstances. This process – labelled 'language intertwining' – is regarded as distinct from both pidginisation and borrowing, however extensive.

According to Bakker, language intertwining is likely to occur primarily in two types of settings. The first involves mixed households where the women and men have separate ethnic and linguistic backgrounds. Rather than assimilate into one of the two parental communities, the young generation forges a new identity of its own. The speakers of Michif belong to this category: they are the offspring of intermarriage between French men who were colonial settlers and traders, and indigenous Cree women. The second type are communities of migrants or other ethnic minorities that undergo a change in their sociocultural environment and are consequently in the process of re-negotiating or re-inventing their group-specific identity. In both types of setting, the younger generation will manifest its mixed heritage by re-assembling structural resources from both parental languages. Typically, the grammar will derive from one language, usually the language of the mothers or the language of the surrounding majority population, while the lexicon will derive from the other, usually the language of the fathers or that of the minority group. Grammatical function words are recruited from either language, or from both.

In contrast to views on gradual language attrition or gradual borrowing, Bakker understands the process of language intertwining as abrupt, much like creolisation, allowing a new mixed language to emerge within just a single generation. Bakker's (1995) hypothesis concerning abrupt emergence has since been corroborated at least in two cases: the younger generation among the Gurindji and the Walpiri, both involving Australian Aboriginal languages in contact with an English-based creole (called 'Kriol'), are in the process of adopting a mixture of the 'old' ancestral language and Kriol, while their parent generation is bilingual in both languages (see McConvell & Meakins 2005, O'Shannessy 2005). Continuing research into mixed languages has furthermore supported the hypothesis that their creation is to a considerable extent a conscious and intentional act of (mixed) identity flagging (cf. Croft 2003, Golovko 2003) and that it is therefore quite different from gradual borrowing, which proceeds subconsciously.

While the corpus of documented mixed languages remains small, several different structural subtypes are identifiable. Only some mixed languages confirm Bakker's (1997) prediction of a consistent split between the source languages for lexicon and grammar. Among them are Media Lengua, a Quechua–Spanish mixture spoken in acculturated rural communities in Peru featuring Spanish lexicon in a Quechua grammatical framework (Muysken 1997), and Ma'a, the in-group language of an ethnic minority population in Tanzania, which features a lexicon of largely Cushitic origin within the grammatical framework of the Bantu language Mbugu (Mous 2003a). Several other cases show a split between the source of verb, verb phrase grammar and verb inflection, and that of nominal inflection and noun phrase grammar. These include Michif itself, which actually derives not just its verb inflection but also most of its verbal roots from Cree; Copper Island Aleut as spoken off the Russian Pacific Coast, which has Aleut noun phrase grammar, Russian verb inflection and a mixed lexicon (Golovko & Vakhtin 1990, Vakhtin 1998); and both Light Walpiri and Gurindji Kriol, which maintain the nominal inflection patterns of the respective Australian Aboriginal language, but adopt the verbal markers of Kriol (O'Shannessy 2005, McConvell & Meakins 2005).

It is noteworthy, however, that none of the recorded cases of mixed languages shows any kind of mixture of sources for finite verb inflection. The diagnostic definition of mixed languages therefore seems to imply that finite verb inflection is drawn from one particular source language, whereas the bulk or at least a significant portion of the basic lexicon (to the extent that lexical roots are identifiable) and possibly other domains of grammar are derived from another. Mixed languages thus constitute a diachronic mixture of the means of initiating the predication of the utterance (finite verb inflection) and the language's referential resources (lexical vocabulary) (see discussion in Matras 2003). This involves a structural distinction between two processing functions that are in all likelihood distinguished during the mental planning of the utterance. The predication permits the anchoring of propositional content in a contextual perspective; it tends to encode features such as the actors involved in the event, the duration and time setting of the event relative to the utterance time, and often also the speaker's perspective on the event. The predication therefore belongs to the more intuitive, context-bound and abstract components of grammar. Referential means on the other hand are labels given to objects. They are often associated with more concrete depictions of objects and are more easily and more consciously substituted and manipulated. I shall return to the role of the predication in language shift and partial language maintenance later on in the discussion.

Based on the above characterisation of mixed languages, it would not seem too difficult to accommodate Angloromani (and other Para-Romani varieties) under the mixed language heading: Angloromani displays a rather consistent lexicon–grammar split among two source languages, as illustrated above by examples (5)–(10); the lexifier language is the ancestral community language of a migrating population; and the motivation for maintaining a mixture as an in-group speech form can be viewed in connection with the maintenance and flagging of a separate ethnic identity and a distinct socio-economic profile, defying full assimilation into the surrounding majority (in this case settled) society. The difficulty lies in determining its precise communicative function – a central aspect of its 'languageness'.

Of the documented mixed languages, only Michif is spoken as an everyday family and community language in isolation from both its source languages, Cree and French. There is no doubt that what might have begun as a playful, deliberate and conscious manipulation of speech patterns has in this case evolved into a highly conventionalised language, separable from both its ancestor idioms. There is ample documentation of Michif conversational material to confirm this. Most other cases of mixed languages are not quite as straightforward. Gurindji Kriol and Light Walpiri appear to be used as the native languages of a young generation of speakers, but these speakers live alongside the older generation of bilinguals who are able to switch between non-mixed varieties of both source languages, and indeed do codemix, drawing on both. While few transcriptions of Media Lengua conversation exist, the language appears to be used as an all-purpose means of conversation among its small number of speakers, and it is reportedly kept separate and structurally distinct from both Spanish and Quechua, and from Spanish–Quechua codemixing. Published documentation of short excerpts confirms the consistency with which Spanish lexicon is embedded into Quechua grammar in Media Lengua conversation (Muysken 1997, 1981). The extent of documentation on Copper Island Aleut does not offer a clear conclusion, but the language is described as a conventionalised mixture of structures from its two source languages, despite the fact that speakers are bilingual and ad hoc mixtures in conversation are therefore also possible.

Alongside these mixed languages, there is a further type that has been recognised essentially as an alternative lexicon that is tightly embedded in a dominant language, one that serves speakers for interactions both outside and quite possibly also within the community. Smith (1995) defines these varieties as 'symbiotic mixed languages', referring to the fact that they exist in inherent symbiosis with their grammar or 'host' language. Ma'a is one of the languages belonging to this type. It consists of a Cushitic-derived lexicon embedded in the grammatical framework of Mbugu, which is the dominant everyday community language. None the less, Mous (2003a) reports that the selection of Ma'a vocabulary items tends to be consistent in conversation.

By contrast, Angloromani lacks such conventionalisation. Excerpts (1)–(2) above have already provided an illustration of the scattered nature of Romani-derived lexical insertions and the fact that such insertions are hardly predictable, let alone conventionalised. The following utterances show that Angloromani is prone to considerable variation even in the use of grammatical lexicon – here, of personal pronouns. Some mixed languages derive their personal pronouns from the lexifier language, others from the grammar or predication grammar language; but the use of pronouns is consistent as long as speakers opt to use the mixed language in conversation. By contrast, consider the frequent alternation in the following examples between English-derived and Romani-derived pronouns:

(11)   *Del* it to him
        'Give it to him'

(12)   I've *chingered lesti*
        'I've annoyed him'

(13)   *Mandi* doesn't *kom lesti*
        'I don't like him'

(14)   I'll do some *hobben*
        'I'll make some food'

(15)   He's not a bad *chor*
        'He's not a bad guy'

(16)   *Lesti's savving* at *mandi*
        'He's laughing at me'

Even in a structural domain that is as tightly defined as the paradigm of personal pronouns, insertion of Romani-derived lexical items appears to be optional and subject to speaker's choice at the level of the individual utterance. This makes it difficult to regard Angloromani as a structurally fixed and fully conventionalised code at a level that is comparable to other documented mixed languages.

1.6 In-group lexicons, argots and 'secret' languages

The occasional insertion of word forms that are not understandable to non-members of the community is precisely the pattern that can be observed in the use of what are often referred to as in-group or special lexicons, 'secret' languages or 'argots'. A research tradition in German linguistics specialising in the phenomenon has coined the term *Sondersprache* (see Möhn 1980, Wolf 1985, Siewert 1996; see earlier Kluge 1901). Special in-group lexicons are usually the property of small populations of commercial nomads or peripatetics – groups that tend to specialise in one or a cluster of service-providing trades and which retain a certain degree of mobility in order to reach their 'sedentary' population of potential customers. Typical trades offered by traditional itinerant communities range from manufacturing and selling small households goods, such as baskets, brooms and brushes, tin- and copperware, drills, skewers and so on, to entertainment and ritual services such as music and dance, performance with animals, fortune-telling, healing and circumcision, and on to both specialised and non-specialised labour such as masonry, seasonal work in agriculture, and many more. Modern trades include dealing in scrap metal, building repairs on a small scale, garden work, car repairs and used car sales, while the traditional trades of vendors, performers and even fortune-tellers continue to survive in rural districts as well as in major cities such as New York, Madrid and Istanbul.

Not only are in-group lexicons the property of commercial nomads, they are even considered a typical, universal feature of the culture of itinerant populations (see Gmelch & Gmelch 1987). The need for a group-internal speech form is often explained in connection with the need to speak in code in order to keep trade secrets and maintain an advantage in trade. This makes in-group lexicons 'bystander-oriented' (see Rijkhoff 1998): their function is to disguise key meaningful elements in order to make the content of key utterances of strategic importance incomprehensible and inaccessible to outsiders who happen to witness the conversational interaction. Situations of this kind might frequently arise when trading goods at markets or when negotiating a price or coordinating a sales approach strategy when approaching clients' homes (hawking), bearing in mind that the service economy of commercial nomads is usually family-based and that clients are often approached by more than one person at a time.

Another key function attributed to in-group lexicons is to convey warnings and to coordinate behaviour that might be regarded from the outsider perspective as a conspiracy against existing social order. This need arises from the social and legal marginalisation of itinerant groups as well as the continuous tension created by their existential dependency on the settled, majority population for basic resources and living space, and their cultural-ideological wish to remain free and protected from the kind of social order that settled society imposes. In fact, the ability to communicate in a mode that is not understandable to the surrounding majority society may be seen as more than just a practical instrument to conceal meaning. It is also symbolic of commercial nomads' constant struggle to escape the control of settled society and its institutions and norms. Much like slang, in-group lexicons serve to symbolise a bond around group attitudes while at the same time allowing users to make a socially and culturally biased statement about an object or state of affairs. This can be either a euphemistic statement, avoiding a dispreferred expression with negative connotations, or a dysphemistic statement, opting to denote the offence caused by the referent or state of affairs, or indeed implying offence towards an audience of bystanders (see Burridge & Allen 1998). In-group lexicons thus do more than just serve as a practical

means to enable secret communication. They are an important way of reinforcing in-group solidarity. Indeed, engaging group members in the design
and implementation of in-group lexicons can be seen as an important social
activity within the group.

The overt and conscious engagement with language as a means of expressing social identity reveals first of all that language, although generally used
in a way that is not overtly conscious in respect of its structural design, may
indeed become the subject of conscious and deliberate manipulation and
engineering, even in the absence of formal institutions such as language acad-
emies, standardisation and codification committees, and spelling reforms.
Various strategies are at the disposal of speakers engaging in such spontaneous, non-institutional language design activities. One of the best-established
strategies is the distortion of the phonological shape of words by altering,
inverting or repeating individual syllables. The French slang code known as
Verlan (from *l'envers* 'inversion'), now associated primarily with the second
generation of North African migrants in suburban council estates, is based
on syllable inversion giving rise to forms like *keuf* 'police officer' from *flic*
and *meuf* 'woman' from *femme*. Adding individual syllables or sounds to
syllables or words is a popular playful slang creation strategy that is universally common among teenagers (often called *Pig Latin*). Irish Traveller
Cant employs sound substitution strategies, some of which continue to be
productive with present-day English words: thus *groilet* from *toilet*. Other
cryptolalic (word camouflage) strategies include the addition of affixes to
common words, disguising their meaning, as in Scandinavian Para-Romani
vårsnus 'us', from Swedish/Norwegian *vår* 'our'. The extent and nature of
distortion strategies often depend on the morpho-phonological typology of
the host language. Arabic cryptolalic formations, for example, often make
use of complex morpho-phonological templates of the general type used for
word formation in everyday Arabic, but specific in their shape to the in-group
lexicon. Thus the speech of the Egyptian Halab commercial nomads has
forms like *mubwābiš* for 'door' from Arabic *bāb*, and *muftāḥiš* for 'key' from
Arabic *miftāḥ*.

A further common word camouflage technique involves the figurative-
associative exploitation of semantic content. English Cant has, for example,
stocks for 'legs', while German Rotwelsch has *Trittling* for 'shoe' (from *Tritt*
'step') and *Zündling* for 'fire' (from *zünden* 'to ignite'). Figurative expressions
can then be combined into compositional formations such as *stock-drawers*
for 'stockings'. Often a 'dummy' or semantically default expression is used
to create attributive compositions, drawing on the figurative meaning of the
attribute to identify the referent, thus English Cant *smelling chete* 'nose',
pratling chete 'tongue', *grunting chete* 'pig', *quacking chete* 'duck'. Dummy
words are often favoured in conjunction with possessive forms for the creation of personal pronouns, as in the in-group lexicon of the Gurbet peripatetics of Iran: *xukī-m* 'I', *xukī-t* 'you', *xukī-mūn* 'we', etc.

Like slangs, in-group lexicons of peripatetic populations may rely equally on external sources of lexical material. These are often dialectal forms or archaisms, or individual words of foreign origin. Polari, a lexicon that was widespread among English seamen, later became the property of the entertainment industry and was subsequently associated with the underground gay community until the 1960s, recruited most of its lexemes from a form of early Romance, possibly deriving from a maritime pidgin or lingua franca that was spoken in and around Mediterranean harbours in late medieval times (cf. Hancock 1984, Baker 2002). The in-group lexicon of the Abdal or Äynu peripatetics – traders, healers and circumcisers – of East Turkistan (Xinjiang province in western China) consists of Persian vocabulary that is embedded in Uygur conversation (Ladstätter & Tietze 1994). In both these cases, it appears that an entire lexicon was recruited from an established trade language, which may well have been used much like a pidgin, relying strictly on its lexical component for the purpose of trade in inter-ethnic interaction settings. Other in-group vocabularies of foreign origin reflect the ethnic origin and traditions of their user populations. Thus Germany had until recently several French-based lexicons that were used within a dialectal German utterance and discourse framework by itinerant masons and musicians who had immigrated from France (cf. Siewert 1996). Jewish cattle-trader jargon in Germany and neighbouring regions in the Netherlands and northeastern France – usually referred to as *lekoudesch* or similar labels, from Ashkenasic Hebrew *loschn ha-koudesch* 'the sacral language' ('Hebrew') – was based on the incorporation of Hebrew-derived lexicon, recruited from the written, sacral language of scholarly and religious literature into the Jewish ethnolectal varieties of colloquial German (see Matras 1991, 1997).

Such 'manufactured' or deliberately recruited lexical reservoirs used by populations of commercial nomads are often referred to in non-specialised discussions as 'Gypsy languages', but they are not to be confused with Romani. In its inflected form, as still spoken today by upwards of 3.5 million speakers across Europe and beyond, Romani is a fully fledged everyday family and community language, much like Bulgarian, Catalan or Welsh, albeit with very weak institutional support or recognition. Maintaining some very archaic inflectional features carried over from a Middle Indo-Aryan ancestor language, it is definitely not (*pace* Okely and Willems) limited to a special lexicon that is used in order to disguise key meanings or for other special effects. None the less, as a minority language that is usually not acquired by outsiders, it can in principle take on similar functions when the need arises. Some Romani dialects show evidence that the language was used for the exclusion of bystanders: Romani dialects in western Europe in particular, where the overall population density of Roma was comparatively low, their social isolation high, and their economy largely limited to itinerant trade, show a preference for internally constructed names for nations and towns rather than replication of the original terms, a proliferation of internal terms for 'policeman' and other official roles like 'mayor' and 'judge', and often also a preference for using internal derivations rather than loanwords for terms denoting occupations, trades and social ranks as well as potential taboo terms such as 'coffin', 'alcohol' or 'church'. This contrasts with the Romani dialects of southeastern and central-eastern Europe, where Romani population density is higher, many more Roma have been settled for many generations and are engaged in a greater diversity of trades, and the above lexical categories tend to be filled with loanwords from the neighbouring contact languages, which are potentially comprehensible to bystanders who are not members of the Romani community.

It is of course tempting to draw a direct connection between the retention of Romani vocabulary in a non-Romani grammatical framework and the socio-economic profile of Gypsy communities, which tends to encourage the creation and use of an in-group lexical reservoir, all the more so since Romani provides a source for the diffusion of lexical vocabulary into numerous lexical reservoirs of diverse populations throughout Europe. The various strategies of lexical camouflaging described above are not necessarily mutually exclusive. Some in-group vocabularies show parallel exploitation of various strategies, sometimes recognisable in the form of different historical layers reflecting in all likelihood periods of interface with other groups and perhaps even social reorganisation or reconstitution of the group itself. Examples of in-group lexicons that rely on a number of different sources are the vocabularies of the southwest German, Swiss and Austrian Yenish (*Jenische*), whose lexical reservoir typically shows a layer of German-based figurative and archaic formations, with additional vocabulary layers of Romance, Hebrew and Romani origin; Bargoens in the Netherlands, which shows a rather similar composition; and Scottish Traveller Cant, which contains English Cant, Shelta and Romani-derived words.

Romani-derived lexical items are thus not limited to the vocabularies of population groups that can claim Romani ethnic origin or inflected Romani as an ancestral language. Moreover, their diffusion is not even limited to in-group lexicons of commercial nomads. Local and regional slangs also serve some of the functions named above, most notably euphemistic and dysphemistic expression, flagging group membership and group solidarity, and signalling defiance towards an imposed social order. The in-group lexicons of peripatetics are protected by tighter social boundaries, being the property of clusters of related families or small ethnic communities. This accounts for their tendency toward lexical conservativism. At the same time, euphemistic and dysphemistic usages are fashion-prone and therefore subject to renewal. The less strict social boundaries within which users of slang bond for a transitional period usually make slang vocabularies more volatile and susceptible to new influences, and hence in search of adequate lexical resources. But as I mentioned in the introductory remarks to this chapter, even the boundaries of Travelling communities are not sealed when it comes to interaction with other itinerant population groups.

As a fully fledged, family language of a tight-knit community, Romani enjoyed a certain amount of prestige in this context and has served as a source of lexical items for a continuum of special speech varieties. It forms the basis for the Para-Romani varieties of itinerant groups that have abandoned inflected Romani. These in turn provide a pool of lexical items from which words are recruited to enrich the in-group vocabularies of other peripatetic groups, such as the Scottish Travellers and the Yenish. Through encounters with marginalised individuals within the settled population who regard Travellers as successful 'conspirators' against the dominating social order, the same lexical pool serves to enrich certain specialised local and regional slang varieties. Among younger people in the Borders area in the Northeast of England it is fashionable to use an inventory of up to several dozen Romani-derived words – such as *nash* 'to run', *chavva* 'guy', *peev* 'drink', *ladjed* 'embarrassed', *gadji* 'man, woman' and many more – in what is often referred to as *chavva talk* or regional adolescent slang (cf. Pistor 1998, Sobell 1999). Users later abandon this vocabulary once they grow out of the relevant age group. Use of Romani-derived slang has been documented for other social groups, including gay communities in Istanbul (Kyuchukov & Bakker 1999) the urban working class in Stockholm (Ward 1936, van den Eijnde 1991, Kotsinas 1996) and more. Finally, local slangs constitute a point of diffusion of Romani-derived elements into colloquial language use by the mainstream settled population. This is the origin of colloquial English expressions such as *pal, chav, kushty* and *minge*, and of colloquial German words such as *Bokh* 'inclination' and *Zaster* 'money'. A much higher density of Romani-derived lexical items is found in colloquial forms of languages of central and eastern Europe, such as Romanian (Graur 1934, Juilland 1952a, Leschber 1995).

Following from the above discussion, it seems reasonable to view Angloromani as part of a continuum of diffusion of Romani-derived lexical elements within the framework of the majority language of mainstream, settled society. Although this impression seems to be confirmed by the discourse excerpts and utterances documented earlier in this chapter, it is not entirely accurate. Consider the following:

(17) *Mush   kek   juns   chichi.*
      man   not   knows   nothing
      '[The] man doesn't know anything.'

(18) *Mandi doesn't kom lesti*
      'I don't like him'

(19) *Pen chichi, muskara akai!*
      'Say nothing, [the] police [are] here!'

Examples (17)–(19) are not quite fully grammatical sentences in any variety of English. In (17) we find both a deletion of the definite article and a re-arrangement of the pattern of negation, missing out the negative auxiliary *doesn't* and containing instead a pre-verbal negation particle, *kek*, inherited from Romani, while the lexical verb carries person and tense inflection. In (18), the first person singular triggers third person singular agreement on the verb; note that the negation pattern attested in (17) is not obligatory, but an option, and (18) follows the English pattern. Finally in (19) we find the omission of both the definite article and the copula verb 'to be'. With the possible exception of the negation pattern in (17), these morphosyntactic features cannot be said to be inherited directly from Romani: Romani does have definite articles, it has obligatory copulas in existential sentences and consistent first person agreement with first person pronouns. What seems to confront us in these examples might be described, rather, as a relaxation of some of the rules on well-formedness of (regional-colloquial) English. In the light of this evidence, we must reconsider once again the 'language' status of Angloromani as more than just a plain English-based matrix for the insertion of Romani-derived lexical elements.

1.7 Language shift and language loss

A final remark in the survey of approaches to the status of Angloromani and other Para-Romani varieties concerns once again the issue of language loss and language shift. As described above, Boretzky (1985; cf. also Boretzky & Igla 1994) had viewed Para-Romani as the products of the abandonment of Romani, followed by a renewed effort to maintain at least some degree of competence in the language (a 'U-turn'). This attempt was effective only in maintaining partial command of the inherited lexicon, while the grammar was lost. This scenario contrasts both with the notion of language main-tenance and gradual wholesale borrowing of grammar, as advocated by Thomason and Kaufman (1988), and with the idea of language acquisition as the main force behind the simplification and consequent abandonment of Romani grammar, as suggested by Hancock (1970, 1984). It is noteworthy that many of the other languages classified as mixed languages have been shown to have arisen in a setting in which an older community language was being abandoned. The Ma'a lexicon, for example, is believed to derive from a Cushitic language that was once spoken by the community as an everyday ethnic language and was abandoned following the group's migration to its present-day location (Mous 2003a). Interestingly, the subsequent creation of a mixed language entailed not just the retention of a Cushitic lexicon, but also recruitment of lexical resources from other sources such as various contact languages of the area, and perhaps also camouflaged lexicon from other in-group vocabularies.

Myers-Scotton (1998) offers a model for such partial language shift, referred to as an 'arrested matrix language turnover'. The idea is that a bilingual group's codeswitching behaviour – inserting lexical content words from the surrounding majority language into the grammatical sentence matrix of the ethnic minority language – is 'flipped' to create a mirror image of the same codeswitching pattern: insertion of lexical content vocabulary from the ethnic language into the majority-language sentence matrix. The new pattern then undergoes conventionalisation or fossilisation, resulting in a mixed language. The prediction is that content vocabulary will derive from the older community language. Several case studies offer partial confirmation of the model, though not in its full detail. Thus the relevant 'matrix' does not usually encompass, as the theory predicts, all grammatical 'system morphemes', but rather that portion of morphosyntax that is relevant for the initiation of the predication (see above). Bearing in mind this modification, the turnover model can be applied not just to Ma'a but also to Copper Island Aleut, where Aleut was the 'old' community language and continues to provide lexicon and nominal morphology, while Russian, the dominant majority language, provides verbal morphology. Indeed, Vakhtin (1998: 321) suggests that a young, bilingual generation of Aleut and Russian mixed origin, whose dominant language was Russian, made a conscious effort to maintain the language of their parent and grandparent generation by replicating Aleut structures, albeit selectively. Copper Island Aleut was thus a kind of 'invention' of the younger generation who wished to restore the 'language of the elders'. Such an attitude towards the old community language is very much apparent as a motivation behind the ongoing formation of the two Australian mixed languages Gurindji Kriol (McConvell & Meakins 20025) and Light Walpiri (O'Shannessy 2005). Here too, the abandonment of the old language is characterised essentially by the loss of the ability to form predications in that language; this ability becomes limited to the dominant language of the surrounding majority population. We thus find that mixed languages may arise, in fact, in situations of competition between languages, in which the winner does not take it all, but does take the predication.

1.8 Towards an integrated scenario: The functional turnover model

In the present section I shall briefly outline the scenario that in my opinion best provides a full account of the motivation behind the formation and retention of Angloromani in its present form. Romani was initially spoken in Britain by a small community of immigrants from continental Europe. From what we know about the structure of Romani society we can assume that this 'community' was in fact comprised of clusters of nuclear families that lived and travelled together as extended households. Romani was their family language, while English served for all interactions outside the extended household, which will have included all business transactions with the settled society but also occasional business and possibly also social interaction with other communities of local Travellers, if and where such encounters took place and if, as we know happens today both in Britain and in other countries, some particular affinity was felt with those Travellers who were not Romani, but to some extent at least shared their social position and destiny with the Romani families. Thus, English may have played a role as a language of social interaction from an early phase in the history of Romanies in Britain. To the extent that fairs and other events provided regular meeting points with other Romani-speaking clans, we can assume that Romani also had a role to play in the semi-public domain, in interactions, whether social or business-oriented, with members of other Romani clans at fairgrounds and other public places. Romani will thus have served as a kind of community language as well, and quite possibly also as the carrier language for any community oral traditions such as stories and songs.

In addition to these functions Romani will have served members of the Romani community as a medium for any internal communication that was to be concealed from bystanders, whether warnings or brief consultation on strategy. This was a secondary function of the language, exploited since a foreign language provided an opportunity to withhold conversational content from outsiders, and since the nature of the socio-economic activity profile in which Romanies were typically engaged provided a need for group-internal communication. The tight-knit structure of Romani communities, the value of individuals' loyalty to one another and of shared spirituality and morality, and the marginalisation and persecution of Romanies all found their linguistic-structural expression in the need for in-group euphemism and dysphemism and the symbolic value of a separate linguistic code that was inaccessible to outsiders. Romani was thus both a vehicle for everyday communication, with all that this entails – narration for the purpose of information sharing and entertainment, social conversation, descriptive discourse and negotiation, and so on – and at the same time a symbolic resource through which in-group structures and values could be strengthened and displayed.

Two principal factors seem to have contributed to the decline of Romani as a language of everyday communication. The vulnerable position of the Romani minority as a visible, immigrant population with foreign customs and language will have created an incentive to abandon any conspicuous use of a foreign language in order not to appear foreign. In addition, interaction with indigenous, English-speaking Travellers will have had a strong impact on the lifestyle of the Romanies and ultimately, through close associations and intermarriage, also on their family structure and so on daily routines. Socialising with English-speaking Travellers will have triggered the use of English as the language of conversation, as is the case with any linguistic minority whose bilingualism is unidirectional rather than reciprocal. Let us assume that even just one single member of an extended Romani family married an indigenous Traveller woman who then joined his household, then English would have become the language of one of just a few nuclear families within the household, and any interaction that encompassed all members of the household would have had to accommodate that English speaker. If such cases were isolated and rare then it might have been likely that pressure would have been exerted on those joining the clan to learn Romani – and quite possibly some of them did. But frequent intermarriage would have created more and more households in which English gradually became the dominant language.

This development did not proceed at full pace in all regions of the country. It appears to have begun in the south, where contact between Romanies and indigenous Travellers was most intensive, proceeding gradually to the north, where Romani was not abandoned until the second half of the nineteenth century or even later. It is likely that the infiltration of English into individual nuclear families as a result of intermarriage led first of all to the weakening of Romani as the language of the relevant nuclear families, and also resulted gradually in a shift to English in the affected extended households, which now needed to accommodate a number of English monolingual members. In practice, this meant that everyday leisure conversation as well as the sharing of information and attitudes through narratives and descriptive and argumentative discourse were carried out more frequently in English. Once this became the pattern in a large number of nuclear families, followed by a large number of extended households, semi-public use of Romani in larger gatherings inevitably declined as well. Romani thus gradually retreated and was replaced by English as a language of the nuclear family, the household and any community-level interaction.

The abandonment of Romani meant that English became the language that most community members used to construct and contextualise utterances. It became the language in which utterances were planned and organised. This meant that English was relied upon for the production of the predication of each and every utterance. It did not necessarily mean that Romani vocabulary was lost. As a tight-knit itinerant group, the community continued to require its own in-group lexical reservoir as a linguistic manifestation of its own social values as well as for intimate warnings and other defiant or bystander-oriented communication. In order to serve as a symbolic resource of this kind, the retention of lexicon was sufficient. This created a motivation to maintain a lexical reservoir that could be inserted into the English predication whenever the need arose.

Romani thus underwent what we might characterise as a turnover of functions: it had been the language of the predication that was required in order to sustain any form of continuous discourse-level interaction, be it at the level of the nuclear family, the extended household or the community in the semi-public domain, and be it for the purpose of negotiation, argumentation,

exchange of information, ritual, or simply leisure conversation and socialising. It now became the linguistic referential resource that was needed in order
to flag group membership and the spiritual and moral values associated with
it, and to disguise key propositional content from outsiders. Serving now as a
lexical reservoir, Romani became subjected to creative processes of manipulation and lexical manufacturing. New word compositions emerged, special
lexicon infiltrated from other sources, and figurative extensions, semantic
analogies and morpho-phonological distortions became the preoccupation of
users. As in the case of other in-group lexical reservoirs, a two-way interface
with slangs and other in-group lexicons came into existence, with Romani
elements enriching these speech varieties while other resources were drawn
upon to enrich the Romani lexicon.

As more and more Romani-speaking households underwent this process
of functional re-allocation, replacing one function of the old language with
another, the inflected Romani dialects of Britain disappeared. The surviving Romani-derived structures now serve only some of the more specialised
and group-specific functions that the old language had had, namely to flag
intimate identification with the group and its norms. This procedure is now
carried out by activating a special mode at the level of the individual speech
act, a mode that triggers associations with a group-internal set of values and
the intimate relationship of loyalty and interdependency that normally exists
between members of the Romani community. This special, *emotive* conversational mode is triggered by the insertion of any number of words from the
special lexical reservoir into an utterance. Unlike conventionalised mixed languages or pidgins, it does not require any consistency in the choice of lexical
items at the discourse or even at the utterance level. Alongside the selection of
words from the special linguistic repertoire, the special conversational mode
is also characterised by a relaxation of some of the rules on grammatical
well-formedness that exist in the everyday English speech of the community.
In the British context, speaking 'Romanes' has thus taken on the meaning of
adopting a particular attitude to English sentence formation along with the
tendency to enrich it, at the user's discretion, with word forms belonging to a
special linguistic repertoire not shared by group-outsiders.

2 The Roots of Romani

2.1 Pre-European origins

The form of Romani that was first documented in Britain (see Chapter 3) was clearly closely related to the varieties of the language that continue to be spoken all across the European continent. By carrying out systematic comparisons of Romani language samples recorded from Gypsies in different locations in Europe with other languages selected almost at random, scholars in the second half of the eighteenth century were able to establish an affinity between Romani and the Indo-Iranian language group, and more specifically with the languages of India (Marsden 1785, Rüdiger 1782). The actual breakthrough came with Rüdiger's lecture delivered in 1777 (and published in 1782). The paper contained for the first time not just a comparison of word lists in Romani and Hindustani, but also a systematic discussion of grammar at the levels of morphology and syntax and an analysis of similarities as well as differences between the two languages along with an attempt to provide an explanatory account of the changes and innovations that have affected Romani. Rüdiger's position was then replicated in Grellmann's (1783) monograph, which, well marketed, became the more frequently cited source for the hypothesis that the Romani language is of Indo-Aryan stock and that the ancestors of the Roma therefore descend from a migrant population of Indian origin. Since Grellmann's other ideas about the Gypsies have generally been discredited – for one, he was an advocate of enforced assimilation, but he also became known for his plagiarism (cf. Ruch 1986) – some writers with no familiarity with the methods of historical linguistic reconstruction have found it appropriate to question Grellmann's Indian origin hypothesis and the linguistic evidence cited in support of the idea (see especially Willems 1997). However, the linguistic evidence stands and has not found a serious contender within linguistics since its was presented and assessed in its original form by Rüdiger (1782).

Less straightforward is the answer to the question of what precisely the linguistic evidence is able to tell us in regard to more specific areas of origin and times of migration. It is generally accepted that little can be said about the circumstances and motivations for migration on the basis of linguistic data alone. Turner's (1926) work established that Romani originated in the Central group of Indo-Aryan languages in a dialect cluster that ultimately gave rise to the predecessor idioms of modern-day languages such as Hindi/Urdu and Gujarati, but that it later broke away from this group and continued its development in proximity to the Indo-Aryan languages of the northwestern subcontinent, notably the so-called Indo-Iranian frontier languages or Dardic languages such as Kashmiri. Turner's method was to examine both the outcome and the relative chronology of a number of major sound developments that divide the Indo-Aryan languages and to try and accommodate the succession of changes in Romani within this comparative grid. Below I will paraphrase some of Turner's observations along with additional descriptions of the succession of structural developments that help lend the language the shape that it has today.

The transition period from Old Indo-Aryan (OIA) to Middle Indo-Aryan (MIA), sometime in the early part of the first millennium CE, gave rise to distinct linguistic changes in various regions of the Indian subcontinent. The outcomes of these changes are the earliest features through which distinct regional dialects in India can be distinguished. In Romani, the outcome of these early changes is closely aligned with that displayed by the languages of the Central group. Syllabic *r* as in OIA *śrn-* 'to hear' develops in Romani into a raised vowel: Romani *šun-* (cf. Hindi *sin-*). The consonant cluster in OIA *akṣi* 'eye' is simplified to *k*: Romani *jakh* (Hindi *akhi*). The cluster in OIA *asmnan, tusme* 'we, you.pl.' loses its sibilant (*s*) segment, giving Romani *amen, tumen* (Hindi *ham, tum*). The initial semi-vowel in OIA *yuvatih* 'woman' becomes an affricate: Romani *džuvel*. This combination of traits places the ancestral form of Romani in close proximity to those of the present-day Central languages of India.

But Romani also shows a number of traits that are more conservative than the corresponding features in the modern Central language and in some cases even more than in their medieval predecessors, indicating that Proto-Romani became isolated from the other Central languages during the early medieval period, perhaps around the middle of the first millennium. The relevant features include preservation of consonant clusters such as *st* in *v-ast* 'hand', *dr* in *drakh* 'grape', *št* in *mišto* 'well' and *tr* in *patrin* 'leaf', as well as the retention of intervocalic dentals as in *gelo* 'gone' (OIA *gata*). All of these are lost or simplified in the Central languages. Since many of these conservative traits are preserved in the languages of the Northwest, Turner (1926) had concluded that the isolation from the Central languages and absence of the relevant innovations in Romani were a result of an emigration away from the Central zone and into the Northwest at a time before the relevant changes spread within the Central languages.

It is noteworthy that other, more widespread changes that affected the whole of the Indo-Aryan-speaking area during the second half of the first millennium did also encompass Romani. These include the general reduction of the older system of nominal case inflection to an opposition between nominative and non-nominative (oblique), the simplification of some consonant clusters, as in OIA *sarpa* 'snake', MIA *sappa*, Romani *sap*, or OIA *rakta* 'blood', MIA *ratta*, Romani *rat*, and the collapse of the old inflected past tense and its replacement through a generalisation of the past participle. These changes could well have reached Romani while the language was being spoken in Northwest India.

There is further evidence of a development phase in Romani that was influenced by the languages of the Northwest: one of the affixes used to derive transitive verbs from nouns and adjectives, *-ar-*, appears to have a northwestern origin and may have been adopted during this phase. The final consonant cluster OIA *-nt* undergoes voice assimilation to *-nd*, as in *dand* 'tooth', a typical northwestern development (cf. Turner 1926). A further feature that stands out is the renewal of the past-tense conjugation through synthetisation of oblique enclitic pronouns. These had been used following the generalisation of the participle to indicate the agent of the action, as in **kerda-yo-se* 'done-which-by him/her', **kerda-yo-me* 'done-which-by me', and so on. From agentive clitics they became person suffixes that were now attached to active past-tense verbs. The development is common in the languages of the Northwest, such as Kashmiri, and appears to have taken an identical path in Romani (Table 2.1): *kerd-j-as* 'he/she did', *kerd-j-om* 'I did', etc. (see Matras 2002: 146–51). This development leads to a loss of ergativity, or perhaps prevents the full development of ergativity in the language – a further contrast to the Central Indo-Aryan languages. At the same time, Romani remains conservative in its retention of the present-tense person conjugation, a Middle Indo-Aryan relic that is preserved in very few languages in such an archaic formation (Table 2.2).

Table 2.1 Romani innovative past-tense person markers and their MIA pronominal predecessors

Person	Participle verb form ('done')	Romani subject concord marker	MIA clitic	Romani full past-tense form
1sg.	*kerd-a*	*(j)om*	*me*	*kerdjom*
2sg.		*(j)al*	*te*	*kerdjal, kerdjan*
3sg.		*(j)as*	*se*	*kerdjas*
1pl.	*kerd-e*	*(j)am <(j)an*	*ṇe*	*kerdjam*
2pl.		*(j)an*	*ṇe*	*kerdjan*
3pl.				*kerde*

Table 2.2 Romani archaic present-tense subject concord markers and their OIA predecessors

Person	Root verb form ('do')	Romani subject concord marker	OIA marker
1sg.	*ker-* (OIA *kar-*)	*-av*	*-āmi*
2sg.		*-es*	*-asi*
3sg.		*-el*	*-ati*
1pl.		*-amas*	*-as*
2pl.		*-en* < 3pl.	*(-athi)*
3pl.		*-en*	*-anti*

2.2 Innovations acquired outside the Indian subcontinent

A series of innovations stand out as separating Romani from the bulk of the Indo-Aryan language group and may be traced quite possibly to the continuing development of the language outside the Indian subcontinent, perhaps as a result of contacts with some of the smaller and more isolated Indo-Iranian frontier languages such as those of the Pamir region, or possibly through the influence of Iranian languages proper or even through that of neighbouring languages of the Caucasus. These innovations include the synthetisation of postposed case markers that are inherited from the late Middle Indo-Aryan period, giving rise to a new set of agglutinating case endings: *rom-es-ke* 'for the man', *rom-es-tar* 'from the man', *rom-es-sa* 'with the man', *rom-es-k-o* 'of the man' and so on. New vocative endings emerge in all likelihood through attachment of deictic elements: *rom-ále!* 'people!'.

In verb morphology, a uniform (person-independent) external tense marker emerges based on the 3SG copula form **-asi*, resembling in etymology and function the external marker of remote tense found in Kurdish and other Iranian languages. It is used to form the remote past (or plurperfect) when attached to the past-tense form, and to form the imperfect (durative or habitual past) when attached to the present-tense form. An older morpheme *-*jov-* (a grammaticalisation of the verb 'to become', OIA *bhuv-*), used to form intransitive derivations (passives and inchoatives), is supplemented by the verb *av-* 'to come', which now takes on similar functions as an auxiliary, much as in the Iranian languages. Loan verbs appear to have been integrated into the language drawing on a pattern that is now widespread in an area stretching from the Caucasus all the way to the Indian subcontinent. This type of system uses the verbs 'to do' and 'to become' as light verbs, differentiating transitive from intransitive loan verbs (see Matras 2002: 129–30). This procedure triggers a grammaticalisation of the verb *ker-* 'to do', which, like *av-* 'to come/ become', becomes a kind of auxiliary or derivational extension to lexical verbs. Some syntactic developments, such as the emergence of prepositions from local relation adverbs, the shift to postposed relative clauses and other subordinations, and the reduction of infinitives might also have been triggered by contacts in this region.

In phonology, Romani undergoes several characteristic changes during this stage, the most outstanding of which are perhaps the transformation of medial dental stops to liquids – *mulo* 'dead' from OIA *mṛta* archaic MIA **muta*; *ker-el* 'he/she does', from OIA/MIA *kar-ati* – and the de-voicing of aspirated stops – *phen-* 'to say' from MIA *bhan-*, *thov-* 'to wash' from *dhāv-*. Both processes agree with developments in the Indo-Iranian transition languages, in Iranian proper and in some of the other neighbouring languages of the Caucasus and Anatolia. There is some evidence to suggest that a series of different retroflex sounds collapsed during this period and merged into a reduced set of, apparently, just two: a simple retroflex, as in Romani *řom* 'man' from *řom*, *ařo* 'flour' from MIA *āṭa*, and *phuřo* 'old man' from MIA *buḍḍha*; and a complex retroflex cluster, as in Romani **maṇḍřo* 'bread' from *maṇḍa* and **aṇḍřo* 'egg' from *aṇḍa*.

The Romani lexicon shows some clearly identifiable traces of both Iranian and Armenian influences. It contains basic vocabulary words, such as *bov* 'oven', *grast* 'horse' and *pativ* 'honour', of Armenian origin, alongside words, like *zor* 'strength', *baxt* 'luck' and *sir* 'garlic', of Iranian origin, as well as a number of words, such as *tover* 'axe', *arčič* 'tin' and *mom* 'wax', that are found both in Armenian and in the neighbouring Iranian languages. While the more traditional view in Romani linguistics had been to interpret this loan vocabulary as an indication of successive migrations, first into Iranian-speaking territory and then to Armenian-speaking territory (cf. Pott 1844–5, Sampson 1923), it is quite possible that this loan vocabulary as well as contact developments in the domains of phonology and morphosyntax were all acquired in a multilingual setting, following Romani settlement in the eastern parts of Asia Minor (eastern Anatolia), where contact with both Armenian and Iranian languages will have been simultaneous.

2.3 The impact of Greek

Another language that could have come into contact with Romani during the same period is Byzantine Greek. Its initial impact on the language seems to have been moderate, leading to the integration of loanwords into existing Romani inflection paradigms. Thus the Greek word *drom* 'way, road' acquires the Romani plural form *drom-á* 'roads' by analogy with inherited (Indic) nouns like *řom* 'man', plural *řom-á*, and the Greek word *kurkó* 'week' acquires the Romani plural form *kurké*, by analogy with inherited (Indic) nouns ending in a vowel, such as *čhavó* 'boy', plural *čhavé*. But subsequent Greek loans tend to retain much of their original inflection. Greek-derived nouns keep their nominative endings, as in the singular forms in *-os*, *-is*, *-as*,

-us, *-o*, *-i,* and *-a* and plurals in *-i*, *-e*, *-es* and *-ides* (thus *fóros* 'town', plural *fóri*). Verbs retain their tense augments, such as present-tense *-in-,-an-*, *-iz-*, *-az-* and so on, and aorist *-is-* and others (thus *jir-iz-ava* 'I return', *jir-is-ajlom* 'I returned'). There is some evidence that even Greek person inflection was sometimes replicated along with Greek verbs, as the Greek 3SG marker *-i* survives in some Romani dialects with loan verbs. A massive amount of vocabulary is borrowed from Greek, including everyday terms such as *luludí* 'flower', *kirvó* 'godson', *skamín* 'chair', *karfín* 'nail', *kókalo* 'bone' and more. Grammatical vocabulary is also borrowed, including items such as *tajsá* 'tomorrow', *pale* 'again', *akómi* 'still', *típota* 'something', *párpale* 'back', as well as the numerals *eftá* 'seven', *oxtó* 'eight' and *enjá* 'nine', and in most dialects also those for 'thirty', 'forty', 'fifty' and above. Along with the vocabulary, derivational markers are borrowed, such as the abstract nominaliser *-imos* (*sasto* 'healthy', *sastimos* 'health'), the participial marker *-imen* (*krestimen* 'baptised'), the adjectival markers *-itiko/-itko* and the ordinal marker *-to*.

Much of this borrowed material is retained in the individual dialects long after emigration out of the Greek-speaking areas. Romani dialects tend to have anywhere between 100 and 200 Greek-derived words in their basic lexicon, and put together the number of distinct Greek lexemes that survive in Romani outside of Greece is around 250, out of a shared lexical pool of around 1,000 word roots. Perhaps the most remarkable impact of Greek has been to equip Romani with a new productive set of inflection markers, nominal and verbal. Many of the affixes mentioned above are retained in Romani and are assigned to new vocabulary from subsequent contact languages. Thus a typical loanword from the contemporary contact languages such as 'doctor' will normally be assigned a Greek-derived nominative ending, e.g. *-is*, *-o* or *-os*, thus *doktoris*, *doktoro* or *doktoros*. Loan verbs are typically integrated into Romani conjugation paradigms with the help of special loanword adaptation morphology, which in some dialects directly continues a selection of Greek-derived tense markers such as *-in-*, *-iz-* or *-is-*: thus Romanian *într-* 'to enter' may be borrowed as *intri-iz-av*, *intri-in-av* or *intri-is-ar-av* 'I enter'. In some dialects of Romani, the Greek-derived 3SG person ending continues to attach to loan verbs from the new contact languages: thus *pomož-in-i* 'he/she helps', of Slavic origin.

The powerful impact of Greek justifies the reconstruction of a distinct period in the history of the Romani language, which we might name 'Early Romani' (see Matras 2002, Elšík & Matras 2006). The Early Romani period was in all likelihood characterised by the same kind of intense and widespread bilingualism that has been typical of Romani communities in Europe ever since. Romani will have served both as the language of the nuclear family and the extended household and, to the extent that there were social or trade contacts among families and clans, as a language of the community used in the private and sometimes in the semi-public domain. Greek, the principal language of administration and commerce in the Byzantine Empire, was the language of work, since work depended on contacts with the sedentary client population. Indirectly, then, the Greek impact on Romani confirms the existence of a service economy as well as the territorial dispersion of Romani communities.

The Early Romani period was also significant for the typological development of Romani as a 'European', and specifically southeastern European or Balkan, language. Greek had an influence not just on the vocabulary and morphology of Romani but also on its syntactic typology. Greek-based word order rules are adopted and Romani becomes essentially a language with Verb–Object default order, the only Indo-Iranian language that does not show obligatory Object–Verb order. The position of the subject becomes variable, alternating pragmatically between Subject–Verb (the default order for clauses with new thematic information) and Verb–Subject (the default order for consecutive or connected events). All clauses are finite, and infinitives and participles become marginal, and non-existent in modal constructions and purpose clauses. Adverbial clauses and complements are finite and are introduced by conjunctions derived largely from interrogatives, and complementation structures show a split between factual or epistemic clauses (those that follow verbs of perception, such as 'I knew that . . .') and non-factual or subjunctive clauses (which follow verbs of volition or intention, such as 'I wish that . . .'), following the model of Greek and the other Balkan languages. The old set of demonstratives in *ov, oj, ol* is used, as in Greek, for third person nominative pronouns 'he', 'she', 'they', while the earlier set of nominative pronouns *lo, li* fall out of use and is only preserved in some dialects as enclitic pronouns in non-verbal predications. Romani also develops a preposed definite article, again based on the Greek model, grammaticalising reduced forms of the remote demonstratives *ov, oj, ol* (quite often *o, i, elle*) for this purpose.

2.4 Towards a chronology of Romani migrations

At this point it is useful to review the linguistic evidence that points to successive development stages of the Romani language in different geographical environments and to try and assess the implications of what is, in effect, a reconstruction of mobility in the early history of the Romani-speaking population. From the outset it is crucial to emphasise that no historical record is known to date that can be linked unequivocally with the ancestors of today's Romani population, nor is there any specific mention of the Rom or their language, nor any other specific citation from the Romani language that would allow us to link any general historical events with the specific population known as Rom. None the less, speculation about the participation of an ancient Romani population in various state institutions, migrations, battles and so forth has been thriving since the second half of the nineteenth century (and partly even earlier). It has recently been given a renewed impetus through the work of a circle of Romani political activists and their supporters engaged in trying to disseminate a historical narrative that is intended to portray the Rom in a way that challenges popular images about them. The principal argumentation line in these essays is that the ancestors of the Roms had occupied a high and privileged status in their country of origin, but were deprived of this status under various circumstances and forced into exile in Europe, where marginalisation and stigmatisation first emerged (see e.g. Hancock 2002, Marsh 2008). Critics of this thesis are often branded justifiers of the social exclusion that is imposed upon the Rom (see Hancock 2008; cf. discussion in Matras 2003).

While the reasons for emigration from India remain inaccessible to investigators, there is some circumstantial evidence to be considered. It concerns primarily the presence of other groups with Indic languages and service economies outside of India, such as the Jat of Afghanistan, the Parya of Central Asia, the Lom of the Caucasus, and the Dom of the Middle East. These groups used to, and in most cases continue to, specialise in the same range of traditional occupations as the Rom of Europe, i.e. in a mobile service economy. The groups maintain a tight-knit community structure based on kin loyalty even when settling in urban districts. The names they give to themselves derive from Indian caste names and many correspond to existing caste names still found in India today, such as that of the *ḍom*, who specialise in a mobile service economy. The names they use to denote the outside, settled population are often cognate with the Romani word *gadžo* and point to a shared conceptual understanding of the roles of outsiders (though not necessarily to a shared ancient language, beyond the fact that all groups speak related modern Indo-Aryan languages). The presence of these various groups outside of India confirms an overall phenomenon of emigration from India of specific caste groups and the maintenance of caste-like identity even after the breakaway from the actual caste-based social system of the Indian subcontinent.

Like the Rom and the Middle Eastern Dom, some of these populations, e.g. the Parya of Afghanistan and Tadjikistan or the *ḍum* of the Hunza Valley in northern Pakistan, speak Central Indian languages. In connection with the linguistic changes discussed above and the periods in which they are documented in writing, the prevailing assumption continues to be that the Rom are descendants of a population belonging to mobile, service-providing castes who migrated from central India northwards in early medieval times, sometime around the middle of the first millennium CE. They remained in the Indian subcontinent long enough for their language to manifest the typical features of the major transitions to Early New Indo-Aryan, thus possibly until the ninth or tenth century CE, at which point the population migrated once again, settling eventually in the eastern regions of the Byzantine Empire, in or around present-day eastern Anatolia bordering the Caucasus.

An origin in service-providing castes in India could well be reconcilable with the view that the Rom left India as camp followers who made their living by providing crafts and services to military forces. This idea was first put forward by De Goeje (1903), and has since offered a middle-of-the-road explanation for the migrations of the Rom: they were neither aimless wanderers, as they are often portrayed in the non-specialised literature, nor a prestigious caste of warriors and priests, as portrayed by some Romani activists (e.g. Kochanowski 1994). Some of the early loan vocabulary, such as the term *koraxaj* (also *xoraxaj*, used for 'Turks' and in some varieties of Romani generally for 'foreigner', from the name of the Turkic *Karakhanide* Empire in Central Asia), the Greek word *kris* ('judgement') used to denote traditional Romani courts, and Iranian *baxt* 'luck, good fortune', hint at a world view that was informed and inspired by the proximity to the military might of the Muslim Turkish armies, by the spirituality of neighbouring peoples, and by the social organisation of Byzantine Greek society. Quite possibly, the linguistic evidence of considerable contact with the populations of eastern Anatolia and the Caucasus and of intense contact with late medieval Greek-speaking society reflects a period during which the dependency on a civilian population was restored and the Rom took on a more permanent economic role in the eastern part of the Byzantine Empire. In any event, the intensity of the Greek linguistic influence prompts speculation that bilingualism and a stable position in Greek-speaking society may have lasted for many generations, perhaps as long as two or three centuries.

Early attestations of Gypsies that can be interpreted as references to the Rom rather than to any other itinerant population appear in the Balkans in the late fourteenth century and testify to the immigration by that point in time of a Romani population westward. Some authors have attributed this movement to the gradual disintegration of the Byzantine Empire and the threat of Turkish invasions. The fate of the Romani population of eastern Anatolia remains uncertain. The only known Romani-speaking populations in the region are the descendants of relatively recent immigrants from the Balkans, who arrived after the establishment of the Turkish Republic in the 1920s. But there are at least three other itinerant populations in the area: the Domari-speaking Dom, the Armenian-speaking Lom (who retain an Indic-derived vocabulary), and the indigenous Abdal, who have an in-group lexicon based partly on Domari as well as Romani. It is possible that the Rom moved out of the area, and that any remaining groups assimilated into neighbouring peripatetic communities or into the settled population. The Romani-speaking Zargar of Iranian Azerbaidjan are believed to have migrated eastwards to their present location from northern Greece sometime in the eighteenth century, indicating that there was at least some Romani presence in eastern Anatolia since medieval times, albeit of a transitory nature.

Much as for the immigration of Roma into the eastern Byzantine Empire, the reasons for their migrations in the fourteenth century into western and northern Europe remain unclear. The only hypothesis put forward so far suggests an attempt to escape from the turbulence surrounding the collapse of the Byzantine Empire and the gradual rise of the Ottoman state in its place. While this certainly might have triggered a movement out of the area by some, we must also note that the majority of the Romani population remained in the Balkans under Ottoman rule.

In all likelihood, judging by the chronicles that depict their arrival in numerous European towns, migration took place in households comprising groups of several dozen persons of all ages. The fact that during the early fifteenth century similar narratives were cited from Rom in different places regarding the reasons for their travel – a pilgrimage from Egypt being one of the more frequent stories recorded – and that possibly even safe-conduct letters were copied or otherwise shared between groups arriving in different locations at different times, indicates that there were contacts between individual households and perhaps even stable social networks across regions and locations. None the less, we must assume that during this period it was the family households, and their closest kin relations with whom they kept contact, that constituted the smallest social unit. Travelling in social isolation from the settled population, these units also constituted tiny speech communities. In the absence of any reports on large-scale settlements or the sudden arrival of larger Gypsy communities in any one location or region, we must assume that the period of migrations lasting well into the late fifteenth century was characterised by the random arrival and settlement of individual households in and around western and northern Europe. Members of kin-related households may have followed and joined those early migrants in places that proved favourable as far as the reception on the part of the settled population and the prospects of earning a livelihood in the short term were concerned, thus creating larger communities.

2.5 Dialect differentiation in Romani

2.5.1 The period of dialect formation

Settlement at a particular location usually meant that Rom were tolerated and given the opportunity to engage in trades for which there was local demand, without competing with local tradesmen. In the Ottoman and Habsburg Empires as well as in the Romanian principalities a general division emerged between itinerant Rom, whose trades required mobility between client populations, and settled Rom, who provided a range of services to local land owners as well as to villagers, including seasonal field labour. The ties and dependencies that were formed between these latter Romani communities and the settled population were of course particularly strong, even if the social distance between them remained enormous. To the

west and north of the Habsburg monarchy, however, there is little evidence
of any large-scale integration of a Romani workforce into local economies.
The Romani populations of these regions remained, often until the twentieth
century and in Britain until this very day, a mobile service economy. When
we speak of 'settlement' in this latter context we therefore mean the adoption
of a routine pattern of trade and services and a network of clients and opportunities based in a particular region and embedded in the economic, social,
geographical and linguistic context of that region.

The period beginning in the middle of the sixteenth century and lasting
well into the Enlightenment and the emergence of modern nation-states is
well known as a period of anti-Gypsy persecution, as testified by hundreds
of royal edicts, regional decrees and police memorandums from across the
European continent. But the absence of security and stability in the lives of
the Romani populations during this period does not necessarily contradict a
gradual process of accommodation to the particular social environment of
their territory of settlement. Indeed, in a period during which long-distance
travel will have been extremely difficult and even dangerous due to severe
limitations, local and regional networking will have been essential for survival. This includes both networking among the Romani households and
clans within a region or territory, and the cultivation of trade contacts with
the local settled population.

Despite the hostility of the state and probably a large portion of the
population too, the descendants of Romani immigrants in individual regions
underwent a kind of integration process: they acquired the regional languages and, without allowing them to interfere with their own group-internal
set of beliefs and values, they adopted each region's religion and even some
of the regional religious practices, such as pilgrimage to recognised locations and participation in certain festivities. They also maintained regional
networks through fairs and regular regional travel, thereby intensifying their
interaction with Rom from the same and the immediately neighbouring
regions. At the same time contacts with Rom in more remote locations were
gradually lost. Romani communities thus began to develop their individual
local identities without necessarily abandoning inherited traditions. Apart
from the differences acquired through partial accommodation to the external
environment, differences also emerged in internal organisation forms: dress
traditions, conflict-resolution institutions and forms of leadership, customs
surrounding marriage and death, and the precise forms of implementation of
an inherited code of honour and spiritual morality that tightly regulates the
mode of interaction among members of the community.

Documentation of the Romani language is rather sporadic until the
early eighteenth century, but becomes more prolific during this period with
growing interest in the movements, social and family networks, customs and
ultimately also the origins of Gypsies on the part of law enforcement agencies
as well as scholars and academics. Even the earliest specimens of Romani,

such as those by Borde (1542; see Miklosich 1879–8), van Ewsum (*c.* 1560; see Kluyyer 1910), Vulcanius (1597; see Miklosich 1879–8), Evliya (1668; see Friedman and Dankoff 1991) and Ludolf (1691; see Kluge 1901), when compared with one another, give a picture of dialect differentiation that greatly resembles the one that is familiar to us from contemporary observations. This picture becomes even more elaborate, covering many new regions, thanks to numerous compilations circulated in the first half of the eighteenth century. It confirms in yet more detail that by this period the major structural developments responsible for dialect differentiation within Romani had already taken place.

One possible way to interpret this is to assume that distinct dialects had already formed prior to migration and settlement in the individual regions. As indicated above, no language is entirely uniform and variation will have occurred within Early Romani too. It is likely that the speech forms of the individual clans that settled in various regions were not identical to one another in each and every structural aspect. However, since the westwards migrations were essentially migrations of extended kinship groups who set out to seek favourable opportunities to engage in local or regional service trade, and not migrations of tribes who took over entire territories, or a coordinated resettlement of populations from one particular district into another, it would require an extraordinary coincidence for larger territories outside the southern Balkans to be targeted exclusively by Romani families whose speech forms resembled one another, while families with different speech forms were attracted to other territories. The hypothesis of an Anatolian genesis of dialect differentiation in Romani as put forward by Boretzky and Igla (2004) and Boretzky (2007) is therefore difficult to accept. For one thing, it is impossible to corroborate such a hypothesis through evidence of any ancient dialect differentiation within Romani found in Anatolia itself. But it is equally difficult to imagine how linguistically coherent subgroups, even if they had existed in Anatolia, might have coordinated their migrations and settlement in western and northern Europe in such a way as to ensure the dominance of a particular Romani dialect in a particular area of settlement in the west. Moreover, many of the structural differences among the present-day dialects of Romani owe their existence directly or indirectly to the influences of the respective co-territorial languages. This concerns not just obvious loanwords, but also changes in the sound system and word stress patterns, lexical semantic developments, and changes in the productivity and frequency of particular inherited morphosyntactic patterns.

For example, the truncation of initial syllables, common to the Romani dialects of the west, affects the internal or inherited Romani structural component: consider German Romani *glan* 'in front' from **anglal*, *vela* 'he/she comes' from **avela*, and *pre* 'above' from **opral*. There is little doubt that this development is set in motion through the adoption of the Germanic initial word stress, and that such a development necessarily followed several generations of Romani–German bilingualism. But even other, genuinely internal changes might have been propagated more easily in the isolated, tight-knit, household-based Romani communities once these began to develop local identities of their own, along with shifting centres of prestige and targets of imitation. Finally, the present-day linguistic landscape of Romani testifies to the successive spread of innovations from a variety of different centres of diffusion, in different directions and to different extents, thus forming a complex web of intersecting territorial isoglosses. Such patterns cannot possibly emerge as a result of the import of coherent dialects into clearly demarcated zones. We must therefore conclude that the most prominent differentiation features separating present-day Romani dialects emerged after settlement and the adoption of a local Romani group identity; in other words, from the early sixteenth century onwards, and that they were well in place by the time documentation of Romani proliferated in the early eighteenth century.

2.5.2 Variation within Early Romani

While no language is entirely uniform, we lack any concrete evidence about any major dialect differences in Early Romani prior to the dispersion and settlement in Europe. There is, however, evidence that some processes that led to dialect differentiation were set in motion at a period prior to the dispersal and settlement in present-day locations. The evidence comes from the historical reconstruction of a variable coupled with an evaluation of the present-day geographical distribution of the complete set of forms representing that variable. The absence of clear geographical patterning, or a random distribution of the forms, in conjunction with the absence of any particular trigger for the various local developments, will indicate that variation existed prior to the dispersion and the formation of the dialects.

A good example is the adoption of the so-called prothetic segments *v-* and *j-* in word-initial position preceding *a-*. While a similar development in positions preceding *u-/o-* and *i-/e-* respectively can be regarded as phonologically conditioned (thus *ušt* 'lip' > *vušt*, *iv* 'snow' > *jiv*), Turner (1932) had identified the development preceding roots in *a-* as a morphological process, namely the fusion of the demonstrative-turned-definite article m. **ov* f. **oj* with the following noun. As evidence, Turner cites the initiation of the process in those three words in which consonant prothesis is uniform across all dialects of Romani: m. *v-ast* 'hand' < MIA *(h)ast*, f. *j-ag* 'fire' > MIA *agi*, and f. *j-akh* 'eye' < MIA *akhi*. It is clear that such a process could only have been set in motion after the emergence of definite articles, and so after contact with Byzantine Greek and therefore in the two centuries or so prior to the dispersal of Romani populations through Europe. At the same time, the initiation of the process will have begun before the definite article form was reduced to its present-day forms m. *o*, f. *i/e*, which is likely to have been long before the

European immigration since no present-day dialects retain full consonantal forms for the complete definite article paradigm. We are thus dealing in all likelihood with a development that began in Early Romani. During the common phase it was firmly adopted in the above three nouns, attaching variably to an additional small number of masculine nouns. Three of those are *v-ařo* 'flour', *v-angar* 'coal' and *v-andřo* 'egg'. The present-day distribution of the forms tends to follow a centre–periphery pattern, with various geographical peripheries (in changing constellations, depending on the individual word in question) selecting the more innovative form in *v-* while the centre ends up rejecting the innovation and opting to generalise the more conservative form. We thus end up with an interaction between the forces of geographical diffusion and the inheritance of variation.

Another case of such interface is the generalisation of copula stems containing the extension *-in-* (*s-in-om* 'I am' etc.) in the southern European periphery, comprising the Romani dialects of western Bulgaria, Macedonia and both sides of the Adriatic coast, while the dialects of Greece show a mixture that can be taken to represent the original variation in Early Romani (see Matras 2004: 102). Apart from the presence of both types of copula form, with and without *-in-*, in the present-day Romani dialects of Greece, additional evidence for historical variation comes from the occasional appearance of copula forms in *-in-* in isolated paradigm positions in other, more remote dialects, such as Finnish Romani and Eastern Slovak Romani, where they appear in the third person present (*hin, hine*). The origin of the formation is likely to be in the re-interpretation of the past-tense stem of the mono-consonantal root *s-/h-* as a present-tense form. The augment in *-in-*, originally an adjectival-participial ending, belongs to the pool of perfective endings that are favoured with ambiguous past-tense forms, such as those that are based on plain participles (third person forms, in particular third person plurals), passives and inchoatives, verbs expressing emotion, and a small set of mono-consonantal verb stems including *s-/h-* 'to be', *d-* 'to give' and *l-* 'to take'. Variation among the dialects thus reflects a stage of variation within Early Romani, where the choice of an augment was optional. After dispersion and settlement, individual varieties of the language opted for a stable setup. The generalisation of forms in *-in-* across a southern belt reflects the region-specific diffusion of a solution to an inherited option.

The co-existence of two separate copula stems in Romani – in *s-* and in *h-* – is itself a further illustration of the way Early Romani variation is inherited into the dialects. There are basically three continuation options. A group of dialects in Macedonia and Kosovo show both sets, directly continuing the inherited variation. Other dialects opt for either one consonantal root or another. In most regions we find that *s-* prevails, but the *h-*set is generalised in the Romani dialects of Germany and neighbouring regions and is also attested in individual dialects in Transylvania and in northern Greece.

The third option is to adopt a mixed paradigm, where forms in *h*- appear in individual slots, most probably in the third person present, and sometimes exclusively in enclitic position. Such mixed paradigms are attested in dialects as far apart as Montenegro, Slovakia and Finland, showing that there are instances of inherited variation for which no geographically coherent preference is visible. Instead, variation appears to be conditioned by local factors, and the geographical distribution is to some extent random. This pertains especially to the choice of lexical items. While some lexical isoglosses split the entire Romani-speaking landscape into large coherent zones, for numerous words neighbouring dialects have conflicting preferences. Most prevalent is a dense variation of preferences in southeastern Europe and the Balkans, the historical diffusion centre of all Romani dialects. Here we find, for instance, forms like *mami*, *baba* and *phuridaj* for 'grandmother', or *men* alongside *kor* for 'neck', side by side in the same region.

The Balkans are also home to numerous different realisations of the historical retroflex cluster *ṇḍ*, including the preservation of a retroflex sound (*maṛo* 'bread'), of various options of a non-retroflex cluster (*mandro*, *marno*, *mando*, *manglo* etc.), and of the simplex *r* that is otherwise prevalent throughout the north of Europe (*maro*). The density of different forms in close proximity to one another makes it quite easy to imagine the prolonged co-existence of different variants continuing the old cluster *ṇḍ* before the migration westwards. Finally, Early Romani appears to have shown palatalisation of dental and velar stops in positions preceding /i/, the results of which survive often in diverse, word-specific realisations of the original segments. Thus *(o)gi* 'soul, heart' may continue as *gi*, *dži*, *zi* and so on. Preference for one or the other continuation of a palatalised segment in one word does not necessarily imply a preference for a similar solution in another word. The outcome is a proliferation of combinations that are often specific to a particular local or regional speech community.

2.5.3 Local and regional changes

While we are able to postulate Early Romani variation for some cases of cross-dialectal differences found today, other cases appear to be the outcome of simplification and levelling processes acting upon the full and coherent Early Romani inheritance, albeit in different ways in different communities. Simplification and functional decline characterise the fate of various grammatical devices, among them the use of enclitic nominative pronouns of the set *lo, li, le*, the use of gerunds in *-indo(j)*, the use of Greek-derived 3SG concord ending *-i* and of Greek-derived numerals from 'thirty' onwards (which are often replaced either by internal formations or by subsequent borrowings), and the collapse of Greek-derived nominal inflection endings and verb integration affixes.

Many changes in the dialects are, of course, directly induced by language contact, and take on different shapes in accordance with the source language. Typical functional domains in which word form or morpheme borrowings occur are comparative and superlative markers in adjectives, nominative plural endings on the noun, indefinite markers and indefinite word forms, conjunctions and discourse markers, conditional and interrogative particles, modal verbs indicating necessity and ability, and prepositions such as 'against', 'between' and 'without'. Romani dialects in contact with Russian, Polish, Czech and Slovak tend to borrow the full set of so-called aspectual (aktionsart) prefixes. Other areas of morphosyntax are frequently subject to restructuring as a result of contact. They include the productivity of definite and indefinite articles, the semantic distribution of nominal cases, the generalisation of a single form of the verb in modal complements (infinitive), changes in word order (affecting especially the position of object pronouns), the productivity of verb derivational morphology, and the lexical-semantic expression of aktionsart. Typical contact-induced changes in phonology include the acquisition of vowel length, changes in stress patterns, the acquisition of additional phonemes and consonant palatalisation.

All this adds up to an enormous pool of potential innovations and so to numerous possible outcome scenarios of a local and regional character. As in any other language, every linguistic structure is potentially open to change and innovation in any community of speakers who use Romani. Many of these changes will remain confined to the domain of lexical preference in the context of family communication, and so they will have little affect on the speech of entire communities. Others will be strongly shaped by the contemporary contact language and will therefore spread more or less along predetermined lines defined by the nature of the multilingual setting. In between, changes might emerge locally and receive acceptance within a limited range of social interaction networks, encompassing perhaps a group of settlements or even a group of related families who interact with one another across greater distances. While all these innovations will contribute to shaping the speech variety of each and every individual and community, they are of little use towards an overall classification of Romani dialects due to the rather limited distribution that they receive. Any approach that chooses to focus on each and every local innovation without identifying a hierarchy of more and less prominent features for comparison will inevitably end up having to define the idiolects of individual speakers as potentially independent varieties. Having identified some of the areas that are particularly prone to variation in Romani, I shall therefore proceed in the next section to outline some of the more prominent developments that receive wide-scale diffusion across larger geographical spaces, and which slice through the Romani-speaking landscape and divide it into larger zones, i.e. into units that provide meaningful indications of historical networks of contacts among speaker communities during the relevant periods.

2.5.4 Territorial developments and major isoglosses

There is ongoing discussion in Romani linguistics whether to regard differences among dialects as territorial, i.e. conditioned by the location of a dialect relative to the geographical spread of a particular structural innovation, or as 'genetic'. The 'genetic' metaphor suggests that certain features must be taken for granted due to ancestry rather than be understood as the outcome of a gradual process of acquisition involving exposure, accommodation and finally adoption of the feature in question. Such an impression of the *Vlax* Romani dialects of northeastern Bulgaria had led Gilliat-Smith (1915) to classify them as 'genetically' distinct from other co-territorial varieties and to postulate that they were not formed in their present location, but had been brought into the region as a result of an immigration of Rom from Romania (specifically Wallachia). The noticeable presence of Vlax dialects in urban centres all across Europe, the outcome of later migrations from Transylvania and Banat from the mid-nineteenth century onwards, made the distinction between Vlax and non-Vlax dialects of Romani a pertinent one in subsequent work on Romani dialectology.

The dispersion of the Vlax, coupled no doubt with the very fact that Romani itself is known to have non-European 'genetic' origins, has created somewhat of a fixation within the study of Romani on interpreting distinctive structural features as proof of a primordial displacement rather than as the outcome of a process of acquisition through interaction and exchange (as an example see Boretzky 2007). In this section I will briefly show how the present-day distribution of major structural features within Romani in geographical space must be interpreted as the outcome of a series of major changes that spread across chains of neighbouring communities, each change subdividing the entire Romani-speaking landscape into a limited number of zones (see Map 2.1). While the spread of some developments follows common pathways creating clusters of linguistic boundaries or isoglosses, the patterns that emerge are by no means uniform. Instead, isoglosses intersect in numerous different ways in a complex matrix. This matrix can be read as an illustration of the ever-evolving targets of social contacts, prestige and imitation that lead speakers from one community to adopt selected features of speech that arise in a neighbouring community.

The geographical diffusion model goes hand in hand with an appreciation of historical migrations of population groups. We must reconstruct the original geographical context for those groups that are known to have migrated to their present locations after the formation period of the dialects had ended, that is from the eighteenth century onwards. To be sure, subsequent changes will have taken place in all dialects, but these must be examined separately. The so-called Southern Vlax dialects that spread among local, settled dialects of the southern Balkans must therefore be examined together with the closely related varieties of the adjoining regions to the north, namely Serbia and Banat and the continuum that they form into the Vojvodina region in the west and Wallachia and Transylvania to the east and north. Northern Vlax dialects that left the Transylvania and Banat regions in the nineteenth century must similarly be considered migrant dialects.

Secondly, there are indeed instances where shared structural features may confirm a breakaway of one group from another and its migration to a remote location. There is little doubt that the similarities between the speech forms of the Lithuanian Rom and those of the Russian Rom of the Urals will have emerged prior to the arrival of Rom in the Urals. They were not, in other words, a result of gradual changes to which a Romani population in the Ural had been exposed and which it adopted, but the result of an exchange that took place while the two groups had been in much closer proximity to one another, somewhere closer to the Russian Baltic coast, and were later on brought to the Urals by a population of migrants. Similarly, features shared by the Romani dialects of Germany and those of Finland are less likely to have diffused gradually from their emergence centre in Germany to reach a Romani population that had already been settled in Finland. It is much more plausible to attribute those features to a period during which the ancestor population of the Finnish Roma resided in or close to Germany. They were then carried in the speech of this group when it migrated to its present location.

Keeping our eyes open for such issues, the plotting of dialectal features on the map allows us to make the following generalisations about the geographical diffusion patterns of structural innovations among the dialects of Romani.[1] A major division is visible between the dialects of western and northern Europe and those of southeastern Europe. The dividing line (also referred to as the 'Great Divide'; see Matras 2005) runs roughly between northern Ukraine in the east and the northern tip of the Adriatic coast in the west (see Map 2.1). It is a cluster of isoglosses, not a single line, and the precise path of individual isoglosses varies somewhat. Some divisions run far enough to the north to include southern Poland and the whole of Slovakia as well as eastern Austria and Slovenia on the southern side of the line; others have a course that cuts across the region farther to the south, leaving either just northern Slovakia or sometimes the whole of Slovakia on the northern side of the line. Transition zones are not uncommon in this area even when we examine just a crude sample that does not take into consideration the full density of settlements or communities. Studies focusing on particular subregions are likely to find even greater variation on both sides of major isoglosses.

---

[1]   The discussion presented here is based on an ongoing evaluation of data from over 200 locations in Europe, compiled and stored as part of the Romani Morpho-Syntax Database (RMS). The resource is freely accessible online: http://romani.humanities.manchester.ac.uk/. For an additional comprehensive source of dialect maps for Romani see Boretzky and Igla (2004).

Even at a superficial glance it is quite clear that the Great Divide reflects the political division and conflict zone between the Habsburg monarchy to the north and the Ottoman Empire to the south, during the crucial period of dialect formation that followed Romani settlement, in the sixteenth and seventeenth centuries. The border separated two major Romani population centres and made it impossible for structural innovations that emerged on one side to be carried over and diffused on the other side. Here too, the presence of a geographical demarcation line does not exclude the possibility that population movements were partly responsible for shaping the precise distribution picture. The absence of a direct continuum between the Arli-type (Southern Balkan) dialects of Macedonia, Kosovo and Albania, and the (Southern Central) dialects of Slovenia, eastern Austria and Hungary, which share some similarities with the first group, might be interpreted as reflecting a displacement of Rom from present-day Croatia northwards, brought about quite possibly as part of the evacuation of civilian populations loyal to the Habsburgs during the seventeenth century. Rom from other regions further to the east will have moved into the region later, carrying with them the Vlax-type dialects that are spoken in Croatia today. Such a scenario must still be confirmed with the help of historical documentation. But even if confirmed it would not place in question the validity of the geographical diffusion model, but would merely add circumstances that could help explain why the division is so clearly pronounced over such a relatively dense zone, and why some of the isoglosses run much farther to the north than the old political borders and conflict zones, thus dividing southern and northern Slovakia.

The Great Divide or north–south division between Romani dialects represents the spread of a series of unconnected structural developments. Germany appears to be the epicentre for a series of innovations on the northern side. Syllable truncation is one of the typical developments in this region, triggered in all likelihood by a shift to word-initial stress as a result of Romani–German bilingualism. The north thus has *mal* 'friend' for *amal*, *khar-* 'to call' for *akhar-*, *sa-* 'to laugh' for *asa-*, often *kana* 'now' for *akana*, and more. Further developments include a preference for prothetic jotation in selected words, among them *jaro* 'egg' and the third person pronouns *jov* 'he', *joj* 'she', *jon* 'they', and the simplification of the historical cluster *ṇd* to *r* in words like *maro* 'bread', *miro* 'my' and *jaro* 'egg', while the south maintains a proliferation of cluster combinations that continue the historical sound (see above). The remarkable coherence of the entire northern area, from Britain to Finland, the Baltics and northern Russia, in relation to these features might be interpreted as an earlier spread among the dialects at a time when their areas of settlement were still closer to one another and social networks among them were tighter, or indeed prior to the split of an earlier group settled around the German–Polish contact area into several subgroups which then migrated in different directions. Note that the Romani dialects of the Iberian peninsula tend to remain conservative with respect of some of these features, indicating that they were not part of the network of contacts that enabled their diffusion of these features in the north.

A number of typically northern developments fail to reach the extreme northern periphery of Finland and appear to have been adopted after the breakaway of the Scandinavian subgroup. They include the loss of the preposition *katar* 'from', which is retained in both British and Finnish Romani, and assimilation of intransitive verbs of motion and change of state into the dominant verb inflection, and the disappearance of gender-inflected past-tense forms or active participles of the type *gelo* 'he went', *geli* 'she went' (retained in Finnish Romani).

A series of lexical preferences spread throughout the north, based on inherited variation that often continues in the south. Thus the north has *xač-* 'to burn' (in the south *phabar-*) and *stariben* 'prison' (*phanglipe* in the south, but also in Finnish Romani), as well as *angušt* 'finger' (*naj* in the south) derivations of *gi* for 'heart' (*ilo* in the south), and *men* 'neck' (*kor* in the south). The south, in turn, has its own non-conforming periphery usually comprising an area along the Black Sea coast and in Greece, and it is here that both *angušt* and *gi* are also preferred, while *men* is found sporadically in the Balkans alongside *kor*.

In the south, the epicentre of innovation appears to be Romania and adjoining regions in all directions. Prominent southern innovations include the loss of the nasal segment at the end of the nominalising suffix *-iben/-ipen*. The emergence of affrication in *tikno* 'small' > *cikno* predominates in the south, though the southern Balkans show a mixed region. By analogy with the preservation of initial *a-* segments, a strengthening of inherited initial segments is observed through addition of *a-* in words like *šun-* 'to hear' > *ašun-*, a development that is contained within the region between Ukraine in the north and northern Bulgaria and Serbia in the south, excluding the southernmost areas of the Balkans. South of the Great Divide, verbs belonging to the perfective inflection classes that had retained a perfective augment *-t-* are re-assigned to the class of verbs with an augment *-l-* (originally representing verb roots ending in vowels): *beš-t-jom* 'I sat' > *beš-l-jom*. Conservative forms occur occasionally in isolation in the south, especially along the Black Sea coast.

Some western innovations are contained and do not spread throughout the north, but continue eastwards, creating a kind of western-central innovation zone that is surrounded by retention zones. Two prominent cases in fact involve selection from a pair of competing Early Romani variants. The 2sg. past-tense and present copula conjugation marker *-al* was probably the older historical form (going back to the 2sg. oblique enclitic pronoun **te*). In Early Romani it appears to have competed with *-an*, an analogy with the 2pl. marker. The form in *-al* is generalised in the western innovation zone in Germany and spreads eastwards into central Europe to include the Romani dialects of the historical Habsburg monarchy and on to some of the dialects of Trans-Carpathian Ukraine, but leaves out the entire western periphery (Britain and Spain) as well as northern Poland and the Baltic areas. A very similar diffusion pattern is found for the predominance of -*h*- over -*s*- in grammatical paradigms and in particular in intervocalic position such as the singular instrumental/sociative case endings (*leha* 'with him' vs. *lesa*). Here too, the variation appears to go back to Early Romani. Note that *s/h* alternation is found in a wide transition zone encompassing the continental side of the Adriatic and stretching all the way to Transylvania (see Map 2.1). Finnish Romani matches this western-central diffusion zone for both items, indicating a rather early development, prior to its separation from the continental dialects.

Other prominent isoglosses divide the Romani-speaking landscape into further zones. Some outcomes of the western developments are contained even further and remain limited to Romani varieties spoken within the German-speaking area and neighbouring regions. These include the shortening of *anglal/angil* 'in front' to *glan/gil*, of *ame* 'we' to *me*, and of the verbs *ačh*- 'to stay' and *av*- 'to come' to *čh*- and *v*- (as examples for numerous other items affected by the process). The areas south of the Great Divide remain unaffected by these developments, but they are not replicated through the entire northern zone either. Instead, a northeastern zone emerges, with its epicentre in northern Poland, comprising the Baltic coast and North Russia and usually reaching northern Ukraine (see Map 2.1). Here, jotation appears consistently so that *ame* 'we' becomes *jame*, and the verbs *ačh*- 'to stay' and *av*- 'to come' become *jačh*- and *jav*-. A partition similar in shape emerges around analogies in the past-tense marker of the 2pl. The original -*an* prevails in the northwest as well as in a central belt connecting Germany all the way to the Romanian Black Sea Coast. The innovation centres are once again the northeastern zone, comprising Poland, the Baltics, Russia and Ukraine, where the predominant form is -*e* (by analogy with the 3pl.), and the southern periphery, from southern Romania through to the Mediterranean coast of France, where a partial analogy renders the form -*en*.

The Great Divide itself is occasionally transitional, with an intermediate central zone separating the north from the south. An illustrative example is the realisation of the word for 'horse', for which we typically find *graj* in the north, the more conservative form *grast* in the south, and an intermediate form *gra* in a central belt from the northern Adriatic to southeastern Ukraine.

Finally, a common pattern of isogloss formation separates centres from peripheries. The generalisation of the copula stem extension in -*in*- prevails within a periphery of a southern belt of dialects stretching from southern Bulgaria through to Macedonia and the northern edge of the Adriatic coast, including the dialects of southern Italy. As mentioned earlier, isolated forms in -*in*- are retained in other dialects as well. Roughly the same area is at the same time a retention zone for the verb *ov*- 'to become'. The north tends to generalise the verb *av*- in the sense of 'to become' at the expense of the older form *ov-*. None the less, some instances of *ov-* remain in the transitional dialects of Slovakia, while a similar development to that carried out in the north is also found in some of the Greek dialects. In effect, then, a three-way zone division emerges, the central one being a retention zone. An area including Ukraine and Romania, and stretching all the way to eastern Austria and southern Poland, serves as a retention zone for oblique forms of the definite article in *l-*, deriving in all likelihood from remote demonstrative/pronominal oblique forms in **oles, *ola, *olen*.

A prominent centre–periphery split appears in the attachment of prothetic segments in *v-*, as in *udar > vudar* 'door' and *ušt > vušt* 'lip'. The historically younger form in *v-* is found in the northernmost dialects of Scandinavia, Britain and western Europe, through to Italy and Greece and the southern Black Sea area. Conservative pockets are found north of the Black Sea coast and along the northern Adriatic, with a mixed zone stretching from southern Bulgaria to Transylvania. A more coherent conservative zone, completely lacking forms in *v-*, appears in Latvia, Lithuania and northern Poland.

The picture for lexical items in *a-* is almost a mirror image. For *angar > vangar* 'coal', the conservative form *angar* prevails in the centre, with the form *vangar* appearing in the Baltics (from northern Poland to Estonia), Britain and Italy. For *ařo* 'flour', the centre has conservative *ařo* in the south and jotated *jaře* in the north, while *vařo* prevails in the entire periphery belt of Finland, Britain, Italy, Greece and Crimea. With *aver* 'other', the spread zone of *vaver* is considerably wider, comprising the entire west and the Baltics as well as Greece, while *javer* appears in the zone with high jotation east of Poland, and the conservative *aver* is limited to the 'traditional' southern zone stretching from northern Bulgaria to southern Poland. By contrast, a three-way division is found for 'egg', with jotated *jaro* in the north, conservative *an(d)ro* in the south and *van(d)ro* only in the extreme southeast, covering isolated dialects of the Black Sea coast in Crimea and Greece, and the dialects of southern Italy.

Further conservative peripheries appear both in geographically marginal and in 'internal' regions. The preposition *vaš* 'for' survives in the Romani dialects of Latvia as well as in the so-called 'Central' dialects of eastern Austria, Hungary, Slovakia, southern Poland and northern Romania. Greek-derived nominal endings in *-is* and *-os* survive in the geographical margins in the Baltics (eastern Finland, Estonia, Latvia), in Britain, along the Black Sea coast from Crimea through to Bulgaria and Greece (primarily *-os*, with *-is* occurring in a smaller region in Bulgaria), as well as in the Northern Central dialects of northern Slovakia and southern Poland.

A similar conservative periphery – Britain, Spain, Italy, and the southern Balkans – shows retention of the original Early Romani demonstrative opposition set in *adava : akava* (with corresponding forms in *-o-*). The centre shows various innovation zones, where the original forms are simplified or reinforced to create opposition pairs such as *adava : dava, kada : kaka, kava:*

kavka and so on. Though zones partly overlap because of the many forms that can become part of the paradigm, a rough geographical split can be identified between a zone in northern Bulgaria and Romania (*kaka*), a central zone around Hungary and Slovakia (*kada*), a northeastern zone comprising Poland and Russia (*dava : adava*) with a unique retention subzone in the Baltics (*kada*), a major zone stretching from the Black Sea coast to the North Sea (*kava*), and a Finnish zone (*tava*).

Finally, we find an illustrative partition into zones involving the fate of Greek-derived tense markers, incorporated into Romani as a means of adapting loan verbs to Romani inflection patterns. The fact that here too we encounter a conservative periphery – proliferation of different forms is preserved in the dialects of present-day Greece, retention of *-isker-* also in Crimean and Zargari Romani, retention of *-isar-* both in Romania-Moldavia and in Spain, and the use of several parallel forms in Welsh Romani – indicates that Early Romani passed on a complex inventory of forms, which were later simplified in the individual dialects. The principal zones that share the same selection are the German–Finnish zone with *-er-/-ev-* (also *-ar-/-av-*), the Black Sea coast, northern Bulgaria and Greece with *-iz-*, Romania–Moldavia and adjoining regions with *-isar-* as well as contracted versions thereof, and a central-eastern zone from the Baltics and all the way down to western Bulgaria and southern Italy with *-in-* (primarily, with additional vocalic variation in the Balkans).

We can try and summarise the emerging picture as follows: in relation to several prominent features in phonology, morphology and lexicon, there is a tendency towards a north–south split. The division tends to follow the older (sixteenth–seventeenth-century) frontier zone between the Habsburg monarchy and the Ottoman Empire, with innovations occurring on both sides of the divide. A southeastern zone comprising Greece and sometimes also the Black Sea coast as well as adjoining inland regions is often conservative and retains either older forms, or a greater range of variants, reflecting its position as the historical centre of diffusion. Many of the features that are specific to other zones are in fact preferences favouring one of the older variants over another, rather than structural innovations in the strict sense. In addition to this southeastern periphery, other geographically marginal zones such as Spain, Britain, Scandinavia and southern Italy also tend to show archaisms as well as non-participation in certain predominant variant selections. With respect to individual features there are of course other retention zones as well; two of the more noticeable ones, which often share retentions, are the central zone (Austria–Ukraine, or sometimes just Slovakia–southern Poland) and the Baltic zone (sometimes just limited to Latvia) (see Map 2.1). Within the core (non-periphery) areas, there are further zones that tend to show coherences with respect to various features. They include the German–Finnish (northwestern) zone, the German–Hungarian (western-central) zone, the Romanian-Moldavian (Wallachian or Vlax) zone (with its

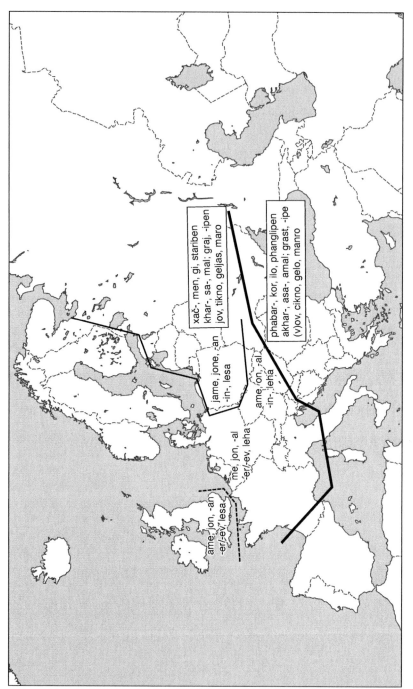

Map 2.1 Some major isogloss clusters in Romani

further penetration into Serbia and Croatia as well as Hungary and migratory spread even beyond these regions during the past two centuries), and the Polish–Baltic (northeastern) zone.

It must be emphasised once again that the participation of a particular region in a 'zone' with adjoining regions is by no means predetermined or static. Different isoglosses show different extents of diffusion, often in different directions, reflecting in all likelihood changing patterns of social networking over time. In some instances these networking patterns will have been influenced by concrete impediments such as political boundaries and the migration of population groups away from their earlier locations. In other cases, they might reflect shifting alliances between groups and consequent shifts in the prestige centre.

The coherences in the distribution patterns of some of the more salient morpho-phonological features have inspired scholars in Romani linguistics to apply a kind of reference grid for the classification of dialects. The prevailing discourse in Romani linguistics, first formulated explicitly in Bakker and Matras (1997; see also Matras 2002 and Elšík & Matras 2006 for an in-depth enumeration of groups and features) has since recognised the following dialect 'groups': Northern, subdivided into Northwest (German–Scandinavian), Northeast (Polish–Baltic); Central; Vlax; and Balkan (see Map 2.2). Aware of the rough nature of this classification, most authors tend to recognise subdivisions, splitting Central, Vlax and Balkan into northern and southern sub-branches respectively. Still, there remain a number of regions and dialects that are not easily accommodated in this reference grid, such as the Romani dialects of southern Italy or some of the Romani dialects of Ukraine, and there are numerous varieties of Romani that show combinations of features that are conventionally attributed to two distinct 'branches'.

All this goes to show that there is no static, predetermined 'membership' in a dialect group. Dialect groups are therefore not 'families' that prescribe an inescapable or unambiguous 'genetic' affiliation. They are, rather, terms of convenience that allow researchers to make generalisations about the distribution of structural features using an economical inventory of reference terms. In this light, the following chapter will deal with the specific formation of British Romani and its connections with the continental dialects.

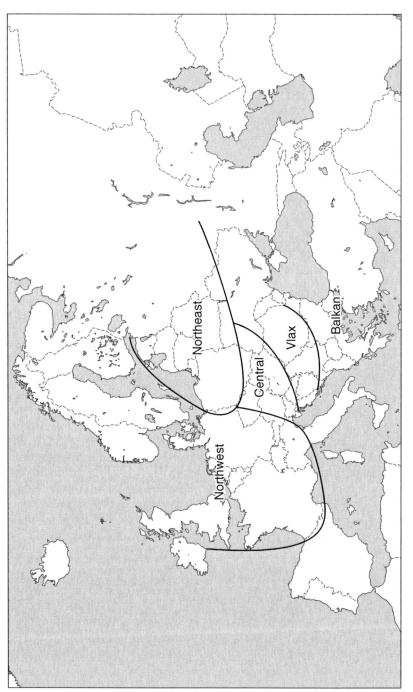

Map 2.2 Conventional dialect classification grid in Romani linguistics

3 The Historical Position of British Romani

3.1 The sources

Romani Gypsies, referred to as 'Egyptian pilgrims' in older sources, are known to have been present in Scotland in 1506 at the very latest, when they sought the protection of the king on a journey to Denmark (Simson 1866: 98), and may have settled in Scotland as early as 1460. According to Winstedt (1915: 129), the earliest reference to Gypsies in England is in a work of Sir Thomas More, who mentions an 'Egypcian' woman who told fortunes in Lambeth in 1514. A subsequent reference from 1687 confirms the wedding of Robert Hern and Elizabeth Bozwell, 'king and queen of the gipsies', at Camberwell. While many subsequent sources speak of 'vagrants' or 'travelling tinkers' who cannot unambiguously be connected with the Romanies, much of the history of the Romani-speaking community in Britain can be traced thanks to sources that provide us both with a description of the community and with a sample of their Romani speech. These offer attestations of the language from regions as far apart as Northumberland, Durham, Derbyshire, Cheshire, Norfolk, Hampshire and Kent. They suggest that families tended to be settled in particular regions, though individuals might move and settle elsewhere, and that families often spent the summer months in a different county, giving rise to immersion opportunities with other families. By and large, this pattern of continuous settlement, travel during the summer, and the occasional breaking away of individuals has been retained among the English Gypsies to this very day.

The sources that testify to the use of Romani among English and Welsh Gypsies vary in the quantity of the data they present as well as in the level of detail and scrutiny that these data are awarded. Many are vocabularies that can be relied on primarily for lexicon and so they leave open the question of whether, at a given time and place, Gypsies in Britain spoke an inflected form of Romani or merely embedded Romani-derived words in their English speech, as is the case today; or indeed, whether both practices existed side by side. Others, however, supply a sufficient number of phrases to allow us to ascertain that inflections and full sentence formation in Romani were indeed in use. Put together, the sources allow us to derive a comprehensive picture of British Romani as it was spoken before it was abandoned and succeeded by the present-day pattern of Romani lexical insertion into English.

The coverage of Romani in Britain begins possibly as early as 1542, with the publication of Andrew Borde's samples of thirteen English phrases with their Romani translations – the oldest documentation of Romani altogether (Miklosich 1872–80, Crofton 1907). No details about the source of the sample are given. It is assumed from the content of the phrases that they were written down during a casual and spontaneous encounter at a bar. The facsimile contains some notation errors, such as the interchange of 'n' and 'u' and of 't' and 'l'. Nevertheless, the short sample provides sufficient material to determine with certainty that it represents an inflected dialect of Romani, with forms such as *av-ava tu-sa* 'I-will-come with-you' (spelt *A bauatosa* in the original). The next source does not appear until 1615, with the publication of the Winchester confessions (McGowan 1996, Bakker 2002). This appendix to a criminal proceedings record documents the Romani vocabulary said to be in use by a group of outlaws. It does not contain examples of inflected Romani, and the brief illustration of Romani words embedded in English prompted Bakker (2002) to argue that the pattern of inserting special lexicon to form a 'mixed' speech variety as it is known to us today from Angloromani was already common in the early seventeenth century, long before the decline of inflected Romani.

Nearly two centuries pass before the date of the next recorded attestations of Romani in Brtiain. In 1785 William Marsden published a Romani vocabulary that incorporated material collected by Jacob Bryant among English Gypsies in Windsor in 1776 (see Sampson 1911). Bryant's list contains over 250 entries, most of them isolated vocabulary items, but also some examples of grammatical inflection, such as *drou panee jal*, translated as 'to bathe', literally 'he's going into the water' (*dro pani dža-l* 'in.the water go-3sg.'), *deas man* 'he gave me' (*dj-as man* 'gave-3sg. me.obl.') (glossed as *give me*), *shunaloe* 'he hears' (*šun-el-o* 'hear-3sg.-m.', with addition of an enclitic subject marker *-o*), *crellis escochare* for 'palace' (*krelis-es-ko kher* 'king-obl.-gen. house'), *prasthem* 'to run' (lit. 'I ran'), *towmah* 'to wash' (*tov-av ma* 'wash-1sg. me.obl.' 'I wash myself'), and a few more. An anonymous text dated 1798 contains what has become known as the 'East Anglian vocabulary of Romani' (Sampson 1930: 136). The manuscript was secured by John Sampson directly from a second-hand book seller in 1928 and contains around forty pages of phrases and word lists organised by semantic domains. Sampson believed it to be original and to show no trace of replication of any earlier published or known sources. A further valuable source is the material collected by Reverend Walter Whiter of Norfolk, who died in 1832. In 1858 it was sent by Goddard Johnson to Reverend T. W. Norwood, who copied the material (in full or in part) into his own notebooks and then returned the manuscript. Nothing is known, apparently, about the origin of the data or the precise date on which they were collected. According to Grosvenor (1908: 165), the material was collected before 1800, making it one of the earliest sources on British Romani.

By the early nineteenth century a number of 'collectors' had taken an interest in the Romani language, recording forms from a generation of speakers born in the late 1700s. A number of collections were published by the collectors themselves, including Frances Irvine's vocabulary recorded in 1819 from the Lee family in Hampshire (N.A. 1925), Samuel Roberts' material collected from his informant Clara Heron in 1836 (N.A. 1912), and Richard Bright's appendix to his book (Bright 1818) containing over forty sentences in inflected Romani obtained from an unidentified family (see also Russell 1916). Many of the manuscripts remained unknown or in private circulation until they were published, often with annotations, in the *Journal of the Gypsy Lore Society* in the early 1900s. Goddard Johnson's collection, completed in 1803, contains words collected at different times from different people, with no precise record of names or places (Scott Macfie & Winstedt 1939). Copsey's vocabulary was collected in 1818 from the Lovell family, whose base during the winter months was in London but who had travelled during the summer to the West of England as well as to Essex (Winstedt 1915). Major-General John Staples Harriott collected his list in 1819–20 in Hampshire from a member of the Stanley clan (Prideaux 1910), and Reverend Samuel Fox obtained his material between 1832 and 1833 in Derbyshire (Sampson 1926a). Sanderson's vocabulary was found in the British Library manuscript collection by John Griffiths. It had been compiled in 1872 by Reverend Robert Nicholas Sanderson working with members of the Boswell, Lee and Lovell families in Oxford and East Anglia (Griffiths & Yates 1934). The collections of T. W. Norwood from Cheltenham include notes taken in the early 1860s and are considered one of the rare sources of contemporary inflected English Romani (Grosvenor 1910).

Probably the most important landmark in the documentation of English Romani is the work of Smart (1862) and of Smart & Crofton (1875). The latter is a monograph-length description with accompanying texts of the English Romani dialect of the Boswell family of Cheshire. The study captures a key transition period in the history of the language and the co-existence of two separate styles of speech, referred to as the 'old' and 'new' dialects. The first still contains Romani inflections and clause-combining elements, while the second relies entirely on English morphosyntax. As we shall see below, even the 'old' dialect documented by Smart and Crofton in Cheshire shows considerable morphological erosion, especially in nominal inflection, compared to the Romani dialects of the European continent. Still, it is one of the last attestations of an inflected dialect of Romani in England. Way's vocabulary, collected in East Anglia in 1900 from the Cooper, Lock and Buckland families, shows only few inflected forms (Francis 1955), and sporadic attestation of some grammatical inflections is contained in various sources from East Anglia and Hampshire collected between 1909 and 1924 (N.A. 1929). Remarkably conservative, by contrast, is the Romani dialect of the Wood clan of North Wales, documented by Sampson in what is probably the most cited, seminal description of a Romani dialect (Sampson 1926b). Sampson was believed to have worked with the few remaining fluent speakers of the dialect in the last decade of the nineteenth century. None the less, the use of some grammatical inflections, albeit inconsistent, is still documented two generations later in the speech of the Boswell and Lee families, camping in 1950 in Caernarvonshire in North Wales (Tipler 1957).[1]

3.2 A structural overview of British Romani

The following sections draw on the sources that document British Romani in its various stages. Their purpose is to reconstruct the inflected dialect of Romani that gave rise to the 'mixed' form of English Romani – Angloromani or English Para-Romani – which can be heard today and which will be described and documented in the following chapters. Word forms are adapted to the general transliteration conventions of Romani dialectology unless there is a particular reason to quote a published source directly.

3.2.1 Lexicon and word formation

Like all dialects of Romani, British Romani inherits a 'Proto-Romani' core lexicon of pre-European origin, along with elements of a lexicon acquired during the 'Early Romani' period through contacts with Greek as well as Balkan Slavic and Balkan Romance. In respect of quite a few lexical items British Romani is conservative, retaining productive roots that are found only sporadically among various dialects of the language in different regions of Europe. Examples are the verbs *parak(er)*- 'to thank' and *prast*- 'to run', which have been lost in many dialects. The self-appellation *romaničel* used by some English Romani families is attested in France (as *romanišel*), in the Basque country (as *errumantxela*) and in Finland (as *romasēl*), but also in Greece (as *romacil*; see Matras 2004), and therefore appears to be an Early Romani word form, retained in a number of peripheral dialects. An example of the exploitation of inherited word roots is the British Romani word

---

[1]   In the following it will be of relevance to distinguish between Welsh and English Romani sources. Tipler's (1957) material, though recorded in Wales, documents the speech of the Boswells, who have traditionally been settled in the Northwest of England, and of the Lees, of whom several clans exist both in North Wales and in Northwest England. It is probably most practical to treat the source as representing a conservative form of English Romani spoken in Wales. The extent to which a strict dialectal subgenealogy among the varieties can be upheld remains unclear.

romado 'married', an adjective-participial form based on *rom* 'husband', *romani* 'wife'. Similar formations are Lithuanian Romani *romanduno*, German (Sinte) Romani *romadino*, and East Slovak Romani *romaduno*. The geographical spread points quite possibly to a regional innovation sometime during the early period of European settlement, replacing the more commonly attested participial form *pandrime* based on the Greek loan *pandr-*, which we may assume to have been the Early Romani word.

In its overall lexical profile British Romani fits well into the group of Romani dialects spoken in the northern and especially northwestern regions of Europe – Germany, France and Scandinavia – often including those in adjoining regions in northern Italy, western Poland, Bohemia and for some structures even the Baltics. Some of these dialects had been argued by Bakker (1999) to constitute a genetic subgrouping within Romani, referred to as the 'Northern' dialect branch. But the northern area has since been shown to be more of a dynamic spread zone for both conservative and innovative features than a static and fixed inheritance (cf. Matras 1999a, 2005). Quite a few of the lexical items shared by the dialects of these regions are the product of selection among competing inherited forms. Thus *xačar-* 'to burn', *traš-* 'to fear' and *men* 'neck' prevail in the north, while *phabar-* 'to burn', *dara-* 'to fear' and *kor* 'neck' appear in the south. In some cases, the shared development involves a semantic extension or specialisation of a word that survives in both sectors but with different meanings: thus *gi/dži* means both 'heart' and 'soul' in the north, but only 'soul' (and sometimes 'belly') in the south; *musi* 'arm' co-exists with *vast* 'hand' in the north, while in the south *vast* alone takes on both meanings, 'hand' and 'arm'. Some of the northern preferences, such as *či* 'something, anything, nothing', are conservative forms that are typically replaced in the south by new formations, loans or semi-loans, such as *ništo* from Slavic, *kati* and *čipota* from Greek, or the new formation *khanči*. Conservative lexical forms encountered in British Romani and the dialects of the north include *rivipen* 'clothes', *gero* 'man' from *goro* 'farmer, non-Gypsy man', and *kaliko* 'yesterday', all of which are found only sporadically in the south, while northern innovations include *stariben* 'prison' from *(a)star-* 'to stop, to detain', and *balevas* 'bacon' from *balo* 'pig'. Noteworthy also is the attested presence among the Welsh Romani community of the group self-appellation *Kååle* 'Gypsies', which has become extinct over the past century or so. Cognate names are still found among the Spanish Gypsies (cf. the language name *Caló* attributed to the use of Romani-derived vocabulary in Spanish and Portuguese) and among the Finnish Gypsies, who use *Kaale* as their principal self-identification tag. The word is also attested historically as the earlier self-appellation of the German Romani-speaking community, before the introduction of *Sinte* in the late eighteenth century (cf. Matras 1999b).

Internal lexical derivation, a feature mentioned by Bakker (1999) as a typical 'northern' trait, seems to have its origin not in a shared inheritance but rather in a similar adaptation to particular sociolinguistic conditions of language use (cf. Matras 1999a). In the northern regions of Europe, Romani communities remained small, socially isolated and mobile kinship groups, often isolated from one another for considerable periods of time. Romani served not simply as a community language but also as a means of protection, limiting communication to insiders. At the same time it became the object of group-internal cultural creativity. This explains the tendency to resist loanwords in certain semantic domains and instead to close semantic gaps through internal creations. Like other northern European Romani dialects, British Romani shows productive place-name formations (cf. Fowkes 1977), as in *hindi-temengro* 'Ireland' (literally 'crap-country') or *tulo-mas them* 'Lincolnshire' (literally 'bacon country'). Creative words are also formed for nationalities, for persons in authority position, and for professional occupations in general, as in *puvengro-gadžo* 'Irishman' (literally 'potato-man'), *prastengro* 'policeman', *grajengro* 'horse-dealer' and *masengro* 'butcher'.

These coinages demonstrate the introduction of two new principles of word formation into the language. The first involves compounding, which is very rarely used for lexical formation in the more conservative dialects of Romani but becomes a key mode of lexical creativity in Angloromani. The second is the derivation of nouns through genitive inflection, attaching a genitive case marker singular -*eskero* or plural -*engro* either to a nominalisation in -*pen*, -*ben* or -*imus*, or else directly to the root of a semantically related word: *kuripe/kurimos* 'fighting' > *kurimengro* 'soldier' ('fighter'), *mas* 'meat' > *masengro* 'butcher', literally 'man of [different kinds of] meat'. The strategy is employed rather marginally in most other northern dialects. For Latvian Romani, a small number of forms are recorded, including *lilengiro* 'teacher' from *lil* 'letter', *masengliro* 'butcher' from *mas* 'meat', *khelibnaskiro* 'dancer' from *kheliben* 'dancing'; attested for Finnish Romani are very few forms, among them *angarengero* 'coal burner' from *angar* 'coal', while in some other words it appears that the genitive ending has become a mere agentive suffix rather than a word formation strategy, as in *juudengiro* 'Jew'. Russian Romani has *pibnaskiro* 'samovar' from *piben* 'drinking', and *maribnaskiro* 'warrior' from *mariben* 'fight'; Swedish Romani too has just a handful of relevant formations, e.g. *bošeprasko* 'musician' from *boš-* 'to play music' (note the metathesis *-paskero* > -*prasko*), *dikkoprasko* 'mirror' from *dik-* to see', *kurramengare* 'fighter' from *kur-* 'to beat'. Next to British Romani, the strategy is by far the most productive in German (Sinte) Romani, where genitive-based word formations are numerous: *kinepaskero* 'customer' from *kin* 'to buy', *sipaskero* 'tailor' from *si(v)* 'thread', *rateskero* 'doctor' from *rat* 'blood', *marengero* 'baker' from *maro* 'bread', *dromengero* 'postman' from *drom* 'road', *sastengero* 'smith' from *saster* 'iron', and many more. One must of course take into consideration that in many instances word formations of this kind are spontaneous, or often limited to a particular tight-knit subgroup of speakers. None the less, we can assume that the existing lexical documentation[2] provides a representative corpus at least for purposes of comparison.

In British Romani, the new word formation strategies are extended even further. Especially prolific are agentive derivations, such as *plastermengro* 'police' from *prast-* 'to run', *petalengro* 'blacksmith' from *petalo* 'horseshoe', *mangamengro* 'beggar' from *mang-* 'to beg', *balengero* 'hairdresser' from *bal* 'hair', *dandengero* 'dentist' from *dand* 'tooth', *kaštengero* 'carpenter' from *kašt* 'wood', *drabingro* 'doctor' from *drab* 'medicine', and countless more. But early nineteenth-century sources such as Harriott's list (Prideaux 1910) already show how genitive derivations are relied on to create words for everyday objects: *pijomengro* 'glass' from *pi-* 'to drink', *giveskro* 'windmill' from *giv* 'wheat' , *povengra* 'potatoes' from *phuv* 'earth', *bašingri* 'music' from *baš-* 'to play music', *dikemingri* 'window' from *dikh-* 'to see', *panengro* 'boat' from *pani* 'water', *bešamengro* 'chair' from *beš-* 'to sit', *jagingri* 'chimney' from *jag* 'fire', *pabamengri* 'cidre' from *pabaj* 'apple', and so on.

Compounding is also prolific in British Romani, a feature shared with Swedish Romani. Examples often show playful creativity in word formation, as in Welsh Romani *hoči-wiči* 'English Gypsies', from the English Romani word for hedgehog *koča-wučus*, from *kočado (< xačardo)* 'burnt, roasted' and *wučus < určus* 'urchin', *bari mači* 'whale' (literally 'big fish'), *kerakni rakli* 'house woman', *livina giv* 'barley' (literally 'beer wheat'), *herengro mačo* 'crab' (literally. 'leg-fish'), and more.

A special affinity can be identified between British Romani and a smaller cluster of dialects comprising German Romani (Sinte) and the closely related Sinte-Manouche dialects of France, Swedish Romani or Scandoromani as attested in the form of a Para-Romani vocabulary by Johansson (1977), Etzler (1944) and recently Lindell and Thorbjörnsson-Djerf (2008) (along with the closely related Para-Romani variety of Norway; Iversen 1944), the now extinct Low German-based Para-Romani of Denmark described by Miskow and Brøndal (1923), and Finnish Romani (Kaale). On the basis of their latest historical location immediately prior to their dispersion into their respective present-day areas of settlement, these dialects might be referred to as a 'Northwestern' European cluster of Romani dialects (see Matras 2002). Alongside the reliance on new word formation strategies involving genitive derivation and compounding, this group of dialects retains a number of forms that are not found in the northern European dialects of the Baltics, such as the indefinites *čimoni* 'something' and *komoni* 'somebody', also found in some Romani dialects of Greece, Italy and Albania, but otherwise replaced by loans or partial loans. The group also shares a number of lexical

---

[2]   Apart from the cited sources, I rely on data from Romlex (http://romani.uni-graz. at/romlex), which in turn incorporates relevant published sources for the various dialects, as well as on lexical data from the RMS database (http://romani.humanities. manchester.ac.uk/rms).

innovations that are based on inherited roots. Among them are *bešto* 'saddle' from *beš-* 'to sit'; *čiči* 'nothing' from *či* 'something, anything'; *kek* 'nothing, not' from *kajekh* 'nothing, nobody'; *moskro* 'police, person in authority' from *mosko* 'voice, face'; *duker-* 'to tell fortunes', which appears in Sinte Romani as *dur-raker-*, literally 'far-talk'; *lač-* 'to find'; and *mokadi* 'defiled', Welsh Romani *måxado*, Sinte Romani *maxado, maxedo*. Some grammatical loans are also specific to the northwestern dialects: the word *nogo* 'own' attested in English and Welsh Romani (Smart & Crofton 1913, Sampson 1926b) is also found in Finnish Romani as *iego* and in Sinte as *ajgeno*, deriving from German *eigen*.

An inventory of early loanwords is retained in British Romani, parts of which are shared with the northwestern dialects in particular, some also shared with other Romani dialects of northern Europe (Poland and the Baltics). Retentions of Greek loans from the Early Romani inventory include *misali* 'table', *čerus* 'time', *kekavi* 'tea kettle', *apopli* 'again', *kommi* 'still', *sapanis* 'soap', *sarla/tesarla* 'morning', *valgora* (< *agora*) 'market', as well as Welsh Romani *filišin* 'castle' and *ravnos* 'sky'. Early Slavic loans, in all likelihood also part of the Early Romani legacy, include *vodros* 'bed', *akonyo, bikonya* 'quiet', *dosta* 'plenty' (from 'enough'), *čelo* 'whole', *kralis* 'king', *mačka* 'cat', *smentini* 'cream', *reca* 'duck', *haro* 'penny, coin', *vodros* 'bed', *skorni* 'boots', *stanya* 'barn' and *zelano* 'green'. A more recent layer of German-origin words strengthens the impression of close contacts with the northwestern dialects prior to, and possibly even following, settlement in Britain. They include *varta* (also *vart-er*) 'to watch' (German *Warte* 'look-out'), *štifo* 'in-law (sibling)' (German *stief-* 'step-'), *selta* 'tent' (German *Zelt*), *čifa* 'boat' (German *Schiff*), *vajla* 'while' (German *Weile*), *šafraben* 'work' (southern German *schaffen*), *stakelengro* 'hedgehog' (Rotwelsch *Stacheling* from German *Stachel[schwein]* 'porcupine') as well as *niglo* 'hedgehog' (German *[ein]Igel*). Words of French origin include *granša* 'barn' (French *grange*), *budika* 'shop' (French *boutique*), and possibly *bitti* 'small' (French *petit*). A layer of more recent loans may well have its source in special vocabularies of other travelling populations, some of them Romance-based. Thus alongside *hora* 'time', British Romani shares with Swedish Romani the words *kakarači* in the meaning of 'magpie' (cf. Smart & Crofton 1913), and *kamora* 'room' (see Lindell & Thorbjörnsson-Djerf 2008), and with the northwestern Romani dialects the form *presta* 'to pay' (elsewhere often *preister-*), apparently from German slang, based on German *Preis* 'price'.

Unique British Romani innovations in the lexical domain include *vasavo, wafedo* 'bad', Welsh Romani *basavo*, and *kučko, kušto* 'good', possibly inspired by *kuč-* 'dear'. There are also numerous characteristic shifts in semantic meaning, such as *goj* 'pudding' (from 'sausage'), the generalisation of *puker-* in the meaning of 'talk, speak' from more specialised meanings (cf. *angle phuk-* 'to tell the future' in Burgenland Romani, *phuk-* 'to admit' in Sinte, and *phukav-* 'to tell' in Hungarian Romani). The word *rakli*, originally 'girl', is extended to mean 'woman'; *tikno*, originally 'small', takes on the meaning 'child' (as 'small' is covered by the loanword *biti*); and *dosta*, originally 'enough', means 'plenty'. On the basis of an English model, nominal roots begin to be used as verbs, as in *jivela* 'it snows'. This tendency proliferates once Romani verbal inflection is lost and roots can be relied on for either word class, thus *buti* 'work, to work'.

The most particular characteristic of British Romani is, naturally, the inventory of English loanwords. Nouns are integrated drawing on the Greek-derived nominative endings *-us/-os* and *-o* for masculines and *-a* for feminines: *badžarus* 'badger', *səmərus* 'summer', *monthos* 'month', *welefantos* 'elephant', *hilo* 'hill', *fello* 'fellow'; *muna* 'moon', *inka* 'ink', *vildža* 'village', *waila* 'while'. The case of *foki* 'nation, people' (from *folks*) confirms the productivity of Greek-derived plurals in *-i*. Adjectives, too, take on Greek-derived endings, thus *grino* 'green (masculine)', *raundo* 'round (masculine)'. Comparative forms of the adjective take the inherited comparative suffix: *useder* 'worse'. Derived adjectives based on English roots may take either the Greek-derived participle suffix, as in *uglimen* 'ugly', or an adjectival ending that is attached to the adapted verb root, as in *tizaso* 'teased'. The most commonly attested loan verb adaptation marker is *-as-* in Welsh Romani, as in *minasava* 'I mean', *hopasava* 'I hope' (Tipler 1957), *thinkas-* 'to think', *wantas-* 'to want' (Sampson 1926b), while for English Romani both *-as-* and *-is-* are attested, albeit sporadically, as in *wantasova* 'I want' (Smart & Crofton 1875), *thinkisova* 'I thought' (from T. W. Norwood's list of 1859). Some examples occur with *-in-*, as in Welsh Romani *thundrin-* 'to thunder' (Sampson 1926b), and some occur without adaptation markers, as in *ričava* 'I'll reach' (Tipler 1957).

3.2.2 Phonology

A series of phonological changes can be identified as typical and constitutive of British Romani. However, there is also considerable stratification and variation among the individual local and family dialects, indicating a continuous and dynamic accumulation of changes among individual groups of speakers. A major split exists between Welsh and English Romani. Welsh Romani continues the inherited consonantal system almost intact (Table 3.1).

The sound /ɣ/ is marginal, being characteristic of the transitional pronunciation of several words like *udar*, *hudar*, *ɣudar* 'door' (English Romani also *vudar*, *wudar*). Other marginal sounds are confined to loanwords, as is /θ/ in *θinkas-* 'to think'. A tendency towards cluster simplification sets off in Welsh Romani, as in *pal* < *phral* 'brother', *kokoro* < *korkoro* 'alone', though many forms are retained, as in *kirčima* 'pub'.

Typical of British Romani (as of German Romani) is the forward shift of stress to root syllables, which often leads either to lengthening of the vowel in the stressed syllable, or to a change in its quality, and to a reduction

Table 3.1 Welsh Romani consonant system (based on Sampson 1926b)

	Labial	Dental	Alveolar	Postalveolar	Palatal	Velar	Glottal
Stop							
Voiced	b		d			g	
Voiceless	p		t			k	
Aspirated	ph		th			kh	
Fricative							
Voiced	v	z		ž		(ɣ)	
Voiceless	f	s		š		χ	h
Affricate							
Voiced				dž			
Voiceless				č			
Nasal	m		n			ŋ	
Lateral			l				
Approximant	w				j		
Rhotic			r				

i, iː				uː
eː	ɪ		ʊ	o, oː
		ə		
ɛ			ʌ	ɔ, ɔː/
a				ɑ

Figure 3.1 Welsh Romani vowels (based on Sampson 1926b)

of the vowels in following, now unstressed syllables: /kangeˈri/ 'church' > /ˈkɔngri/. Welsh Romani retains inherited stress on inflectional segments, as in /phukaˈdas/ 'he spoke'. This is also the picture conveyed by Tipler's (1957) sample, which shows retention of inflectional stress in *kamáva* 'I want', retention of /χ/ in *xàva* 'I eat', but at the same time cluster simplification in *pàpale* 'back' < *parpale*, and *muš* 'man' < *murš*. This conservative pattern appears to erode in English Romani, further weakening the inflected segments. By and large, the vowel system of British Romani as a whole can be characterised as showing a step-by-step convergence with that of English (Figure 3.1).

The following vowel qualities are found in Welsh Romani and can be said to reflect the older or initial stage of convergence:

/a/   continuing inherited and borrowed /a/: /atʃ/ 'stay', /aˈkava/ 'this', /ˈwaila/ 'while', /ˈwɔntas- / 'want'

/ɑ/   continuing inherited /a/: /vaŋˈgɑr/ 'coal', /mɑˈtoː/ 'drunk'

/ɔ, ɔː/ continuing inherited /a/: /jɔg/ 'fire', /ˈgɔːdʒɔː/ 'non-Gypsy man', /ʃɔχ/ 'cabbage', /dʒɔː/ 'go', /ˈmɔχadoː/ 'defiled', /ˈhɔtʃiˈwɪtʃi/ 'English Gypsy'

/o, oː/	continuing inherited /o/: /opˈrēː/ 'up', /iˈʃom/ 'I am', /oːra/ 'hour', /nasvaˈloː/ 'ill'
/ʋ/	continuing inherited /u/: /ʋʃt/ 'lip'
/uː/	continuing inherited /u/: /buːt/ 'many'
/ɛ/	continuing inherited /e/: /dɪˈvɛs/ 'day', /kɛrɪˈbɛn/ 'deed', /bɛŋ/ 'devil'
/eː/	continuing inherited /e/: /neːˈvoː/ 'new', /anˈdreː/ 'inside'
/ɪ/	continuing inherited /i/: /tʃɪb/ 'tongue', /trɪn/ 'three'
/i, iː/	continuing inherited /i/: /bita/ 'little' , /viːˈjom/ 'I came', /kisiː/ 'how many', /oːˈziː/ 'heart', /ˈmandiː/ '(with) me'
/ʌ, ə/	continuing inherited /a/ and /i/: /ʌˈkaɪ, əˈkaɪ/ 'here' as variants of / aˈkaɪ/, /kərˈtʃɪma/ 'pub' alongside /kɪrˈtʃɪma/

The dialect preserves the inherited two diphthongs /aɪ/, as in /phaˈbaɪ/ 'apple', and /oɪ/, as in /joɪ/ 'she', /ʃoˈʃoɪ/ 'rabbit', adding /aʋ/ to the inventory in loans such as /raʋndo/ 'round'. The major innovation in the phonology of conservative British Romani is thus the significant enrichment of the number of vowels, compared to the Early Romani legacy of just a five-vowel system /a, e, i, o u/ with no length opposition. To be sure, in introducing length distinction as well as quality distinctions that accompany them, British Romani follows a similar path to German Romani, and the existing documentation does not enable us to conclude whether the early stage of the two developments might have coincided, triggered by contact with German on the continent, or whether these are parallel but completely independent sets of changes, each triggered in situ by its own contact language.

The direction of change continues in English Romani towards a near-complete convergence with the English system. The inherited consonant system is firstly eroded by the collapse of the aspirate–non-aspirate distinction, and the eventual disappearance of marginal phonemes as well as of /χ/. The latter, though still attested by Smart and Crofton (1875) and some other sources, is usually substituted for by either /h/ or /k/: /χačarˈdo/ > /ˈkɔčədə/ 'burnt, roasted', /šaχ/ 'cabbage' > /šɔk/, /χaˈben/ 'food' > /ˈhɔbən, ˈhɔbɪn/ but also /ˈkɔbən, ˈkɔbɪn/. Note that while Welsh Romani as well as the Sinte and Finnish Romani dialects remain conservative in this respect, a similar development is found in Swedish Romani. English Romani also adopts a more consistent forward shift of stress, losing the inherited accentuation of inflectional suffixes. The result is yet a further reduction of consonant clusters in medial positions and extended reduction of vowel quality towards a centralised vowel: /χačarˈdo/ 'burnt' roasted' > /ˈkɔčədə/, /džuˈkel/ 'dog' > /ˈdžʋkəl/. The following simplified consonant formants are typical of English Romani: *pano* 'white' < *parno*, *baval* 'wind' < *barval*, *beš* 'year' < *berš*, *muš* 'man' < *murš, dan* 'tooth' < *dand, nafalo* 'ill' < *nasvalo*. While unstressed vowels are reduced, stressed vowels are often diphthongised: /mol/ 'wine' >/ moʋl/, /anˈdre/ 'inside' > /aˈdreɪ/. Where inflectional segments are concerned, the two tendencies compete with one another. The reduction of final vowels often leads to loss of gender distinction in English Romani: /'bɔrə/ 'big' < /ba'ro, ba'ri/ 'big.M, big.F'. Alternatively, the inflectional segment is retained but shows a diphthong replacing a back vowel in inherited masculines – /ga'džo/ 'man' >/'gɑːdžoʊ/, /'gɔːdžoʊ/, /ma'ro/ 'bread' > /'mɔroʊ/ – or continues, in the case of front vowels in inherited feminines – /'rak'li/ 'girl' > /'rakli/ 'woman'.

Typically for languages in decline, considerable variation is found both between different families and clans, and as far as can be ascertained from the sources also within them. Variation in the realisation of consonants is mentioned explicitly by Smart and Crofton (1875: 8–9). Concerned are the interchange of labials /v/ and /w/ – *vardo* alongside *wardo* 'cart', *vast* alongside *wast* 'hand' – and occasionally of /b/ and /v/ – *bokočo* alongside *vakaša* 'lamb'. In derivational endings with diminutive function, the segments /č/ and /š/ as well as /k/ and /t/ appear interchangeable, too: *kučko, kuško* alongside *kušto* 'good', *bokočo* alongside *vakaša* 'lamb'. The historical phoneme /χ/ continues to be represented alternately by /k/ or /h/: *kol, hol* 'eat', *kačer, hočer* 'to burn'. Other sources testify to the occasional substitution of vowels, especially /o/ and /i/, /e/ and /i/, and /u/ and /i/, in local varieties: *livena* 'beer' < *lovina*, *čomani* 'something'< *čimoni*, *čeriklo* 'bird' < *čiriklo, zimən* 'soup' < *zumin*. Convergence with regional dialects of English lead to the emergence of region-specific and vernacular features such as the realisation of inherited /o/ as /ʊ/ – /'kʊvə/ 'this' < /kova/ – or the loss of pre-vocalic /h/ – /ʔɔl/ 'to eat' < /χal/, /'ʔɛrə/ 'leg' < /he'roj/.

3.2.3 Nominal inflection

European Romani nominal inflection is characterised by a three-layer system (cf. Matras 2002, Elšík 2000). Layer I case suffixes are inflectional endings that are sensitive to declension class, which in turn is determined by grammatical gender, phonological shape of the final segment, morphological derivation pattern, number and etymology (distinguishing pre-European inherited vocabulary from European loans). Historically, inherited Layer I suffixes continue Old Indo-Aryan case endings. Functionally, they carry the distinction between nominative and oblique (non-nominative) case. Oblique stems of the noun then form the basis for Layer II case formations. A vocative case appears with animates in similar position, i.e. attached directly to the nominal root itself. It is also sensitive to gender and number, and derives in all likelihood from grammaticalised postposed deictic markers. Layer II markers are agglutinating forms that are partly sensitive to the phonology of the preceding segment. Historically, they represent postposed local relations expressions that have undergone grammaticalisation and become shortened and fused to the oblique nominal stem. Functionally, they distinguish semantic roles or types of objects, notably dative, sociative-comitative, locative, possessive-genitive and ablative. Finally, Layer III case modifiers consist of

Table 3.2 Welsh Romani major nominal inflection classes (based on Sampson 1926b)

Declension class	Example	Nom. sg.	Nom. pl.	Obl.sg.	Obl.pl.
Pre-European masculine in consonant	*kher* 'house'		-ā	-es-	-en-
Pre-European masculine in -*ipen*	*čačipen* 'truth'		-ā	-es-, -as-	-en-
Pre-European masculine in -*o*	*šerō* 'head',	-ō	-ē	-es-	-en-
Pre-European masculine in -*i*	*pani* 'water'	-i	-iā	-ies-	-ien-
Pre-European feminine in consonant	*suv* 'needle'		-ī̃ā	-ī̃a-	-ī̃en-
Pre-European feminine in -*i*	*piri* 'pot'	-i	-iā	-ī̃a-	-ī̃en-
European masculine in -*i(s)*	*sapunis* 'soap'	-is	-ī̃	-es-	-en-
European masculine in -*u(s)*	*papus* 'grandfather'	-us	-ī̃	-es-	-en-
European masculine in -*o(s)*	*foros* 'town'	-os	-ī̃	-es-	-en-
European feminine in -*a*	*cipa* 'skin'	-a	-ī̃	-ī̃a-	-en-

a class of prepositions, mostly grammaticalised local adverbial expressions, which precede the noun. Prepositions may govern either nominative or oblique case on the noun, depending on animacy and semantic case role, and subject to dialectal variation.

This conservative system is well documented in Welsh Romani and will have been inherited by all forms of early British Romani (see Table 3.2). It is rather conservative among the inflected dialects of Romani, maintaining three separate masculine inflection classes for European loans, in (Greek-derived nominative endings) -*os*, -*is* and -*us* respectively, while apparently assimilating into them the Early Romani declension class in -*o* which had incorporated Greek-derived neuters. The more productive of these three appears to have been the class in -*os*, which includes, alongside more established European loans such as Greek *čeros* 'time' and Slavic *vodros* 'bed', also contemporary English loans such as *baštardos* 'bastard', *munþos* 'month' and *vāletos* 'wallet'.

Sources on English Romani testify to the presence of most of these inflection classes in the nominative form, but there are hardly any attestations of oblique forms and even nominative plurals are subject to erosion. For consonantal masculines such as *rom* 'husband', *muš* 'man', *beš* 'year' or *kan* 'ear' Norwood's list (Grosvenor 1910), for example, has -*a* plural forms like *mushaw* 'men', *divvusaw* 'days', *boot beshaw* 'many years', alongside a combination of -*a* with an English-based plural as in *kannos* 'ears', *errahs* 'legs'. The retreat of plural formation and its replacement with English endings appears to affect all declension classes. Smart and Crofton (1875: 16–17) report on older plurals for consonantal stems and those ending in diphthongs (originally a subclass), such as masculine *hev* 'hole' pl. *hévyaw*, *grei* 'horse' pl. *gréiaw*, *vast* 'hand' pl. *vástaw*, and feminine *pen* 'sister' pl. *pényaw*, *yok* 'eye' pl. *yókaw*, alongside English-based plurals *pens* 'sisters', *yoks* 'eyes' or indeed the combinaton of the two, as in *báryaws* 'stones'. For vocalic stems, they report on the sporadic retention of archaic, stressed plural formations like *gaíro* 'man' pl. *gairé*, *bókro* 'sheep' pl. *bokré*. Fox's vocabulary (Sampson1926a) shows some preference for the inherited Romani plural ending -*a* with consonantal stems, as in *lav-a* 'words', while vocalic stems show a preference for English plurals, as in *rawni-s* 'ladies'. Tipler (1957) still shows *šošoj-a* 'rabbits'. Groome's (1928: 69–70) material recorded from the East Anglian Smith family during their stay in Scotland in 1881 has the plural forms in -*a* for *gryor* 'horses' and *laviaw* 'words', plurals in -*e* for *chavé* 'boys' and *sheré* 'heads', and the double plural *gillyors* 'songs'.

Inherited gender distinctions similarly decline in English Romani. The only nouns that resist the trend seem to be those that are both paired in the vocalic inflection class and allow inference about natural gender, such as *raklo* 'boy' vs. *rakli* 'girl', still distinguished in Fox's list. Smart and Crofton (1875: 11–12) list a series of word pairs, among them *gairo* 'man' and *gairi* 'woman', *pirino* 'male sweetheart' and *pirini* 'female sweetheart', *grei* 'horse' and *grasni* 'mare', *jookel* 'dog' and *jookli* 'bitch', and *rom* 'husband' and *romni* 'wife', stating pointedly that "usually the gender is determined by that of the corresponding English word", indicating that grammatical gender is practically non-existent as an inflection-relevant category in the dialect. An early word that testifies to gender neutralisation is *matchee* 'fish' (cf. Bryant's list, but also attested by Fox, Harriott and others), which adopts a termination in -*i* replacing inherited *mačho* of the masculine vocalic class in -*o*; the distinction thus seems to have ceased to be meaningful.

The category of abstract nouns in -*ipen* is continued and remains quite productive in English Romani, though the earlier sources show a tendency for the inherited ending to alternate with the Greek-derived abstract nominal ending -*amus* (Welsh Romani -*imus*), covering identical functions. Fox's list, for instance, has both *starrapan* and *starramus* 'prison', and Norwood has both *rokkerpen* and *rokkermus* 'talk'. Sanderson's list, by contrast, gives the impression of a semantic differentiation between the two endings: *jivopen* 'life' but *jivomas* 'living', *rokripen* 'talking' but *rokkomas* 'converse' (Griffiths & Yates 1934). Containing prototypically inanimate nouns, this class rarely appears with any oblique inflection endings.

While essentially the same inflection classes for loanwords are found in English and Welsh Romani, English Romani also shows variants of Greek-derived nominal endings in vowels for the masculine classes. This may be a local innovation, but could also be a retention of a more complex system, involving forms in both -*s* and vowels, as attested in some of the continental dialects. Tipler's (1957) sample, albeit recorded in Wales, shows the old loans *kralis* 'king' and *kokalis* 'bone' alongside the more recent *papiris* 'newspaper', but also older *misali* 'table' and *poatsi* 'pocket' alongside more recent *fouki* 'nation'. The class in -*us* shows older *forus* 'town', *pappus* 'grandfather' and *soponus* 'soap', alongside more recent *səmərus* 'summer' and *murus* 'wall'. Fox's compilation shows masculine loans in -*o*: *bostaro* 'bastard' (cf. *baštardos* in Sampson's documentation of Welsh Romani), *hilo* 'hill'. The class of European feminine nouns in -*a* remains productive and incorporates, at least in the earlier documented period, even English inanimates that lack an 'original' gender; thus Bryant has *plashta* 'cloak' as well as *moonah* 'moon'.

The paucity of textual material in inflected English Romani and the few occurrences of animate nouns in object position within this material mean that it is extremely difficult to identify any attestation of oblique nominal inflection. Usually in Romani, the unmodified oblique serves as the case of the animate direct object. A rare and relatively late attestation is Goddard Johnson's phrase *mordas pes cokeras* 'he killed himself' (Scott Macfie & Winstedt 1939), where both the reflexive pronoun *pes* and the adjective 'alone, on his own', *cokeras*, appear in the unmodified oblique. Russell (1916: 168–9) documents the somewhat ambiguous phrase from Bright's list *chidom, leo gri, dre puv* 'I have taken the horse into the field'. But here it seems that the noun 'the horse' – *o grai* – which appears in the nominative and not in the oblique, is in a dislocated focused position, following an oblique pronoun *le[s]*, i.e. literally 'I have taken it, the horse, into the field'. Smart and Crofton's text collections show nominative endings for animate direct objects (1875: 204): *diktas yoi dooi trin raunya* 'she saw two-three women' (expected in continental dialects and Welsh Romani: *duj-trin ranj-en*). The vocative, too, appears obsolete in English Romani. According to Smart and Crofton (1875: 16–17) the only surviving forms are *déia* 'mother!', *réia* 'Sir!', and *choovále* 'mates!'. Groome (1928) in fact also records *ria* 'Sir!', and Winstedt (1948) records *duvla* 'Oh God!', *raia* 'Sir!', and *čavoli* 'mates!'.

Layer II markers as found in the continental European dialects of Romani are basically continued directly in Welsh Romani, save minor phonological changes (Table 3.3). Attestation in English Romani sources is sporadic and points to their gradual retreat in the dialect. Whiter's vocabulary (Grosvenor 1908) has the dative *devleska* 'for God's sake', Norwood (Grosvenor 1910) has the locative forms *kerrasty* 'in the home' as well as *bishenesty* 'in the rain', and Bright (1818) has *le o giv away gresti* 'take the oats from the horse', confirming the innovation shared with Welsh Romani in the shape of the ablative. Note that these forms also confirm the masculine oblique nominal stem

Table 3.3 Layer II case markers in European Romani and Welsh Romani

Case	Early Romani and continental dialects	Welsh Romani
Locative	*-tel-de*	*-tīl-dī*
Dative	*-kel-ge*	*-kīl-gī*
Ablative	*-tarl-dar*	*-tēl-dē*
Sociative/comitative/ instrumental	*-sa (-ha)l -ca*	*-sa*
Genitive	*-k(er)-l-g(er)-*	*-k(er)-l-g(er)-*

in *-es-*, the basis for Layer II markers. Fox's list from Derbyshire (Sampson 1926a) has the dative form *chavinga* 'for the children', confirming the plural oblique basis in *-in-*. The instrumental is not attested with full nouns. The most commonly cited Layer II marker in English Romani materials is the genitive. Sources such as the East Anglian vocabulary of 1798 (Sampson 1930) have it both as a word-compositional device, as in *sunekiski chiriklo* 'goldfinch', literally 'a bird of gold', or *butti iska besh* 'working season', literally 'year of work', as well as in the function of a genuine possessive, as in *ma duvlas karokraben* (= *ma duvlasko rokraben*) 'the words of my Lord' and *egreski, boshtoi* (= *e greski bošto*) 'the horse's saddle'. Further examples include *gresko* 'of a horse' in Whiter's vocabulary (Grosvenor 1908), *krelisko* '[the] king's' and *kovasko* 'this one's' in Bright's list (Russell 1916), and from later sources *bengesko sap* 'the devil's poison' in Way's list from 1900 (Francis 1955). Note that all attested forms show the shorter genitive morpheme in *-k-* rather than the one with the augment *-ker-*. By contrast, it is the augmented form that normally serves for word-derivational purposes, e.g. *bareskro-grei* 'stallion' (literally 'stone-horse', Smart & Crofton 1875: 13). A frequent alternate to the inherited genitive form is the replacement of the consonantal segment with *-t-*: e.g. *begesto kova* 'lucifer match' in the East Anglian samples of the 1920s (Evans 1929), *chiriklesto-kair* 'bird-cage' (Smart & Crofton 1875: 15). The survival of the genitive is somewhat extraordinary, considering the early adoption of the English possessive-genitive *s* and the frequent alternation between the two strategies, the inherited and the borrowed, even in the oldest sources; thus Fox's list from Derbyshire (Sampson 1926a) *crellisko kir* 'palace', but also *balo's drab* 'pig's poison' and *mo daval's tem* 'heaven'.

The pronominal system preserves a somewhat greater variety of inflectional forms, though here too simplifcations are considerable. From the attested forms as well as the comparison with the full productive set of Welsh Romani, we may assume the following inherited British Romani set of personal pronouns (nominative/oblique): *mel man* 'I', *tul tut* 'you', *jovl les* 'he', *jojlla* 'she', *ame(n)* 'we', *tume(n)* 'you.PL', *jonl len* 'they'. The possessive forms of the pronoun will have been *miro* 'my', *tiro* 'your', *lesko* 'his', *lako* 'her', *amaro* 'our', *tumaro* 'you' and *leng(r)o* 'their'. This set is more or less identical to that of Sinte Romani and Finnish Romani, and generally very closely related to the forms found north of the Great Divide. Layer II nominal endings are attached to this set to form specific case-inflected pronominal forms. The complete paradigm is presented in several sources apart from Sampson's Welsh Romani grammar, for instance in Fox's list, by Whiter, by Sanderson, by Smart and Crofton (1875), by Winstedt (1948), and by Tipler (1957). However, actual exemplification of the use of inflected pronouns is not at all extensive. Borde (1542; see Miklosich 1874–8) apparently has the comitative form *tusa* 'with you'. Bryant has *deas man* 'he gave me' (employing the unmodified oblique, which is the common case for the beneficiary of 'to give' in continental dialects of Romani), Norwood has *dikddum tut* 'I saw you', and Way has *diom tukey* 'I gave you' (in the dative case of the recipient), and in Goddard Johnson's material (Scott Macfie & Winstedt 1939: 12–13) we find *leom lis leski* 'I took it from him'[3] and *mai dik-covalis* 'I see him' as well *as mai comavva lan* 'I love them'. The plural forms of the first and second persons especially suffer from poor attestation; indeed, these are the forms that do not survive in present-day Angloromani. Sanderson, for example, reports in 1872 that both the first and second person plural pronouns are disused (Griffiths & Yates 1934). Winstedt (1948) none the less records *mendi* 'we' as well as *mendi foci* for 'our people'.

It appears that at an early stage in the development of English Romani, a tendency has already emerged to generalise the dative form of the pronoun as a kind of all-function oblique pronominal form. Thus we find in the East Anglian source from 1798 *chum berautote* (= *chumberau tote*) 'I kiss you', *kek ana bish arautote* (= *keker na bishtrau tote*) 'I will never forget you', *ma deval de com eltote* (= *mo devel te kamel tute*) 'love your neighbour' = 'may God love you', all for the direct object, but also *bauchevin tutti a gilli* 'I'll play you a tune', for the beneficiary; Way's list has *pooker mande* 'tell me', Norwood has *katar mandi* 'to me' and *day mandi zee adray tuti's tem* 'give me life in your kingdom', Goddard Johnson has *para karov tude* 'I thank you', and Harriott's list has *penov mandi* 'I say to myself'. At the same time, the possessive-pronominal forms remain productive, as far as can be ascertained; thus Whiter *meer meriben* 'my life', *leski nav* 'his name', *lakko dad te lakky dae* 'her father and her mother', *teero ker* 'your house', Goddard Johnson *mauro gry* 'our horse'. The short forms *mi* 'my' and *ti* 'your' are also sporadically attested and appear to be interchangeable with the full forms, cf. *miro romani an mi chi* 'my wife and daughter' (Bright).

Smart and Crofton's (1875) texts seem to show a transitional stage with some variation. For the 1sg., the most common form is the historical locative *mandi*, which is used for most case relations, sometimes alternating with

---

[3]   What looks like a dative in *leski* 'for him' could either be intended to represent the ablative, or else an expression of the source as a beneficiary in the sense of an individual affected by the action, an involuntary experiencer, and so a genuine dative.

man for the direct object. For the 2sg. the texts show *too* in the subject role, *toot* as a direct object and *tooti* as an indirect object; this is paralleled for the 3sg. masculine and feminine respectively by the forms *yov – les – lesti* and *yoi – la – lati*. Possessive forms are kept apart consistently. For the plurals it is much more difficult to derive a pattern from the texts. Overall, then, there appears to have been a reduction in the pronominal paradigm from a system that differentiates six case roles to one that distinguishes between subject, direct object, indirect object and possessive, or even one that merely distinguishes subject, object and possessive (and in the 1sg just subject/object and possessive).

Much like Sinte Romani, British Romani preserves a set of nominative enclitic pronouns that accompany lexical predications in the third persons. The set appears either with the consonantal base in *l-*, like third person oblique pronouns, or in vocalic form: m. *-o*, f. *-i*, pl. *-e*. The system is productive in Welsh Romani, and we find occasional attestations in the English sources too: Fox *dukaval-o* 'it hurts', Tipler (1957) *šun-el-o* 'he is listening'. As in other Romani dialects in which this set of clitics survives, their distribution seems to be particularly wide with non-verbal or existential predications: *koóshto sas-ló* 'he was good' (Smart & Crofton 1875: 104), Whiter *mishta dousta see-le* 'they are very well', Goddard Johnson *tullo se-llo* 'he is fat' (Scott Macfie & Winstedt 1939: 83), *ši-lo, ši-li* 'he is, she is' (Tipler 1957).

Adjective (and possessive pronoun) agreement in gender, number and case (see Table 3.4) is a further structural feature of European Romani that is continued in Welsh Romani, but interrupted in its English sister variety. Norwood's material seems consistent: *o bitto gav* 'the little village', *pooro gorju* 'old man', *dinle gorje* 'crazy people'. Whiter's vocabulary (Grosvenor 1908) shows *pooro gaujo* 'old man' vs. *poore gauje* 'old people', *lakko dad te lakky dae* 'her father and her mother', but *rinkano chi* 'beatiful girl', indicating that adjectival inflection endings were already losing their distinctive functional value. Thus while Way's list has the gender-inflected forms *goodlo* and *goodli* 'sweet', the East Anglian list of 1798 has *tarn a rocklo* '[young] boy' as well as *tarn a rockla* '[young] girl', and John Harriott (Prideaux 1910) has *beti chavo* 'little boy' (feminine agreement marker with a masculine noun) alongside *baro bar* 'big stone' (masculine agreement marker with a masculine noun). Smart and Crofton (1875: 23–4) are conscious of the agreement pattern and able to provide examples, but note that "the rule is, however,

Table 3.4 Inherited Romani adjective inflection paradigm: *baro* 'big'

	Nom.	Obl.
M.sg.	*baro*	*bare*
F.sg.	*bari*	*bare / bara*
Pl.	*bare*	*bare*

constantly violated by every Gypsy". None the less, borrowed adjectives such as *faino* 'fine' or *bito* 'little' consistently take an inflectional ending. The comparison form for adjectives follows the common Romani pattern: *burrader* 'bigger' (Whiter), *sigader* 'faster', *butider* 'more' (Tipler 1957).

3.2.4 Verbs

European Romani dialects inherit several morphological verb derivation devices. In part, their use is highly lexicalised and not subject to much variation among the dialects. To some extent, however, dialects select individual markers from among the shared inventory of morphemes as productive devices. It is in this domain that we find a rather striking dialectal difference between Welsh and English Romani, as far as can be said from the little information that the sources offer. While Welsh Romani, much like Sinte and Finnish Romani, appears to have preserved both pre-European inherited morphemes, *-er-* and *-av-*, for productive transitive word formation, as in *čumer-* 'to kiss', *baxter-* 'to bless', *gudler-* 'to sweeten', alongside, *trašav-* 'to frighten', *našav-* 'to lose', *sikav-* 'to show', English Romani appears to generalise the affix *-er-*, thus *chumer* 'to kiss' (Harriott), but also *trasher* 'frighten, astonish' (Smart & Crofton 1875), *nasher-* 'to lose' (East Anglian list), and *siker* 'to show' (Tipler 1957). The selection of just one of two potentially competing forms is not unusual. It follows the selection of *-er-* and *-av-* from among a somewhat larger inherited inventory of Early Romani competing forms (which will have included *-ker-*, *-avker-* and possibly more) in the Northwestern dialect cluster. It appears that some dialects of Sinte have proceeded in a similar direction to English Romani, eliminating one of the two affixes from the Northwestern legacy, leading to a preference for *-er-* in eastern Sinte and for *-ev-* in the western zones. Welsh Romani merely retains the Northwestern stage.

None the less, the distribution of *-er-* is of further significance for the dialectological position of English Romani. Alongside its use as a transitive marker or 'verbaliser', it is also attested as an integration morpheme for some loan verbs: *vater* 'to look', from German *wart-*, possibly in *prester* 'to pay' from German *Preis*, and in the nominalisation *shafraben* 'work', from (dialectal southwest) German *schaff-* 'to work', followed by the affix *-er-* and then by a nominaliser *-iben*. It is noteworthy firstly that *-er-* is always used in these instances with loan verbs from German. There is no evidence that the procedure is productive for English borrowings, which are integrated using Greek-derived markers *-as-* and *-is-* as in *wantasova* 'I want' (Smart & Crofton 1875), *thinkisova* 'I thought' (from T. W. Norwood's list of 1859). On the other hand, the use of *-er-* to integrate loan verbs follows logically from its function as a marker of transitive derivation and as an intensifier in predicates such as *paner* 'to shut' (<*phand-*), *mukker* 'to allow' (< *mukh-*) (see discussion in Matras 2009: 175–84). Note that Swedish Romani (Lindell &

Thorbjörnsson-Djerf 2008) follows a similar path, using -*r*- to integrate loan verbs from an earlier contact language, Low German, as in *hilpra* 'to help', *smekkra* 'to taste', *denkra* 'to think', but also as a derivational marker for transitive verbs: *sivra* 'to sew', *sikkra* 'to show'. Whether the German loans in -*er*- represent words that were taken over from a neighbouring Romani dialect rather than directly from German, possibly as a result of the integration of a Romani-speaking population from the continent into the English Gypsies, or whether they represent a stage in the history of English Romani that was shared with Scandinavian and German dialects of the language, is difficult to ascertain; either way, we have clear evidence of intense contacts in the past between the respective speaker communities. The similarities extend, not surprisingly, also to the loss of morphological passives (common to Sinte as well) – in all likelihood a contact development inspired by languages that lack morphological passives. The passive in English (and Welsh) Romani is instead expressed with the help of the auxiliary *v*- 'to become' and a participle: *vel mucklo* 'to be left'.

Clearly the most outstanding feature of inflected English Romani that distinguishes it from subsequent development phases and the emergence of Angloromani is the retention of finite verb inflection. The older sources contain a number of examples large enough to reconstruct the person or conjugation endings of English Romani comfortably as conforming nicely to both Welsh Romani and the continental inflected dialects. Examples in the materials collected by Norwood, Fox, Smart and Crofton and others suggest first of all a general preference for 'long' forms in -*a* in the present indicative, but occasional dropping of the final segment is attested especially in the 1sg: *vov*, *vovva* 'I come', *penov* 'I say', *komava* 'I like'. There is some indication of a weakening of the consonant in the 1sg: *jinaw* 'I know' alongside *jinnova, commaw* 'I love'. In the 2sg and 1pl we find the inherited forms in -*s*-, contrasting with the Sinte–Finnish Romani shift to -*h*- in this position in the paradigm: *jinessa* 'you know', *jassa* 'you go', *ruveress* 'you wear', *vessa* 'you come'; *biknas* 'let us sell', *peerasse* 'we walk'. The 3sg is the inherited -*ela* – *jinela* 'he knows', *shunela* 'he hears', *vella* 'he comes' – contracted to the subjunctive form lacking -*a* in the infinitive: Norwood *to vel mucklo* 'to be left'. Attestation for the 2pl is missing, but there is no reason not to assume that, as in all other Romani dialects, it was identical to the 3pl, for which we find *dikenna* 'they look', *jinenna* 'they know', *janna* 'they go', etc.

Documented forms of the past-tense set of person markers once again matches that of Welsh Romani and probably also the most conservative stage of the set across Romani dialects, inherited directly from Early Romani (Table 3.5). The 1sg ends in -*om*/-*um*: *veum* 'I came', *geum* 'I went', *kerdum* 'I did'; a unique occurrence of *prasthem* 'I ran' in Harriott is in all likelihood not indicative of any major shift in vowel quality. In the 2sg we meet the more widespread form -*an* rather than the form in -*al* found in Sinte and Finnish Romani as well as in the Central European dialects: *kedan* 'you did', *gean*

Table 3.5 Attested person conjugation forms for English Romani

	Present	Past
1sg.	*-åv(a)*	*-um, -om, (-em)*
2sg.	*-es(a)*	*-an*
3sg.	*-el(a)*	*-as, -ol-i*
1pl.	*-as(a)*	*-am*
2pl.		
3pl.	*-en(a)*	

'you went', *dictan* 'you saw', *viyan* 'you came'. Smart and Crofton (1875: 37) report on the occasional extension of the past-tense 3sg marker to the 2sg: *bisserdas too?* 'hast thou forgotten?', *diktassa too?* 'did you see?'. The 3sg itself shows the expected inflection form in *-as* – *dikdas* 'he saw', *romadas* 'he married', *perdas* 'she fell' – but also, as in Welsh Romani, conservative person-inflected forms with selected verbs indicating change of state: *perdī* 'she fell', *suti* 'asleep', *uštyas* alongside *uštilo* 'he stood up' (Tipler 1957). The only attested plural form is *oiam* 'we ate'.

The copula shows a sound shift from **sj > š* which affects the first and second person forms and may be said to be diagnostic of British Romani (a similar change is attested only from Parakalamos Romani in northwestern Greece): *šom* 'I am', *šan* 'you are', *se/si* 'he is/they are'. For the past tense, the forms *shimmus* 'I was' and *sis/sas* 'he/she was' are attested. As in most of the northern European dialects of Romani, the future form of the copula is recruited from the verb **av-* 'to come', via the meaning 'to become': thus Norwood *boot mushaw venna motte kerate* 'many men will be drunk tonight'.

Romani verbs have a rather prolific past-tense inflection class formation. Examples primarily from Norwood's material and from Smart and Crofton (1875), but also from other sources, allow the reconstruction of the following picture. The class of verb stems ending in dentals and in *-v-* behaves in much the same way as in the other conservative varieties, continuing the Early Romani perfective marker *-d-*: *kerdum* 'I did', *rokkerdum* 'I spoke', *nasherdas* 'he lost', *perdas* 'she fell', *pandas* 'he said', *kindas* 'he bought', *jindas* 'he knew', *jivdas* 'he lived'. The resulting consonant cluster is rarely simplified: *kaidom* 'I did'. Stems with the underlying transitive augments *-av-* or *-er-* and the irregular past of *per-* 'to fall' similarly take *-d-*: *dookodum man* 'I hurt myself', *romadas* 'he married', *romadum* 'I married', *pedas* 'he fell'. The archaic marker *-t-* is retained, again as in the more conservative dialects, in stems ending in dental sibilants /s/ and /š/ as well as in the irregular past-tense stem of the verb *sov-* 'to sleep': *prasthem* 'I ran', *beshto* 'he sat', *lasthom* 'I found', *suttum* 'I slept'. Stems in velar consonants, labials and affricates agree with Welsh Romani in aligning themselves with the above group, rather than with formation of inflection classes of vocalic stems. We thus find *dikdas* 'he saw', *mookdas* 'she left', *dictan* 'you saw', *camdom* 'I wanted', *pučdas* 'he asked'. Note that the notations *d/t* are sometimes interchangeable here. There follows a class of verbs that do not take perfective markers at all. These correspond roughly to the classes that take either historical *-l-* or a derived palatalised variant *-j-* in other dialects. They include the vocalic stems, as in *oium* 'I ate', *oiam* 'we ate', and the mono-consonantal stems, as in *veum* 'I came', *geum* 'I went', *gjas* 'she went', *diom* 'I gave', *lias* 'he took'. We might take the notation to indicate the traces of a palatal glide, indicating the loss of historical *-l-* in positions where it will have preceded a palatalised person ending. The segment in *-l-* remains, however, in the participle form: *mucklo* 'left', *panlo* 'shut'. The irregular *ušti-* 'to stand up' shows two alternate forms – *uštiyas*, *uštilo* 'he stood up' – while the particular inflection class of vocalic stems in *-a* that indicate mental states take the past-tense marker *-nj-*, as testified for *saniom* 'I laughed' (Tipler 1957).

Apart from the past-tense copula form *shimmus* 'I was', there is no evidence in English Romani for the use of the remoteness marker *-as* or any related form for the formation of imperfect and pluperfect tenses on the basis of the present and past respectively; the procedure is, however, productive in Welsh Romani, and we might assume that the absence of documentation for English Romani stems from the paucity of the source material.

The imperative form of the verb continues to consist of the inherited verb stem. There is evidence from Harriott for the continuation, optionally, of the emphatic imperative particle **-tar* in *dikta* 'look!', *šunta* 'listen!'. The stem of mono-consonantal verbs, however, is not the inherited stem but an augmented one, which serves as the imperative, too: *lel* 'take!' (European Romani *le*). A phonotactic rule requires monosyllabic verb roots to end in a coda. Inherited mono-consonantal verbs like *l-* 'to take' and *d-* 'to give', as well as those ending with a vowel nucleus like *xa-* 'to eat', *pi-* 'to drink' and *sa-* 'to laugh', are amended to incorporate a consonant deriving either from the 3sg. present-tense person ending *-l* (*lel* 'to take', *del* 'to give', *hol* 'to eat', *sal* 'to laugh') or, more rarely, from the 1sg. present-tense person ending *-v* (*sav* 'to laugh' alongside *sal*, *piv* 'to drink'). Evidence that this process takes place even before the loss of Romani verb inflection is the attestation by Smart and Crofton (1875) of forms such as *deldom* 'I gave' alongside inherited *diom*. A relaxation of the rule is found with the verb *dža-* 'to go', for which we find *dža* alongside *džal*, *džel* and *džov*, and partly with the verb *pi* 'to drink', which may also occur without an augment.

By contrast, there is evidence for the emergence of a modal infinitive in the form of the verb root, unlike European Romani, where the embedded verb must occur in a finite (subjunctive) form: *trašado šan te dik* 'you are scared to look' (Tipler 1957), *jal ta duruck* 'she is gone to tell fortunes' (East Anglian vocabulary of 1798), *maw mook mandi dik toot* 'don't let me see you' (Smart & Crofton 1875: 205) (but also: *so shom te keraw* 'what must I do?' with finite person inflection; ibid.: 31), *mussa jaw* 'I must go' (Copsey, in Winstedt 1915). Note that some Sinte and Polish Romani varieties introduce a quasi-infinitive, but that even this form is based on the 3sg finite form, not on the bare verb root.

Negative forms of the verb show the retention of a distinct negative imperative particle *ma* – *ma pen* 'don't say' (Fox) – while in the indicative there is on the one hand retention of inherited *na*, but on the other hand reinforcement through the negator *kek* that is typical of the Northwestern dialects: *more pen kek kokopen* 'don't tell any lies' (East Anglian list from 1798), *na junav me kek* 'I don't know' (Whiter), *kek na jinova me* 'I don't know' (Smart & Crofton 1875: 48), *kek nanei yek kohst* 'not a single stick' (ibid.: 113), *kek yon te wel panlo* 'they will not be locked up' (ibid.: 194).

3.2.5 Grammatical vocabulary and morphosyntax

While the sources provide attestation for the continuation of much of the inherited grammatical vocabulary, the decline of both definite and indefinite articles stand out. The indefinite article is replaced early on by English *a*: *bauchevin tutti a gilli* 'I'll play you a tune', *ava coushcou chau* (= *av a kušku čhav*) 'Be a good boy' (East Anglian list from 1798). This is in all likelihood triggered by the asymmetry in the use of indefinite articles in European Romani and in English. Romani dialects tend to use indefinite articles strictly in order to introduce new topical entities, while otherwise no overt article is used. This older pattern appears to continue in the inflected dialect, as confirmed by Smart and Crofton (1875: 11): *dikkova gairo* 'I see [a] man' in the inflected ('deep') dialect, but *mandi diks a gairo* 'I see a man' in the uninflected ('new') dialect. As for the definite article, Smart and Crofton report on the occasional use in Romani of the English article, pronounced *de*. In the other sources, occurrences are limited to a few forms such as *o bitto gav* 'the little village' (Norwood), *le o giv* 'take the oats', and *e greski bošto* 'the horse's saddle' (Bright), *o chum te cam* 'the moon and sun', (Goddard Johnson), representing the nominative and oblique forms, respectively. Note that the Welsh Romani definite article paradigm is similarly reduced to an opposition of two forms – *o* for the masculine singular and optionally plural nominative, and *i* for all other forms.

Demonstratives, by contrast, show the inheritance of a complex system, in both Welsh and English Romani. The Early Romani legacy is that of a unique four-term system of demonstrative pronouns, which tend to survive in the peripheral zones comprising the Balkans, Italy, earlier attestations of Iberian Romani, and Welsh Romani. The system is based on an opposition of consonantal stems in *-d-/-k-* and vocalic stems in *-a-/-o-*: *adava, akava, odova, okova*. In a simplified analysis, stems in *-d-* indicate immediately accessible objects while those in *-k-* denote specific referents; and stems in *-a-* indicate objects that are present and visible while those in *-o-* denote those that are remote or imagined or retrieved primarily from the discourse context. European dialects of Romani outside the Balkans, Wales and southern

Italy typically restructure the paradigm somewhat. A frequent restructuring pattern, encountered for instance in the Polish-Baltic dialects, is to eliminate one of the consonantal stems but to rely instead on the semantically distinctive presence or absence of an initial vowel (*dava, adava, dova, odova*). The path taken in English Romani appears to have been instead to employ the contrast +/− initial vowel in order to reinforce the vocalic opposition, which is weakened as a result of fluctuations in the quality of pronunciation of the inherited phonemes /a/ and /o/ as [a, ɑ, ɔ, ʌ, ʊ] etc. The resulting pattern is *akava, kova, adova, dova* (potentially inflected for gender, number and case). Reduplicated forms are also attested, carrying the augments 'here', 'there': *dəva dai, dəva doi*. The parallel place deixis expressions are *(a)kai* 'here' and *(o)doi* 'there', similarly derived from an original four-term system (*akaj, adaj, okoj, odoj*).

The inventory of indefinite expressions is partly old and retains Early Romani compositions such as *chomoni* 'something', *kommoni* 'somebody' and *chichi* 'nothing', sporadically found in the Balkans and otherwise preserved especially in the dialects of northern Europe. A further Early Romani inheritance is *vareso* 'any, whichever', attested both in Welsh Romani and in English Romani (Sampson 1926b, Smart & Crofton 1875). The indefinite marker on the expression goes back in all likelihood to the early influence of Balkan Romance, and a set based on the marker has spread especially around the Romani dialects of Transylvania and central Europe. Two significant innovations characterise the system of indefinites. The first is the negative indefinite *kek-*, which is shared with the other Northwestern dialects (the German and Scandinavian dialects of Romani). It is extended to form expressions such as *kek-komoni* 'nobody', *kek-komi* 'never' and *keker* 'never, none'. The second appears to be a more local innovation, and is based on the composition *sa-kon* 'every', literally. 'all-who', as a marker of universality: *sawkon kova* 'everything', *sawkon cherus* 'always'. Inherited interrogatives that survive in English Romani include *so* 'what', *savo* 'which', *sår* 'how', *kaj* 'where', *kon* 'who', *soski* 'why' and *kana* 'when'. A rare innovation is *sar kizzi* 'how much', modelled on the structure of the English counterpart expression.

A rather complete inventory of prepositions and local relation expressions is attested, continuing the inherited inventory. Noteworthy is the co-existence of both full and shortened forms for *adre/dre* 'in' and *aglal/glal* 'before, in front', attesting to a stage that is somewhat more conservative than that found in the German and Polish dialects, which show short forms only. Conservative retentions of lexical items are *perdal* 'through, across' and *tresal* 'around'. The short form *ke* is found in the meaning 'in, at' – *ke teero ker* 'in your house', and *kety* in the sense of 'to, towards' (Bright). Note the absence of inherited prepositions indicating source, movement away from, or a completed phase. These are borrowed from English: *le o giv away gresti* 'take the oats from the horse' (Bright), *romadum romane juval boot beshaw ago* 'I married a Romani wife many years ago', *ky shan since dikddum tut?* 'where have you been since I saw you?' (Norwood).

Among the set of numerals, Welsh Romani shows a series of unique innovations for figures above 'five': *duvari trin*, literally 'twofold three', for 'six', *trin t'a štår*, literally 'three and four', for 'seven', *duvari štår*, literally 'twofold four', for 'eight', and finally *deš bi yek*, literally 'ten without one', for 'nine'. The system is confirmed by Tipler ((1957) as well as in part by Smart and Crofton (1875: 45), who have *trin ta stor*, literally 'three and four', alongside *dooi trinyaw ta yek*, literally 'two three and one', for 'seven', *dooi storaw*, literally 'twofold four', for 'eight', and *dooi storaw ta yek*, literally. 'twofold four and one', for 'nine'. Other sources confirm *dui trins ta yek* for 'seven' (N.A. 1929) and *dui shtors* for 'eight' (Winstedt 1949). The presence of inherited *šov, efta, oxto, enja* (the latter three Greek-derived) is also well attested, however, and suggests some fragmentation within British Romani, quite possibly a result of continuing contacts with continental varieties of Romani on the part of some British Romani clans but not others.

While the picture for English Romani syntactic formations is far from full, especially when compared to Welsh Romani, both dialects appear to maintain a series of inherited conjunctions such as *kana* 'when', *soske* 'because', and the complementiser *te*. Welsh Romani is a rare case among the dialects of Romani in having abandoned a separate complementiser **kaj*, originally limited to introducing factual complements, and having merged both the subjunctive and the factual and conditional functions in *te*. Tipler's (1957) examples confirm this: *Phukadom me i juviaki te kamav i Wålši* 'I told the woman I like Wales'. The continuation of *te* is attested in sources such as the East Anglian list – *jal ta duruck* 'she is gone to tell fortunes' – and Smart and Crofton *te wel mandi te mer* 'should I die'.

That full morphosyntactic convergence with English is certainly missing is testified to by the persistence of constructions that are quite distinct in their typology form their English counterparts. Thus Smart and Crofton's (1875: 204) texts show word order patterns such as *diktas yoi dooi trin raunya* 'she saw two-three women', with overt verb-subject order (*diktas yoi*, literally 'saw-she') indicating the inherited Romani resultative-continuative mode. Sanderson's list similarly shows 'verb focus' word order as typical of the depiction of surprising events and the introduction of new, unknown topics in *avella gorgio* 'a stranger is coming' (Griffiths & Yates 1934). To cite just one further example, consider the persistence of continental Romani case assignment in *deas man* 'he gave me' (Bryant), where the case of the direct object (the unmodified oblique) also serves the beneficiary of 'to give'.

3.2.6 The impact of English

The impact of English on the English dialect of Romani especially is considerable. In addition to loanwords, Romani replicates lexico-semantic patterns, as in *ke divous* 'today' (literally 'to-day'), *avri se yog* 'the fire is out', *sår o čeros* 'all the time', *mai shom sill* 'I am cold'. A major addition to the language's inventory of constructions is the formation of a progressive, based on the English model of employing the verb 'to be' as an auxiliary, accompanied by the Romani inflected present-tense or embedded subjunctive: *caishin de jasher?* (Fox) = *kai shan te dzhasa?* 'where are you going?', *šom beravav mo bal* (Tipler) 'I am combing my hair', *shum to jaw to peerov avree* (Norwood) 'I am going to walk out'. Note in the last example the merger of the inherited Romani complementiser *te*, which introduces the complement or target predicate, with the English *to*, which introduces the infinitive.

The earliest indications of morphological borrowings pertain to the indefinite article, a number of conjunctions – cf. Bright's *miro romani an mi chi* 'my wife and my daughter' – and prepositions (discussed above), but also bound morphemes: the plural ending *-s* appears regularly alongside the inherited Romani ending (either doubling it or with a word-specific preference or in variation): cf. Norwood's *errahs* 'legs', *kannos* 'ears'. The English genitive-possessive *s* is also replicated: cf. Norwood's *mandy's tchavvy* 'my boy'. Derivational morphemes replicated from English include *to* as in *to divus* 'to-day' (Bright) and the adverbial ending in *ladjfully* 'shamefully' (Smart & Crofton 1913). Finally, a further inflectional ending appears to enter the language at a stage before the actual decline of inherited verb inflection: the progressive construction replicated from English takes on the English gerundial verb ending *-in*: *kaliko raati mandi sas wel-in' keri* 'Last night I was coming home' (Smart & Crofton 1875: 254).

We might summarise by saying that English influence on Romani in England leads in the first instance to a loss of categories rather than to the adoption of morphological material: the distinction between declension classes is blurred, grammatical gender is eroded, nominal case marking is reduced and morphological agreement becomes redundant – all this while its sister variety in Wales, as documented by Sampson (1926b), remains conservative. Where adoption of morphology is concerned, we find here too a split between the varieties, with English Romani taking on in a systematic manner English plural endings, the English genitive-possessive ending, an indefinite article and some prepositions and conjunctions.

3.3 The position of British Romani among Romani dialects

Our use of the term 'British Romani' appears justified in the light of the close resemblances between the densely documented variety spoken by the Wood clan from Wales in the second half of the nineteenth century (Sampson 1926b), the description of the variety of Romani spoken by the Boswells of Cheshire two generations earlier (Smart & Crofton 1875), and the various, albeit much more fragmented specimens of English Romani varieties found in other sources. Among the characteristic features that set British Romani apart from other Romani varieties are the convergent sound development triggered through contact with English, a number of characteristic lexical features such as *wafado* 'bad', *kučko/kušto* 'good', *bita* 'a little' and *puker* 'to speak', ablative marker *-ti*, the merger of factual and non-factual complementisers in *te*, renewal of the numerals 6–9, the retention of both *-ipen/-iben* and *-imus/-amus* as abstract nominalisers and of *-is-/-as-* as loan verb adaptation markers, the retention of demonstrative sets in both *(a)kava* and *(a) dava*, and a combination of features typical of the Northwestern European dialects such as negation in *kek*, the exceptional sound shift in **ogi > *dži > (o)zi* 'soul', and several distinct lexical developments.

English Romani sets itself apart from the conservative Welsh dialect primarily through extensive cluster reduction in words like *beš* 'year' and *muš* 'man', consistent shift of stress, loss of *-l-* as a past-tense marker, the emergence of a variant genitive marker in *-to*, reduction of nominal inflection categories, and reliance primarily on *-er-* as transitive verbal augment.

In its relation to the continental dialects of Romani, British Romani shows first of all those developments that are typical of the Romani dialects that emerged to the north of the so-called 'Great Divide' (see above, Map 2.1, and Matras 2005): *j-* in *jaro* 'egg' and *jov* 'he', cluster reduction in *raker-* 'to speak' (from **vr-*), retention of *-n* in the abstract nominal ending *-pen/-ben*, contraction of initial *a-* in *mal* 'friend', *sa-* 'to laugh', *rakh-* 'to find', simplification of the historical cluster /ṇḍ/ to /r/ in *maro* and *jaro*, and the selection of a range of lexical items as outlined above: *xačar-* 'to burn', *stariben* 'prison', *dži* 'heart', *heroj* 'leg', *men* 'neck', *rukh* 'tree' and so on. Further features shared with dialects of northern Europe – Germany, Scandinavia and the Baltic area – include the stem vowel in *džin-* 'to know' (elsewhere *džan-*), the syllable structure in *džuvel* 'woman' (elsewhere *džuvli*), the presence of /x/ in *kaxnji* 'chicken' (elsewhere *khanji*) and of /v/ in *čovaxani* 'witch', and in the morphological domain the stability of past-tense markers in *-d-/-t-* with most consonantal verb stems and the limited distribution of markers in *-l-*.

Among the Northern European dialects, British Romani is conservative, along with Latvian Romani, in maintaining the class of masculines in *-is* and *-os* for European loan nouns (the latter is also shared with Finnish Romani and with some conservative varieties of Sinte; see discussion in Matras 1999b); in maintaining, along with Sinte, a semi-productive use of subject clitics with lexical predications; and in maintaining, along with Finnish Romani, some use of gender-marked active participles in the 3sg of verbs of motion and change of state.

In respect of a range of modifications to initial segments (Table 3.6), the northern European region offers a varied, transition area. British Romani is consistent in its adoption of initial *v-* (also realised as *w-*). It stands out on its own in showing prothetic *v-* in *vangust* 'finger' (and *vangusti* 'ring'), agrees with the Baltic dialects in showing *vangar* 'coal', agrees with Scandinavian

Table 3.6 Word-initial segments in British Romani and other Romani dialects

	'flour'	'finger'	'tear'	'now'	'stay'	'other'	'coal'	'egg'	'door'	'lip'
Angloromani	voro	wongust	swa	akno, kenau	atch	vaver	vongar	joura	vudar, wudar	wishta
Welsh Romani	vārdō, vārō	vangušto	swā	akana, kana	ačh-	vaver	vangar	jāro	hudār, xudār	(v)ušt
Swedish Romani	varo	gustro		[nii]	asj-	vaver		jaro	vurda	vust
Finnish Romani	vāro	angux, angus	svaal	kān, kā	čh-	vaver	angar	jāro	vūdar	lippos
Sinte	jarro	gušto	sva	kana	ačh-, čh-	vaver	angar	jāro	vudar	vušt
Polska Roma	jažo	gušč	jasfa	kana	jačh-, čh-	vavir, javir	vangar	jaro	vudar, udar	vušč
Lithuanian Romani	jažo	[pal'co]	jasva	kana	jačh	vavir	vangar	[parnoro]	udara	ušt
Latvian Romani	jažo	angušt	jasva	kana	jačh	vavir, javir	vangar	jaaro	udara	ušt
Molisean Romani	vare	ungušte		kana	čh-	vaver	ngar	vare	vuddar	vušt
Caló	xaroi	angusti		acaná	[sin-]	aver		anro	bundai	

Table 3.7 Initial palatalisation of inherited segments in Angloromani and other Romani dialects

	'soul'	'butter'	'boot'	'how much'
Angloromani	zī	kil	čoka, čirka	kisi
Welsh Romani	ōzy	khil	čiox	kisi
Swedish Romani	si	kił	tirak	
Sinte	zi	khil	tirax, kirxa	kici
Finnish Romani	či	čil	tiehi	
Latvian Romani	dži	kšil	tirax	kicy
Lithuanian Romani	dzi	kšil		kicy
Polska Roma	dži	kšił	terax	kicy
Molisean Romani	gi		trijax	
Caló	orči		tiraxajče	kiči

Romani on *varo* 'flour' and with most of the western zone on *vušt* 'hand' and *vaver* 'other'. Welsh Romani is most probably conservative in not showing a stable labial consonant in *hudar* 'door', in all likelihood reflecting a transitional stage from *udar* to *vudar*. British Romani agrees with Sinte and the Scandinavian dialects in dropping original initial *a-* in *swa-* 'tear' (as in the contraction of *av-* 'to come' to *v-*), but is somewhat more conservative in maintaining variants in an initial vowel for words like *akana ~ kana* 'now', *adrej ~ drej* 'in', *asa-* and *sa(v)-* 'to laugh' (and likewise in maintaining variants like *avri* and *vri* 'out', *adre* and *dre* 'in', etc.), and in consistently maintaining the vowel in *ač-* 'to stay'.

A further salient domain of structural variation in Romani is the word-specific palatalisaiton of dentals and velars (Table 3.7). British Romani agrees with the western European conservative zone in retaining *g-* in words like *gili* 'song', *giv* 'wheat' and *k-* in *kil* 'butter' (where Finnish Romani undergoes a special development as a result of contact with Swedish) as well as the absence of palatlaisation in *buti* 'work', *tiro* 'your', *tikno* 'small' and *dives* 'day'. Within the western groups of dialects, British Romani stands out in palatalising the initial segment in 'boot' (*čirka* etc.) and in the de-affrication of the dental in *kisi* < *kici* 'how much'. It agrees with Sinte and Swedish Romani in showing *zi* 'heart, soul' (from **g'i* > **dži*, as in Lithuanian and Polish and Finnish Romani), realised similarly as *si* in Swedish Romani (the same development is seen for *iz* 'clothes', Swedish Romani *is*, elsewhere *idž*; see Table 3.7).

British Romani shares two morphological innovations with Sinte (German Romani) and the Scandinavian Romani dialects. The first is the negation particle *kek*; the second is the productive use of *-er-* as a verb derivation marker. There is some indication that *-er-* was also used as a loan verb adaptation marker to integrate loans from German, and so here a special affinity stands out between English Romani and Swedish Romani.

Finally, returning to the lexicon, we note once again close similarities between British Romani and the German (Sinte) and Scandinavian dialects of the language. Shared specifically with Sinte and Scandinavian are lexical features such as *gavvers* 'police' (Swedish Romani *gav* 'man'), *muskro* 'policeman', and *puker* 'say', which also appears in Swedish Romani, while the seeds of British Romani formations in *-engro* are already found in Sinte *kanengre* 'earrings', *grajengro* 'horse dealer', *masengro* 'butcher', and to a lesser extent also in Swedish Romani *kurrmengare* 'fighter' (contaminated, in this case, with the Swedish agentive marker *-are*). Table 3.8 illustrates how individual lexical items are shared within the larger lexical pool of Romani varieties to the north and west of the Great Divide, with the Baltic varieties more closely, and specifically within the more tightly linked network of the Northwestern dialects (Sinte, Swedish Romani and Finnish Romani). The variant words for 'clothes' and for 'hedgehog' represent nicely how Angloromani incorporates lexical variants that link it simultaneously to several different dialects.

In the light of these findings, it is necessary to revise somewhat the impression conveyed in relation to British Romani in Matras (2002: ch. 2) as an independent dialect cluster rather than part of the Northwestern group. Not only do we now have a more detailed understanding of the structures of some of the dialects involved – owing in particular to extensive fieldwork on both Angloromani (by the author and the Manchster Romani Project) and Swedish Romani (by Gerd Carling and Lindell & Thorbjörnsson-Djerf 2008) – but we also have a better understanding of the relations among dialects as much more dynamic (see Matras 2005). In this regard, British Romani is as much 'independent' as it is the product of a network of contacts, both historical (in the sense of 'origin') and continuous (in the sense of maintenance of social networks and migrations), with geographically neighbouring communities of Romani speakers in the North Sea area.

The selection of data presented in the tables of this section provide a clear picture of a tightly related branch of British Romani, consisting of the closely affiliated Angloromani and Welsh Romani. This 'branch' shares the greatest number of features with neighbouring Swedish Romani (which is, as far as the Romani component is concerned, more or less identical with Norwegian Romani) as well as with Sinte Romani, followed by Finnish Romani. With some margin, there is also an affinity with the dialects of the Polska Roma of Poland, itself something of a transitional variety between the Baltic (Lithuanian and Latvian) dialects of Romani, to which it is closely related, and the neighbouring Sinte variety. Similarities then follow in decreasing order of prominence with the dialects of the Baltics, with other dialects on the same side of the Great Divide, and finally with those across the Great Divide:

British Romani > Swedish Romani > Finnish Romani > Sinte > Polska Roma > Lithuanian and Latvian Romani > other dialects north/west

Table 3.8 Selected lexical items in Angloromani and other Romani dialects

	'soldier'	'arm'	'bed'	'clothes'	'find'	'hedgehog'	'cat'	'saddle'
Angloromani	kulimengro	musi	wodros	iz, rivoben	lač	hoči-wiči, niglo, štakelengro	mača	boshto
Welsh Romani	kūramangerō	mušī	vodros	rivipen	lat	určos	mačka	beshto
Swedish Romani	dākkaskiro, kurrmengare	mussing	våddro	is	lattja		masskra	
Sinte	lurdo ~ kurmangari	musi	čiben	ripen, feci	hač-	niglo, štaxelengro	mačka	zen
Finnish Romani	dekakiro, xelado	mussi	vuodros	koola	lač-		mahka	baxta
Latvian Romani	zaldatus	vast	čiben	rizi	lač-	ježus	kotka	zen
Lithuanian Romani	xalado	vast	loško	idži	latx-	ježo	khaca	zen
Polska Roma	helado	vast	čhiben	uripen	rakh-	ježo	khaca	
Molisean Romani	panjiluro	uast	oddr	xulivja	rakk-		cica	
Caló	seroy	murcia	cheripén	dicló	alachar	uchabaló	machicai	

of the Great Divide > southeastern dialects of Romani (south of the Great Divide)

Naturally, British Romani remains uninfluenced by developments that are specific to the Balkans or southeastern Europe in general. Some conservative features in morphology, such as retention of demonstratives in *akava*, *okova* etc., of subject clitics *lo* etc., of active participles such as *uštilo* 'stood up', and of Early Romani Greek loan morphemes such as *-mus* and *-as-* as well as *-os* and *-is* create a superficial impression of similarities with specific dialect groups such as Balkan, Vlax, Northern Central or Baltic Romani, but these are non-diagnostic archaisms that are not particularly meaningful as far as the reconstruction of any shared development history is concerned.

It is partly the presence of such archaisms in British Romani that requires us to postulate a clear demarcation between the British Romani population and that of neighbouring North Sea regions in continental Europe, rather than simply an unbroken continuum of a single group. For a start, both physical boundaries and language-cultural boundaries (in the sense of immersion with distinct settled populations) will have had their impact in safeguarding distinct community structures. Two important structural features of the Northwestern dialect group – the shift from /s/ to /h/ in intervocalic position in grammatical paradigms (and in Sinti also in function words and the copula), and the preference for 2sg -*l*- – do not reach British Romani, but are shared with the Central dialects immediately to the east. We might speculate that the bond between the Romani communities in Britain and the continent was no longer sufficiently strong by the time this development took place to allow it to spread into British Romani. The likely historical scenario therefore points to an immigration, and possibly to successive immigrations, of Romani-speaking 'communities', i.e. extended families or 'clans', from the North Sea area (northern Germany and Scandinavia) into Britain, as well as, possibly, back again. Of particular interest in this respect is a safe-passage letter cited by Simson (1866: 99–100). It was issued by King James IV of Scotland, addressed to the King of Denmark, in 1506, and recommends the undisturbed passage from Scotland to Denmark of a group of "Egyptian pilgrims" led by one "Antonius Gawino, Earl of Little Egypt". This documented interest on the part of British Gypsies in maintaining links with networks on the continent might indicate that British Romanies continued to absorb a modest degree of lexical influence even after settlement in Britain. Nevertheless, the separation across geographical and political borders enabled the maintenance of some conservative structural features in British Romani, as well as the failure to adopt structural innovations that were to spread on the continent and in Scandinavia; it also paved the way towards the cumulative loss in English Romani of entire structural categories, and ultimately to the decline of inflected Romani in Britain.

3.4 The decline of inflected Romani in Britain

Before drawing conclusions from the above discussion it is useful to return to the debate surrounding the emergence of Angloromani. Recall first the weakness of the arguments put forward by Hancock (1970) in favour of the emergence of Angloromani as a kind of contact variety used for in-group communication among a mixed population of Travellers of Romani and non-Romani origin; it is fairly clear that whenever such contacts emerged, English provided an adequate means of inter-group communication and there was no need for a special contact variety. None the less, Hancock's scenario may be valuable in postulating at least the social setting in which inflected Romani was being abandoned yet a Romani vocabulary was being retained as an in-group lexical reservoir: mixed marriages and the absorption of individuals who were not Romani speakers into the community will have strengthened the position of English as the language of the family; yet at the same time the community did not abandon its tight-knit structures and sense of identity, and the retention of Romani vocabulary served to strengthen and to flag this identity.

Recall as well that Kenrick (1979) had suggested that this transition to the 'broken' language was gradual and involved a step-by-step structural attrition of the old inflected language. Bakker (2000) reviews a number of the sources discussed above that record the inflected variety, and concludes that Kenrick is partly justified in recognising a gradual structural attrition in the language. However, Bakker contends that the final transition from inflected Romani to Angloromani was abrupt and that it took place within no more than a single generation. In support of his argument he points to the absence of any attestation of a "transitory stage" (Bakker 2000: 28) between the two variety types. It is not entirely clear, however, what kind of transitory stage might have been expected and what its structural characteristics might have been.

An interesting scenario is presented by Coughlan (2001: 6–51). With Kenrick's suggestion as a point of departure, Coughlan argues that by the late eighteenth or early nineteenth century the number of fluent speakers of Romani in England had declined considerably. This was due to the small size of the population and its dispersion over considerable distances, as well as its remoteness from any larger Romani-speaking population centres. English, which had served alongside Romani in the organisation of daily life, began to play an ever more important role within the community as well as outside it, and English structures began to penetrate Romani speech even more intensively, leading to a gradual reduction in competence in Romani and ultimately to language shift. Welsh Romani, it is argued, broke away from English Romani before this process of attrition. None the less, the emotional value of the language enabled the creation of the "new reduced variety" by those who preferred English but did not wish to abandon Romani entirely as a family language. This reduced variety will have existed alongside the inflected variety for quite some time, until the latter completely disappeared in the mid-nineteenth century. Coughlan concludes by suggesting that the reduced variety continuted to undergo changes and was finally redefined functionally as a specialised in-group code as opposed to a mother tongue.

To conclude this chapter I wish to present a scenario that integrates some of the ideas presented in these various approaches. Briefly, I propose that population mixing and the integration of Travellers of non-Romani origin into the Romani community led to the decline in the everyday use of Romani as a family and community language. This process merely accompanied the growing structural impact that English had on the English Romani dialect, and which had led to some significant changes in its structure, but not to its abandonment altogether. Thus, gradual structural attrition and language shift must be seen as two independent processes, with separate outcomes. The disappearance of the inflected language was the outcome of language shift, and this process of language shift is likely to have taken place within a single generation, as is the case in most situations: an older generation fails to transmit its languauge to the younger generation, and the language is thus abandoned. In this respect, the hypothesis of a gradual structural attrition and that of an abrupt decline of the inflected language can both be supported. As for the so-called 'reduced' variety, it is in fact not at all a reduced form of the inflected language, but an *alternative* to the inflected language, one that relies on English for its grammar and in particular for the initiation of the predication and so for verb inflection. The practice of inserting Romani vocabulary into English sentences may indeed, as argued by Bakker (2002), have been very old and well established – possibly as a humorous code, possibly also as a way to initiate non-Romani speaking Travellers into a shared in-group code (in a setting that resembles the one proposed by Hancock, albeit not for purposes of intra-group communication but rather for the flagging of an in-group bond). This variety continues to survive and becomes the carrier of the more emblematic and more subtle, emotional functions previously associated with the inflected language, while the function of default everyday conversation is taken over by English. While the abandonment of inflected Romani is fairly abrupt, some evidence of a transitory stage does indeed exist in the form of utterances that contain verb inflection from both Romani and English, thus showing a mixture of inflected Romani and Angloromani. To the extent that the prevalence of Angloromani has a structural correlation, it is the loss of the ability to form the predication using Romani inflection and the replacement of predicational morphology by English grammar that constitutes the decisive turning point.

Welsh Romani as documented by Sampson (1926b) testifies to the existence of an early, and later of a conservative, form of British Romani that retains the full inherited inflectional potential of European Romani. We might postulate a first and early phase of English influences consisting primarily of the partial adoption of English phonology, the adoption of English loanwords and lexical semantics. We have attestation from the south of England that by the late eighteenth century the impact of English extended to include further phonological convergence, the replication of English progressive aspect and an uninflected infinitive, the adoption of the indefinite article *a*, and simplification of the pronominal system with a tendency even at this stage to generalise just one object pronoun (East Anglian list of 1798; Sampson 1930). Just a generation or so later we already find a new phase in the influence of English, characterised by the adoption of the nominal plural marker -*s* as well as the possessive-genitive *s*, the erosion of nominal case and in some instances also of nominal gender, the borrowing of conjunctions and local relation expressions, and even the adoption of the gerundial suffix -*in*.

Throughout this period, the language retains its finite verb inflection and so the ability to form predications without reliance on the contact language. A third phase in its contact development, however, is a crucial 'flip' stage in terms of the system-internal integrity of Romani: verb inflection is lost and with it the ability to distinguish unequivocally between a predication that is initiated in Romani and one that is initiated in English. This inevitably results in some ambiguity in defining propositions and speech actions, and hence also entire interaction contexts, as consistently 'Romani'. It is from this stage onwards that we can speak of a Romani component that is hosted within the utterance and discourse framework of English, rather than of English elements or constructions that are adopted and hosted within the framework of Romani. Romani–English bilingualism becomes, at this stage, essentially a choice between English with or without a Romani component. It is noteworthy that the loss of verb inflection is accompanied by the loss of conjunctions and an independent clause structure, as well as the loss of plural pronouns and the complete decline of inherited plural formation in nouns.

It is not easy to put a precise date to the emergence of this third and crucial phase in the development of English Romani. According to Bakker (2002), the second-oldest British source on Romani, the Winchester Confessions recorded in 1615–16 (McGowan 1996), already provides evidence of such a 'mixed language'. The documents consist of testimonies of prisoners, which include a word list referred to as *a note of such Canting words as the Counterfett Egiptians use amongst themselves as ther Language*. The list contains just over 100 entries, but these are mainly isolated words, which makes it impossible to draw any conclusions about the shape of Romani utterances. The reference to the 'canting tongue' is also ambiguous, and although 'Cant' and the language used by Gypsies among themselves are portrayed as identical, we cannot exclude the possibility that the list documents, rather, Romani-derived words as adopted and used by non-Romanies. The only grammatical feature found in the list is gender agreement with adjectives, which tends to fluctuate: *bong-o vast* 'right hand (M)', *cubney gaggey* = *khabn-i gadži* 'a pregnant woman'; but also *trickney ruckelo* 'a little boy' alongside *trickney ruckey* 'a little girl' (European Romani *tikn-o raklo* vs. *tikn-i rakli*). This latter feature could represent the use of Romani words outside a Romani grammatical framework.

Of particular interest are three phrases in the list which show Romani words embedded in English phrases: *Swisht with a sayster in the end*, translated as 'A staff with a pike'; *Coore the Gorife*, translated as 'goe beate the Cow'; and *to be corde*, translated as 'is to be whipped'. Bakker (2002) interprets these phrases as evidence of the existence at this early period of a mixed form of speech, containing Romani-derived vocabulary in an English grammatical framework. Once again, it is difficult to say whether these examples testify to the use of a mixed code in Romani households, or simply to the adoption of Romani-derived vocabulary as a special lexicon among other population sectors, a usage pattern which may well have arisen independently of the decline or the structural 'erosion' of inflected Romani itself.

More striking, therefore, is the evidence that suggests that some speaker communities alternated randomly between the use of Romani verb inflection (carrying with it, normally, also the use of Romani pronouns and conjunctions) and the embedding of Romani verb roots in English verb inflection (usually accompanied by a choice of English pronouns and sentence organisation). Thus Goddard Johnson, collected sometime before 1803 (Scott Macfie & Winstedt 1939: 12–13), has *leom lis leski* 'I took it from him' (using both Romani verb and pronominal inflection) alongside *ar rackyas are tuvvin ar chicklo easers* 'The maids are washing the dirty clothes' (using English nominal plural and English auxiliary and gerundial suffix) and *nashar'd mauro gry* 'Lost our horse'. Copsey's list from 1818 (Winstedt 1915: 159–60) has *nah falée shum* 'I am sick' (with Romani verb inflection and conservative adjective-verb word order) alongside *pen your naave* 'say your name'. Fox, collected between 1832 and 1833 (Sampson 1926a: 86–7), cites inflected *yek raunee weller* (= *jek rani avela*) 'A lady is coming' and *vieomy vry Yorkshire* (= *avijom avri Yorkshire*) 'I've come from Yorkshire' alongside *I am jallen to the gave* 'I am going to the village', *I dowker raunees* 'I tell fortunes [to] ladies' and *I go káta kongrée* 'I go to church'. The collections of T. W. Norwood from 1859–64 (Grosvenor 1910) abound in such mixtures. We find *thinkisovva mandy's tchavvy was adray odoi* 'I thought my child was in there', combining Romani inflection on the borrowed English verb *think* with the English copula *was*; *I shan't vov kery till rate* 'I shan't come home till evening' (with *vo-v* 'I come'); *we shall jassa kallako* 'we shall go tomorrow' (with *jassa* 'we go'); and *I used to kerob booty* 'I used to work' (with *kerob* 'I work'). The overall pattern here is to employ Romani lexical verbs along with their inherited Romani inflection, but to use English auxiliaries along with their inflection. Note that it is the auxiliary that anchors the predication of the sentence.

Considering that the compilers of this material were on the search for 'pure Romani', it appears that what speakers were willing to regard and define as 'Romani' included a range of different degrees of mixing and integration of grammatical constructions deriving from both languages. Mixtures in verb inflection appear even in Smart and Crofton's dialogues in the 'old' dialect (1875: 254ff): *yov dels mandi soar mandi pootches* 'He gives me all I ask[s] for', *mandi penova yoi'll mer* 'I say she'll die'. Smart and Crofton admit that "It is scarcely necessary to observe that there is no precise line of demarcation between the old and new dialects" (1875: 273). The two varieties are thus analytical idealisations, which in practice form a continuum. The term 'new' dialect is used with reference to the consistent absence of Romani inflection, as can be seen by comparing Smart and Crofton's (1875: 219–21) presentations of the same passage in each of the two varieties:

'Old dialect':

Mandi	pookerova	toot	sar Petalengro
I	say.1sg.	you.obl.	how

	ghias	kater	mi	Doovelesko	keri
	went.3sg.	to	my	God.3.sg.m.gen	house

'I will tell you how Petalengro went to my Lord's house'

'New dialect':
Mandi'll poker tooti how the Petalengro jal'd andre mi Doovel's kair

The characteristic feature of the 'old' dialect is the retention of Romani verb inflection, prepositions, inflected or partly inflected personal and possessive pronouns, genitive endings, and subordinating conjunctions (introducing adverbial clauses and embeddings). Most of these features are lost and replaced by English structures in the 'new' dialect. The principal Romani component in the 'new' dialect is lexical vocabulary, which is accompanied by some personal pronouns in a fossilised form, and occasionally by other elements of grammatical vocabulary such as demonstratives and negation particles. This is the shape of 'Romanes' or 'Angloromani' as documented in most of the material collected in Britain from the early 1900s onwards: Romani inflected forms are rare, and are limited to fossilised expressions of the type *dova si mandi* 'I have that' (Winstedt 1948: 103). This picture indicates a loss of competence in the use of Romani grammatical inflections and a reliance instead on English for the grammatical organisation of utterances and discourse. At the same time, the appearance of fossilised expressions containing some inflectional material suggests that speakers are replicating more than just vocabulary. They are, to some extent at least, activating recollections and impressions of entire salient speech acts.

I suggest therefore that the period of turbulence in the shape of the Romani predication indicates a period during which the language was undergoing a turnover of functions: from a language used in the community and the family to exchange, contextualise and evaluate information, it shifts to an emblematic instrument used primarily to flag solidarity among family and group members. In other words, from a structural framework used by speakers in order to construct separate Romani-context predications (and by chaining predications, to construct Romani-context discourse), it shifts to a structural reservoir that is *embedded* in English-context predications and discourse for special effect. Predication grammar thus becomes a functionally negligible part of the Romani repertoire and hence obsolete, while the acquisition process instead becomes focused on merely the selective replication of structures that have a role to play in conveying a special effect – primarily lexical items, but also grammatical material that is from a semantic-pragmatic viewpoint *salient* to the propositional context, such as negation, direction and so on (so-called *salient grammar*).

The various historical phases of grammatical borrowing from English merely represent the gradual stablisation of a licence for speakers to relax somewhat the boundaries between the selection of structures within their bilingual repertoire when communicating in the family or community setting, and should not be confused with language 'attrition', i.e. the inability to retrieve structures in order to communicate effectively in the language. The infiltration of English modal auxiliaries into Romani is perhaps the latest phase in this development. It follows universal regularities of structural borrowing, whereby modal auxiliaries are borrowed before the grammar of lexical predications (see Matras 2009: 175ff). Norwood's examples cited above show that by the time English modal auxiliaries were freely used in Romani, they were also accompanied by English pronouns and other structures. Thus, the stage of language maintenance reflected by the relevant examples can be said to be at or past the point of *functional turnover*, where communication becomes secondary to emblematic display, and where native acquisition of the family language gives way to *selective replication* of content-salient structures.

4 The Structural Composition of Angloromani

4.1 The data corpus

The discussion in the following two chapters (as well as the documentation of Romani vocabulary in Appendix I) drawns on a corpus of interview recordings, carried out mainly between 2005 and 2008 with around forty individuals who describe themselves as English or Welsh Gypsies. They live in various parts of England and Wales, including the Northeast (County Durham and West Yorkshire), the Northwest (Lancashire and Cheshire), south Wales, West Midlands, Staffordshire, Leicestershire, Oxfordshire and Surrey. The great majority reside in mobile caravans ('trailers') but have usually been based in the same caravan site for a generation or even longer. Some have moved from caravans into houses sometime during the past decade but still keep caravans alongside the house, which they use either continuously for some members of the family, or just seasonally, when they travel to other parts of the country. Others, by far a small minority of those interviewed, tend to stay on one site for periods of between several months and two or three years and then move on to a different site in another part of the country. Seasonal travelling in caravans especially during the summer months and occasionally to fairs and other gatherings is common among all participants.

All interviewees refer to themselves in casual speech as 'Gypsies'. Asked to define themselves more specifically, they emphasise that they are 'Romani Gypsies', and some use or are at least familiar with the term 'Romanichals'. They draw a strict boundary between themselves and the Irish as well as Scottish Travellers, whom they regard as separate populations. By contrast, most feel some kind of affinity with Romani immigrants from central and eastern Europe, whom they describe as 'Roma'. All those interviewed are engaged in the kind of traditional occupation portfolio that is typical of British Gypsies, varying from road construction work (specialising in tarmac surfaces for private driveways), external house and garden work (especially assembly of PVC or aluminium pipes, gutters and window frames, and cutting and trimming trees and bushes) to scrap metal collection and occasional trade in second-hand cars or furniture and sometimes in horses and antiques. Work is organised within the extended family, which also tends to constitute the co-residential household, i.e. closely related nuclear families (those of several brothers or first cousins) tend to occupy a cluster of neighbouring trailers on a site, sharing cooking and washing facilities and often living as one economic household.

The traditional occupation of the women in these households was fortune-telling, and families relied significantly on income from this trade until fairly recently. The retreat of fortune-telling is usually due not to a decline in demand but to a ban imposed by the evangelical missionary movement, to which many of the families belong. The Light and Life mission has been active exclusively among English and Welsh Gypsies since the early 1980s and plays a key role within the community of British Romani Gypsies as a whole and in the lives of many of those interviewed. Some interviewees are even officers of the church, spend much of their time working in its service within their own community and among Romani communities abroad, and depend on the church for a considerable part of their income (the preferred description being 'compensation for loss of earnings' while away on church-related work).

All interviews were carried out by a team of researchers working on the Manchester Romani Project.[1] A complex and original interview technique was called for to cater for a rather paradoxical situation: Angloromani is not a language of entire conversations, but a code used to mark out individual utterances. Its employment is usually triggered either by reactions to outsiders, or by the emotive content of a speech act. It is therefore nearly impossible to ask speakers simply to 'engage in conversation' in AR for the benefit of a recording. Nor is it effective to try and elicit entire sentences in the language; speakers may lack an equivalent for a particular structure, which in turn might cause them embarrassment and jeopardise their readiness to continue the interview. The fact that we are dealing with an in-group, intimate code that is usually used only within the family makes documentation a literal challenge in terms of the 'observer's paradox'. Indeed, many speakers are not willing to share information on the language, regarding it as something that is 'private' or even 'secret'.

In identifying suitable and willing interviewees, the team relied initially on individuals who contacted the project on their own initiative out of an interest in the project's documentation work, as well as on networks of contacts and recommendations between one speaker family and another (the so-called 'snowball effect'). In this way, contacts were acquired around the country

[1]   See   http://romani.humanities.manchester.ac.uk/.   The   documentation   of Angloromani was supported by ESRC grant no. RES-000-23-1495. Interviews were carried out by the author and by Hazel Gardner, Ruth Hill, Charlotte Jones, and Veronica Schulman.

and the survey could be based on cooperation with speakers who not only fully consented to participate, but were also proud of the fact that institutional interest was shown in their language.

In order to ensure comparability of the results, a word list was designed that served as an initial reference point in the data elicitation. Its purpose was firstly to establish the extent to which Romani-derived words that have been documented for AR as well as for other Para-Romani varieties in the past are familiar to present-day users of AR. The wordlist was therefore composed by putting together words documented in various published sources on AR and other Para-Romani varieties, and then reversing the list to make the English translations the point of departure. A further purpose was to document the extent of vocabulary coverage that is available to speakers in AR. To this effect, a 'basic vocabulary' list of 1,400 items was adopted from the Intercontinental Dictionary Series and the Loanword Typology Project at the Max Planck Institute for Evolutionary Anthropology, leaving out items that were obviously of no relevance, such as certain fauna, foods etc. The two compilations rendered a list of altogether around 1,500 lexical items. These were grouped by semantic domains in order to facilitate self-prompting by association on the part of the consultants. Speakers were then asked to translate the English words into their variety of Romani.

Quite often, words triggered associations of language use. The limitations on actual use-in-context of AR in the presence of an interviewer/investigator meant that other means of eliciting language in context had to be pursued. Inspired by the successful elicitation of Lekoudesch (Jewish Cattle Trader Jargon in southwest Germany; Matras 1991, 1997) via anecdotes, speakers were often asked to reconstruct episodes in which they remembered using AR. Unlike Lekoudesch, however, AR is still in active use, albeit to various extents, among the majority of the consultants, and most episodes of language use go unnoticed and are not necessarily recorded in speakers' memory and recounted to others as humorous anecdotes. Nevertheless, this kind of prompting was often successful in triggering a simulated account of occasions on which the language might be used, rendering the intended 'authentic reconstruction' effect. Moreover, on some occasions this kind of reconstruction had the effect of integrating the project team members into the speaker's discourse, transforming the interview situation into a spontaneous conversation in which AR assumed its natural function as an intimate code marking out the emotive value of individual speech acts, thus allowing the documentation of its authentic, spontaneous use.

The typical duration of interviews was between one and two hours. All interviews were digitally recorded, transcribed and stored in the Romani Project Archive. A special database was constructed for the AR material. It lists all words retrieved from the interviews that were identified by the speakers as belonging to their 'Romani' vocabulary. Each lexical entry is tagged for speaker (and accompanying speaker metadata) and accompanied by information on its phonetic realisation, its method of retrieval (e.g. whether prompted or volunteered), an English translation, a Romani or foreign etymology, a dialect-specific etymology where appropriate (i.e. where the word form allows the identification of a connection with a particular Romani dialect or dialect branch or sub-branch), and the time of its occurrence in the recording. Utterances and usage examples are also recorded and linked to the individual word entries; they too carry a time indication, allowing the analyst to review the context in which they are employed in the full transcript or recording. In addition to the material from the interviews, seventeen major published sources were evaluated and the data stored and annotated by the same principles for the sake of comparison (see list of sources on the Manchester Romani Project online dictionary of English Romani: http://romani.humanities.manchester.ac.uk/angloromani).

In identifying and noting Romani etymologies, the point of orientation was a somewhat abstract entity that might be referred to as 'European Romani'. By and large, this contains the reconstructed entity referred to as 'Early Romani' (Matras 2002, Elšík & Matras 2006), along with any modifications that can be assumed to have emerged in the particular forerunner dialect of British Romani. Thus, a form such as *divvus* ['dɪvəs] 'day' is related to European/Early Romani *dives*, while the form *wovva* ['wʊvə] 'other' is traced back to European Romani *vaver*, a regional variant arising from Early Romani *aver*. European loanwords that entered the language prior to the isolation of British Romani and which are widely attested in other dialects of the language are considered part of the European Romani legacy. The only items that are considered non-Romani etymons are therefore those that have entered the language during or following the decline of inflected Romani in Britain, through direct contact with the source language. This includes dialectal, archaic or vernacular English as well as special vocabularies such as (Irish) Shelta and (English or Scottish) Cant, and also items of German and French origin, which may have been transmitted either via neighbouring Romani dialects or through direct or indirect contact with these source languages.

In evaluating the data (as well as in the technical labelling of data categories in the database), the following conceptual representations are used. A *meaning* is the English meaning assigned by the speakers to a particular item of their Romani vocabulary (irrespective of its actual etymology). In effect, it is the English translation of a word, or the semantic concept that a Romani word represents. The meaning of *wovva* is thus 'other'. A *word form* is the specific phonological realisation of a given Romani word by a given speaker; *wovva* ['wʊvə] is thus an example of a realisation of a word by a particular speaker. Each word form may be related to other word forms; i.e. other speakers (or indeed even the same speaker) may have other ways, morphological and phonological, of realising a cognate word with the same meaning, for example *wavvo* ['wævəʊ] or *waffa* ['wæfə]. Related word forms form a cluster by sharing both *meaning* and their *predecessor*, which in this case is the European Romani expression *vaver* 'other'. The predecessor in turn has an etymology, which in this case leads back to an Early Romani form that is slightly different in structure – namely *aver*. The sum of the same predecessor, its various descendant word forms in present-day Angloromani, and their shared contemporary meaning is referred to as an *expression.* On the list of expressions, we would thus find 'other' alongside the various word forms deriving from *vaver*, all in a single entry (see Appendix I). Now, there might be another way of expressing the meaning 'other'; or perhaps a word form deriving from the predecessor *vaver* might also be used in a separate meaning. In such a case, these would be associated with a separate *expression.* Note that predecessor expressions may also be loanwords from European languages into Romani (see above), in which case the recon-structed predecessor form is based on the appearance of the word in other Romani dialects, while the original form in the source language constitutes its *etymology*.

4.2 Phonology and phonological variation

In designing a notation system for AR, a major consideration was to make it both consistent and coherent and at the same time allow it to conform as much as possible to English orthography so that it would be more accessible to a non-academic audience. Since AR phonology basically corresponds to (dialectal) English phonology, the principal challenge is the notation of vowels – both vowel quantity and quality. The system adopted differentiates between open and closed syllables. In open syllables, the use of a single conso-nant indicates a long vowel, while a double consonant indicates a short vowel. An example of an open syllable word is *rati* 'night', which is found in variable pronunciations (long and short vowel): *rati* 'night'= ['ɹɑːti], *ratti* 'night'= ['ɹæti]. Exceptions to this rule are unstressed syllables. These are reduced to schwa and so no vowel length distinction is necessary. For example, the spelling *Romani* ['ɹəʊməni] is used, rather than *Romanni*. In closed syllables, it is the vowel rather than the consonant that indicates length. The English spelling of long vowels is used for this. For example, *eev* [iːv] 'snow' rather than *iv*, which latter would be short [ɪv], and *boot* [buːt] 'much/many/very' rather than *but*, which latter would be short [bʊt, bʌt]. Diphthongs that are ambiguous when written in English are spelt in the following way: [aɪ] = {ai}, e.g. *grai* 'horse', [eɪ] = {ey}, e.g. *aprey* 'up', [eə] = {ae}, e.g. *chaerus* 'time'. In consonants, the only unique feature of Angloromani is the retention of the phoneme /ʒ/ in a small number of words, which we render here as 'zh', as in *yoozha* 'clean'.

Perhaps the most striking structural feature of AR vocabulary is the extent of random phonological variation. This is not surprising, but is in line with observations on language decline and the relaxation of normative control on the realisation of lexical items and their structural components. While speakers may have some individual preferences and in some instances even associate certain pronunciations with certain families or regions, by and large there seems to be an acceptance of a wide range of shapes for words and the syllables they contain. It seems therefore that only a few general characteristics can be extracted to describe the overall nature of phonological variation. To begin with, some consonant phoneme pairs are particularly prone to alternation and substitution: /f~s/, /v~w/, /b~v/, m~w~v/, /r~l/, /n~l/, as well as /k~h~tʃ/ as reflections of historical /χ/. Volatility among vowels in neighbouring position is even greater. Clusters include /a~ɑ~ɔ/, /æ~ɛ~ɪ/, /ʊ~uː/ and in unstressed syllables /a~ə~ɪ~e~əʊ/ and /ə~ɪ~eɪ/. Syllable configurations also alternate frequently; typical variants include CVCCVC ~ CVCVC, VCCV ~ CCV, CVCV ~ CVC, CVCVCCV ~ CVCVCV. Finally, phonological variation interacts with the tendency to form morpho-phonological analogies and especially to manipulate the endings of words. Volatile suffixes include *-us*, *-is*, *-as*, recognisable to speakers as inflection and sometimes derivational affixes within the Romani component, and to some extent also the (historical) derivational endings- *(a)lo*, *-ni*, *-in* and *-do*. Table 4.1 provides an insight into the degree of phonological variation found in the corpus for a selection of words.

Lenition and fortition are common phonological changes in AR. Two illustrative instances are *rat* > *rati* > *radi* 'blood' and *čib* >*jib* 'language, tongue', where /t/ and /tʃ/ have mutated to their voiced counterparts (lenition). Another example of lenition is *bal* > *val* ('hair'), where the plosive /b/ becomes a fricative /v/. Examples of fortition are even more extensive. The fricative /v/ commonly changes to a plosive /b/, as in *avri* > *abri* 'outside', *dova* > *duvva* > *dubba* 'that' or *devel* > *dibəl* 'God'. /v/ also changes to its voiceless counterpart /f/, as in *avral* >*fral* 'beside, outside' and *iv* > *eef* 'snow'. It appears, in fact, that /v/ is highly unstable and is commonly changed to another consonant. The outcome of the change from /v/ – either /b/ or /f/ – is not predictable by phonological environment and is subject to variation among speakers. Thus we find, for example, two variants for 'snow' (Romani *iv*) – *eef* is used by some speakers, while others say *gib*. Occasional cases of consonant harmony and metathesis can be found in the data, as in the cases of *men* 'neck', also realised as *nen* as well as *mem*, and of *nilaj* 'summer', which appears as both *naili* and *lenna*, with metathesised vowels and consonants respectively. Another case of variation is the interchange of /v/ and /w/, as in *wudder* vs. *vudder* 'door' (already noted by Smart & Crofton 1875). These appear to go back to various changes that took place within British Romani and may indeed be indicative of a rather lax norm accompanying the gradual decline of conversational language use, giving way to individual linguistic creativity.

A notable feature of dialectal English, commonly found in the English speech of Gypsies, too, is the disappearance of initial /h/. Due to low levels

Table 4.1 Variation in the shape of selected word forms

Meaning	Recorded word forms	Predecessor
'above'	*apra, aprey, oprey, opro, prey*	*upre*
'across'	*paddel, pardel, parl, pawdel, pedal*	*perdal*
'apple'	*pab, paba, pabbo, pava, pob, pobba, pobbai, pobbi, pobbo, pobra, poppoba, povva*	*phabaj*
'bacon'	*ballamas, ballavas, ballomas, ballovas, ballowas, bawlomas, bawluva, bawluvva, vallavas, villivas*	*balavas*
'bed'	*vadros, voddaras, vodros, vodrus, vuddus, vudrus, wuddus, wudlus, wudrus, wudrussin*	*vodros*
'beer'	*lavvana, lavvinong, levvernay, livna, livni, livvena, livvina, livvinda, livvini, lovvina, vinni*	*lovina*
'big'	*baro, barri, bawla, bawro, bora, bori, borri, borro, bowro*	*baro*
'cake'	*malliki, mannikli, marrakel, marraki, marrakli, marreki, marrika, marriki, marrikli*	*mařikli*
'church'	*kangeri, kongeri, kongla, kongling, kongra, kongri, kuggari*	*khangeri*
'coal'	*vanga, vangar, vonga, vonger, vongeri, wangar, wonga*	*vangar*
'coat'	*chaho, chokka, chokko, chokwan, chotcho, chowfo, choxa, chukka, chukko*	*coxa*
'cow'	*gorovvi, gorrif, grazna, grovveni, growv, grumni, gruvni, gruvveni, gruvverni, gurni, gurruv, gurummin, guvni*	*guruvni*
'dirty'	*mokkadi, mokkadowi, mokkati, mokkerdo, moshadi, motchadi*	*maxado*
'dog'	*jakkel, jokkel, jonkul, juggal, juk, jukkel, yakkal*	*džukel*
'door'	*wodda, wodder, wooder, wudder, wudrus*	*vudar*
'fair'	*valgorus, varringera, waggawlus, walgerus, welda, welgora, welgoru, wesgorus*	*valgora | agora*
'food'	*gobbin, habben, hobben, hobbin, obben, obbin, ovven*	*xaben*
'gold'	*sonakai, sonnakai, sonnaki, sonnokai, sonnokoi, suhaki, sunakai, sunnakai, sunnather, sunnikai, zollakai*	*sonakaj*
'head'	*cherro, serro, sharro, sharrus, sherra, sherro, shira, shirro, shurra, shurro*	*šero*
'hungry'	*bokkalo, bokkoli, boklo, boktalo, booklo, bukelo, bukkalo, bukla, buklo, buklu*	*bokhalo*
'ill'	*naffalo, nafla, nafli, naflo, naflu, nashfelo, nashval, nasvalo*	*nasvalo*
'old'	*parro, pora, pori, poro, porri, pura, purna, purno, purra, purri, purro*	*phuro*
'plate'	*char, charo, charra, cherrah, cherro, chorro, chowr*	*čaro*
'prison'	*staeripen, staerpen, staraben, starapen, stardi, stariben, staripen, starrapan, starriben, starripen, sterriben, sterripen, stirripen*	*staripen*

Table 4.1 (continued)

Meaning	Recorded word forms	Predecessor
'rain'	*bisha, bishen, bishin, bishno, breshin, brish, brishendo, brishiben, brishin, brishindo, brishno, brishum, briskeno, mishum*	*brišind*
'ring'	*vangasti, vangustri, vawnustri, vokkishna, vong, vonga, vongasha, vongashi, vongista, vongrushni, vongusha, vongusti, vongustri, vonnishin, wangustri, wongesta, wongushi*	*vangrusti*
'sheep'	*bakra, bakral, bawkaro, bawkero, bawkra, bokkasha, bokkencha, bokkenshi, bokkero, bokkishna, bokkoro, bokra, bokro, okri*	*bakro*
'sugar'	*dudli, googlo, gudla, gudlam, gudli, gudlo, gudlu, gugli*	*gudlo*
'summer'	*lenna, lilai, lillai, linnai, maili, neel, nyli*	*nilaj*
'time'	*chaero, chaeros, chaerus, chellus, cherris, chiris, chiro, chiros, chirrus, chirus, churnus, shaerus*	*čiros*
'white'	*parna, parno, pawli, pawni, pawno, porna, porno*	*parno*

of education, low proficiency in reading and writing, and little exposure to institutional English, Gypsies tend to be especially insecure in their use of initial /h/, and as a result, hypercorrection is especially common. This affects the entire lexical repertoire and no differentiation is made between English and Romani-derived vocabulary. Speakers will thus often produce forms such as *Hinglish* for 'English', *Hirish* for 'Irish', *hill* for 'ill' or *halcoholic* for 'alcoholic', as well as AR forms such as *heef* 'snow' (Romani *iv*) and *hav* 'to come' (Romani *av-*).

Ad hoc phonological modification is sometimes applied in support of lexical differentiation. For example, the loss of the original aspiration contrast in *ker* 'make, do' and *ker* 'house' has led speakers to create a new distinction by using either *ken* for 'house' (possibly inspired by the corresponding Cant word) or *kel* for 'do' or 'make'. In another case, the voicing of /t/ is applied only selectively to the word *rati*, originally both 'night' and 'blood'; and to consider a final case, once the word 'church', *kongri*, became extended to mean 'school', a change to *kongli* was adopted to create a contrast. Table 4.2 illustrates the changes seen in these three word pairs. Note that Pairs 1 and 3 are found with most speakers, while Pair 2 occurs only with some speakers (many retain the original pair).

4.3 Word formation and word classes

Broadly speaking, the AR vocabulary consists of three layers of vocabulary items: those carried over directly from inflected Romani, those borrowed

Table 4.2 Recreating minimal pairs in Angloromani (based on Matras et al. 2007: 164–5)

Pair 1	'do/make'	'house'
Predecessor form	*ker*	*kher*
Anglo-Romani form	*ker*	*ker*
New pair option (a)	*ker*	*ken*
New pair option (b)	*kel*	*ker*

Pair 2	'blood'	'night'
Predecessor form	*rat*	*rati*
Anglo-Romani form	*rati*	*rati*
New pair option (a)	*radi*	*rati*
New pair option (b)	*rati*	*radi*

Pair 3	'church'	'church' (> 'school')
Predecessor form	*khangeri*	*khangeri*
Anglo-Romani form	*kongri*	*kongri*
New pair option	*kongri*	*kongli*

from other languages, and creative formations. An in-between category comprises items that have been inherited or borrowed but may have changed their meaning. Since Romani-derived vocabulary is basically employed in AR within an English sentence and discourse framework, it is not obvious that we should encounter any word forms other than content lexemes. In fact, disregarding frequency of distribution in actual conversation, 90 per cent of the special vocabulary that constitutes AR consists of content lexemes (59 per cent nouns, 19 per cent verbs and 12 per cent adjectives). Only 10 per cent belongs to the category of 'function words', including numerals, personal pronouns, indefinites, interrogatives, deictic and other adverbs, demonstratives, conjunctions, exclamations and so on.

4.3.1 Word derivation

Evidence of the productive incorporation of at least two English word forma-tion markers into Romani exists as early as the documentation of inflected British Romani; their relevance increases in AR: The (originally adverbial) prefixes *a-* and *to-* accompany Romani-origin words calquing the correspond-ing English models: *rakli's a-trash* '[the] girl's afraid', *a-sutti* 'asleep', *a-drum* 'away', *a-ladj* 'ashamed', *to-divvus* 'today', *to-rati* 'tonight', *to-sawlo* 'tomor-row'. In the case of *to-*, the English marker actually appears in positions that in some earlier sources are attested as composed of two Romani inherited elements calquing the English formation, namely *ke-divvus* 'today', *ke-rat* 'tonight'. On the other hand, the occasional decomposition *taley* 'below' to *aley, ley* appears to hint at a re-analysis of the inherited component in *t-* etc. as representing English *to-*. A further, albeit isolated example of productive English derivation is *fawdel* 'forgive', based on *del* 'to give' (< Romani *d-el* 'give-3sg.'). Semi-bound English aktionsart markers occasionally accompany fossilised Romani verb forms, as in *jassan* 'come on' (<Romani *dža-s* 'go-1pl.'). Such procedures reveal an attitude to the inherited Romani vocabulary as embedded in and subjected to the word derivation rules of English, and thus to Romani and English as being essentially inseparable systems.

None the less, AR also preserves internal, and in part inherited, Romani word formation procedures. Perhaps the most prolific of those involves the nominaliser *-(m)engr-*, which, as discussed in Chapter 3, is productive not just in British Romani but also in other Romani dialects of northwestern Europe. The source of the ending is the genitive plural suffix *-engr-*, indicating strictly speaking 'things belonging or pertaining to' the object of the derivation. Its variant in *-m-engr-* is originally associated with the nominaliser *-imos/-amos*, which apparently had been reserved to derivations from activity names or nouns derived from verbs. This distinction no longer appears productive and in fact the two formations seem randomly interchangeable, as can be ascertained by comparing the derivations *mass-engra* 'butcher' from *mas* 'meat' with *mora-m-engra* 'baker' from *maro* 'bread'.

The semantic functions of *-(m)engr-* can be classified into several categories:

1 Instrumental, enabling an activity depicted by the word stem: *beshamengra* 'chair' from *beš-* 'to sit'; *dikkamengri* 'mirror' from *dik-* 'to see'; *hotchamengra* 'frying pan' from *xačar-* 'to burn, to fry'; *rokkermengri* 'telephone' from *raker-* 'to talk'.
2 Productive-objective, presenting the object of a depicted activity, or the product derived from the depicted material or matter: *pimengra* 'coffee, tea' from *pi-* 'to drink'; *chinnamengra* 'letter' from *čin-* 'to carve, write'; *puvvengra* 'potato' from *phuv* 'earth'; *pobbamengri* 'cider' from *phabaj-* 'apple'.
3 Agentive, indicating a preoccupation with the depicted activity, goal or product: *bokramengra* 'shepherd' from *bakro* 'sheep'; *kuramengra* 'soldier' from *kur-* 'to fight'; *massengra* 'butcher' from *mas* 'meat'; *berramengra* 'sailor' from *bero* 'boat'.
4 Descriptive, drawing on one or several concepts characterising the referent: *bavvalpoggermengri* 'windmill' from *balval* 'wind' and *phagger-* 'break'; *dur dikkinengri* 'telescope' from *dur* 'far' and *dik-* 'to see': *waffatamengra* 'foreigner' from *vaver them* 'other country'.
5 Associative-figurative, evoking some concrete association with the referent: *dantimengra* 'pepper' from *dand* 'tooth'; *kannengra* 'hare' from *kan* 'ear'; *rukkamengra* 'monkey', 'squirrel' from *rukh* 'tree'.

See Table 4.3.

Table 4.3 Word formation with *-(m)engra* found in the corpus

Word form	Meaning	Predecessor	Predecessor meaning
aeramengri	'apron'	*heroj*	'leg'
ballamengra	'ghost'	*balval*	'wind'
bavvalpoggermengri	'windmill'	*balval, phagger-*	'wind', 'break'
berramengra	'sailor'	*bero*	'boat'
beshamengra	'chair'	*beš-*	'to sit'
bokramengra	'shepherd'	*bakro*	'sheep'
borapukkamengri	'magistrate'	*baro, pukher-*	'big', 'to speak'
boshengra	'violin player'	*bašav-*	'to play a musical instrument'
chinnamengra	'letter'	*čin-*	'to carve, write'
choramengra	'thief'	*čor-*	'to steal'
dantimengra	'pepper'	*dand*	'tooth'
dikkamengra	'crystal ball'	*dik-*	'to see'
dikkamengri	'mirror'	*dik-*	'to see'
drabbengra	'doctor'	*drab-*	'medicine'
dur dikkinengri	'telescope'	*dur, dik-*	'far', 'to see'
erramengri	'bicycle'	*heroj*	'leg'
gavvengra	'farmer'	*gav*	'village'
givvengra	'farmer'	*giv*	'wheat'
graiengra	'horse dealer'	*graj*	'horse'
gruvvengra	'farmer'	*guruv*	'bull'
hotchamengra	'frying pan'	*xačar-*	'to burn, to fry'
jinnamengra	'clever'	*džin-*	'to know'
kannengra	'hare'	*kan*	'ear'
klissemengri	'locksmith'	*klisin*	'key'
kuramengra	'soldier'	*kur-*	'to fight'
massengra	'butcher'	*mas*	'meat'
moramengra	'baker'	*maro*	'bread'
mottamengra	'drunk man'	*mato*	'drunk'
mutramengri	'tea'	*muter*	'urine'
pimengri	'coffee, tea'	*pi-*	'to drink'
pobbamengri	'cider'	*phabaj-*	'apple'
poramengra	'miller'	*parno*	'white'
possamengri	'pitchfork'	*pusi*	'straw'
prastamengra	'policeman'	*praster-*	'to run'
pukkamengri	'lawyer'	*phukker-*	'to speak'
puvengra	'potato'	*phuv-*	'earth'
rokkermengri	'telephone'	*raker-*	'to talk'
rukkamengra	'monkey', 'squirrel'	*rukh*	'tree'
sastermengra	'frying pan'	*saster*	'iron'
sikkamengra	'showman'	*sikar-*	'to show'
tattamengri	'vinegar'	*tato*	'hot'
tattramengra	'frying pan'	*tater-*	'to heat'

Table 4.3 (continued)

Word form	Meaning	Predecessor	Predecessor meaning
tuddamengra	'milkman'	*thud-*	'milk'
varramengra	'miller'	*varo*	'flour'
vastamengras	'handcuffs'	*vast*	'hand'
vatermengris	'glasses'	*vater*	'to watch'
veshengra	'forest keeper'	*veš*	'forest'
vongermengra	'coal man'	*vangro*	'coal'
waffatamengra	'foreigner'	*vaver them*	'other country'
yoggamengra	'forester', 'gun'	*jag*	'fire'

Such intense exploitation of a word derivational technique is reminiscent of procedures in other in-group and secret vocabularies, as in the case of derivations in the archaic derivational suffix *-ling* in German Rotwelsch and Jenisch (*Trittling* 'show', from *tritt-* 'step', *Funkling* 'fire', from *Funk* 'spark', and so on), or the 'dummy' marker *chete* in English Cant (*prattling chete* 'tongue', *listening chete* 'ear', etc.). The most indicative feature of such internal, cryptolalic formations is their extension to associative-figurative derivations. This stage testifies on the one hand to the acceptance of creative and humorous word play as a means of forming new expressions that make it into common use in the community's in-group vocabulary, and on the other to a need to camouflage even the most ordinary, everyday expressions. Language-internal cryptolalic systems of course rely almost entirely on such procedures. In AR they are an added bonus that allows the extension and enrichment of the inherited Romani vocabulary.

Marginally productive is the inherited word formation strategy involving the nominalisation suffix *-ipen/-iben*. There does not seem to be any recognisable complementary distribution of the two markers; *-imus* appears alongside both as an additional variant. The derivation strategy is analysable to speakers owing to the high frequency of formations that employ it: *kelliben* 'a dance' from *kell* 'to dance', *tamlapen* 'darkness' from *tamlo* 'dark', and so on (see Table 4.4). While some of these are no doubt directly inherited from the inflected language, individual cases testify to the strategy's productivity. Thus we find *boklipen* 'hunger' from *bokla* 'hungry', while European Romani has *bokh* 'hunger'; *delliben* 'gift' from *del* 'to give' is modelled on English *give* > *gift*, and draws as a base on the inherited 3sg. form *del*, which in AR becomes the default form of the verb root for 'give'; *savvapan* 'laughter' is likewise modelled on the verb root *sav*, originally the inflected 1sg. from the inherited root *asa-* 'to laugh'; finally, *brishiben* appears alongside *brishum* for 'rain' (Romani *brišind*), apparently the result of an association of the final sound in *brishum* with the English gerundial suffix *-ing/-in*, leading to a re-analysis of *brishum* as 'raining' and ultimately as a nominalised verb.

Compounding, which arises as a feature of the inflected forerunner variety of Romani in Britain and partly elsewhere in northwestern Europe,

Table 4.4 Formations in -*ipen*/-*iben* from the corpus

Word form	Meaning	Predecessor	Predecessor meaning
boklipen	'hunger'	*bokh*	'hunger'
bollapen	'bath time'	*bold-*	'baptise'
brishiben	'rain'	*brišind*	'rain'
chingamos, chingerpen	'war'	*čhinger-*	'fight'
chummaben	'kiss'	*čumi*	'kiss'
delliben	'gift'	*del*	'give'
dukrapen	'fortune-telling'	*dokrapen*	'fortune-telling'
gilliben	'dance, song'	*gili*	'song'
habben, obben	'meal'	*xaben*	'food'
hotchipen	'burn'	*xač-*	'burn'
jiaben	'life'	*dživiben*	'life'
jinnaben	'clever'	*džin-*	'know'
kellapen, kellipens	'commotion, dance'	*khel-*	'dance'
kelliben	'do'	*ker-*	'do'
kuriben, kurriben	'fight'	*kur-*	'fight'
merriben, merripen	'life, death'	*mer-*	'die'
mitchipen	'trouble'	*midžax*	'bad'
mongipen	'hawking'	*mangipen*	'beg'
mushipen	'child'	*murš*	'man'
naflipen	'sickness'	*nasvalo*	'ill'
okkapen	'lie'	*xoxavipen*	'lie'
otchaben, otchraben	'venereal disease'	*xačariben*	'burn'
piapen	'drink'	*pi-*	'drink'
purroben	'age'	*phurol-i*	'old'
rokkerpen	'talk'	*raker-*	'talk'
ruddaben	'dress'	*urado*	'dressed'
savvapan	'laugh'	*sav*	'laugh'
shafraben	'work'	*šafreben*	'work'
sherraben	'bridle for horse's head'	*šero*	'head'
starriben, starripen	'prison'	*staripen*	'arrest'
tamlapen	'darkness'	*tamlo*	'dark'
tatchapen, tatchipen	'truth'	*čačo*	'true'
tatchipen	'burn'	*tato*	'hot'
tulliben	'fat'	*thulo*	'thick'

is expanded in AR to become the most relevant word formation strategy. Several strategies constitute regular patterns, namely those involving the words *divvus* 'day', *mush* 'man', *gaera* 'man, person' and *fowki* 'people'. The first serves to create a closed class of calendar expressions (Table 4.5). The others show greater distribution and are used to form labels for agentives, professions and nationalities (Table 4.6).

Table 4.5 Compounds in *divvus*

Word form	Meaning	Predecessor	Predecessor meaning
bollesko divvus	'Christmas day'	*bol-*	'to baptise'
devla divvus	'Sunday'	*devel*	'God'
kamdivvus	'Sunday'	*kham*	'sun'
kedivvus	'today'	*ke*	'to'
kinning divvus	'Saturday'	*kin-*	'to buy'
latchi divvus	'good day'	*lačho*	'good'
mas divvus	'Sunday'	*mas*	'meat'
mul divvus	'Christmas'	*mol*	'wine'
paladivvus	'midday'	*palal*	'after'
shov divvus	'week'	*šov*	'six'
todivvus	'today'		
tuvvin' divvus	'Monday'	*thov-*	'to wash'
wavver divvus	'tomorrow'	*vaver*	'other'
wavver divvus	'yesterday'	*vaver*	'other'

Table 4.6 Compounds in *mush*

Word form	Meaning	Predecessor	Predecessor meaning
lavvengremush	'a man who speaks different languages'	*lav*	'word'
kawlamush	'black person'	*kalo*	'black'
matchkamush	'fisherman'	*mačho*	'fish'
dur-aver-tem mush	'foreigner'	*dur, them, vaver*	'far', 'ountry', 'other'
duvver-tan mush	'foreigner'	*than, vaver*	'place', 'other'
temeskamush	'foreigner'	*them*	'country'
wovvatemmush	'foreigner'	*them, vaver*	'country', 'other'
yogmush	'gamekeeper'	*jag*	'fire'
jungalo mush	'greedy man'	*džungalo*	'ugly'
Romanichal mush	'Gypsy man'	*čalado, romani*	'family', 'Gypsy'
bangla mush	'left-handed man'	*bango*	'crooked'
gavmush	'official'	*gav,*	'village'
purri mush	'old man'	*phuro*	'old'
gavvamush	'policeman'	*gav, garav-*	'village', 'hide'
muskramush	'policeman'	*mujeskero*	'policeman'
paningramush	'sailor'	*pani*	'water'
kongri mush	'school master'	*khangeri*	'church'
bokra mush	'shepherd'	*bakro*	'sheep'

Some of the compounds in *gaera* replicate those in *mush: matchigera* 'fisherman', *kongligaera* 'school teacher', *kulingaera* 'black man'. Additional forms include *kistagaera* 'jockey' (from *klisto* 'riding') and even *poggaera* 'monkey' (presumably from *phager-* 'to break'). Corpus attestations of compounds in *fowki* include *wavvertemfowki* 'foreigners' ('people of other countries'), *shinafowki* 'Jews' (from *čin-* 'to cut' = 'circumcised'; cf. Polish Romani *čindo* 'Jew') and *lavna foki* 'Welsh people' (from *lav* 'word, speech'). The need for an internal marker for persons and groups of persons derives from the need to employ the in-group language to categorise and identify outsiders and is a universal structural device in in-group and secret languages. In AR, compounding with the help of these suffixes serves in addition to agentive derivations in *-(m)engr-*.

Proper compounding, involving two semantically independent concepts, is also common and applies to around 10 per cent of the meanings attested in the recorded corpus. The most common are combinations of nouns, whereby the second noun figures as a generic type, and the first modifies it, specifying a particular subclass: *vesh jukkel* 'fox' (literally 'forest dog'), *atchin' tan* 'camp' ('stopping place'), *saster cherikla* 'aeroplane' ('iron bird'), *kali cherkla* 'crow' ('black bird'), *veshni kanni* 'pheasant' ('forest hen'), *bori lun pani* 'sea' ('big salt water'), *sikkering kosh* 'signpost' ('showing stick') and so on. This procedure is complemented by genitive-possessive compounding, directly attributing the second noun to the first: *grai's chokki* 'horseshoe', *duvla's pani* 'rainbow' ('God's water').

As hinted above, compounding is an overt way of lexical creation for the purpose of camouflaging in-group vocabulary. It is the most obvious indication that AR has gone beyond a stage of mere lexical retention from an earlier heritage language and has turned functionally into an independent system that offers its users communicative advantages in situations where it is purposeful either to keep propositional content undisclosed to bystanders, or to flag the availability of means of expression that are exclusive to community members. A good indicator for the adoption of such functions is the presence of creative strategies to construct place-names. Place-names (as well as names of nations) are perhaps the most prototypical universal word forms, which tend to remain consistent across language boundaries, apart from phonological and rarely morphological adaptations. In-group and secret languages, by contrast, often adopt their own creative place-names, both as means of flagging internal coherence and belonging to the group ('insider' knowledge) and as a way of making destinations and salient points of geographical reference incomprehensible to eavesdroppers.

Our interviews indicate that internal place-names have largely fallen out of use during the past generation; the only retrievable place-names in the corpus were *panigav* ('water-town') for 'Manchester', *guiallameskrapen* ('pudding-eating')[2] for 'Yorkshire', *apreytem* ('above-country') for 'Scotland', *kora*

---

[2]   It appears that here the speaker confused the nominal ending *-(a)pen* with *gui allameskra tem* 'eating country'. Note that *tem* ('country') is a common ending in internal place-names.

pani ('black water') for 'Blackpool', and *kawlagav* ('black-town') for both 'Birmingham' and 'Blackpool'. These naming strategies are obviously based on a combination of literal translation from English, where this is possible, and semantic associations with the particular location. Manchester is thus associated with rain, Birmingham with industry and hence 'black', while Blackpool is associated with 'black' because of its English name. The fact that the same name might be used for several different towns indicates that place-name camouflaging was a highly contextualised strategy that was used in a particularly tight-knit group of speakers, with reference to immediately proximate locations that had a salient relevance in the daily lives of the interlocutor. Internal place-names cited in earlier word lists of AR include *wudrusgavtem* ('bed-village-land') for 'Bedfordshire', *chikkinotan* ('cement-place') for 'Brickfield', *tavveskro gav* ('weavers' town') for 'Nottingham', *lullo piro* ('red foot') for 'Retford', *bikkensbi waggores* ('selling-bi market') for 'Selby fair', and *matchkani gav* ('fisherman town') for 'Yarmouth' (cf. Winstedt 1949, Smart & Crofton 1875).

Semantic extension is a further means of internal lexical creativity. Some extensions merely involve a widening of the pragmatic context of application, as in *dusta* in the sense of 'many', deriving from European Romani *dosta* 'enough' (a Slavic loan). Other extensions are associative-figurative. Thus European Romani *xačardo* 'burnt, roasted' is used in AR to denote a 'roasted hedgehog', from which the general word for 'hedgehog', *(h)otchi*, is then derived. Romani *xev* 'hole' becomes AR *(h)ev* 'window', which then extends to 'mirror' as well as to 'glass' as material, and on to 'glass' as a 'drinking vessel'. The word *shuliki* 'sour' lends itself as a term for 'orange'; the word *beshtaw* 'saddle', from *beš-* 'to sit', extends to mean 'leather'; and more.

In some cases the extension involves an abstraction from the inherited meaning of the word onto a more generic meaning, which covers an entire set; from this, in turn, the same term is used for other individual members of the set: thus *kongri* 'church' extends to mean 'school' (via the abstract notion of an 'institutional location specialised in learning and regulating community behaviour'), *goi* 'sausage' extends to mean 'pudding'. A particular subtype of the latter kind of extension derives meanings from their literal opposites. The word *divvus* 'day' is attested in the meaning 'night', *rawni* 'lady' can also mean 'gentleman', *kutch* 'dear' is extended to 'cheap', *sav* 'to laugh' is also attested as 'to cry', *dad* 'father' and *dai* 'mother' both assume interchangeable meanings, *latch* 'to find' takes on the meaning of 'to search', *mishtipen* 'good' is attested as 'bad', and *mer* 'to die' takes on the meaning 'to live'. The use of identical lexical roots to derive opposite meanings is of course not exceptional (cf. Hebrew *šáxar* 'dawn', but *šaxór* 'black, dark'). But in connection with the rapid shift in meaning in the in-group lexicon of a tight-knit, marginalised community there are two key conclusions to be drawn from this phenomenon. The first is the degree of liberty that speakers claim for themselves when applying radical innovative and creative strategies to the inherited in-group lexicon; this testifies to a high level of awareness of individual ownership of language and the confidence to intervene and shape linguistic forms and usage patterns in a creative and almost playful manner. The second is the tight-knit, highly presuppositional, context-bound use of this lexical repertoire, without which such radical, associative shifts in meaning are likely to trigger misunderstandings if not indeed a breakdown in effective communication.

The counterpart to individual ownership of language and linguistic creativity is trust in the interlocutor and confidence in the well-formedness of the interlocutor's discourse and in his or her benign communicative intentions. Without this basis of trust and without a high degree of presuppositional knowledge against which the interlocutor's communicative intentions can be gauged and anticipated, neither creativity nor the extreme extent of variability and volatility – phonological, morphological and semantic – in the lexical repertoire would be sustainable. We can tell from this that the tight-knit community within which AR is employed as a communicative medium is a social prerequisite for the viability of a volatile and varied system of structures that is inherited without the normative framework of a native speaker parental generation.

4.3.2 Grammatical vocabulary

The characterisation of AR as a 'mixed' language usually takes for granted that grammatical operations are represented strictly by English structures, and yet a range of functional expressions is inherited from Romani and remains productive, to some extent. A nice illustration is the exclamation *dordi!*, which is unique to AR. A series of grammatical word classes is carried over from the inherited inventory. On the borderline between 'lexical' and 'grammatical' we find a set of adverbs in the corpus; they include local and temporal relation expressions such as *palla* 'again', *anglo* 'before', *kanna* 'now', *pawley* 'behind', *teley* 'down, under', *avri* 'out', *uprey* 'up', *pasha* 'next to', *opro* 'above' and more. Their conversational use appears to be limited; they are found occasionally in adverbial function as verb augments:

(1)   Besh teley
        'Sit down'

(2)   Lel pawley
        'Take [it] back'

Even more rarely, they are used as prepositions:

(3)   Mandi sutti abri mandi's wudrus
        'I slept outside my bed'

Table 4.7 Location deixis for four speakers

Speaker	'here'	Example	'there'	Example
A	*akai*	*he's avin' akai* 'he's coming here'	*adoi*	*vater adoi* 'look over there'
B	*akai*	*divya chavvi akai* '[there are] wild children here'	*adai*	*kek jel adai, mush chingerpen* 'don't go there, [there is a] man shouting'
C	*akai*	*pen chuchi muskara akai* 'say nothing [there is a] policeman here'	*akai*	*mush's jolled akai* '[the] man's gone there'
D	*akai*	*vater the mush akai* 'look at the man here'	*adowi* 'close there' *adai/adoi* 'over there'	*vater the mush adowi* 'look at the man (right) there' *vater the mush adai* 'look at the man (over) there'

(4)   Mandi atched abri the gav desh baersh
        'I stayed outside the village [for] ten years'

(5)   Adrey duvva kaer
        'Inside this house'

A number of deictic adverbs also remain productive and widespread in conversation. The historical system of Romani possesses a four-term distinction of place deixis, based usually on the alternation of consonantal stems in *-d-/-k-* and vocalic stems in *-a-/-o-*: *adaj, akaj, odoj, okoj*. AR shows some variation among speakers (Table 4.7).

Among the 'genuine' classes of grammatical word forms we also find a productive and widespread use of demonstratives. AR retains *duvva* and *kuvva* from the original four-term set (see Chapter 3). The first, *duvva* (also *dovva*), functions as a demonstrative adjective, as a situational deixis referring to persons, and as a discourse deixis:

(6)   Mandi kom dovva chavvi but kek kom dovva chavvi.
        'I like this child but [I] don't like that child.'

(7)   Dik at duvva.
        'Look at him/this-one.'

(8)   I was gonna del duvva, I felt like morin' him.
        'I was gonna hit this-one, I felt like killing him.'

(9)   Vater duvva's yoks!
        'Look at this-person's/his/her eyes!'

(10)   Kekka pen dovva, rakli's trash!
        'Don't say that, [the] girl's scared!'

Note the focus in (8) with *duvva*, and the later resumption via the English anaphoric *him*. The other deictic expression, *kuvva*, has an extended, quasi-lexicalised meaning, as a substitute for a named object. This meaning is attested in various dialects of inflected Romani (see Matras 2002: ch. 5). It is continued in AR, where *kuvva* has a prolific use indicating a contextually retrievable referent that remains unspecified:

(11)   Del mandi the kuvva akai.
        'Give me that thing/thingy here.'

(12)   Gavva the kuvva akai!
        'Hide the thingy here!'

(13)   Kek kel kuvva akai!
        'Don't do this kind of thing/anything here!'

(14)   Dik at the rakli's kuvva!
        'Look at the girl's thing/look at what the girl's got!'

(15)   I might just rokker to you go put some puvvengras in a kuvva, bit
        of mas.
        'I might just say to you go put some potatoes in a thing, a bit of
        meat'.

(16)   This little rakli is asking me all these kuvvas and I don't know what
        she's manging.
        'This little girl is asking me all these things and I don't know what
        she's asking.'

The decline of personal pronouns in English Romani is documented as early as Smart and Crofton's (1875) work. Present-day AR retains a selection of case-neutral pronouns, which continue the Romani locative forms: *mandi* 'I'/'me', *tutti* 'you', *lesti* 'he, him', *latti* 'her', *lendi* 'them'. Forms for the first and second plural persons are conspicuously missing from the paradigm; they are seldom found in other Para-Romani varieties (cf. Matras 2002: 247). In addition to the 'standard' AR set of pronouns, individual speakers show familiarity with the historical nominative forms *me/mei/mi* for 'I', *yo* and *yoy* for 'he' and 'she', and *tu* for 'you', as well as with the historical oblique or direct object form *tut* for 'you' and with the possessive forms *miro, mirra* 'my'. Forms of the third person occasionally appear as *leski* 'he', *lakki* 'she' and *lengi* 'they', continuing the historical dative forms, but these are marginal. Many speakers are unfamiliar with the third person plural form, and some with any of the third person forms. We can thus postulate a hierarchy of pronoun retention: 1sg.

and 2sg. are more likely to be retained from Romani than 3sg., which is more likely to be retained than 3pl.. The retention hierarchy thus favours simplicity (singular over plural), egocentricity (first over other persons), deixis (participants over non-participants) and topicality (thematic saliency). It should be emphasised that, like any use of AR vocabulary, the use of Romani-derived pronouns is never obligatory, even when the utterance is marked out by other Romani-derived material. Instead, we find considerable variation:

(17)   Del it to him
        'Give it to him'

(18)   I've chingered lesti
        'I've annoyed him'

(19)   Mandi doesn't kom lesti
        'I don't like him'

(20)   I'll do some hobben
        'I'll make some food'

(21)   He's not a bad chor
        'He's not a bad guy'

(22)   Lesti's savving at mandi
        'He's laughing at me'

Familiarity with interrogative pronouns is generally limited to the words *saw* 'what', *kon* 'who' and *savvo* 'which', but there is no indication of active use of these words and it cannot be excluded that they have only recently been 're-acquired' through contacts with inflected Romani speakers from central Europe. Indefinites, by contrast, are in frequent use. AR retains the forms *chommani* 'something, anything' as well as *chichi* and *niksis* 'nothing'. By far more common in conversation is the use of the negative indefinites ('nothing'), providing an indication of the use of Romani vocabulary to express what might be understood as dispreferred propositional content (negative replies and prohibitions).

(23)   Did you kaer chumni today? Did you lel some luvva?
        'Did you do anything today? Did you make some money?'

(24)   I've got chichi
        'I've got nothing'

(25)   Chichi, oh, jaw adrum!
        'Say nothing, oh, go away!'

(26)   Pen chuchi, muskara akai!
        'Say nothing, [the] police [are] here!'

(27)   Mush kek juns chichi.
      '[The] man doesn't know anything.'

(28)   Rokker niksis!
      'Say nothing!'

(29)   Coz he wouldn't kaer chichi wrong would 'e?
      'Coz he wouldn't do nothing wrong would 'e?'

(30)   The poor fowki that haven't got a poshaera to their name and want
      to take money off 'em they haven't got chichi.
      'The poor people that haven't got a half-penny to their name and
      want to take money off 'em they haven't got anything.'

In some instances, the demonstrative *kuvva* may take on an indefinite meaning:

(31)   And, er, me dad used to say, low life fowkis, oh, don't want chichi,
      never will have any kuvva.
      'And, er, me dad used to say, low life people, oh, don't want
      nothing, never will have anything.'

The most frequent and productive use of a grammatical marker in the corpus is that of the negative markers *kek* and *kekka*. The first, *kek*, appears in the printed sources and is cognate with the marker of the same shape found in the Sinte and Scandinavian Romani dialects (from **kaj-jekh* 'any-one'). The second, *kekka*, does not seem to appear in any of the published sources, but is widespread in the corpus:

(32)   Kekka pen dovva, rakli's trash!
      'Don't say that, the girl's scared!'

(33)   Kek pogger dovva!
      'Don't break this!

(34)   Mandi kek sutti.
      'I'm not asleep/I haven't slept'

(35)   Mush kek juns.
      '[The] man doesn't know.'

(36)   Kekka pukker hokripens, rokker tatchipen!
      'Don't tell lies, tell [the] truth!'

(37)   Kekka rokker romanes up the gav.
      'Don't talk Romanes in the town.'

In prohibitive constructions, double negation is occasionally found, with *kek/ kekka* appearing alongside English *don't*:

(38)   Kekka don't mess with that gawdja, dordi, nash on!
        'Don't mess with that man, really, move on!'

(39)   Kek don't mang no kushti in her, she's chikli this rakli is!
        'Don't look for no good in her, she's dirty this girl is!'

Occasionally, one also encounters the prohibitive marker *maw* (Romani *ma*):

(40)   Maw rokker, let mandi rokker, til ya jib!
        'Don't speak, let me speak, hold your tongue!'

(41)   Maw be rokkering in front of the mush and rakli!
        'Don't be talking in front of the man and [the] girl!'

Numerals form part of the AR repertoire, though their use is surprisingly limited and a very small number of interviewees showed familiarity with any numerals at all (see Table 4.8). The decline of knowledge of numerals might be interpreted as a further indication of the decline of the use of AR in the context of trade and its growing confinement to family-based interaction. Not surprisingly, the rate of retention of individual numerals is hierarchical and matches the retention of inherited numerals in situations of borrowing, i.e. it is the mirror image of the borrowing hierarchy for numerals in contact situations (cf. Matras 2009: 201–3). Knowledge of the lowest numerals up to 'five' is most common, followed by knowledge of 'ten' and 'twenty', followed by other numerals under 'ten', and so on:

(42)   Hierarchy for numeral retention:
        1–5 > 10, 20 > 6–9 > 11, 100 > 12–19 and above

Interestingly, almost all numerals reflect the inherited European Romani forms and there is no trace of the British Romani innovations for the values between seven and nine, except, indirectly, in the numeral 'sixteen', which one single speaker rendered as *deshdeduitrin*, literally 'ten and two threes'. For the numerals between 'fifty' and 'ninety' recollection is obviously weak and the forms are rather impressionistic replications of the inherited Romani forms, not direct continuations.

4.3.3 Retention of grammatical inflection

AR is generally characterised by the insertion of Romani-derived lexical items into an English grammatical framework, and so by the loss, by and large, of Romani grammatical inflection. There are, however, some traces of productive or semi-productive use of inflectional material. Above, we have already discussed the productivity of derivational word formation in -*(m)engr*- and in -*ipen*/-*iben* and -*imos*. Nominal inflection proper is still

Table 4.8 Angloromani numerals documented in the corpus

Meaning	Word forms	Predecessor	No. of speakers
one	yak, yeg, yek	*jekh*	12
two	du, dui, dun	*duj*	13
three	trien, trin	*trin*	8
four	doostar, shor, shtar, star, stor, stun	*štar*	9
five	panch, pandj, pansh, pawnch, pendj, pengi, ponch, punch	*pandž*	13
six	chov, sharn, shik, sho, shob, shor, shov, showv	*šov*	5
seven	afta, eft, efta, ekka, hefta	*efta*	5
eight	oitu, okt, okta, okto, otter	*oxto*	5
nine	enga, enna, ennia, enya, hina, ina	*enja*	5
ten	desh	*deš*	7
eleven	deshdeyak, deshdeyek, deshtayek, deshtuyek	*dešthajekh*	4
twelve	deshdedu, deshtadui, deshtudui	*deštaduj*	2
thirteen	deshdetrin, deshtatrin, deshtutrin	*deštatrin*	2
fourteen	deshtastor, deshtushtar	*deštaštar*	1
fifteen	deshtapansh, deshtupanch	*deštapandž*	1
sixteen	deshdeduitrin	*dešthajduj trin*	1
seventeen	deshtahefta	*deštaefta*	1
eighteen	deshdeokta, deshtaokta, deshtuoct	*deštha(j) oxto*	2
nineteen	deshtaenna, deshtuindya	*deštaenja*	1
twenty	beesh, besh, bis, bish	*biš*	7
twenty-one	beeshtuyek	*bišthajekh*	1
twenty-two	beeshtudui	*bištaduj*	1
thirty	trianda, trinda	*tr(i)anda*	2
forty	shtada, shtardo, storanda	*saranda*	1
fifty	pancha, panchdo		1
sixty	shobda, shobdo		1
seventy	defredesh		2
eighty	okta		1
ninety	endo		1
one hundred	shel	*šel*	4
five hundred	posh miya	*paš, mija*	1
one thousand	yek meel	*jekh, mil*	2

partly represented in the frequent tendency to assign an ending -*us*/-*is* to words belonging to the special lexical reservoir, as a kind of marker of integration. The procedure is no doubt inspired by the earlier practice, in inflected British Romani, of attaching the Greek-derived endings of similar or identical form to masculine loanwords. Words like *chaerus* 'time', *fongrus* 'fork', *kokollus* 'bone', *sappenus* 'soap' and *wudrus* 'bed' all contribute to an overall impression of -*us* as a typical Romani word ending, as does the coincidental similarity with the endings in words like *divvus* 'day' (Romani *dives*), *Rumnus* 'Romani language' (*romanes*), and the combination of a Romani plural in -*a* with an English plural ending in -*s*, as in *dandus* 'teeth' and *vastus* 'hands', or of a plural re-analysis of a Romani word, as in *dostus* 'lots', from *dosta* 'plentiful, sufficient'. The use of -*us* is further reinforced by its presence as a Latinate legacy and form of camouflaging suffix in Cant: *mammus* 'mother', *daddus* 'father', *niksus* 'nothing'. As a result we find an extension of the ending to selected lexical items: *kokkodus* 'uncle' (Romani *kako*), *tiknus* 'baby' (*tikno*), *walgerus* 'fair' (originally a feminine loan *valgora*), *vongus* 'gold' (*vangar* 'coal') and more.

While nominal plural endings are generally English – *muskra* 'policeman', *muskras* 'policemen'; *yora* 'egg', *yoras* 'eggs'; *mush* 'man', *mushes* 'men' – there is some tendency towards retention of the Romani plural ending, which is then reinforced by the English plural suffix: *vastas* 'hands' (Romani *vast* 'hand', *vasta* 'hands'). In some rare cases, Romani productive plural endings continue to appear, alternating with 'double plurals': *izaw*, *izers* 'clothes', *yokkai*, *yokkers* 'eyes', *jukler*, *jukkels* 'dogs'. Gender and number agreement has generally disappeared and adjectives take uniform endings: *bori luvva* 'much money', *bori mush* 'a big man', *bori rakli* 'a big woman'. None the less, there appears to be some underlying appreciation of a morphological marking at least of natural gender, and while most speakers adopt a uniform pronunciation of the word *gawja* ['gɔːdʒə] and do not differentiate *gawjo* 'man' from *gawji* 'woman', and there is no distinction between the endings in *rakli* 'girl' and *chavvi* 'boy', the notion of gender distinction mapping on to masculine -*o* and feminine -*i* is something that speakers often claim to be familiar with through exposure to the more 'purist' or 'archaic' speech of other speakers. Other examples of nominal inflection appear only in the form of fossilised constructions. Thus we find the genitive forms *bollesko divvus* (also *bullesta divvus*), literally 'baptising day', for 'Christmas', and the genitive *palleska*, literally 'of the brother', in the meaning 'nephew'. The latter is replicated in a stereotypical way, i.e. using the same masculine singular (instead of feminine singular) genitive ending in *penneski* 'of the sister' to form the word 'niece'. A further case is *romnis dadeskra* for 'father-in-law'; here too, the masculine genitive is replicated stereotypically, attaching to the head ('father') rather than the possessor ('woman') and thus merely reinforcing the actual English genitive (literally 'the woman's father.gen.').

Verbs are also fully integrated into English inflection. The Romani 3sg.

present-tense inflection ending -*(e)l* continues, however, in cases where the original 3sg. form was monosyllabic, though the ending has become part of the root itself and is no longer functional but is followed by an English inflectional ending: *to del* 'to give', *lesti dels* 'he gives'; *to lel* 'to take', *mandi lelled* 'I took'; *to jal* 'to go', *tutti jals* 'you go'; *to ol* 'to eat'; etc. (see Chapter 3). Inflected forms are occasionally heard from speakers in fossilised expressions, often replicating situative speech acts. Thus we recorded *shom shillo* 'I am cold' (Romani *š-om* 'be-1sg.'), but from the same speaker *tutti's shillo* 'you're cold'; *lesti jinel* 'he knows' (Romani *džin-el* 'know-3sg.'), but from the same speaker *mandi jins* 'I know'. One descendant of a Welsh Romani family was able to recall the expressions *hollem* 'we ate' showing a past-tense person inflection (*xa-l-am/*xa-l-em* 'eat-past. 1pl.), reported as an expression used by his parents. Occasional inflected verb forms are recorded in the corpus, such as *ruvel* 'cry/cries' and *jas* 'go/you go', but the inflection does not appear to be productive and the form can be used at random with different persons. There is a trace of the emphatic imperative in *-tar* in the exclamation *shunta!* 'listen up!' (Romani *šun-tar!*), and a frozen inflected form is embedded in the greeting *sarshin!* (Romani *sar šan?* 'how are you?').

4.4 Morphosyntactic characteristics

In Matras et al. (2007), reference was made to Muysken's (1981) relexification hypothesis and the possibility that AR might be explained as an insertion of lexical tokens into predefined slots within the English sentence. We would have to assume that the utterance is to some extent pre-planned and pre-processed in English, but that for special effects and by deliberate choice, lexical types are selected and substituted by token from the Romani lexical reservoir of lexical forms. This would suggest that Romani-derived words are not types in their own right, but merely substitute tokens for English lexical types. Many of the data presented in the previous sections can be viewed as evidence in support of this hypothesis: the combination of Romani tokens with non-productive English derivation markers, as in *a-trashed* 'afraid', *to-divvus* 'today', *a-drum* 'away', the application of English inflection, and the extension of Romani tokens to cover the same word class functions and meanings as their English counterparts, as in *it's ivin'* 'it's snowing', from Romani *iv* 'snow' (but no verb *iv-* 'to snow' exists in European Romani).

While there is little doubt that token substitution is a *possible* strategy for which speakers resort to their AR lexical reservoir, the assumption that AR is entirely 'parasitic' on the pre-structured English utterance must be dismissed. Rather, AR is a mode of speech that entails several different strategies. Lexical token substitution is just one of those. A further strategy might be referred to as 'expressive utterances' (see Matras et al. 2007: 172). 'Expressive utterances' is a label given to utterances that convey a propositional meaning, but are not well-formed grammatically. We find in the corpus numerous utterances that are not structurally compatible even with the dialectal English spoken by the consultants on an everyday basis. The principal 'deviations' from well-formed English sentences are mainly 'omissions', primarily of definite articles, aspectual and existential auxiliaries, and co-referential pronouns. The structural difference from grammatical English can basically be described as follows: AR allows greater flexibility in the omission of overt reference, indicating that information is contextually highly retrievable. Consider the examples by category:

a) Omission of copula auxiliary in existential predications

(43)   Mush akai
        '[A] man [is] here'

(44)   Mandi boktalo, del mandi obben.
        'I [am] hungry, give me food.'

(45)   Pen chuchi muskara akai!
        'Don't say anything, [the] police [are] here!'

b) Omission of presentative copula

(46)   Kek jel adai, mush chingerpen
        'Don't go there, [there is a] man shouting'

(47)   Divya chavvi akai
        '[There are] wild children here'

c) Zero anaphora

(48)   Mandi kom dovva chavvi but kek kom dovva chavvi.
        'I like this child but [I] don't like that child.'

(49)   Kek jel there, lel the otchaben!
        'Don't go there, [you'll] get VD!'

d) Omission of definite article

(50)   Mush kek juns chichi.
        '[The] man doesn't know anything.'

(51)   Kekka pen dovva, rakli's trash!
        'Don't say that, [the] girl's scared!'

(52)   Maw be rokkering in front of the mush and rakli!
        'Don't be talking in front of the man and [the] girl!'

e) Other omission

(53)   *Dikka the mush's moi nafli zi!*
        Look [at] the man's face [he's got a] bad heart!'

Universally, languages form a continuum in the extent to which they require overt structural encoding of such properties and devices as definiteness, present-tense copula or existential expressions, or co-referential pronouns; AR is thus not exceptional, certainly not in any way 'deficient' or 'simplified'. There is furthermore nothing at all to indicate that this structural feature of AR is in any way connected to historical bilingualism or language contact in the community, in the sense that it is contact that might have led to any simplifcation or erosion of grammatical competence. Indeed, all the structures that are subject to 'omission' are found in the speakers' everyday English, and even their omission in AR is optional. But the feature does indicate that speakers subscribe to a slightly different set of grammatical rules, however subtle the differences, when structuring utterances in AR. It appears that the relative ease with which overt reference to contextually retrievable information of this kind is omitted in AR is indeed connected to the conversational functions of AR, and so to the attitudes surrounding it: it is not a primary means of conveying propositional content, but one that emphasises the emotive aspects of the message. Indeed, Binchy (1993: 92) notes the frequent absence of the definite article in Shelta, and concludes that it is based on a somewhat 'simplified' variety of English. But the Jewish Cattle Trader Jargon Lekoudesch similarly shows omission of the (German) copula and definite article (Matras 1991). Such relaxation of the rules on overt connectedness appears therefore to be not uncommon in in-group emotive registers of this kind.

A further feature of AR morphosyntax, not unconnected to the 'omissions', is the absence of consistent marking of verb inflection. Taking into account that dialectal verb inflection in British English differs from the standard, AR differs from both in treating the first and second person subjects as third persons, or generalising third person present-tense inflection across the paradigm:

(54)   Mandi jins
        'I know[s]'

(55)   Tutti jins
        'You know[s]'

(56)   Tutti's shilo.
        'You are cold.'

(57)   Mandi's delled a mush.
        'I've hit a man.'

(58)   Jel coz mandi's gonna del dubba.
         'Run coz I'm gonna hit this one.'

One might relate this feature to the somewhat humorous and theatrical key that is achieved by activating the AR repertoire: even participants who are present in the interaction are regarded as remote actors, and the statement is a distant and non-engaged commentary. In the same spirit as the 'minimal information' strategy observed above, tense and aspect inflectional marking is sometimes entirely absent from the sentence:

(59)   Dovva mush kek dik
         'This man [does]n't see'

(60)   Foki jel akai.
         'People [are] com[ing] here.'

(61)   Mandi dik tutti wavver divvus.
         'I [will] see you another day.'

(62)   Mandi buti all mandi's jiaben
         'I [have] work[ed] all my life'

4.5 Lexical composition and lexical distribution

This final section is concerned with a characterisation of the lexical inventory of AR, as documented in the corpus of recordings. An initial point of interest – closely connected with the question of 'languageness' referred to in Chapter 1 – is the extent of the vocabulary, in the sense of the quantity and range of different meanings (or concepts) for which users of AR have a separate, in-group word form at their disposal. The question is of theoretical relevance, since it reveals something about the expressive range of the vocabulary, and about the potential consistency with which speakers can avail themselves of in-group vocabulary in actual communication.

The sum of recordings with all interviewees, including both elicitation and evaluation of recorded free conversation in which speakers make use of AR vocabulary, yields a total of around 1,000 different meanings, i.e. conceptual representations captured through a distinct English translation. The counting procedure is not, however, entirely straightforward and requires some clarification. The approach taken was to assign separate meanings to concepts that were lexically differentiated by the speakers as primary concepts only. Derivations and compositions, such as 'Gypsy boy' and 'Gypsy girl', or 'female' and 'male' animals (cf. English terms like 'bitch' and 'mare'), were treated as separate concepts when and if speakers had no hesitation in assigning one meaning to a Romani concept rather than the other, indicating the stability and transparency of the Romani word. Concepts such as 'to run' and 'to run away' are similarly counted as separate entities, as are meanings such as 'half-penny', which can be considered as fixed rather than ad hoc compositions. On the other hand, inflectional counterparts such as 'marry' and 'married' were not distinguished and were counted as one single concept. Numerals were excluded from the statistics because of their entirely compositional (as well as potentially infinite) nature.

The procedure is thus basically designed to eliminate from the count repetitions of an English concept, or cases where the same conceptual meaning is represented in several different ways, drawing on various Romani words. All this means that the significance of the quantification of the inventory of meanings is a matter for interpretation, and that no absolute measure can be used to compare different languages, since the balance between inflectional and compositional material and 'primary' expressions may be significantly influenced by the languages' morphological typology. None the less, the count gives a rough impression of the extent of lexical differentiation that AR offers. The count also possesses some implications for the notion of 'basic vocabulary'. Most discussions of basic vocabulary to date tend to rely on the stability of inherited vocabulary as opposed to the borrowing of loanwords. The case of AR is in a certain sense a mirror image of such case studies. Here, we are talking about the retention of vocabulary from another source following language shift and the adoption, in practice, of the basic vocabulary of the contact language (English) as the primary means of communication. Which concepts continue to have semantic-pragmatic saliency in in-group communication, so as to require or benefit from the retention of a special lexical inventory, is a question that is related to, but by no means identical with, the question of which semantic concepts are likely to resist borrowing in conventional situations of contact.

Moreover, a vocabulary such as that of AR offers interesting insights into the division between 'primary' or 'prototype' semantic concepts and those that are derived. For example, in line with universal patterns we find that agentives are treated as case-particular whereas the subject of their activity or its objective is normally the prototype (see above on derivations in *-(m)engr-*); similarly, kinship terms denoting more remote kin tend to be derived (*palleska* 'nephew' = 'belonging to the brother'); products derive from their source, as in *puvvengra* 'potato' from *puv* 'earth'; and basic colours tend to help modify the meaning of prototypes rather than be derived themselves with reference to relevant entities, thus *lellopammingra* 'carrot' = 'red potato', *porno-kawla cherkli* 'magpie' = 'white-black bird'. On the other hand, the formation of 'grapes', *mulleskras* = '[things] from wine]', defies the conventional rule that source is primary in its relation to product, and shows how lexical prototypes are culturally constructed.

The inventory of *c.*1,000 lexical meanings alluded to is represented by around 1,600 individual expressions altogether, that is, combinations of a meaning with one or several related (cognate) word forms that can be traced back to the same predecessor. Thus, there are often several different lexemes or expressions that are used for the same meaning. Occasionally this comes about by projecting a similar basic meaning onto a set of historically differentiated Romani expressions: for example, the meaning 'a lot' is expressed by *bora* (Romani *baro* 'big'), *boot* (Romani *but* 'many'), as well as *dostus* (Romani *dosta* 'sufficient'); the meaning 'girl' is expressed by *rakli* (Romani *rakli* 'non-Romani girl'), *chai* (Romani *čhaj* 'Romani girl'), *juvel* (Romani *džuvel* 'woman'), *monishna* (Romani *manušni* 'female') and so on. Proliferation of expressions is partly also the result of individual creativity with respect to non-inherited concepts. Thus 'pheasant' is expressed by *borrikanni* 'big chicken', *divya kani* 'wild chicken' and *veshni kanni* 'forest chicken'.

Altogether, around 500 different Romani-derived predecessor expressions are represented in the corpus, along with up to 60 predecessors of other origins, notably English slang expressions, Cant, Shelta, German and French (see Appendix II). The overall ratio of predecessor expressions to meanings as well as to individual expressions thus shows that the lexicon is rather differentiated semantically, and the reliance on internal derivational procedures is modest, accounting for only around two-thirds of lexical expressions, on average, and for fewer than half of the individual meaning-concepts. A representative sample of written sources on English Romani was also surveyed (for a list see Manchester Romani Project online dictionary of English Romani, http://romani.humanities.manchester.ac.uk/ angloromani). Significantly, fewer than fifty Romani expressions are attested in those sources which are not also represented in the recorded corpus: *an-* 'bring', *asva* 'tears', *bijando* 'born', *čelo, celo* 'whole', *čerxen* 'star', *čhad-* 'vomit', *čham* 'cheek', *čhungar-* 'spit', *čuči* 'breast', *čupni* 'whip', *duxo* 'ghost', *džung(ar)-* 'wake', *feder* 'better', *haj(av)-* 'understand', *kašuko* 'deaf', *kež* 'silk', *khilav* 'plum', *kindo* 'wet', *kir* 'ant', *kotor* 'piece', *kuči* 'pot', *kukli* 'doll', *langalo* 'lame', *loš* 'joy', *melalo* 'dirty', *mrazo* 'frost', *naj* 'nail (anatomy)', *papus* 'grandfather', *paruv-* 'change', *pendex* 'nut', *phar* 'silk', *pori* 'tail', *šelo* 'rope', *šing* 'horn', *šuko* 'dry', *šuvljardo* 'swollen', *tasav-* 'choke, strangle', *trad-* 'drive, chase (away) 'expel', *učar-* 'rise, raise', *ušt-* 'get up', *vazd-* 'lift', *xandž-* 'itch', *xaning* 'well', *xanřo* 'sword', *xarkum(a)* 'copper', *xulaj* 'host'.

This indicates a relatively high rate of continuity, and gives the impression that only around 10 per cent of lexical roots may have been lost in the community during the past century and a half. The observation, however imprecise and impressionistic, is consistent with Boretzky's (1998) observation on the extraordinary extent to which Para-Romani vocabularies seem to preserve inherited vocabulary. One should in this connection take into consideration that the core inherited vocabulary that is shared by inflected Romani dialects is often estimated at not much more than between 600–800 lexical roots. Speakers' individual knowledge of Romani vocabulary presents, of course, a very different picture. For the twenty speakers with the largest count of unique or exclusive expressions in the corpus – i.e. expressions identified as 'Romani' – the average count of expressions is 254, the average count of meanings is 200, and the average count of predecessors is 150. Figures vary among those 'top twenty' between 100 and *c*.800 expressions, between 90 and 600 meanings, and between 75 and 360 unique predecessors. This can be considered a representative picture for the middle-aged generation, and so in a sense also representative of the community's 'collective' knowledge of Angloromani. There is a very clear age gap, whereby elderly speakers have a much wider knowledge of Romani expressions than do younger speakers. Taking into account the limitations of the interview and the likelihood that not all lexical items known to speakers could be elicited, it is probably fair to expect the typical middle-aged user of Angloromani to have a knowledge of around 350–450 Romani expressions, and elderly users to have around double that figure.

This inventory of expressions includes a number of synonyms. Synonyms may come about either as a result of the collapse of semantic nuances differentiating inherited lexemes, a further sign of the semantic volatility of expressions belonging to the in-group lexical reservoir, or else as a result of variation in the innovative strategies employed by individual speakers to create new meanings drawing on inherited components. Thus, for the meaning 'bad' the corpus has *waffado* and many cognate word forms that go back to British Romani *vasado (Welsh Romani *basavo*), *dinla* going back to Romani *dinilo* 'crazy', *beng* from 'devil', *nafli* from *nasvalo* 'ill', *kek kushti* literally 'not good', and *gammi*, an English slang expression; for 'drunk' we find *mato* continuing the Romani word for 'drunk', its agentive derivation *mottamengra*, alongside *livvinda* from *lovvina* 'beer', and *peeved* from *pi-v* 'I drink'; 'farmer' is derived by the same procedure from at least four alternative base lexemes, namely *gavvengra* from *gav* 'village', *givvengra* from *giv* 'wheat', *gruvvengra* from *guruv* 'bull' and *puvvengra* from *phuv* 'earth'; the words for 'grass' are *char*, from Romani *čar* 'grass', *kas* from *khas* 'hay' and *poov* from *phuv* 'earth'; and 'frying pan' is *sastermengra* from *saster* 'iron', *tattramengra* from *tato* 'hot', or *hotchamengra* from *xač(ar)-* 'to burn, roast'. (Synonyms are listed as adjoining entries in Appendix I.) Once again it is worth emphasising that the seeming lexical 'luxury' of maintaining a relatively high number of synonyms is connected in two different ways to the history and functionality of the Para-Romani lexical reservoir that constitutes Angloromani. On the one hand, competence declines and speakers are left with a range of different associations on the basis of which they reconstruct and re-assign meanings to expressions. On the other, normative pressure is relaxed as speakers take over individual ownership of language as a creative and innovative activity to which they contribute through their own personal associations while tolerating a range of individual variants.

A geographical division appears with regard to the influence of Cant and

English slang vocabulary, which is more often associated with 'Romani' by younger speakers in the south. Of the ten speakers who provided the largest number of words deriving from Cant, Shelta or dialectal or slang English, six were based or had spent longer periods in Oxfordshire, Kent and Surrey; the others were in West Yorkshire, Lancashire, Staffordshire and Nottinghamshire. While the sample is too small to make detailed statistical calculations worthwhile, this remains an observation that is worthy of further investigation in the future. It is possible that the geogrpahical distribution indicates a higher degree of immersion and intermarriage between the descendants of Romani immigrants and indigenous English Travellers some generations ago. A number of items with Cant predecessors, however, are widespread and not limited to this subgroup of speakers, but are identified by most speakers as belonging to their 'Romani' repertoire. They include the expressions *daddus* 'father', *mammus* 'mother' and *niksis* 'nothing', as well as *skreev* 'car' and to a lesser extent *jigga* 'door'. Words with dialectal English predecessors that are widespread are *foki* 'people' and *vikkels* 'food'.

Against this background, it is interesting to note that despite considerable variation both in personal preferences and in the number of vocabulary items that individuals have at their disposal, competence in the in-group lexical reservoir is not random but pretty much hierarchically structured in relation to specific expressions and their meanings. Table 4.9 compares the total number of tokens of a particular expression in the corpus, i.e. the number of occurrences of an expression (irrespective of word form variation) in all recorded example sentences and free speech samples), the number of tokens involving a particular predecessor (irrespective of word form or meaning) in the corpus, and the number of meanings (irrespective of expression, word form or predecessor), taking into consideration top twenty values only.

Throughout, the predecessor counts are higher, since they capture occurrences of the same predecessor in a variety of semantic functions, including compositions. Thus the predecessor *murš* 'man' occurs both in the expression token *mush* 'man' (and its inflected variants such as *the mush's*) and in the expression token *wovvatemmush* 'foreigner'. The expression token *mandi* 'I' will occur only in this function, while the predecessor token *mande* will also cover inflected forms like 'me' and 'mine'. The predecessor count is thus a useful way to measure the relative productivity of a Romani-derived word in the corpus, while in the expression column we find a number of etymologically and semantically related tokens, such as *jal* and *jel* 'go', or *mandi* in the meanings 'I' and 'me'. The meaning count, in turn, will take into consideration occurrences of the meaning token 'man', whether realised by the expression *mush* or another semantically equivalent one like *gaera*. Despite the variation in the mapping of expressions, predecessors and meanings, a cluster of forms appears consistently among the top twenty in all three groups: *mush* 'man', *mandi* 'I', *kushti* 'good', *rakli* 'girl', *akai* 'here', *dik* 'look', *kuvva* 'thing', *luvva* 'money', *gawdja*

Table 4.9 Corpus frequency of expressions, predecessors and meanings (top twenty)

	Expression count			Predecessor count			Meaning count	
Expression	Meaning	No. of tokens		Predecessor	Meaning	No. of tokens	Meaning	No. of meanings
mush	'man'	144		*murš*	'man'	266	'man'	198
mandi	'I'	94		*mande*	'me (obl. loc.)'	248	'go'	113
kushti	'good'	70		*dikh-*	'see'	186	'I'	106
rakli	'woman'	63		*rakli*	'girl (non-Gypsy)'	167	'woman'	97
akai	'here'	61		*kek*	'not'	153	'look'	85
dik	'look'	61		*džal(a)*	'go (3sg.)'	143	'good'	82
kuvva	'thing'	53		*akaj*	'here'	136	'here'	73
luvva	'money'	52		*kuč*	'dear'	134	'don't'	73
gawdja	'non-Gypsy'	40		*mulo*	'dead'	129	'money'	73
fowki	'people'	37		*raker-*	'speak'	111	'non-Gypsy'	70
duvva	'that'	34		*(a)kova*	'that'	110	'thing'	60
mandi	'me'	33		*(alo)dova*	'that'	106	'come'	58
grai	'horse'	31		*mer-*	'die'	102	'nothing'	58
jel	'go'	31		*čhavo (-i)*	'boy (/girl)'	94	'dirty'	55
jal	'go'	30		*vaxtr-*	'to watch/look'	94	'food'	52
kek	'don't'	30		*love*	'money'	93	'girl'	52
tutti	'you'	30		*lel*	'take (3sg.)'	91	'that'	49
yog	'fire (n.)'	30		*ker-*	'make, do'	90	'policeman'	47
jukkel	'dog'	29		*gadžo (-i)*	'non-Gypsy'	88	'you'	46
rai	'gentleman'	29		*jag*	'fire'	86	'boy'	43

Table 4.10 Speakers' knowledge of expressions (variable word form)

Predecessor	Meaning	Speakers
murš	'man'	29
dikh-	'see'	27
jag	'fire'	26
kuč	'dear'	26
raker-	'speak'	26
akaj	'here'	25
jakh	'eye'	25
ker-	'make'	25
mande	'me (obl. loc.)'	25
rakli	'girl (non-Gypsy)'	25
čhavo	'boy'	24
džal	'go (3sg.)'	24
džukel	'dog'	24
muj	'face, mouth'	24
pani	'water'	24
tirax	'shoe'	24
graj	'horse'	23
gadžo	'non-Gypsy'	22
kek	'not'	22
love	'money'	22
mulo	'dead'	22
raj	'gentleman'	22
baro	'big'	21
(o)kova	'that'	20

'non-Gypsy', *duvva* 'this', *jal* 'go' and *kek* 'not'. These seem to be among the most 'productive' words in the Angloromani vocabulary. As Table 4.10 shows, these expressions are not just used more frequently by a selection of speakers, but they are also the ones found to be known to a larger number of speakers.

Finally, we find that a form's frequency in the corpus and speakers' familiarity with it also correlate with its retrievability. When evaluating interview recordings, all data were tagged for the mode of retrieval. Expressions that were elicited via a word list with (English) meanings were tagged as either 'immediately' retrieved, i.e. the speaker was able to provide Romani expression matching that meaning immediately, or 'delayed' or 'prompted', in cases in which the expression was offered only after some reflection or a prompt (from the interviewer or another speaker). Expressions that were mentioned by speakers not in response to the elicitation of meanings – either because they occurred to speakers spontaneously or by association without appearing on the word list, or because they appeared in usage examples or free conversation – were entered as 'volunteered'. Clearly, a higher density of volunteered words appears in recordings of free conversation, whereas retrieval

Table 4.11 Retrieval patterns: most frequent immediate retrievals and volunteered expressions

Immediate retrieval			Volunteered expressions		
Expression	Meaning	Speakers	Expression	Meaning	Tokens
mush	'man'	29	*mush*	'man'	102
mandi	'I'	24	*dik*	'look'	51
akai	'here'	16	*kushti*	'good'	49
yog	'fire (n.)'	15	*mandi*	'I'	48
kushti	'good'	14	*rakli*	'woman'	46
rakli	'woman'	13	*akai*	'here'	41
gawdja	'non-Gypsy'	12	*kuvva*	'thing'	41
del	'give'	11	*luvva*	'money'	39
grai	'horse'	11	*duvva*	'that'	28
jukkel	'dog'	11	*fowki*	'people'	28
mandi	'me'	10	*gawdja*	'non-Gypsy'	27
mullered	'dead'	10	*jel*	'go'	27
wudder	'door'	10	*jaw*	'go'	23
yoks	'eyes'	10	*mandi*	'me'	21
dik	'look'	9	*tutti*	'you'	20
ker	'do'	9	*vater*	'watch'	20
kek	'not'	9	*kek*	'not'	19

patterns are relevant to the elicitation procedure. The relevant comparison is therefore not between retrieved and volunteered words, in the first instance, but among the individual meanings and expressions that are retrieved and volunteered, respectively (Table 4.11).

Overall, then, a small cluster of expressions emerges that shows the highest retention rate and viability, and which in many ways symbolises the purpose of the in-group inherited lexical reservoir: *mush* 'man', *mandi* 'I', *jal* 'go', *kushti* 'good', *rakli* 'girl', *dik* 'look', *akai* 'here', *gawdja* 'non-Gypsy', *luvva* 'money', *kuvva* 'thing', *kek* 'not'. These are basic vocabulary expressions that allow deictic reference to the speaker (*mandi* 'I'), the immediate speech situation (*akai* 'here') and salient objects that belong to it (*kuvva* 'thing'); to draw attention (*dik* 'look') and direct motion (*jal* 'go'); to refer to salient individual actors categorised by gender (*mush* 'man', *rakli* 'girl, woman') and by group membership (*gawdja* 'non-Gypsy'); to assess and evaluate states of affairs (*kushti* 'good', *kek* 'not'); and to make reference to work and earnings (*luvva* 'money'). This small representative set nicely summarises the essence of what Angloromani is about, functionally speaking: a means of adding an in-group flavour to communication about the most basic everyday situations, and where necessary to maintain private, in-group communication when assessing basic states of affairs surrounding economic transactions with clients (who are invariably group-outsiders).

5 The Conversational Functions of Angloromani

5.1 Back to 'languageness'

A central role in the formation process of mixed languages has been attributed by many writers to the conscious, emotional flagging of identity and group solidarity in small populations. Bakker (1997) regards mixed languages as an opportunity to flag ethnic admixture in populations of mixed households such as the Cree-French Michif (Métis) of Canada and in socially isolated peripatetic communities, while Golovko (2003) sees playful language mixing for the purpose of entertainment as a key tool in the formation of mixed in-group codes such as Copper Island Aleut. Thomason (1995, 1999), too, makes some remarks in a somewhat similar direction, alluding to the role of speakers as conscious 'engineers' of language and proposing a connection with language-manipulation strategies that lead to the emergence of mixed idioms. More explicit is Vakhtin (1998), who identifies a conscious effort on the part of speakers to 'resurrect' a moribund language, resulting in the creation of a mixed code in the case of Copper Island Aleut. Taken for granted in most of these studies is the eventual stabilisation of ad hoc, stylistic mixing to form a coherent and consistent language system with a mixture of historical components. Mous (2003a, 2003b), for instance, acknowledges the role of lexical manipulation in the process that leads to the creation of Ma'a (the special, partly Cushitic lexicon used by the speakers of the Bantu language Mbugu in Tanzania) but emphasises that the 'parallel lexicon' that constitutes Ma'a is used as an all-purpose code and in some households even as the 'unmarked' option.

In a separate tradition, in-group lexicons have been regarded as lexical camouflage strategies created and maintained primarily for secret communication amidst non-affiliated bystanders (see already Avé-Lallemant 1858–62, Kluge 1901). The controversy surrounding Angloromani is connected not least to its position in relation to both mixed languages and in-group lexical reservoirs used for limited purposes. The proliferation of studies of Angloromani in Britain during the first half of the twentieth century was to a considerable extent motivated by a wish to document as thoroughly as possible all traces of the earlier Romani, often misleadingly referred to in the naive terminology of lay investigators of the time as 'pure' Romani – an inflected and all-purpose minority language that had once been spoken in Britain and had become moribund or indeed extinct, save in the form of a Romani-derived, in-group, parallel lexicon. An anonymous source, for example, writing in the *Journal of the Gypsy Lore Society* (N. A. 1929: 109–10), reports that the Smiths and Garrats of East Anglia "used Romani with the utmost freedom in ordinary conversation". One of the Garrats reportedly even wrote letters to the authors that contained many Romani words in them. At the same time the authors report on other families whose Romani was "not particularly good". Most discussions of AR since the 1940s have relied either on replication of earlier material, or on material composed for the purpose of illustration, such as the Lord's Prayer in AR (see Hancock 1984), or, indeed, on no data exemplification whatsoever. Barthelemy (1979), for example, publishes a short text supplied by Donald Kenrick, composed with the help of a speaker, a young girl named Sandra Price; it is quite clear that an effort was made to include as high a density of Romani-derived words as possible. Such depictions of AR have often led to the impression, reproduced in works such as that by Thomason and Kaufman (1988), that AR might be an all-purpose mixed language. At the same time Kenrick (1979) himself, basing his comments on participant observation, notes how use of AR is largely confined to warnings and similar acts of defiance, while Okely (1983), also writing on the basis of first-hand observations (albeit among an unspecified community of 'Travellers'), notes the use of individual in-group words but denies any connection to a separate 'language', whether historical or contemporary.

In a seminal paper on Para-Romani languages and secret languages, Bakker (1998) draws a clear demarcation line between the two, relating the emergence of Para-Romani varieties invariably to the predetermined process that gives rise to mixed languages as the languages of households that are in the process of redefining their group identity. Bakker defines these languages, potentially and from historical perspective, as all-purpose languages, quite distinct from secret lexicons. Structural manifestations of the distinction are, according to Bakker, elements of independent grammar within the structure of the grammatical 'host' language in the first, and strategies of lexical camouflaging in the second. Bakker (2000, 2002) does not dispute the possibility of the co-existence of the two varieties – inflected Romani and English Para-Romani (Angloromani) – in the period attested in the Winchester Confessions of 1615 (see McGowan 1996). Interestingly, though, these documents hint at the use of Romani words within the English-speaking framework in the specific context of subversive communication, while they do not contain any direct samples of inflected Romani. If the two varieties existed side by side, in the same period but amongst different populations, then the question needs to be addressed of whether they might have served different purposes.

A new direction in the analysis of so-called secret languages is offered by Binchy (1993, 1994, 2002) in her discussion of Shelta, the in-group lexicon of Irish Travellers. The study is based on participant observation and recordings of in-group speech with the Traveller community. Binchy points out that Travellers constitute a closed network community and that they share considerable background knowledge with one another. She proposes that Travellers 'codeswitch' from English to Shelta when discussing matters that are highly contextual and so require a high degree of shared background knowledge. As candidate domains for the use of Shelta, Binchy mentions making a living among non-Travellers (i.e. secret communication for work purposes), maintaining boundaries between Travellers and settled people (statements made about settled people, often triggered by their presence), and communication within the Traveller community, the last including intimate domains and "things which can only be spoken about in an oblique way", such as women's health (Binchy 1993: 160). Secret communication is thus a by-product of a code that symbolises the tight-knit social structure and strict moral code of the community.

Romani Gypsies too share a specific moral-spiritual code. They also tend to share a pool of attitudes to events, actors, modes of behaviour and states of affairs. These attitudes are shaped in part by the moral-spiritual code that among other things provides guidelines as to what is considered honourable and pure, and what is, by contrast, a case of misfortune or defiled (see Okely 1983, Engebrigtsen 2007). It is also shaped by a very particular shared life experience and a common pattern of evaluating events and states of affairs.

My claim in this chapter, following up on an idea presented in Matras et al. (2007), is that Angloromani, much like other in-group vocabularies in groups with a similar socioeconomic profile, serves as a kind of formalisation or conventionalisation of a mode of communication that calls on the hearer in a rather explicit way to activate a specialised presuppositional domain when processing an utterance. Presuppositions are often regarded as logical constraints on the contextual relations among utterances (see Karttunen 1974, Levinson 1983, Keenan 1998). In the Conversation Analysis tradition, however, this is seen as a derived function of presuppositions: they help the participants narrow down the possible meanings of utterances by taking into consideration factors such as their jointly perceivable surroundings and their cumulative discourse to that point, as well as knowledge that each of them brings with him or her to the encounter (see Goffman 1983). By their very definition, presuppositions are pragmatic constructions. But that is not to say that there are no formal means of activating presuppositional information. Evidentials, for example, are a typical conventionalised device in many languages of the world which triggers explicit processing of presuppositional background in relation to an articulated proposition. And as it happens, Romani dialects tend to have a formalised set of deictic expressions that indicate the source of knowledge and so help guide the hearer through the relevant presuppositional domain when referring to entities (cf. Matras 1998a).

My proposal for an interpretation of the conversational function of Angloromani is this: members of the English and Welsh Romani community, through their linguistic socialisation, acquire a repertoire of linguistic structures that contains a special inventory consisting mainly of lexical elements, but accompanied by certain conventions of presentation and utterance structure (mainly noticeable from an English perspective as the omission of certain connectivity and predicate-anchoring devices). Speakers generally have a choice whether to make use of this inventory when interacting with fellow group members, or to make do with the same set of structures that are used in interaction with non-group members. In this respect, the choice between English and Angloromani differs from codeswitching in bilingual situations, where there is normally an unmarked choice that is favoured in group-internal interaction. The choice of the special lexical inventory is therefore a statement, but not one that is limited to the social effect of flagging solidarity among fellow group members. It is, rather, a call on the hearer to interpret the propositional content of the speaker's utterance in the light of a specialised or exclusive presuppositional domain. In this respect, the overt marking of presuppositional relevance is not necessarily to be seen as restrictive, but rather as more focused, directed or specified. Use of the special lexical inventory activates an exclusive, group-specific presuppositional domain as the background against which an utterance is to be processed.

5.2 Angloromani as a speech-act device

It follows from the above that Angloromani is not a consistent code that is selected as the preferred choice for the entire duration of conversational interaction in a given setting. Rather, it is a conversational or discourse device – a more subtle way of modifying the delivery key for individual speech acts by signalling to the hearer that a 'specialised', in-group perspective is to be taken in processing these acts. As an in-group perspective I consider the cumulative sum of particular attitudes and experiences that the participants share in their specific role as members of the 'group'; in most situations, the 'group' comprises members of the extended family or related individuals, though it may also extend to include other acquaintances who are part of the Romani community, and less frequently even strangers who are known to the speaker to have been raised in a Romani environment.

Since the effect created by the insertion of in-group vocabulary helps shape the entire speech act, it is potentially achieved through the selection of any number of words from this vocabulary. Speakers thus have the liberty to insert a lower or a higher density of 'special' words; an utterance is an

Angloromani utterance irrespective of the density or consistency of Romani vocabulary that it contains. In practice, though, we might distinguish two types of lexical insertion. The first is intended merely to create the in-group 'flavour' or key of the speech act and can be achieved through the insertion of any Romani word. The second is geared more specifically towards the design of a message that will reflect the relation between group attitudes and particular aspects of the depicted state of affairs – actors, referents or events. The most frequently available expressions cater for both types of needs, singling out individuals and activities, locating referents in a setting, and assessing situations (see Chapter 4). Following Matras et al. (2007) we can thus define Angloromani as an *emotive mode* that expresses an emotionally engaged evaluation of an event or state of affairs. Here, the choice of AR elicits the hearer's identification with the speaker's emotional involvement – a sense of solidarity that has its base in the activation of an exclusive presuppositional domain of experiences, attitudes and interests that are shared by group members.

Consider first the following examples, observed by the author in interaction with Gypsies in the Northwest of England. At Appleby fair, an annual gathering of Gypsies and Travellers from all over the country that takes place in Cumbria in the first week of June, two young women with their small children walk across the bridge in the town centre. The bridge overlooks the location where horses are washed in the river and is thus the centre of events connected to the three-day fair. One of the women comments to the other on the display of traditional horse-drawn wagons on the road leading from the town to the nearby hill, where most of the stalls and trailers are based. The other responds: "Yeah, that was really *kushti.*" There is nothing secretive at all about the evaluation of the event, and so no external need to camouflage meaning in any way. The word *kushti* 'good' is selected from the pool of more readily available items in the special lexicon in order to emphasise mutual group membership and belonging, against the background of an ongoing event that is devoted to displaying and celebrating Romani identity, culture and tradition publicly. We might even speculate that any other word in the same utterance might have had exactly the same effect if said in Romani. In practice, it is the concept *good* that is the salient content element in the utterance and which is being predicated; and the word *kushti* has in turn a higher retention and availability rate among users/speakers than any items covering the content of any of the other words in the utterance. The choice of *kushti* here therefore achieves both the goal of packaging salient content in Romani and thus highlighting it for special attention and evaluation, and that of assigning the entire speech act a group-internal flavour, calling on the hearer to accept the content not just in any capacity but in her specific capacity as a fellow member of the community who is sharing the experience of the annual fair with all its implications.

In the next two examples, the author is speaking to a Romani friend of many years. Their friendship revolves in part around a mutual interest in and appreciation of Romani language and culture and an active involvement in various activities to promote them. In this respect, the author is treated as an 'honorary' group-insider. The first setting is in the friend's trailer home on a caravan site in a small town in Lancashire. The friend had been looking into buying a house for quite some time in order to escape the pressures of living on the organised council site. He reports on recent developments, and how on the previous day he had been close to signing an exchange contract for a house. The following exchange then takes place:

(1)   Author: Did you get it?
        Friend: No.
        Author: Why not?
        Friend: I got trashed.

The expression *trashed* 'scared, frightened' (no connection to English 'trash') is used to capture the speaker's hesitation faced with a life-changing transaction that would have an effect not just on a key aspect of his lifestyle, but through that also on both practical and symbolic connections to Romani culture – giving up life in a caravan, surrounded by members of the extended family, in favour of life in a house, isolated among non-Gypsy people. Clearly, such hesitation has a distinct meaning when interpreted from the particular perspective of the speaker's Romani roots and collective cultural and historical experience rather than just from the personal angle of the speaker as a potential investor in property. It is this cultural context that is conveyed by the choice of a Romani word.

Another sample interaction involving the same friend takes place at a public event to mark the official 'Roma, Gypsy and Traveller History Month' in a small town in Lancashire. Local Romani activists, in conjunction with the municipal council and the local Traveller Education Service, had organised information stalls and an exhibition in the town's main shopping area, which draws a crowd of visitors. Among them is a local police officer, who engages in conversation with the author. Some five to ten minutes into that conversation, the author's friend appears. The author excuses himself from the conversation with the police officer and turns to his friend, while the officer continues to examine the nearby stalls, just a few yards away. After a brief exchange, the friend says: 'Right, I'll leave you to *rokker* with the *muskra*' ('I'll leave you to talk to the police officer'). Here again, no secrecy or deliberate camouflaging of content is involved. Rather, the key is that of a personal message between the speaker and the addressee, concluding the brief exchange between them and expressing the speaker's withdrawal from the interaction in acknowledgement that he had interrupted an ongoing exchange with a stranger. The use of Romani here marks out the turning point in the conversation. But it also establishes a hierarchy of personal loyalties, signalling recognition that although the speaker is yielding to the addressee's earlier conversation with the stranger, the bond between the speaker and the addressee is stronger than the one between the addressee and his other interlocutor, the police officer, and that the speaker is withdrawing for practical and perhaps tactical reasons, recognising the utilitarian benefits of showing respect to a representative of the authorities.

The final example derives from observations during a visit with a Gypsy family at a caravan site in Lancashire. A four-year-old girl draws the attention of her aunt, who is sitting among a group of adults in the trailer, after she had taken, silently and at first unnoticed, a piece of bread from a dinner tray that was being prepared for guests. Her aunt asks her, in a very friendly and not at all accusing tone, where she got the bread from. The girl smiles and says somewhat shyly: 'I *chored* it' ('I stole it'). Once again, secrecy or an attempt to conceal meaning from bystanders has absolutely no relevance in this particular case, which shows a speech act in its most natural setting of the home environment. The girl is also, in all likelihood, entirely unaware of a *category* of words that are only used in in-group communication and are not intelligible to group-outsiders, as she has not yet had any immersive contact at all with outsiders, save a few non-Gypsy family friends who to all intents and purposes are regarded not as outsiders, but as regular interlocutors. But she does recognise the particular lexeme *chor* as one that triggers a particular emotive key, and she therefore chooses this expression over possible alternatives such as 'took', 'stole', 'grabbed' etc. Aware, as part of her linguistic socialisation to date, that *chor* is reserved for intimate contexts that convey a high degree of trust and solidarity, she employs the term strategically to cover her embarrassment and guilt at having to admit that she has taken something without permission, while at the same time expressing a general endearment of the state of affairs and her confidence that, owing to the bond of solidarity, trust and love with the people around her, inclusive of the addressee (her aunt), she will not be held to account for this minor offence.

This latter example illustrates a rather frequent use of the emotive speech mode for a euphemistic depiction of faults, eliciting the hearer's sympathy, solidarity or understanding. Often in such cases, the use of Romani expressions is not random but targets the key concepts that are the potential source of shame, blame or embarrassment. The following are examples from the corpus of recorded interviews:

(2)   He delled him in the mui.
        'He hit him in the face.'

(3)   The mush tried to chor the trailer.
        'The man tried to steal the trailer.'

(4)   Everybody has a dindla in the family.
        'Everybody has a crazy person in the family.'

(5)   Oh, dik at the state of my bal, oh I'll have to jaw somewhere to
        somebody could do a hairdresser to get me bal done, ooh dik at the
        state of it!
        'Oh, look at the state of my hair, oh I'll have to go somewhere to
        somebody could do a hairdresser to get me hair done, ooh look at
        the state of it!'

AR may be used euphemistically to encode a taboo word or concept. Here,
the emotive mode is used to appeal to the hearer's solidarity and to request
an exemption from the sanctions that would normally follow the overt
use of such expressions. By coding the concepts in the emotive mode, the
speaker thus escapes embarrassment. While the content remains the same,
the speech act used to convey it has a different effect on the conversational
interaction when it is marked for the emotive mode. Note that in the case
of some of the concepts, the associated embarrassment is very much a result
of culture-specific attitudes, and this too is captured by the culture-internal
code:

(6)   And it wasn't long after that, she mored.
        'And it wasn't long after that, she died.'

(7)   And she used to say: "Count this luvva", you know, and we used to
        count the luvva.
        'And she used to say: "Count this money", you know, and we used
        to count the money.'

(8)   Coz you'd think you were gonna get juvs off her head.
        'Coz you'd think you were gonna get lice off her head.'

The AR insertions signal that the speaker expects the hearer to agree that
concepts like 'death' and 'money' constitute key words whose overt mention
in conversation is to be avoided. In Romani culture in particular, direct
mention of certain taboo topics such as those related to illness, death or
sexuality is considered disrespectful to the addressee. Issues relating to
money may cause discomfort since they allow the listener, during the narration, insights into the private circumstances of the actors, and so involve
an element of exposure. Use of the emotive code for relevant references
reinforces the 'cultural contract' between speaker and hearer and elicits the
hearer's solidarity and loyalty, and at the same time provides an acceptable
means of packaging concepts that may trigger discomfort or loss of face if
mentioned directly. The tendency is reinforced whenever reference to such
taboo topics is intensified:

(9)   She's a chikli rakli – look at the chik everywhere!
        'She's a dirty woman – look at the dirt everywhere!'

(10)   And you said "He's chikla and he's a luvni gera and he's had more
         monnishins on the end of his kawri".
         'And you said "He's dirty and he's a whore-man and he's had more
         women on the end of his penis".'

(11)   We call a bad rakya what likes loads of mushes "a chikla luvni",
         you know, what likes goin' with these different mushes, and we'll
         say "don't rokker to duvva it'll have the otchraben".
         'We call a bad girl what likes loads of men "a dirty whore", you
         know, what likes goin' with these different men, and we'll say
         "don't talk to this one, she'll have VD".'

A further type of speech act that is often marked by AR material is
attempts by the speaker to direct the hearer's behaviour. Binchy (1993, 1994)
describes a similar function, which she labels 'directives', for which Irish
Travellers employ Shelta. The expected goal of these speech acts is compliance with the speaker's prompt. Such prompts are sometimes accompanied
by threats, though these are not necessarily to be taken literally. The use of
the emotive mode signals the speaker's view that the hearer's behaviour does
not conform to a set of expectations. The fact that the speaker may take the
liberty of reprimanding the hearer, and that there is a certain standard of
expected behaviour in the first place, brings us back to the domain of particular shared presupposition and the bond of attitudes and solidarity that exists
between speaker and hearer. In this light, the threat is to be interpreted as an
expression of concern for the hearer's fate, reinforcing the intervention with
the hearer's behaviour. The emotive mode indicates the speaker's expectation
that the hearer should show understanding for the speaker's viewpoint and
comply with the speaker's prompt. The action that the speaker is prompting
is classified as being in the mutual interest of speaker and hearer, or of third
parties who are close to or dependent on them. Here too, then, the emotive
mode activates a sense of solidarity and shared responsibilities.

(12)   Ol the obben coz when the raklis jels I'm gonna mor yas.
         'Eat the food coz when the girls go I'm gonna kill you(pl.).'

(13)   Don't jaw over there coz I'll mor ya.
         'Don't go over there coz I'll kill you.'

(14)   Lel the stardi off the chavvis.
         'Take the hat off the kids.'

(15)   Come and lel ya obben.
         'Come and get your food.'

(16)   Putch the rakli for a tuvla
         'Ask the woman for a cigarette'

(17)   Varta the chavvis.
        'Look at the boys.'

(18)   I'd tell 'em not to chor in the burrika
        'I'd tell 'em not to steal in the shop'

(19)   Stor akai or I'll mor you when I jel out this tan.
        'Stay here or I'll hit you when I come out [of] this place.'

(20)   You're going to jal with that monnishin aren't you?
        'You're going to go out with that girl aren't you?'

Directives of this kind are the most likely speech acts to attract the attention of ethnographers and other observers of Gypsy culture who are not focused in particular on the use of language, perhaps while they are most likely to be cited by speakers themselves as examples of their in-group speech form. Buckler (2007: 59–61), for instance, describes how Gypsies in the Northeast of England introduced her to an inventory of Romani words as a display of their own culture, while illustrating their practical use by citing instructions and warnings.

A subtype of the call for compliance with the speaker's prompt is the frequently mentioned function of AR as a 'secret code' used to warn group-insiders of external threats (see e.g. Kenrick 1979). Warnings can be subdivided into different types. Those where AR serves most obviously as a 'camouflage' strategy are pronounced in the presence of, and can potentially be overheard by, outsiders. One might interpret such speech acts as signals to the hearer that the content is conveyed, with the speaker having the hearer's own interest in mind, amid a threat to the hearer's interests within the immediate surroundings. This too reinforces an existing bond between speaker and hearer that puts them both in opposition to the environment. Secrecy is here a by-product of the use of the special code. Consider the following examples (mainly deriving from episodes in which speakers reconstruct their usage of AR):

(21)   Dik at the mush over there.
        'Look at the man over there.'

(22)   Mok it, you'll be lelled.
        'Leave it, you'll be caught.'

(23)   Pen chuchi, muskra akai!
        'Say nothing, [the] police [are] here!'

(24)   There's a gaera akai.
        'There's a man here.'

(25)   The konligaera's avvin', gavva ya kukkeri.
        'The teacher's comin', hide yourself.'

(26)   Kek chinger, the muskras'll lel ya.
       'Don't shout, the police'll get ya.'

(27)   Kekka rokker in front of the rakli.
       'Don't talk in front of the woman.'

(28)   Mandi's rom is gonna rokker waffadi kuvvas.
       'My husband is gonna say bad things.'

Naturally, the availability of a linguistic resource that is not accessible to outsiders makes it possible for communication to be exclusive and disguised among bystanders. Derrington and Kendall (2004: 102), for instance, describe how Gypsy schoolchildren admit to using Romani in order to exclude non-Travellers deliberately from their conversations, but emphasise how secrecy is, here too, a secondary effect, and how in the first instance Romani is used as a "source of support between Traveller students, an affirmation of shared identity, and also as a form of protection, allowing Traveller students to mark the boundaries between themselves and others".

Warnings may also be of a more subtle type, not necessarily uttered when facing an immediate threat or in the presence of a threatening third party, and so not encoded in AR in order to disguise or camouflage meaning. Rather, in this type of warning the speaker is conveying to the hearer his evaluation of the situation with reference to a domain of shared attitudes, values and interests. Here too, the implicit reference to common interests serves to reinforce the bond and solidarity between speaker and hearer against external threats:

(29)   Mush jins everything ya rokkerin' anyway.
       '[The] man knows everything you're sayin' anyway.'

(30)   Gavva from the muskras, they're vellin'!
       'Hide from the police, they're comin'!'

(31)   Kek jal akai, you'll be mullered!
       'Don't go there, you'll be killed!'

Example (32) provides a nice illustration of how the solidarity effect may operate at several levels. In the quotation presented by the speaker as an illustration of family-internal communication, we find a warning delivered by a parent to children, as in some of the previous examples:

(32)   You'd say to the chavvis: "Rokker niksis, don't give them ya nav!"
       'You'd say to the children: "Say nothing, don't give them your name!"'

This quotation itself is bracketed by an utterance in which the speaker is reconstructing, for the benefit of the hearer, a context in which the quotation would be employed. That context is characterised as one that features family-internal communication. The speaker is conveying to the hearer that he trusts the hearer to understand and accept group-internal norms, and so to accept that part of parental guidance to children is to warn them not to cooperate with the authorities and not to say anything if questioned, even their name. This trust that the speaker is expressing towards his immediate interlocutor is represented by the choice of *chavvis* 'children' in the matrix part of the utterance. The bond within the family is represented by the Romani words in the bracketed quotation.

5.3 Angloromani in narration

The examples presented in the previous section showed how AR is employed at the level of the individual speech act, often embedded in an isolated speech act in a given situational context. Embedded in narration, speech acts marked in Angloromani can achieve three separate goals. Firstly, they provide speakers with a means of marking out and authenticating reports on events in which Angloromani played a role as the choice code in a reconstructed speech act. In this respect they do indeed fulfil one of the typical conversational roles of codeswitching, and that is to contextualise reported speech, often by switching into the code in which the original speech segment had been delivered (cf. Gumperz 1981, Auer 1984). Such reports are also useful to us since they provide further insights into the authentic, situation-bound usage of the in-group variety. Secondly, these speech acts may serve as tools to help organise the narration as a speech event, foregrounding salient, controversial or complicated events, or highlighting the resolution and evaluation positions in the narrative structure by gauging attitudes and strengthening speaker-hearer solidarity in an effort to arrive at a shared evaluation of the events reported on (cf. Labov & Waletzky 1967, Labov 1981). Finally, in line with the assumptions of so-called Third Wave Variation Theory (cf. Eckert 2008), we might view the entire narration which contains Angloromani segments as a performance mode that is embedded in the indexical field of the ongoing speech situation. Highlighting portions of the narration by activating Romani vocabulary may thus serve a purpose that is external to the narration and related to the relations between the speaker and the interlocutor or audience of interlocutors.

In the following excerpts, speakers recall individual events in which Angloromani was used in conversation:

(33)
a. Or if I was in a place with me dad years ago, and he'd say to me/ before we'd go in this place he'd say to me: *Maw rokker*, let *mandi rokker*, *til ya chib*. {Don't talk, let me talk, hold your tongue.}

b.   And I could never say nothing until I went outside.
c.   Let *mandi rokker*. {Let me talk.}
d.   Then he used to say: *mol muk' us jaw*, you know {let us go}.

Note the build-up, however brief, of the background describing the setting before the climax of the short narration is presented in the form of a direct quotation from the speaker's father, authenticated in Angloromani. In the narrative structure AR marks out the climax of the event – the use of Angloromani to warn the boy before the encounter with strangers (note the fact that the warning is given in Romani not *in front of* the strangers, to prevent them from understanding, but *before* the actual encounter, as an act of warning/solidarity, in line with the characterisation given in the previous section). The use of AR also authenticates the original quotation. At the level of the shared indexical field of speaker and addressee, it delivers a piece of information that is worth sharing and thereby reaffirms the participants' shared interest in the Romani language and the particulars of Romani life. It also signals the speaker's confidence in the interlocutor who, despite being a group-outsider, will be able to contextualise and understand the Romani segment. Note the repetition of the key instruction from the climax of the story – *let mandi rokker* – in segment (c), instigating further reflection and a shared evaluation of the relevance of the sample as an example of the authentic use of Angloromani in conversation.

In (34), once again the reconstruction of the original speech event in Angloromani serves as an illustration of a reportable event (cf. Labov 1981), as an authentication of the original utterance, and as a way of flagging the speaker's repertoire and competence in response to the addressee's enquiry about usage patterns of Romani:

(34)
a.   *Mandi's* with *adella mush akai* {I'm a-hitting the man here}, it means like we've hit the man there,
b.   That is what we used to say.
c.   If one was young boys, if w'was roguish, we'd say like/
d.   If/ if w'was amongst a load of *gawja* people, whatever, we'd say:
e.   *Jel* cause *mandi's* gonna *del dobba*. {Go cause I'm gonna hit this man.}
f.   *Mandi's* gonna *mor dobba akai*. {I'm gonna hit this man here.}

A similar structure is found in the following example:

(35)
a.   I can remember one time I went to see me dad's family in Wales, maybe twenty year ago, over twenty year ago,
b.   and I got to me granddad's place in South Wales, down the middle of nowhere in South Wales,

c.   so we knock on me old granddad, bang bang bang bang, knocked him up, me, Dave and uncle Ervin,

d.   'Get up', I heard me old granddad whisper, 'Get the *kosh*' {stick}

e.   'Get the *kosh*'

f.   Get the stick to hit me with,

g.   We were running in fits laughing.

h.   Me uncle was like it's me, it's me Ervin.

Here too, we have a gradual build-up of the story background and setting (segments a-b), a complicating action (segment c), and a climax that contains a direct quotation, authenticated through the use of Angloromani and at the same time marked out in Angloromani as the climax of the story. Within the internal progression of the story line, the use of Angloromani marks out an instruction conveyed by the grandfather to somebody close to him to comply in the interest of both. At the level of the speaker's performance in telling the story, the use of Angloromani marks out irony: the grandfather's suspicion of the innocent visit by his nephew and grandchildren is symbolised by his defiant choice of Angloromani, as if embarking on a clash with strangers, while his whispered words were in fact both heard and understood by the visitors. Angloromani is thus a major tool in delivering the humorous key of the story and so in allowing the speaker to carry out his performance successfully in front of an audience of listeners. More than just share experience through narration, Angloromani also serves as a device for delivering entertainment through narration. A crucial role is played by the symbolism of Angloromani for insider-outsider mapping, and the potential for irony and embarrassment when insiders are wrongly categorised as outsiders and the language is stripped of the protective function for which it had been selected.

In the following excerpts, the insertion of Romani expressions similarly accompanies quotations from reconstructed events. These are often introduced by explicit cues: 'and we'll say', 'and she used to say to me', 'you say', 'and they'll say', and so on. Here, however, the purpose is not to single out complications in a chain of events, but rather to share with the listener insiders' appreciation and evaluation of entire situations. Angloromani segments here are direct quotations from reconstructed situations, but they are also a way to perform attitudes and approaches to everyday situations and to invite the listeners to associate themselves with this, the group-insiders' view of the world:

(36)

a.   And- and we'll say, '*dik* at *duvva*'s *izers*, ooh i'n't she *kushti* she *diks* ooh *todivvus*' eh {look at this one's clothes, ooh, i'n't she pretty she looks ooh today},

b.   Oh, doesn't she *dik kushti*, a high born *rawni* {doesn't she look nice, a high born lady},

c.   And that means she could be a lady or a film star the way she's dressed.

(37)

a.   Say you see somebody with loads of beautiful jewellery,

b.   You don't look at them and stare, you say, oh, lovely, *kushti kuvvas* {pretty things} look at the lovely *vongashis* {rings} and gilders *duvva yek's* {this one's} got on,

c.   This is how our kind of people talk.

d.   A *rawni rakya* {lady girl}, you know, *kushti*. {pretty}

(38)

a.   When I was a, maybe ((laughs)) a bad little lass, when I was little,

b.   I was always getting in mischief and she used to say to me, 'I'll *mor* ya, *jaw adrum* {I'll beat you, go away} come 'ere',

c.   and I'd say 'no don't! let/ *muk* me *jaw*' that means say 'let me go'.

d.   And she'd say 'no, come 'ere I'll *mor* ya, *jaw* over *akai*' ya know, '*jaw* over *akai*, *lel* to me' {I'll beat you, go over there, ya know, go over there, give to me}

e.   and then I'd say 'no mum *muk* me *jaw*' {let me go}

f.   Well when I did let go I got slaughtered! ((laughs))

(39)

a.   B: Like if we/ say we was goin' on a bus or summat, you know,

b.   And 'stead like some people just show your pass or pay whatever, [you know]

c.   H: [Yeah].

d.   B: And they'll say don't *pukker* your *nav*, *mong* the- the *gaera* how much *luvva duvya* is {don't say your name, ask the- the man how much money this is},

e.   You see, instead of saying oh well I'll get the fares, I don't- you know, how much it is,

f.   H: [Yeah]

g.   B: [how-] pay in *luvva* {money}, but that's/ we *rokker* {say} it in Romanes

h.   H: Yeah ((laughs))

In (36)–(37) the listener is given an illustration of how the group would assess a lady's beautiful appearance; in (38) the speaker is sharing a typical childhood scenario; and in (39) the speaker is demonstrating how group solidarity acts to conspire against the mainstream behaviour norm ('And 'stead like some people just show your pass or pay whatever') and how Romani words are used among members of the group in order to encourage one another to remain protective of themselves and distanced from others. Once again there is an element of authentication of the original speech event and setting in the repetition of Romani words in the direct quotation; and there is a strategic organisation in the narration in promoting the direct quotations to a position of a topical highlight of the reconstructed event. At the same time, though, each narration segment serves a performative function in allowing the speakers to display their loyalties, identities and attitudes to group norms, preferences and values. The use of Angloromani lexicon, embedded in key segments within this performative discourse, is part of the key of the message, inviting the listener to share the speaker's perspective and emotional assessment of the kind of situations dealt with in the narration.

We finally turn to a different type of use of Angloromani in narrative discourse. While in the previous examples the declared purpose of the narrative was to provide examples for the use of Romani, in the following excerpts the performative aspect is itself foregrounded, as speakers use Romani expressions spontaneously to communicate their points of view and assessment of events and situations. The distribution of Romani expressions is not, however, random, but targeted specifically for the packaging of taboo or other concepts that are controversial. Such taboo material is flagged against the background of the exclusive presuppositional domain and a set of attitudes, norms and values to which speaker and listener both subscribe; and it is this background that provides the basis upon which the participants can engage cooperatively and harmoniously in assessing the states of affairs depicted in the narration:

(40)
a. Believe it or not, not givin' 'im something - we'd have *bad bokri* {bad luck},
b. For not *dellin'* {giving} that man something, for not giving 'im something, that *rashai* {priest}.
c. So what we'd do then, we'd think, right, well badness is coming upon us,
d. So we used to class it as a good deed, we'd actually take something to that man, to give 'im.
e. And we'll say, right, that's put us right with the Lord.

(41)
a. When our mam used to *durrik* {tell fortunes} these high/ high born *rawni foki* {lady-folk},
b. Well, I could afford it, they had tons of money,
c. They used to give me mam a ring if they couldn't afford/ like they'd say, I haven't got a lot on me,
d. Some of them didn't carry a lot of money, you know what I mean,
e. They'd write a cheque out or they'd give her something in gold, and you should've seen the stuff she got give!

In example (40), the notion of 'bad luck' (*bad bokri*) is introduced as a culture-specific, internal concept, triggering associations with the group-internal system of values and attitudes. Note that in what follows, throughout segments (a) and (b), there is a process of language negotiation as the speaker alternates between introducing other terms in plain English and highlighting them in Romani. Thus the notion of 'giving' is repeated three times, once in Romani; and the seemingly neutral (initially) reference to 'that man' is promoted to the *rashai* 'priest'. In (41), the highlighted terms are once again a group-specific activity, *durrik* 'to tell fortunes', and once again the characterisation of the key person, an outsider, who is the target of the transaction, namely the *rawni foki* 'lady folk'. Romani expressions are thus used in both examples not in order to avoid overt mention of the concepts per se and achieve a subjective qualification of these concepts without doing so explicitly. Instead, the procedure is to allow the listener to draw conclusions by triggering a particular world of associations, one that represents the in-group culture and the complexity of its relations with outsiders – be it persons in high institutional office and the procedures they represent, or clients with their preferences.

The following two examples provide a more specific illustration of 'taboo' in the sense discussed by Burridge and Allen (1998), namely as an X-phemistic qualification of a content-meaning:

(42)
a. And you know I used to *chor* {steal} everything in the jumble sale,
b. Me granny used to put a stall up, you know for the poor little *chavvis* {children} mmm,
c. And she said, be thankful to the Lord, and get down and pray she said to the *shadai* {the Lord},
d. And thank him she says you've plenty o' *izers* {clothes} on yer back and plenty to *ol* {eat},
e. And you've been brought up to know what's *yoozha* {clean} and what's *chikla* {dirty}, *vater* {look} these she said, there's nobody to *tuv* these *tiknases* {wash these kids}
f. And she says they're going to be put in *kaers* {houses}, that meant they were orphans, no mothers no fathers,
g. The mothers had been *luvnis* {whores} tha' dumped 'em,
h. And either the fathers didn't want 'em, they couldn't keep 'em and go out and get their livin' an' all,
i. So me granny used to do collections for money, and she'd buy clothing.

(43)
a. K: And me Aunt Alice was crying.
b.   Our Debbie she said I've summat to *pukker* {tell} you she said,
c.   Oh it's *mored* {killed} me I can't lift me *sherra* {head} up everybody's *rokkerin'* {talking} she said among our *fowki* {people}.
d.   Why she said, our Debbie she said, she's *bori* {pregnant}, *bori* means with child.

e.   H: Yeah.
f.   K: Mmm, she said oh she said/ she said: and she can't *pukker* {tell}
          me, she said the *chor* {poor}.
g.   She said who's the father of the *tiknas* {child}, coz she'd been with
          that many,
h.   She'd had that many different *mushes* {men}, and, oh, and me
          mam used to say you know if you take any *izers* {clothes} off
          Debbie, *yog* 'em. {burn 'em}

Taboos are defined as meaning domains that cause embarrassment or discomfort when discussed directly, and which therefore require modes of evasive communication (cf. Burridge and Allen 1998). In this sense, the strategic use of Romani expressions in excerpts (40)-(41) might qualify as a form of euphemism, since it accompanies the discussion of the problematic relations between in-group members and outsiders – church officials and clients. Recall that the concepts for which Romani was used were the terms for outsiders and the terms for the related activity through which group-insiders complied with the expectations of outsiders or rendered them services.

In (42)-(43), Romani expressions create the overall euphemistic 'flavour' of the discourse in its entirety by flagging the usual themes of solidarity, shared experience and values, and by calling on the listener to process what is being said in the light of those. Thus, the speaker is able to present difficult content material that might cause discomfort. In addition, there is a strategic distribution of Romani expressions. It covers concepts that represent activities or notions that cannot be mentioned directly as they are tightly regulated by behavioural norms, and the slightest implication that these norms are being negotiated might cause discomfort and insecurity. The expressions that appear in the two examples can be divided into several thematic areas: behavioural taboos set by the surrounding society – *chor* 'to steal', *luvnis* 'whores'; functions and institutions of mainstream society – *kaers* 'homes (=orphanages)'; drastic action that violates balanced, harmonious well-being – *mor* 'kill', *yog* 'burn'; bodily appearance and functions and associated concepts – *izers* 'clothes', *ol* 'eat', *sherra* 'head'; community-internal norms on cleanliness and sexuality – *yoozha* 'clean', *chikla* 'dirty', *tuv* 'wash', *bori* 'pregnant', *mushes* 'men' (as sexual partners); and finally endearment of concepts representing relations and interactions with fellow group members – *chavvis* 'children', *tiknases* 'kids', *fowki* 'people', *vater* 'look', *pukker* 'tell', *rokker* 'speak'.

Along with the above examples of speakers' characterisations of their own Romani language use, these conversation excerpts provide us with some overall answers to the question of the functions that a Romani lexicon represents in the particular context of the Romani Gypsy community in Britain, and the community's historical motivation for maintaining an in-group lexicon: these are invariably connected with the kind of relations that exist between community members and the surrounding, majority population.

The in-group is a tight-knit community that is highly protective of its strict norms and values, many of which are targeted at maintaining a sense of moral-spiritual purity and cleanliness and to protect members from contamination. In the same spirit, these norms tightly regulate points of interaction with group-outsiders. This system of attitudes and values is reinforced, in turn, by majority society's wholesale exclusion and suspicion of the in-group and its own practice of reserving only very narrow and highly regulated slots for interaction with the group. These points of interaction invariably involve economic transactions, and more specifically the provision of a very specific portfolio of services by the in-group to the surrounding majority population, as well as, by necessity, a limited range of interaction points with the majority's institutions and authorities.

The Angloromani lexical inventory helps process this dichotomy between loyalty to in-group norms and the constraints imposed on individuals and their everyday behaviour and activities. At the level of the entire discourse, it provides an emblematic instrument of flagging separateness and so encouraging loyalty to in-group values and norms. It also provides a mode for separate and private in-group communication in mixed settings. As a conversational and discourse device, it marks out salient positions in narration, especially those that symbolise potential conflict or a clash of values. But it also protects the stability of group norms and values by encoding, and thereby seemingly neutralising, any negotiation of the boundaries of accepted behaviour. In this way, the in-group lexicon helps maintain both symbolic and practical boundaries between group-insiders and outsiders, between accepted behaviour and taboo, between pure and defiled, and between endearment/solidarity and rejection/exclusion.

The Romani-derived lexicon thus continues to be of value to the community once inflected Romani is abandoned. As the inventory of linguistic structures erodes, the in-group code can no longer be relied on for all-purpose communication. In particular, the loss of verb inflection as a way to anchor predications means that no independent sentences can be formed, and hence no separate, coherent propositions can be conveyed in the code; the system can therefore no longer be utilised for any communicative function that requires sequencing or chaining of coherent propositional units, such as conversation or narration. The remaining structures, primarily lexical, are then exhausted as a discourse device that is triggered through insertion of isolated words, if necessary, modifying the interpersonal and emotional delivery key at the level of the speech act, rather than carrying the full content of a proposition. One might say that the language itself has undergone a process akin to that described for individual structures of language as 'grammaticalisation' (Hopper 1991, Hopper & Traugott 2003): the structural means have been eroded, but their intrinsic or internal function has been exploited for a much more subtle or abstract, specialised meaning, one that helps modify other structures rather than simply convey an independent, self-contained

meaning. The historical process leading from Romani to Angloromani is thus
a kind of 'grammaticalisation of a language'.

5.4 Speakers' perspectives on language loss and revitalisation

During interviews and encounters with Romani Gypsies one is constantly
confronted with a self-image of linguistic semi-competence. This is on the one
hand in line with speakers' quite realistic self-assessment of their *Romani* as
a mixture of English and Romani, or as the insertion of Romani words into
English conversation. But it goes further in the tendency to attribute greater
competence to 'others' whose identity is either somewhat vague – such as a
Romani family that lives in a remote area of northern Scotland and supposedly still speaks 'fluent' Romanes – or who are generally unapproachable
– an uncle or a grandmother who have passed on and who supposedly were
able to say 'everything' in Romanes. The image of a 'lost language' thus
constantly accompanies speakers' narrative about their own present-day
speech form. Genuine competence in the language is something that is generally attributable to others and usually associated with past generations; but
this image is not directly connected with any specific point in time or place;
understandably, nobody is able to specify which generation, in which family
and in which area in the country were the 'last' to speak 'fluent Romanes'.
The only cases where 'fluency' is objectively contextualised is through recent
encounters with Romani immigrants from central and eastern Europe, who
speak Romani as their everyday household and community language. These
encounters strengthen the awareness among English Gypsies of the existence
in principle of a stable, self-contained Romani language.

Some individuals, like the speaker in (44) – a retired horse breeder in
County Durham – even go as far as to suggest a decline in their Romani-
language competence during their own lifetime, taking a somewhat nostalgic
approach to the topic of knowing and using the language:

(44)

a. P: Yes *bish ta pansh besha* twenty-five years I've never really *rokkered
         in Romani jibb* {talked in Romani language}
b. M: No.
c. P: My mind works in English these last *do trin divvis* {two three
         days} I've been trying to *pench* {think} in Romani because I knew
         you were=
d. M: Oh right
e. P: =and all the time it just comes slowly, what's that *lav* {word}? Ah
         right yes and it comes back to me.
f.   And if you don't/ if you went abroad and you could speak French
         and you'd never spoken to anybody in French for twenty-five

years you wouldn't just be able to switch if you hadn't been using it.

g. I just *adge here kokkero*, stay here alone right so other than when I go away *lena*, summer and meet a few people and *sash in* {how are you} you know,

h. and exchange one or two words with them, never really get into conversation.

The 'languageness' ambiguity that one encounters in theoretical perspective mirrors in some respects a kind of ambiguity that can be found in speakers' attitudes as well. Thus the speakers in (45)-(46) – both tradesmen based in Lancashire – are adamant that Romanes is inherently connected to work and that it is acquired by children accompanying their fathers on sales negotiations:

(45)

a. N: Me personally, I'd only use me language if I was getting me living or if I was in the conversation with somebody and I didn't want nobody to understand,

b. V: Mhm,

c. N: you know what I mean
   ((. . .))

d. If me dad was dealing with somebody and I'd talked to me father in Romanes, me dad would get upset, if it wasn't anything to do with the deal do you know what I mean.

(46)

a. Like, my children only picked it up with going out working with me, that is where they pick it up,

b. Like if I'm talking to a man, and he's a complete fool I'll say oh look at the *chuvno* {guy}, this is much as a *diddler* {fool}, let's *jel* {go}, do you know what I mean,

c. Or different things, like, you know what I mean, just like single words there's no grammar to it, it's just single words, you know what I mean, just single words,

d. But me boys are learning it from going out working with me, and that is where they are picking bits up.

Note that Hancock (1984) presents a similar picture of Angloromani as a code that is acquired in adolescence, outside the home. Alongside the realistic description of the language as consisting of 'just single words', however, as in the above example, one also encounters claims that the language can, or could in the past, be used for entire stretches of conversation, even though it is described as 'broken' – that is to say, incoherent, non-self-contained and 'intertwined' – to use Bakker's (1997) term – with English:

(47)

a.   M: It would be all broken.

b.   C: Yeh, sure but-

c.   M: It would be broken like you know, if I was with my family, my people, I could sit down, you know what I mean, you could talk away, it would just be natural,

d.   But a lot of words you don't have for things, you know what I mean.

This ambiguity – a 'broken' language consisting of single words and even lacking terms for certain concepts, on the one hand, but a 'natural' mode of conversation in the family context that people were once able to speak coherently, on the other – surfaces in other discussions of Angloromani, too. Kirk and Ó'Baoill (2002), for example, present a forum that is devoted mostly to Cant or Gammon (Shelta), as used by Irish and Scottish Travellers. The volume includes a documentation of speakers' attitudes towards their language, and among them are speakers of Angloromani. The views taken there also appear contradictory: some speakers claim that the language is used only as a secret code in the presence of group-outsiders, while others claim to have entire conversations in it.

The ambiguity no doubt rests in part on an existing tradition that is conscious of a lost language, as indicated above. This issue is highly controversial especially among a circle of ethnographers specialising in Romani/Gypsy cultures, who question whether Gypsy communities have historical collective memory, and on that basis go on to question whether they constitute a 'nation' or an 'ethnicity'. Various arguments in this or a similar direction can be found in the works of Okely (1983), Stewart (1995), Gay-y-Blasco (1999), Lemon (2000) and others. At least with respect to language, there is certainly among the English and Welsh (Romani) Gypsies a collective memory of loss of language as a cultural asset, and so of an erosion of culture and distinctiveness. In part, we can assume that the feeling of loss is also gauged by the comparison with other ethnic minorities who do have their own fully fledged language, and specifically with the Roms of central and eastern Europe, who are regarded as a related population that have managed to preserve their language and traditions better than the English Gypsies have done. From this stems the need to try and portray a 'normalised' state of affairs in what concerns language; in other words, to 'perform' a form of language that has or pretends to have the qualities, functions and characteristics of a 'full' (i.e. not 'broken') everyday community language. Consider the following excerpt from a speaker based in Leicestershire:

(48)

a.   I was supposed to lel some luvva back to the varda but it was no kushti so i couldn't jel the luvva,

b.   The mush kept the luvva and mandi jelled back with niksis.

a.   I was supposed to take some money back to the trailer but it was no
      good so I couldn't bring the money,
b.   The man kept the money and I went back with nothing.

The example is consistent with the use of common Angloromani expressions
and word forms, but compared to the examples cited earlier in this chapter
and in the preceding chapter, it is quite obvious that the emotional key that
normally accompanies Romani word insertions is missing. Contrasting with
the engaged mode of typical speech acts that contain Romani insertions,
this excerpt comes across as a neutral descriptive report. Indeed, its purpose
is merely to illustrate the speaker's competence in Romani. It succeeds in
replicating Romani material on the formal-structural side, but not on the
conversation-functional side.

      Some speakers even go further than this in an attempt to forge for them-
selves and for others an image of a language that is not 'broken' or incoherent, as other speakers described it in the quotations above, but self-contained
and coherent to the highest possible degree. The following is from a speaker
who descends from a Welsh Romani family and who appears to have
exceptionally extensive familiarity with some conservative Welsh Romani
forms. Addressing the occasion of a visit by two members of the Manchester
research team, the speaker makes an effort to speak in a form of Romani that
might have been referred to in earlier scholarship as 'deep' or reminiscent of
the 'old' dialect:

(49)
a.   Shom sor tatcheni rumnichels rokkerbun, rokkerin' gawdja raklis,
b.   They've jassed avri from bori gav Manchester,
c.   beshin' akai mandi's varda shunnin' rumnichel's rokkerbun.
d.   This is sor tatcheni rumnichel's rokkerbun,
e.   Not waffadi rokkerbun - raklis doesn't jin the difference

a.   I am how real Romanichals speech, speakin' [to] non-Gypsy girls,
b.   They've come out from [the] big town Manchester,
c.   sittin' here [in] my trailer listenin' Romanichal's speech.
d.   This is how real Romanichal's speech,
e.   Not wrong speech – [the] girls don't know the difference.

In fact, this is not inflected Romani, and the effect that is rendered via the
English translation pretty much conveys the genuine impression given by the
original as far as grammatical coherence and consistency is concerned. But
this sample is also quite different from the usual forms of Angloromani that
one encounters in the community. For a start, it is, once again, emblematic of

the speaker's competence in and feelings towards the language itself, rather than emotive in the sense that it might employ Romani insertions in order to support the flagging of loyalty to values and norms, or pragmatic in the sense that it might support the internal organisation of discourse and the high-lighting of turning points, quotations, taboos and the like. Structurally, it is organised in such a way as to avoid as far as possible an English grammatical framework, with the outcome that most phrases in fact lack an organised and coherent grammatical framework altogether, for there is no inflected Romani morphosyntax to compensate for the English structures that have been left out.

The speaker begins with two archaisms: the inflected form of the British Romani copula *shom* 'I am' and the conjunction *sor* 'how'. But the con-stituents of the first sentence are put together through mere juxtaposition. In the second utterance the speaker resorts to English morphosyntax, but note the exceptional form of *jassed* 'come, arrived, gone', which uses as its base the historical 2sg. inflected form *džas* rather than the more common 3sg. *džal* (*jalled*). Note that the speaker is making an effort to rely on Romani verbs throughout, but in fact he is (not surprisingly) unable to form any predications in Romani. The conjunction *sor* is repeated again in the follow-ing utterance (segment d).

This entire effort to convey a sample of supposedly 'genuine' Romani is of course flagged not just in the selection of words and the organisation of phrases, but also in the content of the excerpt itself: the speaker goes as far as to claim that this, unlike other forms of Romani that one hears, is a coherent sample of the 'old' language, or as near to it as one can get.

This brings us to the prestige that is associated with knowing Romani. The images of ancestors or living elderly relatives who are 'fluent' in Romanes are communicated by members of the community not just for information's sake, but also with some admiration and envy: those whose command of the language is thought to be firmer naturally have an advantage if and when they are required to conceal messages from bystanders. But it is their repertoire as such that lends them prestige, along with the fact that they are held to be more consistent in their culture and that this, in turn, gives them a reason to feel proud and self-confident. Conversely, the image of a 'broken' language is associated with the self-image of a broken nation that has lost an important part of its identity. Re-affirming one's commitment to language both privately and in public is a way of gaining respect and so of accumulat-ing social capital in the recent context of an identity-revivalist trend.

The trend has been around since the late 1960s and the beginning of politi-cal campaigns to defend the rights of Gypsies and Travellers – campaigns which in the UK were preoccupied mainly with the right to be allocated stopping opportunities along with associated services at protected caravan sites (see Kenrick & Clark 1999: 84ff, Evans 1999: 118ff). Acton and Davies (1979: 101) cite an essay written by a Gypsy child in a state school in 1976. The essay describes Appleby fair, and makes use of numerous Romani terms such as *vardo* 'waggon', *grais* 'horses', *kitchema* 'pub', *raklis* 'women', *mushes* 'men', *jiv* 'to live', *kin* 'to buy', *gilly* 'to sing', *drom* 'road' and many more. This dense use of Romani expressions is clearly a manifestation of the child's self-confidence in openly displaying her family's cultural heritage.

Two generations on, overt displays and discussions of Romani identity are now inspired by an established transnational network of Romani activists throughout Europe, by numerous websites and other communication outlets and by regular events and conferences devoted to issues of Romani status and identity. Shared flagging of Romani identity has even become a feature of social networking among strangers of Romani background, much of it on the internet, and language plays a vital role in this display as a badge of authenticity and overall loyalty to one's origins and identity (rather than to any particular set of traditional values). The following are excerpts from an online moderated message board set up by the BBC in Kent in 2005, with the original intention of eliciting readers' and radio-listeners' queries and comments on the content of various Romani-related features. As can be seen from the excerpt, the list soon took on the function of a social forum. The list appears to have been shut down in 2008, though at the time of writing it was still being archived online with no restrictions on access. Several other sites operate social forums that target an international audience of Romani people – some in English, others in Romani or in various other languages. The BBC Kent list appears to have attracted exclusively English and Welsh Gypsies. The selected examples are presented in their original sequence of appearance, codenamed for author and date and numbered sequentially (181–283) as they appear on the website; some messages were omitted since their content was not of interest to the present study:

(50)
(http://www.bbc.co.uk/dna/england/F2770282?thread=1370341)
Message 181 - posted by ggf, 7 November 2005
wot did you saye *rownie* {lady} say it agen
Message 183 - posted by Rawnie_Rommi, 7 November 2005
Tobias translated it beautifully . . . so it may save the moderator looking in the Romani *lil* {book} to figure out what its saying!
Message 186 - posted by Tobias_nevowesh, 7 November, 2005
Mind you, most of today's *chavvies* {boys} have trouble with English, or so it seems
Complain about a message
Message 187 - posted by Rawnie_Rommi, 7 November 2005
Tatcho {correct}, and its a shame too. Most leave school at 11, which I also feel is a shame. (This may be the start of a whole new debate now!)
Message 191 - posted by Tobias_nevowesh, 7 November 2005
See you later *bang* {devil}, it was *Kushti* to *rokka* with you *mush* {it was good to talk with you man}

Message 197 - posted by xxMaryxxKentxx, 7 November 2005
Cori sherros {dick head} let them censor that LOL
Message 198 - posted by Rawnie_Rommi, 7 November 2005
LOL!
Well I suppose I'd better go sort out some *hobben* {food} now! See ya later Tobias, and thanx again biggrin
Message 201 - posted by Tobias_nevowesh, 7 November 2005
What yer havin'??? *hotchi witchi* {roasted hedgehog}??? LOL
Message 202 - posted by xxMaryxxKentxx, 7 November 2005
Hello Risha im ok thx m8 im still evil tho steam
hoes you i can see uv ad a rite laugh im gutted i missed it
Message 203 - posted by Tobias_nevowesh, 7 November 2005
What you evil about??? I'm ready for a *cor* {fight}!!!!
Message 206 - posted by xxMaryxxKentxx, 7 November 2005
Hello Tobias im evil coz me boy got dashed up the other nite by 4, 5
chavvies {boys} hes alrite he ad a fight with 2 of em but there was to many 4
of em kicked him in the head. im tryin to find out who thay r
Message 208 - posted by Tobias_nevowesh, 7 November 2005
Sorry to hear that, how old is your *chavvo* {boy}?
Message 212 - posted by Tobias_nevowesh, 7 November 2005
I bin *corrin'* {fightin'} all my life and it don't do you any good. It seems
today's *chavvo* {boy} can only *ruk* in a group. pick em off one by one, no
sorry, don't listen to me, he'll end up in *stir* {jail}!!! LOL
Message 228 - posted by Rawnie_Rommi, 7 November 2005
I totally understand Mary, when someone hurts your kids its worse than
them hurting you, and hard to let it go.
Enjoy your *hobben* {food} and we'll *chin* {write} again later! xxx
Message 233 - posted by ggf, 8 November 2005
hi hay how you doing kan i ask ar you a *mush* {man} or *rakly* {woman} no
offens
Message 235 - posted by ggf, 8 November 2005
hi tammy im a *mush* {man} last time i looked lol cant say my name to
trashed {scared} . . .
Message 278 - posted by TillyLSurrey, 8 November 2005
alright all i'm back. Mary you know what our problem is we are *div's*
{crazy}. If it happened the other way around we'd all be looked up!!
There's this *divvness* {craziness} ammoungst us not to be *gavvers* {not to
hide}. The way i see it , that would be the best thing to do with em. One
carn't do nothing against two or three let alone that many little *sovvers*
{fuckers}!!
Message 281 - posted by TillyLSurrey, 8 November 2005
hello *phen* {sister} how was ya day out?
Message 283 - posted by Rawnie_Rommi, 8 November 2005
That's *tatcho* {correct} Tilly I agree with you there!

As far as one can tell, the users display an 'authentic' knowledge of Angloromani, i.e. one that was acquired in a family context. This is apparent through the makeshift system of writing Romani words as well as their semantics and context of use. The density of Romani insertions and the selection of expressions very much resemble the patterns described above for oral usage, and indeed serve as an illustration of the manner in which computer-mediated written communication replicates orality. At the same time the forum itself is one that attracts and facilitates communication among strangers, a setting that is rather untypical of Angloromani oral usage. This gives the Angloromani insertions added value, or, from the reverse perspective, motivates the insertion of Romani items in the first place: they serve as tokens of solidarity and shared destiny and interests among strangers who, on the basis of their shared self-identification as Romanies, are seeking bonds with one another despite the fact that they are strangers. Romani insertions are thus a demonstration of an emotional and ideological state of mind and of individuals' need to display and celebrate publicly their pride in their Romani identity and ancestry.

Note that alongside the general pattern, which is to spell Romani words in an ad hoc and improvised fashion, Message 281 in the sequence replicated in example (50) begins with the words 'hello *phen*' meaning 'hello sister'. The transliteration *phen* is replicated from academic conventions of writing Romani, where consonant aspiration is indicated by the double grapheme {ph} etc. This system is also used in various popular initiatives for writing Romani in central and eastern Europe. It appears that the author has had some exposure either to academic materials on the Romani language or else to materials written in the inflected language in the context of continental European initiatives. We thus have some indication of a link between use of Angloromani in a new, public electronic forum, and interest in written forms of inflected European Romani used in media produced in other countries.

This kind of active interest in European, inflected Romani is partly also documented in our corpus of interviews. A number of speakers produced inflected forms such as *miro* 'my', *mansa* 'with me', lexical items such as *mišto* 'good', *lačhes* 'well', and European loanwords such as *časo* 'hour' and *vorba* 'talk' that have no roots in British Romani and have clearly been adopted through contacts with speakers of European dialects of Romani. (These forms were not taken into account in the compilation of the Angloromani dictionary and usage statistics.) All speakers who used these forms have had contacts with Romani immigrants from eastern Europe, and some have travelled abroad and visited Romani-speaking communities there. The following example is from a speaker who travelled widely and has had occasional contacts with speakers of inflected Romani dialects for over twenty years. During the interview he demonstrates his knowledge of Romanes:

(51)

a. Boot besh palpali, mandi a bitti chavvi, miro mamma, miro dadda, bootey the rushni,
b. Mamma she jal mongipen, dukrapen the gadjo,
c. Dad, kel chi, chichi, chi, miro dad, boot mato,
d. del pogger mandi mama, kek mishto mush, miro dad

a. Many year back, I [was] a little boy, my mum, my dad, work the flower,
b. Mum she go begging, fortune-telling the non-Gypsy,
c. Father, do nothing, nothing, nothing, my father, a lot drunk,
d. gives break me mum, not good man, my father.

Although this is not a sample of any grammatical form of inflected Romani, it is not consistently Angloromani, either. For a start, the speaker makes an effort to use only Romani words. Furthermore, he tries to avoid the use of English verb inflection. Unable to use proper Romani inflection, he either leaves out the verb – 'I [was] a little boy' – or employs nouns and nominalisations – *bootey the rushni* 'work the flower' = 'made a living by selling flowers' – or combines those with a verb root in Angloromani that represents fossilised inflection – *she jal mongipen, dukrapen* 'she went begging, fortune-telling', *del pogger mandi mama* 'gives break (= beat) me mum'. Finally, the speaker adopts words like *miro* 'my' and *mishto* 'good' that are not part of the inherited Angloromani stock but were acquired in interactions with European Roms.

This trend towards enriching the Angloromani vocabulary through European Romani is gaining legitimacy even in documentary material devoted to English Romanes. Hayward (2003: 111), for instance, in his dictionary of what he calls the *Gypsy Jib*, inserts under the English entry 'to have' the comment that "possession is expressed by the verb to be, e.g. Si man ker meaning (there) is to me a house, or I have a house"; though this type of construction is absent from contemporary English Romanes and is found only in the inflected Romani dialects of the European continent. Hayward, much like our speaker in (51), provides himself with a licence to enrich English Romanes with relevant expressions from European Romani, revealing a language ideology that favours a symbiosis of the two and looks to European Romani as a potential source of enrichment, both structural and functional, of the Angloromani used by English Gypsies.

5.5 The prospects of a 'language revival'

The quest to regain the lost language is a recurring theme in discussion forums devoted to English Romani culture. Consider the following selection of readers' comments posted on the BBC's 'Voices' website in reaction to a contribution by the author on Angloromani, in 2006 (http://www.bbc.co.uk/voices/multilingual/romani.shtml):

(52)

a. Jan Kurpiel katar {from} Sheffield
    Hiya. I am trying to learn as much of the language as possible, so
    that i can pass it on to my children in the future. It's great being able
    to communitcate with Romanes from all over the world and i would
    recommend learning it to anyone.
b. Len Smith from New Forest
    [. . .] Those of us who speak the jib {language}, very much encourage its
    use, and would be happy to see a joint effort with speakers of Eastern
    European Romani dialects, to repair our dialect where it is wearing
    somewhat thin.
c. Bryn Heron, Northampton
    My Puri dai {grandmother} and the Rom spoke the pure, inflected chib
    {language}. Their grandchildren, me included, have only the pogerdi
    chib {broken language}, now. I married away from the kawlo rattee
    {black breed}, a gawji {non-Gypsy} whom I love to this day. Apart
    from my grandparents, I have never heard the pure chib {language}
    spoken I agree with Jacqueline, though – if you want the pukkered
    chib {spoken language}, go to the kawlo ratte {black breed}, not the
    Romanes Rai or Rawnee {Romani gentleman or lady}.

Both the mere notion of speaking consistent or coherent Romanes, and the adoption of Romani expressions from continental dialects, are products of the exposure to European inflected varieties of Romani and an identification among British Romani Gypsies with this form of speech as representing something that is perceived as more authentic and original, something that is close to the ancestral language that is regarded as 'lost', and something that one would like to acquire and be able to display as one's own.

Encounters with speakers of inflected Romani varieties will have taken place for generations, since English Gypsies occasionally travelled to Germany and France. It is also known that Romani-speaking families from the continent travelled through England and Kelderash families (of central European background, originating in Transylvania) even settled in the London area. But the beginnings of a trend towards trying to acquire inflected Romani seem to go back to the early beginnings of the Gypsy evangelical missionary movement in Britain, in the late 1970s. During this period, an English-speaking missionary couple was sent to Britain from France by Pastor Jean Le Cossec, the founder of an evangelical mission that operated among Gypsies in France and Spain. Their task was to try and spread their version of Christianity specifically among British Gypsies. Le Cossec's work had begun in Normandy in the 1950s as a mere attempt to support a small number of Romani families and to bring them closer to his church. His success in integrating a growing number of Romani families alienated the church establishment, and he was given the choice between abandoning his activities among the Gypsies and leaving his post. He opted for the latter, and established the 'Vie et Lumière' Gypsy mission.

By the late 1970s the church had many thousands of followers in France, and became closely affiliated with Romani evangelist movements operating in Spain, where it was called the 'Philadelphia Church' (see Williams 1991, Gay-y-Blasco 2000), and in the United States. Its scope of activities covered huge outdoor conventions to which members and interested non-members arrived in trailers, camping for several days; a Bible college and church buildings where services were held exclusively for Gypsies; and printed material in the form of videos and audio CDs with religious content and religious music, much of it in various dialects of Romani. It also offered individuals opportunities to become active and to rise within its ranks in a fairly informal way.

Le Cossec himself visited Britain in 1979 and met extensively with Romani families around the country. Among them was a charismatic young English Gypsy man who had been interested in Bible studies before the encounter with Le Cossec, and had also learned French and so was able to communicate directly with the French pastor when he arrived in Britain. A small circle of followers gradually emerged, attributing their new conviction to a series of 'miracles' that they had experienced. Through frequent participation in international missionary conventions in France in the early 1980s some of them began to learn European dialects of Romani. They were inspired by Matheo Maximoff, a Kelderash Romani author based in Paris who in this period translated the Gospels into Romani. These people also made contact with Kelderash Romani followers of the missionary movement in London and asked for support in learning their dialect of Romani. By the late 1980s, the Light and Life mission in England had several thousand followers and began collecting funds from its own members in order to buy buildings and open its own churches. The movement's leadership continued to maintain very close ties with its sister organisations, especially in France but also in other countries. To the activists it became clear that they were involved not just in what they regarded as a religious 'revival', but also in a new form of organising their people as a people, culturally, and creating a momentum of cultural unity among Romani people across state boundaries.

To many new followers of the Light and Life movement, the attraction was thus manifold. Firstly, the new church offered an experience of religion that was personal, spiritual and emotional, rather than intellectual. Next, it offered this experience in the familiar setting of the Romani community, adapting to its values and structures rather than demanding that individuals should integrate and accommodate to new rules and ways. While imposing some constraints on the traditional lifestyle, such as a ban on alcohol and tobacco as well as on fortune-telling, which had been an important source of income to traditional Romani families in Britain, the Gypsy church welcomed entire families, offered an open style of community worship that allowed people to enter and exit the hall as they pleased, and organised much of its missionary work around outdoor conventions that took on a shape similar to traditional Gypsy fairs. Its leadership was not overtly hierarchical, but emphasised engagement at the local level and offered individuals who showed commitment opportunities to take on further responsibility without any formal training procedure. In flagging links with other Romani communities abroad, the evangelical mission gave its followers an opportunity to experience their culture in an institutionalised context and to gain the self-confidence of a transnational people with an old and firm tradition. The Romani language became one of the symbols of this tradition, and knowing more Romani became prestigious in a new, institutionalised context.

The political transition in eastern Europe in 1990 gave the missionary movement a new momentum. The church's leadership recognised the opportunity to expand into Romani communities in central and eastern Europe. These communities now acquired freedom of association and could entertain missionary visits, organise conventions, take on donations and raise and administer their own funds. At the same time they became desperate for support because of ideological confusion, growing economic hardships, and a new wave of overt hostility and social exclusion directed against them. In Britain, as in other western countries, the Gypsy missionary movement began to organise visits to Romani communities in central and eastern Europe in an attempt to gain followers. These trips were accompanied by the circulation of audio CDs with religious music in Romani and of videos depicting the life of Jesus and other biblical episodes with a voiceover in various Romani dialects. Many of these CDs and videos were produced in situ in central and eastern Europe with funds and technical support from sources such as the Wycliffe foundation for Bible translation and other US-based evangelical organisations.

In this new context, basic conversational knowledge of European Romani became an important skill that enabled UK-based church activists to join missionary trips abroad. Within the subtle hierarchy of the movement, participation in missionary activity abroad and absence from family and work for this purpose were rewarded both in the form of promotions through the ranks of internal distribution of responsibilities within the movement, and in the form of compensation for 'loss of earning', which itself of course constituted a new form of earning. Knowing Romani has thus become a skill that is directly linked to career opportunities.

From the mid-1990s Romani immigrants started arriving in the UK from central and eastern Europe, first as asylum-seekers from Poland, the Czech and Slovak Republics and Romania, then eventually, following the first round of EU accession in 2004, as immigrants from Poland, Lithuania,

Slovakia and the Czech Republic, and in 2007 also from Romania. Their arrival created a new incentive among English Gypsies to acquire some conversational competence in an inflected form of Romani. For a start, many Romani immigrants found part-time employment working for English Gypsies in various services, from road construction to gardening and more. A bond of mutual trust was formed that enabled and encouraged such working relationships. Since the immigrants spoke little or no English, many English Gypsies found themselves relying on their own Romani vocabulary but limited in not being able to use it to construct whole sentences. A quite exceptional situation arose in which the 'local' English Gypsies had the home advantage with all its social and economic implications, but the immigrants enjoyed the prestige of having kept their language. A fashion emerged among many English Gypsy employers who began to imitate or even acquire the immigrants' Romani dialects.

For the missionary movement, too, the arrival of Romani immigrants became a challenge. The church opened its doors to the immigrants, and these often attended its meetings in large numbers, if for no other reason than to have a point of contact for meeting local people and setting up local networks. Church activists had a new incentive to learn to communicate with newcomers in order to integrate them into the congregation. By 2000, churches in Birmingham and London were offering Sunday meetings in Romani for Romani immigrants. Informal language classes were offered on Sundays and on weekdays in the afternoon for English Gypsies, mostly church activists, who wanted to strengthen their knowledge of European Romani. As a basis, the Kelderash Romani dialect was used, which is spoken both in numerous urban diasporas in western and eastern Europe and in the Americas, and by immigrants from Romania and Hungary. Many of the church activists became familiar with Kelderash through their contacts in France and the US, and competent Romani immigrants from Romania were selected to teach the courses. By 2002–3, the movement was operating several churches in the Midlands and the Northwest that offered services in Romani. At first, these meetings were held by local, English Gypsy preachers who had acquired a basic knowledge of European Romani. Gradually, as congregations grew and as the religious movement gained momentum in central and eastern Europe and recruited local clergy in those countries, Romani-speaking preachers were engaged from the countries of origin.

Immigration and the expansion of the Gypsy evangelical movement contributed to the rise in interest in European Romani among English Gypsies. The first created opportunities to meet speakers and to learn and use the language. The second contributed to the process of learning. As the church grew, new followers were confronted with role models – persons in positions of authority within the movement – who had some knowledge of European Romani, who encouraged the process of learning, and who could even offer career advancement prospects to those who became active in preaching (or 'witnessing', as the procedure is called internally) to others, especially through missions to Romani communities abroad. The momentum created by the church combines a spiritual revivalism with a strong and institutional framework with effective organisation structures, audiovisual resources and energetic networking activities, all of which revolve around a sense of belonging to a transnational, self-confident Romani identity. This momentum did not, of course, by-pass even those members of the English Gypsy community who have not become followers of the church.

From 1999, when it was first advertised that research on Romani linguistics was being carried out at the University of Manchester and that a course unit in Romani linguistics was offered there, the author began receiving phone calls from individual Gypsies from different parts of the country asking for support and personal guidance on learning European Romani. Many emphasised that they were able to use much of the vocabulary they had acquired at home to communicate with Roma from eastern Europe, but that they lacked the grammar necessary to speak in proper sentences. Some calls came from individuals who were not involved in any way in religious work, but who admitted that the interests that the born-again Christians were taking in the Romani language had given them the courage to do the same, explaining that the act of looking up books in the library or contacting a university professor was otherwise regarded as a '*gawdja* thing to do', hence inappropriate for a 'true' Gypsy. Many callers were directly associated with the church, and requested help in setting up structures to teach European Romani to their fellow congregation members as well as to their children. In response to one of these requests, a two-hour audio recording was produced in 2001 that provided sentence examples in several different Romani dialects, surveying all areas of grammar in a systematic and exhaustive manner but using the plainest and simplest terms to explain and define the rules. The recording was sent to several people on a CD. Within a few weeks it was reproduced by the Light and Life mission and distributed in several thousand copies at its conventions, while requests for copies continued to arrive at the University's Romani Project office for several years. The idea of a medium of this kind was then replicated by several English Gypsy church activists who had gained a fairly good knowledge of a European Romani dialect, usually Kelderash; they produced their own recordings, which were also circulated widely.

The exact number of individuals who have in the past few years acquired a relatively good knowledge of inflected Romani is difficult to estimate; it is possible that it is somewhere between fifty and one hundred. In a community of possibly up to 20,000 or more – there are no reliable figures about the size of the Romani community in Britain – this does not seem like a significant number. But in the context of local leadership, role models and fashions, it does point to a trend. The number of people exposed to the use of inflected Romani in public gatherings, the rising popularity of Romani-language religious music, and the production and scale of distribution of learning resources for Romani all indicate that the trend is widespread.

It is therefore worthwhile to conclude with some observations on the nature of the process. For the moment it might be too early to speak of an organised revitalisation effort affecting the entire Romani Gypsy community. But the fact that a revitalisation of the language is taking place among individuals and their close networks of family and friends is undeniable. The term 'revitalisation' is justified for two main reasons. Firstly, the enthusiasm towards European dialects of Romani is fuelled by the notion of a gap that exists within the community and by the awareness, alluded to above, of a 'lost' language. The accessibility of European Romani dialects is seen as an opportunity to fill this gap and in this way also to strengthen self-confidence and elevate the position of the Romani Gypsies in Britain from its prevailing image as a 'Travelling population' to what is regarded as a 'genuine' minority that can take pride in its own language. Secondly, despite the differences between the present-day Angloromani lexicon that is in use among English Gypsies and the various inflected dialects of European Romani that are the target of acquisition and imitation, speakers are confident about the close affinity between the two, and many are happy and eager to be able to identify with the European dialects as 'their' language. This process takes place not without discussion; some individuals within the English Gypsy community have expressed scepticism towards learning the European varieties and called for a revival of their own 'English Romanes'. But these calls are usually rejected as impractical. Those people who are engaged in the effort see themselves as learning a language that is close enough to the lexicon used in their homes to be able to embrace it as their own. In this regard they view the adoption of European Romani dialects as a renewal of the Romani language that had been lost in Britain.

Thirdly, while there is no evidence as yet that English Gypsies are adopting European Romani as their family language, the numbers of Romani-speaking immigrants from eastern Europe have been rising during the period between 1995 and 2010, and at the time of writing some observers were claiming that the number of immigrants reached or even surpassed that of the local English Gypsies. This is not implausible. In the Greater Manchester area alone, a population of no fewer than 3,000 individuals of eastern European Romani background was known to the author at the time of writing from first-hand encounters. This population is subdivided into clusters of extended families. The typical size of an extended family is between 100 and 150 individuals; clusters of up to 400–500 individuals, comprising anywhere between one and five extended families, all originating from the same location in eastern Europe, usually take up residence in the same or adjoining streets in one of the districts in the area. Groups of Roma in the Manchester area include, at the time of writing, family clans from (the EU countries of) Romania, Slovakia, the Czech Republic, Hungary, Poland, Lithuania and Latvia, with some nuclear families from Macedonia on a visitors' visa trying to obtain a more permanent residence status. There is no doubt that in other areas of the country, most notably London and Birmingham, the numbers of Romani immigrants are significantly higher. Overall, then, it is certainly possible that in 2010 the number of immigrant Romani speakers in Britain may reach or even exceed 20,000. Given even some degree of interface and immersion between this immigrant community and the community of English Gypsies, and the strong sense of the latter's identification with the language as representing their own cultural heritage, it is clear how Romani can make an impact even as a second community language.

A remarkable feature of the 'language revival' process is that it is not one that is centrally planned or that involves the participation of any major institutions, either within or external to the community. The Traveller Education Services – a national network of support services under the direction of the educational authorities of individual counties, but which also fall under the responsibility of the Ethnic Minorities Achievement Unit in the government Department for Children, Schools and Families (DCSF) – have produced many publications in which the existence and use of Angloromani as a kind of community language is acknowledged. These publications even include workbooks that support the acquisition of literacy and contain Romani words, evidently in an attempt to help Gypsy children identify with school content, and other materials in which Romani words are employed in narratives and headings. The DCSF also supported the production of a series of audiovisual learning materials on Romani by the Romani Project at the University of Manchester, in 2007–9. There is in addition a wide range of private publications that deal with Romani life and folklore and which document Angloromani in various ways. All of these have certainly contributed to maintaining an awareness of Romani, while the materials produced by the Manchester Romani Project were the only ones that explicitly promoted awareness of European Romani and its links with Angloromani. None the less, none of these materials has, to our knowledge, served so far either as the basis for a coherent curriculum for the teaching and learning of Romani, or as an agenda for a language revival programme.

Instead, revitalisation is driven in the first instance by the personal motivation of individuals to be able to interact with Romani speakers from the European continent; the process of revitalisation of Romani in Britain is thus the sum of these individual learning processes. It is true that many individuals' motivation is also inspired by the direction and the personal role models provided by a number of persons who constitute the leadership of the evangelical movement, and that some 'career' opportunities within the movement are informally linked with individuals' ability to succeed in forging links with European Roma communities, and so with their language skills. Nevertheless, the acquisition of Romani is not the outcome of any formal decision taken by an institution, and appointments or responsibilities within the church are not linked explicitly to language skills. Learning Romani, and so the revitalisation of Romani in the community context, remains a bottom-up process that is set in motion by the will and initiative of individuals, and in which institutional support is merely a secondary factor. One is reminded somewhat of Nahir's (1998) conclusions concerning the revival of Hebrew (arguably the only genuinely successful case of language revitalisation) and its strong dependency not so much on the official policies of institutions in the domains of education, broadcasting and so forth, but on the practical choices that (potential) speakers had to make when interacting with one another; the success of Hebrew revitalisation was, accordingly, due to the fact that it successfully assumed the role of a lingua franca among persons of various linguistic backgrounds, in addition to its institutional role and prestige.

This role of a practical necessity, rewarded by successful communication, is what motivates English Gypsies to learn and to use European Romani. This also means that, inevitably, the 'community' of speakers of European Romani is likely to remain contained. Interactions with Romani people abroad remain limited to a small number of people within the community, and even interactions with immigrant Roma in England are not sufficiently widespread to motivate the adoption of inflected Romani as a longer-term lingua franca; second generation immigrants are very likely to opt for English when communicating with English Gypsies. And of course neither domain affects family communication among English Gypsies. But this is precisely where another key factor in Nahir's (1998) analysis of Hebrew revival enters the picture, namely language ideology and its adoption by individuals. Those English Gypsies who are now making efforts to record European Romani phrases and to teach them to their children are doing so out of a conviction that they are reinstating part of a lost cultural heritage. This view may be supported and inspired by the missionary movement, but it is not being imposed by any institution. The need for practical communication with immigrant Roma, and the emotional value attached to the language, both combine to produce a bottom-up, individual motivation for engaging in the process of active language learning.

This brings us to a further feature of the process, and that is the motivation to engage in what is, at least to some extent, an intellectual procedure of learning for the sake of knowledge, rather than acquiring experience in practical, real-life situations. While the procedures of learning European Romani are largely non-guided and non-institutional, making use of interaction opportunities and a minimum of learning resources, mainly in the form of semi-formal audio guides, they are none the less clearly procedures that are reminiscent of school-like, intellectual learning – precisely the kind of activity that most Romani people would regard as a '*gawdja* thing to do'. This is not to deny in any way that there are many among the English Gypsies who do pursue 'intellectual' careers and who train, read and acquire skills in formal and institutional contexts. Some of those may also be engaged in learning inflected Romani. But the point I am making here is that the motivation for engaging in a learning activity extends to those who do not otherwise typically embrace such opportunities. To be sure, the church has played a role here too in inspiring intellectual learning in the form of Bible reading sessions and study sessions. The revival, however contained, of Romani in the English Gypsy community brings with it changes in attitudes and practices, and a licence to engage in new kinds of cultural activities.

Finally, this bottom-up process of language propagation is also pluralistic in its choice of target variety. A number of English Gypsies, in particular among the missionary movement's leaders, have had some exposure to Kelderash thanks to their links with urban missions in France and the United States, where there is a high presence of speakers of Kelderash and related varieties. Immigration of Kelderash-speaking Roma from Romania has reinforced the interest in this particular dialect of Romani, as have the numerous CDs with religious music that have Kelderash Romani texts. At the same time, those English Gypsies who have come into contact with speakers of Baltic Romani dialects or Central European dialects such as Slovak Romani have noticed the greater similarity between many forms in these dialects and their Angloromani counterparts. These people have also developed a practical curiosity towards other dialects, and the same goal – to be able to communicate effectively with speakers of other dialects – motivates them to learn various forms of inflected Romani. It is noteworthy that many of the religious video productions circulated in Romani among members of the evangelical movement have versions in several dialects. To the extent that language planning takes place within missionary institutions, it thus favours pluralism and a direct approach to communities in their own variety of Romani over any kind of uniformity or standardisation of the language. This approach is very much in line with the overall trend in the codification of Romani, which gives some advantage, often just numerical, to the Vlax dialects of southeastern Europe, among them Kelderash, but which is essentially pluralistic in the choice of variety and pragmatic in the choice of mode of codification.

6 Conclusions: The Decline, Death and Afterlife of a Language

Opinions are split as to what constitutes the most appropriate format for describing Para-Romani varieties. The more traditional mode of documenting them has been in the form of a dictionary or word list, perhaps accompanied by some example phrases indicating the manner in which words are embedded structurally in sentences in the mainstream or 'host' language. Others have attempted to write proper reference grammars of Para-Romani varieties, emphasising both the presence of creative word formation strategies and some features that differ from the typical structures of the host language (see Ladefoged 1998, Carling's contribution to Lindell & Thorbjörnsson-Djerf 2008). In a brief contribution to the BBC's online language documentation programme *Voices*, published in 2006 (http://www.bbc.co.uk/voices/), I referred to Angloromani as a 'phenomenon' that involved the use of Romani-derived lexicon in an English conversation framework. At least one reader was apparently irritated by my use of the term 'phenomenon' and posted a comment on the website emphasising that "Far from being a "phenomenon" the language is alive and well > I wish the BBC had asked a British Traveller for a view and they would have got it from the Gry's mui {the horse's mouth}" ('Jacqueline from Suffolk', http://www.bbc.co.uk/voices/multilingual/romani.shtml; last accessed December 2009).

The fact is that neither a grammatical sketch nor a list of lexical items can adequately cover the intricate usage conventions and functions of contemporary Angloromani, nor, most likely, those of other Para-Romani varieties. In the case of Romani in Britain we are fortunate to have both a corpus of text material documenting the historical stages of the language, and a community of speakers willing to share their time and reflections to help document its present-day usage. This combination has made it possible to review Angloromani in its historical and present-day sociolinguistic and discourse context, in addition to taking stock of its structures and lexical composition. In this concluding chapter I review the main findings of this investigation and their relevance to a general appreciation of key questions in the fields of language contact, language death, and the formation of mixed languages and of in-group or special lexicons.

6.1 The historical decline of inflected Romani

The survey of earlier documentation of Romani in Britain leaves no room for doubt that the variety known to us today as 'Angloromani' descends from an inflected dialect of Romani that was spoken in England up to the mid-nineteenth century and perhaps even a generation or two later. This dialect was closely related to the Welsh Romani dialect documented by Sampson (1926b), which continued to survive, retaining even more of the conservative features shared with the continental dialects of European Romani, until the late nineteenth century and perhaps even a generation later. The similarities between the two dialects, the English and Welsh, in a series of internal innovations, even disregarding those that are the outcome of contact with English, are beyond coincidence and point to the existence of a shared forerunner speech variety, which we have termed 'British Romani'. The latter was situated both geographically and structurally at the far end of a continuum of Romani dialects stretching from the southern Balkans westwards. The varieties most closely related to it were also its nearest geographical neighbours: Swedish Romani and German Romani, and to a somewhat lesser extent Finnish Romani. More remote connections can be established with the Romani dialects of the Baltic regions, while some features were shared even more widely with the Romani dialects of northern and central Europe, i.e. those situated north of the so-called Great Divide (Matras 2005) – the historical border area between the Habsburg and Ottoman Empires, which hosts a dense cluster of isoglosses dividing the Romani dialectal landscape. This position in the dialect continuum excludes the possibility that British Romani was the speech form of a population that arrived directly from the Balkans during a period after the initial Romani settlement in northern Europe in the fifteenth century. Structural features that happen to be shared by British Romani and the Romani dialects of southeastern Europe but are not common elsewhere are invariably archaisms inherited directly from Early Romani: the demonstratives *okova* and *odova*, the Greek-derived nominaliser in -*imos* and nominal endings in -*is*, -*us*, -*os*, the enclitic pronoun *lo* in non-verbal predications, and more. With respect to these and other features, British Romani constituted a retention zone or a conservative geographical periphery.

The similarities between English and Welsh Romani also suggest that both speaker populations descended from the same group or migration wave, or at the very least from two closely related groups immigrating into Britain roughly from the same areas, by a similar route. The fact that shared British Romani innovations appear consistently in present-day Angloromani vocabulary rules out the possibility that this vocabulary could have been diffused either from continental European dialects of Romani into the English speech of indigenous Travellers in Britain, as suggested by Okely (1983), or through imitation of the speech of a new wave of Romani-speaking immigrants, one that followed the decline of inflected British Romani, as hypothesised by Boretzky and Igla (1994).

Nor is there any evidence to suggest that Angloromani was formed through a process of creolisation or language simplification. In order to address this question we must focus on at least two separate issues. The first involves the possibility that Romani might have been a target language for acquisition by non-Romanies and that this acquisition process, as a second language, led to the simplification of the target language and the emergence of Angloromani. This kind of scenario was entertained as part of the hypothesis that the emergence of Angloromani was connected to the rise in intermarriage and population mixing between Romanies and indigenous English Travellers (cf. Hancock 1970). To be sure, increased immersive contact with English Travellers is likely to have contributed to the abandonment of inflected Romani and to a shift from Romani to English as the language of the community, the language of oral traditions, and subsequently also as the language of the family. In this context there is, however, no room for creolisation in the strict sense, since the language that was being adopted as a common language of the community was English and not Romani. The maintenance of Romani vocabulary as a token of identity is not a result of outsiders joining the group and acquiring Romani, but of insiders insisting on the maintenance of a group-particular form of speech, coupled with the functionality of an in-group lexicon in the social context of a tight-knit peripatetic group. Thus, population mixture was in all likelihood a key trigger for the abandonment of Romani as an everyday family language, but it did not lead to a mass acquisition of Romani or to its simplification as a target language.

The second aspect concerns cross-generation transmission of the language. Creolisation is defined as the transmission, to a young generation, of a simplified lingua franca, which is then adopted by the young generation as a native language and undergoes in most cases radical structural expansion. In the case of Angloromani, the process is quite the opposite: the older generation, which spoke inflected Romani, failed to transmit it to the younger generation. Instead, accommodating to the growing reality of population mixtures and the growing impact of English within their own community, they transmitted only Romani-derived vocabulary emdedded in English discourse, and this too not as the primary means of everyday communication, but as a specialised in-group code that accompanied the principal language of interaction, English. Thus there is no evidence for the need for, or for the existence of, a makeshift or simplified code on which speakers of different backgrounds were dependent for inter-ethnic communication, and so no basis or evidence for either pidginisation or creolisation.

The structural facts of Angloromani and the documentation of English Romani throughout its various stages also fail to provide any evidence of a sudden simplification of grammar. Instead, there is evidence of gradual erosion of certain grammatical categories as a result of a process of

convergence with English. This involved the destabilisation of the phonological system, an erosion of the system of nominal case marking and gender
and case agreement, the borrowing of a limited number of morphology
and function words (possessive endings, indefinite article, plural endings,
conjunctions, prepositions and adverbs), and influence on the structure and
form-meaning mapping in collocations, aspectual constructions and lexical
semantics. All these are fairly typical of the influence of contact languages
on individual dialects of Romani throughout Europe and the Balkans. In
English Romani, the most far-reaching effect of contact is probably to be
seen in the domain of nominal inflection, where there is considerable erosion
of synthetic case markers and their distinctive functions. This, too, is not
unprecedented, and a similar erosion of nominal case markers can be found
in the Romani dialects of southern Italy, where the process is not accompanied by any noticeable decline in language use. While we might be able to
distinguish two phases of attestation of English influence on English Romani,
before and after the beginning of the erosion of nominal inflection, as well as
the more conservative stage represented by Welsh Romani, it is important to
note that there is otherwise no evidence of a gradual increase in the impact
of grammatical borrowing, and certainly no evidence of gradual borrowing
of English inflection (in the verbal system) or of other forms that are less
likely to be borrowed, such as personal pronouns. In other words, despite
some borrowing in lexicon and grammar, the overall coherence of grammar
and lexicon in English Romani remains intact and we find no support
for Thomason's (2001) assumption of a gradual replacement of inherited
Romani grammar by English grammar, resulting, at the very end of the
process, in a form of Romani that has completely adopted English grammar.

The documented material from earlier sources does provide some evidence for the co-existence of two distinct forms of speech, both containing
Romani vocabulary: the first relying primarily on English verb inflection
('Para-Romani'), the other on Romani verbs (conservative Romani). There is
occasional mixture of the two, indicating that there might have been a transition period during which some speakers may have had both registers at their
disposal. Smart and Crofton (1875) certainly suggest this, as they attribute
some of their texts in both the 'old' and the 'new' dialect to the very same
source. Otherwise, the material testifies to a consistent use of either inflected
Romani, which preserves its inherited verb inflection, or Angloromani, in
which Romani words are inserted into English finite predications. From this
we may conclude that the transition from inflected Romani to Angloromani
was characterised by a loss of the commitment to organising the predication
consistently in Romani. This development may not have been abrupt, for
we can find evidence for the random employment of English and Romani
predications even within the same utterance. It is in fact very likely that the
transition followed the incorporation, in the first instance, of English auxiliary verbs along with their English inflection (see Chapter 3), a borrowing

procedure that is not uncommon in other dialects of Romani as well as in other languages of the world (see Matras 2009: 185–7). Such borrowings may have created a licence to include English predications in utterances produced in Romani interaction contexts, which then began to occur more frequently, though in random distribution. There is, however, as stated above, no evidence to show that there was any gradual borrowing of individual English inflectional markers to replace inherited Romani markers, and so no adoption of English grammar, but rather an emerging alternation between Romani and English predication grammar within the utterance.

This kind of development, characterised by a random preference for one language over another in the construction of the predication of the utterance, will have destabilised the grammatical system in interaction contexts hitherto defined as 'Romani', i.e. where Romani was the preferred and default language of conversation, e.g. in the family domain and among Romani individuals. In bilingual settings, the most obvious marker of the chosen language of a given interaction context is arguably the choice of grammar for the predication, which in turn anchors the entire propositional content of the utterance. The random use of English as an alternative for predication building even in Romani contexts will have blurred the distinction between interaction contexts defined as 'Romani' and those defined as 'English', and will have thus begun to push Romani into a symbiotic relationship (cf. Smith 1995) with English, one that is characterised by a consistent dependency on an English grammatical framework. The result is an asymmetrical relationship that characterises the symbiosis: while the absence of Romani from English contexts can easily be achieved, 'Romani' contexts are not just inherently mixed, but remain entirely dependent on English even for the most basic pragmatic function of anchoring the predication as the core of the proposition of an utterance.

The loss of the ability to define any interaction context as a strictly Romani context means that use of Romani becomes limited to much more subtle functions such as flagging emotions at the level of the speech act, rather than defining entire interaction settings as in-group settings. The sociolinguistic motivation behind this development will have been the increased acceptance of English as an insider language and as a language of the family, not just a language of interaction with outsiders; and this in turn was in all likelihood a product of increased intermarriage and absorption into the community of individuals who were English monolinguals, whether of settled or of Traveller background.

6.2 Bilingualism after language shift

Our historical scenario thus postulates a period of bilingualism, lasting roughly until the mid-nineteenth century. During this period English was the language of outsiders while Romani was the language of the home. Given what we know about linguistic minorities, especially those whose heritage language is strictly oral and lacks the backing of institutions, group-internal interactions will have often been bilingual, allowing insertions from and codeswitches into English. None the less, Romani and English interaction contexts could be distinguished socially through the composition of participants, and structurally through the ability to form utterances whose predicational core was structured or 'anchored' using the predication grammar (i.e. finite verb inflection) that was uniquely Romani. Romani will have thus served functions of everyday communicative interaction in the extended family domain, as well as occasional interaction with individuals belonging to other Romani families. In all likelihood, community oral traditions were also transmitted in Romani. In addition to these functions, Romani will have served as a marker of ethnic and family identity, as a language of affection and a symbol of the experience and values shared by the tight-knit group and separating it from outsiders, and wherever necessary also as a mode of communication that was exclusive of bystanders and could serve to deliver in-group, concealed or 'secret' messages.

As the relevance of monolingual English speakers grew within the community, Romani will have lost first of all its function as the default language of communication between Gypsies of different family backgrounds and so also its function as the carrier of community oral traditions. As more families began to include individuals of English background, Romani lost its position as the default language of the family context, too. This is the point at which the use of English predications will have become generalised in all situations and the ability to define an interaction context as exclusively Romani was lost. It is this point that we can most clearly define as the point of language shift, or the abandonment of inflected Romani. Regardless of other changes that may have affected the language in earlier periods – the borrowing of certain morphemes and semantic patterns, the erosion of nominal inflection and so on – it is the loss of the independent predication that indicates the loss of the ability to define separate interaction contexts, and so the loss of the language's viability as an independent vehicle of communication.

The extraordinary case of Angloromani is the survival of parts of the language after and despite this loss of viability. Triggered by the social organisation of the community as a tight-knit group, strongly reliant on kinship-based economic organisation, socially isolated and marginalised yet dependent on commercial relations with clients who are invariably group-outsiders, language played an emblematic role in symbolising group membership and flagging shared values and a particular pool of experiences. It also served a practical role in enabling exclusive, in-group communication in the presence of bystanders. The motivation for maintaining a Romani vocabulary is inherently linked to the motivation for maintaining these functions of language. In other communities of comparable social organisation

– indigenous populations specialising in itinerant trades in various parts of the world – such emblematic and practical functions are assigned to a specially designed lexicon assembled through various creative techniques such as phonological distortion of syllables, figurative extension of meaning, morphological camouflaging of words, borrowing from other languages and so on. In Angloromani, they are mapped onto the lexicon that survives from what had been the everyday family and community language. While the lost functions of inflected Romani – the vehicle of family conversation and carrier of community oral traditions – required the ability to form coherent utterances and so the ability to form distinct predications, the now remaining functions – to display identity and emotions, to mark out individual speech acts and to disguise selected meanings – merely require a selection of lexical content-elements and at most some pragmatically salient functions of grammar such as the facility to point out directions, to identify participants and to express negation. Angloromani in its contemporary form is thus a functional resource that fills the specific communicative needs of the community that are not adequately covered by what is now its everyday language of conversation, English.

In addition to these needs, Angloromani provides 'added value' in two additional ways. Firstly, it constitutes not just a marker of group identity but a symbolic means of flagging the borderline between insiders and outsiders and so of maintaining contrast with the majority society. Identifying with a linguistic code, however modest its actual expressive functions may be, provides the group with valuable symbolic capital and a confident sense of identity. Secondly, the in-group vocabulary is a cultural asset and the creative preoccupation with it is itself a cultural activity. Its functions are primarily aesthetic-emotional in nature; its decoding is highly contextual and situative, and is dependent on an extremely high degree of specialised presupposition, making its use between strangers extremely unlikely. Regulation of form and structure is accordingly lax and words are open to pragmatic interpretation. Speakers are licensed to adopt individual ownership of the lexicon and to apply creative and innovative processes such as lexical derivation, figurative meaning extension and structural analogies, thereby increasing variation. Up to 10 per cent or more of the lexicon actually consists of non-Romani elements that are replicated from other sources – often from the vocabularies of other Traveller groups – and absorbed into the Romani core reservoir. This reflects a preoccupation with the language as a source of playful creativity, targetting what is regarded as much as a personalised resource as it is as a symbol of collective identity.

A further question to be addressed is therefore whether users of Angloromani are bilingual in English and a form of Romani. The answer depends, of course, on our definition of 'bilingual', and this in turn depends on our notion of what a 'language' is, or more precisely, of where the boundaries lie between individual 'languages'. In practical terms, it might be obvious that users of Angloromani are bilingual, since they are able to produce utterances and even entire stretches of discourse that are not fully comprehensible to speakers of English, and since they are able to distinguish such utterances from a form of English speech that does not contain Romani. From a formal perspective, on the other hand, we might argue that speakers of Angloromani are not bilingual since their form of 'Romani' does not constitute an independent language system with its own grammar, though this could be contested by claiming that their form of Romani is a 'mixed language' whose grammar happens to be more or less identical to that of English.

Yet a third option is to regard bilingualism as the speaker's command of a broad and complex repertoire, elements of which are carefully selected to accommodate to different sets of interaction contexts. Unlike the stylistic continuum within the linguistic repertoire of most monolinguals, the selection and inhibition constraints governing the use of structural elements within the bilingual repertoire are strict and failure to observe them is likely to lead to a complete breakdown of communication, and not just to loss of face. Within the linguistic repertoire that users of Angloromani have at their disposal, the components are not symmetrical or of equal status in that there is only a single mode of initiating predications and so no way of marking out an entire interaction context as 'Romani'. Instead, Romani elements are largely limited to the pragmatic and more subtle level of modifying the speech act. None the less, Angloromani constitutes a part of a complex repertoire of linguistic structures that are governed by strict constraints on selection and inhibition. With this in mind, we can define the multilingual repertoire without necessarily expecting bilinguals to show command of two separate languages, and we can define language contact without the need to identify fully independent and parallel language 'systems'. Rather, bilingualism manifests itself here through the command of a multilayered repertoire of structures with both practical and symbolic value to the community.

Recapitulating, we can state that due to the absence of resources for forming predications exclusively in Romani, there is no context in which an interaction can be defined strictly as Romani. Instead, the function of Romani structures is emblematic, and involves assigning a kind of Romani 'flavour' to individual speech acts or speech events. What Angloromani has now become cannot simply be described as a mixed language, for two reasons. Firstly, the mixture of structures that we see in Angloromani utterances is entirely inconsistent and remains fully at the speaker's discretion. The choice of one Romani element in an utterance does not in any way automatically trigger the choice of another element in the same utterance, even if an adequate form is readily available. Secondly, the term 'mixed language' disregards the very particular functionality of mixing at the utterance level and the fact that the communicative goals achieved by mixed utterances are fundamentally different from those pursued in non-mixed utterances. In Angloromani, the choice between mixed and non-mixed code is triggered by more than just addressee and setting. It relates instead to the emotional side of the message at the level of the individual speech act. In this respect Angloromani cannot be regarded simply as a language 'system' that is equivalent to English; rather, it is a component of speakers' repertoires that supplements their English language system.

This position of the Romani lexicon as a special structural reservoir that is part of speakers' overall repertoire of communicative structures also facilitates our appreciation of the way speakers claim individual ownership of this special lexicon, its composition and its employment patterns. As well, it helps interpret speakers' tendency to adopt a lax attitude to certain aspects of English grammar and sentence well-formedness, which are similarly iconic of the use of the special emotive mode for an individualised, lax form of communication. In Chapter 5, I suggested a parallel between the history and functional development of Angloromani, on the one hand, and the process known in historical linguistics and in linguistic typology as 'grammaticali-sation', on the other. In both, there is in the first instance a pragmatically defined inference that is assigned to a structure or set of structures. This infer-ence becomes the principal function of the structure as its older, underlying meaning undergoes 'bleaching' and its formal appearance undergoes erosion. Its new meaning is subtle and more abstract, and in particular, it is typically no longer directly referential but serves to modify other, external structures and chains of structures; in other words, it becomes 'grammatical'. With this analogy in mind, Angloromani might be a case of a 'grammaticalisation of a language', i.e. one in which an entire linguistic 'system' is reduced, or indeed promoted, to a more subtle device that serves to modify the delivery key of messages that are anchored in a separate language (English), and is now bare of much of its earlier, historical, referential and expressive potential, both structurally and pragmatically.

In any event, the existence of speech forms such as Angloromani should draw our attention to the need to adopt a much more fine-tuned apprecia-tion of what 'language' – as an organised set of structures used for human communication – is; depictions of Angloromani as either a 'mixed language system' or a mere 'lexicon' both tend to miss its functionality, which is not only essential to any definition, but also crucial to an understanding of its historical emergence and the manner in which it can furnish an essentially dead or abandoned language with a vigorous 'afterlife'.

Appendix I Lexicon of Angloromani

The vocabulary is based on the corpus of recordings with speakers/users of Angloromani in England and Wales. All word forms have been retrieved directly from transcriptions of oral recordings of interviews, covering both English-to-Romani word elicitation (where speakers were asked for a Romani translation of English meanings) and free conversation. The vocabulary does not take into account material from published sources. An extended version of the vocabulary which combines materials from the corpus of recordings with material extracted from published sources can be found online, on the Manchester Romani Project website: http://romani.humanities.manchester. ac.uk/angloromani. The vocabulary is arranged by listing English meanings, as it is intended to capture those English concepts for which a distinctive word in Angloromani exists. For a list of Romani-derived words that are carried over into Angloromani, as well as the various non-Romani sources of word forms, see Appendix II.

Each entry identifies first a meaning (in English) along with its word class, followed by a set of etymologically related word forms given by the speaker consultants as translations of this meaning. No attempt is made to arrange these word forms into 'primary' or 'secondary' variants, on the basis of either frequency or shape. The phonological value of the word form is derivable from the spelling system that is used (see Chapter 4). A phonetic representation of the precise rendering of the word forms by speakers can be found in the online dictionary along with, in due course, sound examples. The set of related word forms (i.e. word forms with a common meaning and origin) constitutes the Angloromani *expression*. This is followed by the predecessor expression or etymology. Romani etymons are indicated by the abbreviation 'ER' (European Romani). A translation of the original predecessor expression follows. Thus in the first entry, '(an)other', the abbreviation 'adj.' for 'adjective' appears, followed by the word form *woffa* representing the Angloromani expression. The abbreviation 'ER' indicates a European Romani etymology of the following predecessor *vaver*, the meaning of which is 'other'. Some Angloromani expressions are compounds and have two- or even three-word compositions as their underlying predecessor form. In such cases, the relevant words are listed as individual predecessor expressions separated by semicolons, and their translations follow the order of appearance of the predecessor expressions; thus 'another country' is a noun (n.), and is represented in Angloromani by the word forms *du-ever-tan, duvver-tan, wavver-tan* and *wavvotam*, all of which are composed of the European Romani (ER) expressions *than; dur; vaver; them*, which mean, respectively, 'place'; 'far'; 'other'; 'country'.

a little n. *bitti* Cant *bitti* French *petit* 'little'

a lot adj. *bori, borra* ER *baro* 'big'

a lot adj. *byoot* ER *but* 'much, many'

a lot adj. *dostus, dowsa, dowsis, dustra* ER *dosta* 'enough'

a lot to do n. *kaerdi, kellapen, kelliben, kellipen, kellipens* ER *ker-* 'make, do'

above prep. *apra, aprey, oprey, opro, prey* ER *upre* 'on'

ache n. *dukkel, dukker* ER *dukh* 'pain'

across prep. *paddel, pardel, parl, pawdel, pedal* ER *perdal* 'through, across, over'

aeroplane n. *saster cherikla, saster cheriklo* ER *čirikli; sastri* 'bird'; 'iron'

afraid adj. *adar* ER *dar* 'fear'

afraid adj. *atrash, atrashed, trash, trashed, trashlo* ER *traš-* 'frighten'

after prep. *palal, palla* ER *pala(l)* 'behind'

after adv. *pawley* ER *pale* 'back, backwards, again'

again adv. *palla* ER *pale* 'back, backwards, again'

age n. *poro, purra, purroben* ER *phurol-i* 'old man'; 'old woman'

alcohol n. *livvinda* ER *lovina* 'beer'

alcohol n. *peev* ER *piv* 'drink (1sg.)'

all adj. *sa, sala, sar, saw, so, sor* ER *sa* 'all'

all together adv. *sowkaten* ER *sa khetane* 'all together'

alone adj. *kokkero, kukkeri, kukkeru, kukro* ER *korkořo* 'alone'

am v. *shom, shum* ER *som* 'I am'

and conj. *da, ta, te, ti* ER *taj* 'and'

angry adj. *chingerpen* ER *čhinger-* 'quarrel, shout'

angry adj. *roshta* ER *rušto* 'angry'

angry adj. *waffadi* ER *basavo, vasavo, wafedo* etc. 'bad'

another adj. *woffa* ER *vaver* 'other'

another adj. *awovver, waffa, wavver, wovver* ER *vaver* 'other'

another country n. *du-ever-tan, duvver- tan, wavver-tan, wavvotam* ER *than; dur; vaver; them* 'place'; 'far'; 'other'; 'country'

ant n. *pishun* ER *pišom* 'flea'

anything n. *kowi, kuvva* ER *kova* 'thing'

apple n. *pab, paba, pabbo, pava, pob, pobba, pobbai, pobbi, pobbo, pobra, poppoba, povva* ER *phabaj* 'apple'

apron n. *aeramengri* ER *heroj* 'leg'

arm n. *vast, vasti, wast* ER *vast* 'hand, arm'

arms n. *nurses* ER *musi* 'arm'

arrested part. *lelled, lellelled* ER *lel* 'take (3sg.)'

ashamed adj. *aladj, ladj, ladjed* ER *ladž-* 'be ashamed'

ashes n. *chik* ER *čhik* 'mud, dirt, earth'

ask v. *mong* ER *mang-* 'beg, ask, demand'

ask v. *pukker, pukkered* ER *phuker-* 'tell'

ask v. *putch, putcha* ER *phuč-* 'ask'

ask v. *rokker* ER *vraker-* 'speak'

asleep adj. *asutti, suggi, sutti, sutto* ER *suto* 'sleeping, asleep'

aunt n. *bibbi, bibi, mibi* ER *bibi* 'aunt'

awake adj. *jongi, yonga* ER *džungado* 'awake'

away adv. *adrom, adrum, drom* ER *drom* 'way, road'

away adv. *arri, avrey, avri* ER *avri* 'out, outside'

axe n. *tobar, tovver, towba, tuvva* ER *tover* 'axe'

baby n. *babbi* English slang *babby* 'baby'

baby n. *chavvi, little chavvi* ER *čhavo; čhavi* 'boy'; 'girl'

baby n. *tikkino, tikna, tiknas, tiknus* ER *tikno* 'small'

back (anatomy) n. *dommo, dumma, dummo* ER *dumo* 'back'

back (time/space) adv. *korporli, palpali* ER *palpale* 'back, backwards'

back (time/space) adv. *pala, palla, pawla, pollaled* ER *pala(1)* 'behind, after'

back (time/space) adv. *pawley, pawli, pori* ER *pale* 'back, backwards, again'

bacon n. *ballamas, ballavas, ballomas, ballovas, ballowas, bawlomas, bawluva, bawluvva, vallavas, vassavo, villivas* ER *balavas, balevas* 'bacon'

bacon n. *mas* ER *mas* 'meat'

bad adj. *awna* ER *xoli* 'anger'

bad adj. *baffadi, vaffadi, vaffati, vafti, vasful, vassavo, waffadi, waffati, waffedo, wasali, wasalo, wassedo, wufferdu* ER *basavo, vasavo, wafedo* etc. 'bad'

bad adj. *beng, bengalo* ER *beng* 'devil'

bad adj. *bilatcho* ER *bilačho* 'bad'

bad adj. *dinla* ER *dinilo* 'fool'

bad adj. *gammi* English slang *gammy* 'injured, painful, infected'

bad adj. *kek kushti* ER *kuč; kek* 'dear'; 'no, none'

bad adj. *nafli, nasal* ER *nasvalo* 'sick, ill'

bad adj. *suvvalo* ER *sov-* 'swear an oath'

bad luck n. *bad bokri* ER *baxt* 'luck'

bad luck n. *bi bok* ER *bibaxt* 'without luck'

bad luck n. *chuvvikanon* ER *čovexani* 'witch'

bad luck n. *nashval buk* ER *baxt; nasvalo* 'luck'; 'sick, ill'

bad luck n. *naslo buk* ER *baxt; nasvalo* 'luck'; 'sick, ill'

bad people n. *wafti fowk* ER *basavo, vasavo, wafedo* 'bad'; English *folk* 'people'

bad person n. *muller* ER *mulo* 'dead'

bad smell n. *kanda, kandel* ER *khan(d)* 'smell'

bad smell n. *sum* ER *sung* 'smell'

badness n. *mishiben* ER *midžax, mižax* 'bad, wicked, wrong'

bag n. *gunna, gunno* ER *gono* 'bag, sack'

baker n. *mawrengro, moramengra, morangra, morengro, moringra* ER *maro* 'bread'

bald adj. *belsherrud* ER *bal; šero* 'hair'; 'head'

baptise v. *baldo* ER *bold-* 'baptise'

bargained v. *mongered* ER *mang-* 'beg, ask, demand'

barley n. *juv* ER *giv* 'wheat, barley'

barn n. *gran, granz, granza, greynsi* Sinti *granša* French *grange* 'stable'

barn n. *stannia* ER *stanja* 'barn, stable'

basket n. *tushna, tushni* ER *košnica* 'basket'

bastard n. *bastardo, boshtadi, boshtardus, bostardo, bostaro, bostris* English *bastard* 'bastard'

bath time n. *bollapen* ER *bold-* 'baptise'

bathe v. *tuv* ER *thov-* 'wash'

bean n. *bobba, bubbi* ER *bobo* 'bean'

beard n. *bal* ER *bal* 'hair'

beard n. *bara, barba* ER *barba* 'beard'

beard n. *moi-bal* ER *bal; muj* 'hair'; 'face, mouth'

beat v. *mar, mor* ER *mar-* 'hit'

beautiful adj. *lastri* ER *lošano (-alo)* 'glad'; 'joyful'

beautiful adj. *rinkedi, rinkeni, rinkeno, rinkni, ritchini* ER *ranikano* 'beautiful'

beautiful adj. *shukka, shukkari, shukkaro* ER *šukar* 'beautiful'

bed n. *vadros, voddaras, vodros, vodrus, vuddus, vudrus, wuddus, wudlus, wudrus, wudrussin* ER *vodros* 'bed'

bedroom n. *wudrus* ER *vodros* 'bed'

bee n. *gudlapish, gudlo-pisham, gudlo-pishamma* ER *gudlo; pišom* 'sweet, sugar'; 'flea'

beer n. *lavvana, lavvinong, levvernay, livna, livni, livvena, livvina, livvinda, livvini, lovvina, vinni* ER *lovina* 'beer'

beer n. *peev* ER *piv* 'drink (1sg.)'

before adv. *agal, aglal, anglo, gal, glal* ER *anglal* 'in front, before'

before adv. *palley* ER *pale* 'back, backwards, again'

beg v. *mang, mong, monger* ER *mang-* 'beg, ask, demand'

beggar n. *mong, mongamengro, monger* ER *mang-* 'beg, ask, demand'

begging v., n. *mong, monganus, monging, mongipen* ER *mang-* 'beg, ask, demand'

behave v. *mokka konya* ER *spokonya (?); muk-* 'peace'; 'let, allow'

behind adv. *apoli* ER *palpale* 'back, backwards'

behind adv. *palli, pawley, pawli, poli* ER *pale* 'back, backwards, again'

believe v. *pass, patch, patser* ER *pača-* 'believe'

belly n. *dumma* ER *dumo* 'back'

belly n. *ji* ER *dži* 'soul, heart, belly'

belly n. *paer, pur* ER *peř* 'belly, stomach'

below prep. *aley, ley, teley, tulli* ER *tele* 'down'

beside prep. *fral* ER *avral* 'outside'

bicycle n. *erramengri* ER *heroj* 'leg'

bicycle n. *saster grai, sesta grai* ER *graj; sastri* 'horse'; 'iron'

big adj. *baro, barri, bawla, bawro, bora, bori, borri, borro, bowro* ER *baro* 'big'

big adj. *dusta* ER *dosta* 'enough'

big gentleman n. *bori rai* ER *raj; baro* 'gentleman, lord'; 'big'

binoculars n. *dur dikkiningris* ER *dikh-; dur* 'see'; 'far'

bird n. *cherikla, cherrikel, cherrikla, cherrikli, cherriklo, chillikel, chirkla, chirklo, chirrekla, chirrekli, chirrikla, chirriklo, chukro, churra, churraka, churrika* ER *čirikli* 'bird'

Birmingham n. *kawlagav, kawlogav* ER *kalo; gav* 'black'; 'village'

bit n. *bitti* Cant *bitti* French *petit* 'little'

bite v. *dan, danda, danya, darya* ER *dandar-* 'bite'

bite v. *dand* ER *dand* 'tooth'

black adj. *akowla, kala, kali, kalli, kallo, kalo, kawla, kawliban, kawlo, kawlu, kora, kowlo, kula* ER *kalo* 'black'

black man n. *kawlagaeri, kuligaera* ER *kalo; goro* 'black'; 'man'

black man n. *koolmush, kora mush, kulamush, kalamush, kawlamush* ER *kalo; murš* 'black'; 'man'

black person n. *kawla, kora, kuli* ER *kalo* 'black'

black woman n. *kora rakli* ER *kalo; rakli* 'black'; 'girl'

Blackpool n. *kawlagav, kawlogav* ER *kalo; gav* 'black'; 'village'

Blackpool n. *kora pani* ER *kalo; pani* 'black'; 'water'

blacksmith n. *petlenga, pettalangra, pettalengro* ER *petalo* 'horseshoe'

blanket n. *kawpa, kawpi, klappa, koppa, koppi* ER *kapa* 'blanket'

bleed v. *rattavella* ER *ratavel* 'bleed (3sg.)'

blind adj. *gammy yoks* ER *jakh* 'eye'; English slang *gammy* 'injured, painful, infected'

blind adj. *kawro, kordi, koredo, korro, korrodo, kurdi, kurra* ER *kořo* 'blind'

blind adj. *kek dik* ER *kek; dikh* 'not'; 'see'

blind adj. *yokki* ER *jakh* 'eye'

blood n. *nafti* ER *nasvalo* 'sick, ill'

blood n. *rat, rati, ratti, rawt* ER *rat* 'blood'

blow v. *poov, pud* ER *phurd-* 'blow'

boat n. *baero, baro, barra, barro, berra, berri, berro, berromeskro* ER *bero* 'ship, boat'

boat n. *chifa* Sinti *šifa* German *Schiff* 'ship'

body n. *trup, trupos, truppo, truppus* ER *trupo* 'body'

boil v. *kaer it, kerrav, kerrov, kerru* ER *kerav-* 'cook'

boil v. *lel adrey tatta pani* ER *pani; andre; lel; tato* 'water'; 'in'; 'take (3sg.)'; 'warm, hot' bone n. *kellesso, kokkalos, kokkolus, kokla, kokollus* ER *kokalo* 'bone'

book n. *lavvolil* ER *lav; lil* 'word'; 'letter, book'

book n. *lel, lil, lils* ER *lil* 'letter, book'

boot n. *chok, chokka* ER *tirax; čiox, kirax; tirax, tirax, tijax* 'shoe, boot'

born v. *barno, borno* English *born* 'born'

bottle n. *vallin, vellin, villin, wallin* ER *valin* 'glass, glass (material), bottle, window'

bottom (anatomy) n. *bool, bul* ER *bul* 'buttocks, bottom'

bowl n. *char, charo, charra* ER *čaro* 'bowl, plate'

box n. *mokto, moxto, mukto, musta, mutchta* ER *moxto* 'box, chest'

boy n. *chavingra, chavva, chavvi, chavvo* ER *čhavo* 'boy'

boy n. *chor* ER *čhoro* 'poor'

boy n. *pral* ER *phral* 'brother'

boy n. *tikna, tiknus* ER *tikno* 'small'

brainless adj. *goggi, goggi's* ER *godi* 'mind, brain'

branch n. *kosh* ER *kašt* 'wood'

brave adj. *kek trash* ER *traš-; kek* 'frighten'; 'no'

bread n. *amora, mallo, maro, marro, mawro, moira, mor, mora, morro, motto, ora* ER *maro* 'bread'

break v. *pagger, pogger* ER *phager-* 'break'

breakfast n. *sala* ER *tajsarla* 'morning'

breakfast n. *salhobben* ER *xaben; tesarla, tajsarla, tehara, teharin* 'food'; 'morning'

breast n. *bark, burk* ER *brek* 'breast'

breath n. *poov* ER *phurd-* 'blow'

bridge n. *porji, pudge, pudj, puggi* ER *phurd* 'bridge'

bridle for horse's head n. *sherraben* ER *šero* 'head'

bring v. *kaer* ER *ker-* 'make, do'

bring v. *lel* ER *lel* 'take (3sg.)'

broken adj. *paggered, poggadi, poggado* ER *phagardo* 'broken'

broken language n. *poggadi chib* ER *čhib; phagardo* 'tongue, language'; 'broken'

broken winded adj. *povva bavvolgrai* ER *phager-; balval; graj* 'break'; 'wind'; 'horse'

brother n. *pal, palla, pel, pral, prala, pralla, pulu* ER *phral* 'brother'

brother-in-law n. *stiffa pal, stiffo pal* ER *phral* 'brother'; Sinti *štif* German *stief* 'step-'

build v. *kaer* ER *ker-* 'make, do'

building n. *tan* ER *than* 'place'

bull n. *grov, gruv, gruvveni, gruvverno, gurro, gurroni* ER *guruv; guruvni* 'bull'; 'cow'

burn n. *hotchipen* ER *xač-* 'burn'

burn n. *tatchipen* ER *tato* 'warm, hot'

burn v. *hotch, hotcher, hotchi, kotchi* ER *xačar-* 'burn'

burn v. *yog* ER *jag* 'fire'
burning hot adj. *pobbor* ER *phabar-* 'burn'
burnt v. *hotchi, hutch, hutchet, otchi, utch, wutch, wutchet* ER *xač-* 'burn'
burnt v. *otchadi* ER *xačardo* 'burnt'
burnt-out adj. *yogged* ER *jag* 'fire'
bury v. *purras, purrav, pushna* ER *praxo-* 'bury'
bush n. *rukka* ER *rukh* 'tree'
butcher n. *massangra, massengero, massengra, massengri, massengro, massingra* ER *mas* 'meat'
butter n. *chil, fril, kal, kel, kib, kil, killi* ER *khil* 'butter'
butter n. *churna* English *churn* 'churn'
button n. *kafni, kenafni, krafni, kratton* ER *karfin, krafni* 'nail'
buy v. *bikkin* ER *bikin-* 'sell'
buy v. *kin, kinnen* ER *kin-* 'buy'
by prep. *adrey* ER *andre* 'in'

cabbage n. *kanarfri* ER *karfiol* 'cauliflower'
cabbage n. *shak, shok, shokyaw, shuk* ER *šax* 'cabbage'
cake n. *malliki, mannikli, marrakel, marraki, marrakli, marreki, marrika, marriki, marrikli* ER *mařikli* 'cake'
call v. *pen* ER *phen-* 'say'
came v. *jelled* ER *džal* 'go (3sg.)'
camp n. *atchin' tan* ER *ačh-; than* 'stay'; 'place'
camp v. *atch* ER *ačh-* 'stay'
candle n. *eb* ER *xev* 'hole'
candle n. *mommali, mumbla, mumbli, mumli, mummali* ER *momeli* 'candle'
cannabis n. *kuvva* ER *kova* 'thing'
cap n. *staerdi* ER *stadi(k)* 'hat'
car n. *kisda, kista, kistavarda* ER *klisto* 'riding'
car n. *sasner grai* ER *sastri; grai* 'iron'; 'horse'
car n. *skreev* Cant *skreev* 'car'
caravan n. *varda* ER *vordon* 'cart, wagon'
carpet n. *sovvahari, sowvaharri* ER *sov-* 'sleep'
carrot n. *lellopammingra* ER *lolo; phuv* 'red'; 'ground, earth'
carry v. *rig* ER *liger-, irigr-, igar-* 'carry'
cart n. *varda, vardo, wardo* ER *vordon* 'cart, wagon'
carve v. *chin* ER *čhin-* 'cut'
cat n. *madjka, mancha, manksha, mashkel, maskel, maskrel, matcha, matcheku, matchi, matchian, matchika, matchka, matchko, mutsa* ER *mačka* 'cat'
catch v. *lel* ER *lel* 'take (3sg.)'
chain n. *vengri, verkel, verriga, verriglo, werriga, werriglo* ER *veri, veriga, verklin, verni, verid'a* 'chain'
chair n. *besha, beshamengra, beshengra, beshestra, beshomengro* ER *beš-* 'sit'
chair n. *beshaleyta* ER *tele; beš-* 'down'; 'sit'

chair n. *skammawl, skammeen, skammi, skammin, skavvin* ER *skamin* 'chair'

change v. *kaer* ER *ker-* 'make, do'

cheap adj. *chitti luvva* ER *či(či); love* 'nothing'; 'money'

cheap adj. *kutch* ER *kuč* 'dear'

cheap adj. *latcha, latchi, latcho* ER *lačho* 'good'

cheek n. *mu* ER *muj* 'face, mouth'

cheese n. *kal, keers, kel, keril, kerral, kiel, kil, kiral* ER *kiral* 'cheese'

cheese n. *kas, kasm, kassem* Cant *kasum* possible German *Käse* Dutch *kaas* 'cheese'

chemist n. *drabbingra* ER *drab* 'medicine'

chest n. *bek, bekki* ER *brek* 'breast'

chicken n. *kani, kanni, kannis, kenni* ER *kaxni* 'hen'

child n. *chabbo, chavingra, chavo, chavva, chavvi, chavvo* ER *čhavo* 'boy'

child n. *mushipen* ER *murš* 'man'

child n. *tikkeno, tikna, tikno, tiknus* ER *tikno* 'small'

christening n. *bolla* ER *bold-* 'baptise'

Christmas n. *mul divvus* ER *dives; mol* 'day'; 'wine'

Christmas day n. *bollesko divvus, bullesta divvus, bullivan divvus* ER *bold-; dives* 'baptise'; 'day'

church n. *kangeri, kongeri, kongla, kongling, kongra, kongri, kuggari* ER *khangeri* 'church'

churchyard n. *kongripuv* ER *phuv; khangeri* 'ground, earth'; 'church'

CID n. *chavvingra* ER *čhavo* 'boy'

cider n. *pobbamengri, povvamengri* ER *phabaj* 'apple'

cigar n. *tugla* ER *thuvalo* 'tobacco'

cigarette n. *tugla, tuv, tuvla* ER *thuv* 'smoke'

city n. *bora gav* ER *gav; baro* 'village'; 'big'

clean adj. *kel* ER *ker-* 'make, do'

clean adj. *nevya* ER *nevo* 'new'

clean adj. *porno* ER *parno* 'white'

clean adj. *roodjo, roodjoi, yuso, yuzha, yuzo* ER *užo* 'clean'

clever adj. *jinnaben, jinnamengra* ER *džin-* 'know'

clock n. *ora, yora* ER *ora* 'hour'

close v. *pan, pand, pander, panner, panni, pappanda, parner* ER *phandar-* 'close, lock'

cloth n. *dikla, diklo* ER *diklo* '(hand)kerchief, shawl'

cloth n. *mizli* ER *mesali* 'towel, scarf'

cloth n. *partan, poktan, poxtan, proktin* ER *poxtan* 'linen'

clothes n. *izaw, izers* ER *idža* 'clothes'

coal n. *vanga, vangar, vonga, vonger, vongeri, wangar, wonga* ER *vangar* 'coal'

coal man n. *vongermengra* ER *vangar* 'coal'

coat n. *chaho, chokka, chokko, chokwan, chotcho, chowfo, choxa, chukka, chukko* ER *coxa* 'skirt'

coat n. *smuvva* English *smother* 'smother'

cock n. *bosherro, boshni, bosseno, busno* ER *bašno* 'cockerel'

cockerel n. *banchno, bashno, boshena, boshlod, boshno, roshna, vashni* ER *bašno* 'cockerel'

cockerel n. *kokni* ER *kaxni* 'hen'

coffee n. *kalapani* ER *kalo; pani* 'black'; 'water'

coffee n. *pimengri* ER *pi-* 'drink'

coffin n. *mullamokta, mullamuchta, mulleni mukta, mullo moxto* ER *mulo; moxto* 'dead'; 'box, chest'

coin n. *bar* ER *bar* 'stone, rock'

coin n. *ora* ER *xajera; xajri; xajro, hal'ris* 'penny'

cold adj. *chilla, shillino, shillo, shirillo* ER *šilelo* 'cold'

cold adj. *chilri, shil, skil* ER *šil* 'cold'

cold blooded adj. *nesher* ER *našar-* 'lose'

comb n. *konga, kongli, kongri, kundla* ER *kangli* 'comb'

combed v. *kongried* ER *kangli* 'comb'

come v. *ab, av, avred, avva, avver, hav* ER *av-* 'come'

come v. *jal, jalled, jel* ER *džal* 'go (3sg.)'

come v. *jas, jassed* ER *džas* 'go (2sg.)'

come v. *jaw* ER *dža-* 'go'

come v. *vel, wel* ER *vel* 'come'

come back v. *jalpollal* ER *pala(1); džal* 'back'; 'go (3sg.)'

come here v. *jawri* ER *dža-* 'go'

come on v. *jassan* ER *džas;* 'go (2sg.)'; English *(go) on* > 'on'

come on v. *jawra* ER *dža-* 'go'

coming v. *akaia* ER *akaj* 'here'

coming v. *av, avley, avvin'* ER *av-* 'come'

coming v. *jallin', jellin'* ER *džal* 'go (3sg.)'

coming v. *vella, vellin'* ER *vel* 'come'

commotion n. *kallaben, kellapen, kelliben, kellipen, kellipens* ER *khel-* 'dance, play'

cook v. *kaer, kaer it, kel, kerrav* ER *kerav-* 'cook'

cook v. *pekt* ER *pek-* 'roast, bake'

cooked meat n. *pek mas* ER *pek-; mas* 'roast, bake'; 'meat'

copper n. *kawlder* ER *Kalderaš* 'coppersmiths, kettle-makers', also *caldera* 'kettle'

copper wire n. *saski* ER *sastri* 'iron'

copulate v. *suv* ER *sov-* 'sleep'

corn n. *giv, givvi* ER *giv* 'wheat'

correct adj. *chatchi, tatchi, tatcho* ER *čačo* 'right, true'

correct adj. *chatcho, tatcha, tatcheni, tatchi, tatchiben, tatchipen, tatchno, tatcho* ER *čačo* 'right, true'

count v. *gin, ginja, ginya* ER *gin-* 'count'

country n. *tam, tem, temma, temmas* ER *them* 'country, land'

country n. *wavvertan* ER *than; vaver* 'place'; 'other'

country n. *wavvertem* ER *them; vaver* 'country, land'; 'other'

cow n. *gorovvi, gorrif, grazna, grovveni, growv, grunni, gruvni, gruvveni, gruvverni, gurni, gurruv, gurummin, guvni* ER *guruvni* 'cow'

cow n. *grasna* ER *grasni* 'mare'

cow's milk n. *guvverni tud* ER *thud; guruvni* 'milk'; 'cow'

crazy adj. *dindla, dingla, dinglo, dinla, dinlo, dinnilla* ER *dinilo* 'fool'

cream n. *smantunna, smentin, smenting, smentini, smeutino, smintino, smintni, smitten, spentani* ER *sme(n)tana* 'cream'

cream n. *tud* ER *thud* 'milk'

crooked adj. *bango, bongo* ER *bango* 'crooked'

cross n. *trushel, trussel, tushel* ER *trušul* 'cross, trident'

cross-eyes n. *bangri yokt* ER *bango; jakh* 'crooked'; 'eye'

crow n. *kakkaratchi* ER *kakaraška* 'magpie'

crow n. *kali cherkla* ER *kalo; čirikli* 'black'; 'bird'

cry v. *rov, rovvin', rowv, ruv, ruvva* ER *rov-* 'cry'

cry v. *roval* ER *rovel* 'cry (3sg.)'

cry v. *sav* ER *sav* 'laugh (1sg.)'

crying v. *ruvva, ruvvin'* ER *rov-* 'cry'

crystal ball n. *dikkamengra* ER *dikh-* 'see'

cup n. *korro, kurra* ER *khoro* 'jug'

cup of tea n. *mukkamangri, muttermongri* ER *muter* 'urine'

curse n. *chuvvion* ER *čovexani* 'witch'

cut v. *chin, chinned, chivved, chivvi* ER *čhin-* 'cut'

cut v. *chiv* ER *čhiv-* 'put'

dad n. *da* ER *dad* 'father'

dad n. *mai* ER *daj* 'mother'

damp adj. *waffadi* ER *basavo, vasavo, wafedo* etc. 'bad'

dance n. *gilliben* ER *gili* 'song'

dance n. *kellapen, kelliben, kellimus* ER *khel-* 'dance, play'

dance v. *kel, kella, kil, killin* ER *khel-* 'dance, play'

dancing v. *kelliben, kellimus, kellipen* ER *khelipen* 'dance'

dark adj. *kekdud* ER *dud; kek* 'light'; 'no'

dark adj. *rati* ER *rati* 'night'

dark adj. *tamla, tamlo* ER *tamlo* 'dark'

darkness n. *tamlapen* ER *tamlo* 'dark'

daughter n. *chai* ER *čhaj* 'girl'

daughter-in-law n. *bori* ER *bori* 'bride, daughter-in-law'

day n. *devvis, devvus, deyvis, divrus, divvus* ER *dives* 'day'

day of judgement n. *divvus g'divvus* ER *dives* 'day'

dead adj. *mored, mur* ER *mar-* 'kill'

dead adj. *mulla, muller, mullered, mullo, mulo* ER *mulo* 'dead'

dead body n. *mullered* ER *mulo* 'dead'

deaf adj. *kek shun* ER *kek; šun-* 'not'; 'hear'

deaf adj. *mullo* ER *mulo* 'dead'

dear (expensive) adj. *dowsta* ER *dosta* 'enough'

death n. *maer, mar, merriben, merripen, mirraban, mirrapen* ER *mer-* 'die'

death n. *mollu, mulla, mullo* ER *mulo* 'dead'

deported adj. *bitchadipani* ER *pani; bičhar-* 'water'; 'send'

deported adj. *bitchadipardi* ER *bičhar-; perdal* 'send'; 'through, across, over'

devil n. *bang, beng, benga, bengla, bing* ER *beng* 'devil'

devil n. *mulla, muller* ER *mulo* 'dead'

diamond n. *bavlabar* ER *bar; barvalo* 'stone, rock'; 'rich'

diamond n. *dudbar* ER *bar; dud* 'stone, rock'; 'light'

diamond n. *tatchibar* ER *bar; čačo* 'stone, rock'; 'right, true'

did v. *kaered, kelled* ER *ker-* 'make, do'

die v. *maer, mer, merrer, mor* ER *mer-* 'die'

die v. *muller, mullu* ER *mulo* 'dead'

died v. *mored* ER *mar-* 'kill'

dirt n. *chik* ER *čhik* 'mud, dirt, earth'

dirty adj. *chikla, chikli, chiklo* ER *čhikelo* 'dirty'

dirty adj. *hindi, hinditti, hint* ER *xindo* 'lousy, shitty, bad'

dirty adj. *mokkadi, mokkadowi, mokkati, mokkerdo, moshadi, motchadi* ER *maxado* 'dirty, defiled'

dirty people n. *ettimengri* ER *xind-* 'defecate'

dirty people n. *mokkadi fowki* English *folk; maxado* 'people'; 'dirty, defiled'

dirty-looking thing n. *muttermengri* ER *muter* 'urine'

dirty-mouthed adj. *chikla-moied* ER *čhikelo; muj* 'dirty'; 'face, mouth'

disco n. *kellipen* ER *khelipen* 'dance'

ditch n. *poov* ER *phuv* 'ground, earth'

do n. *kelliben* ER *ker-* 'make, do'

do v. *del* ER *del* 'give (3sg.)'

do v. *kaer, kaera, kel, kur* ER *ker-* 'make, do'

doctor n. *drab, drabbengra, drabbengro, drabbingra, drav, dravvengra, dravvingra, gravvi* ER *drab* 'medicine'

dog n. *jakkel, jokkel, jonkul, juggal, juk, jukkel, yakkal* ER *džukel* 'dog'

donkey n. *maila, mailo, mila, millan* English *mule* 'mule'

don't v. *kaerka, kaka, kakka, kek, kekka* ER *kek* 'not'

don't v. *kekna* ER *kek; na* 'not'

don't v. *ma, maw* ER *ma* 'not, don't'

don't v. *nai* ER *na* 'no, not'

door n. *jigga* Cant *jigger* 'door, gate'

door n. *panda* ER *phandar-* 'close, lock'

door n. *wodda, wodder, wooder, wudder, wudrus* ER *vudar* 'door'

door lock n. *klisnev* ER *xev; klisin* 'hole'; 'key'

dordi excl.

down adv. *aley, ley, li, talley, teley, tuley* ER *tele* 'down'

dress n. *chukki* ER *coxa* 'skirt'

dress n. *ridda, ridder, ruddaben, ruddi* ER *urado* 'dressed (adj.)'
dressed adj. *ridda, ringi, ruddai, ruddom* ER *urado* 'dressed (adj.)'
drink n. *pani, panni* ER *pani* 'water'
drink v. *peev, piva* ER *piv* 'drink (1sg.)'
drink v. *pi, pia, pina* ER *pi-* 'drink'
drink v. *piapen* ER *piben; pi-* 'drink'
drop v. *pier* ER *per-* 'fall'
drunk adj. *livvinda* ER *lovina* 'beer'
drunk adj. *mati, mato, matti, morta, morti, morto, motta, motti, motto, mutti*
  ER *mato* 'drunk'
drunk adj. *peeved, pivi* ER *piv* 'drink (1sg.)'
drunk man n. *mottamengra* ER *mato* 'drunk'
drunkard n. *motsimengri, muttamengra* ER *mato* 'drunk'
dry adj. *kos* ER *khos-* 'wipe'
dry adj. *trushlo, trushna* ER *trušalo* 'thirsty'
dry adj. *trushni* ER *truš* 'thirst'
duck n. *herretzi, ratchkro, retchka, retza, rotchka* ER *raca, reca, reč(k)a*
  'duck'
duck n. *pappin* ER *papin* 'goose, duck'
dung n. *ful* ER *ful* 'excrement'
dust n. *char* ER *čar, čar, čhaar* 'ashes, grass'

ear n. *gan, kam, kan* ER *kan* 'ear'
ear n. *shunningro* ER *šun-* 'hear'
early adj. *bori charus* ER *baro; čiros* 'big'; 'time'
early adj. *sala, salo* ER *tesarla, tajsarla, tehara, teharin* 'morning, early'
early morning n. *sowla* ER *tesarla, tajsarla, tehara, teharin* 'morning, early'
ears n. *kanchis, kannadas, kanyas, kon* ER *kan* 'ear'
earth n. *poof, poov, povvi, powv, pu, puv* ER *phuv* 'ground, earth'
eat v. *al, hal, hol, kol, kolla, kollo, ol* ER *xal* 'eat (3sg.)'
eat v. *has* ER *xas* 'eat (2sg.)'
eat v. *skran* Cant *skran* 'food'
eaten v. *hollem* ER *xal(j)am* 'eat (1pl. past)'
eater n. *oller* ER *xal* 'eat (3sg.)'
egg n. *ora, yarro, yora, yorra, yorro, yowri* ER *jaro* 'egg'
eight num. *oitu, okt, okta, okto, otter* ER *oxto* 'eight'
eighteen num. *deshdeduistar* ER *thaj; duj; deš; štar* 'and'; 'two'; 'ten'; 'four'
eighteen num. *deshdeokta, deshtaokta, deshtuoct* ER *deštha(j)oxto* 'eighteen'
eighty num. *okta* ER *oxto* 'eight'
eleven num. *deshdeyak, deshdeyek, deshtayek, deshtuyek* ER *dešthajekh*
  'eleven'
embarrassed adj. *ladjed* ER *ladž-* 'be ashamed'
English Gypsy n. *Romanichal* ER *čalado; romani* 'family'; 'Gypsy (adj.)'
English Gypsy girl n. *Romani chai* ER *romani; čhaj* 'Gypsy (adj.)'; 'girl'

enough adj. *dosta, dotta, dowsa, dowsis, dowsta, dowstas, dusta* ER *dosta*
  'enough'
everything pr. *chommani* ER *čomoni* 'something'
everything pr. *kukkeri* ER *korkořo* 'alone'
everything pr. *kuvva* ER *kova* 'thing'
evil adj. *baffadi, vaffadi, waffadi, wufferdu* ER *basavo, vasavo, wafedo* etc. 'bad'
evil adj. *beng* ER *beng* 'devil'
ewe n. *bukri* ER *bakro* 'sheep'
excrement n. *chin, inga, kinder* ER *xind-* 'defecate'
expensive adj. *dusta luvva* ER *dosta; love* 'enough'; 'money'
expensive adj. *kootch* ER *kuč* 'dear'
eye n. *yak, yok, yokki* ER *jakh* 'eye'
eye reading n. *durriking* ER *dokrapen, dorikeripe, dorikaripe, dorikiriben*
  'fortune-telling, far seeing'
eyebrow n. *yokba* ER *bal; jakh* 'hair'; 'eye'
eyes n. *yakkai, yokkas, yokkers, yoks* ER *jakh* 'eye'

face n. *moi, mowi, mu, mui* ER *muj* 'face, mouth'
fair n. *valgorus, varringera, waggawlus, walgerus, welda, welgora, welgoru,*
  wesgorus ER *valgora, agora* 'fair, market'
fall v. *paer, pier* ER *per-* 'fall'
family n. *dia* ER *daj* 'mother'
family n. *fowki* English *folk* 'people'
far adj. *dor, dur, durra* ER *dur* 'far'
far seeing adj. *durriking* ER *dokrapen, dorikeripe, doricaripe, dorikiriben*
  'fortune-telling, far seeing'
farmer n. *gavvengra* ER *gav* 'village'
farmer n. *givvengra* ER *giv* 'wheat'
farmer n. *gruvvengra* ER *guruv* 'bull'
farmer n. *puvvengra* ER *phuv* 'ground, earth'
farthing n. *posh-aera* ER *xajera, xajri, xajro, hal'ris; paš* 'penny'; 'half'
fast adj. *sig* ER *sigo* 'fast'
fat adj. *bori* ER *baro* 'big'
fat adj. *chubba* English *chubby* 'chubby'
fat adj. *tallo, trullo, tulla, tulliben, tullo* ER *thulo* 'thick, fat'
fat (f.) adj. *tulli* ER *thulo* 'thick, fat'
fat (m.) adj. *tullo* ER *thulo* 'thick, fat'
father n. *dad, daddi* ER *dad* 'father'
father n. *daddarus, daddus* Cant *daddus* 'father'
father n. *dai, daia* ER *daj* 'mother'
father-in-law n. *romnis dadeskra* ER *dad; romni* 'father'; 'wife'
father-in-law n. *sastaro* ER *sastro* 'father-in-law'
father-in-law n. *stiffa daddus* Cant *daddus* 'father', *štif* German *stief* 'step-
  (relation by marriage)'

feather n. *por, porengri, pori, porra* ER *por* 'feather'

feet n. *perra, perri, pieri, piri, piris, pirro* ER *piro* 'foot'

female n. *rakli* ER *rakli* 'girl'

female cat n. *matchka* ER *mačka* 'cat'

female dog n. *jukkles, jukkli, jukli* ER *džukli* 'female dog'

fence n. *baw, ber* ER *bar* 'hedge, garden'

fence n. *stigga* Cant *stigga* 'gate, fence'

fiddle n. *bash, bawchamongri, bosh, boshamengri, boshamungeri, boshedi, boshimangri, boshri* ER *bašav-* 'to play an instrument'

field n. *chowvi* ER *čhar-alol-akol-ano* 'grassy'

field n. *poov, powf, puv, puvva* ER *phuv* 'ground, earth'

fifteen num. *deshtapansh, deshtupanch* ER *deštapandž* 'fifteen'

fifty num. *pancha, panchdo* ER *pandž* 'five'

fight n. *kor, kora, korben, kuriben, kurriben* ER *kur-* 'beat up'

fight v. *ching* ER *čhinger-* 'quarrel, shout'

fight v. *kor, kuer* ER *kur-* 'beat up'

fight v. *mor* ER *mar-* 'hit'

fight v. *pagger, pogger* ER *phager-* 'break'

filthy adj. *hinditti* ER *xindo* 'lousy, shitty, bad'

filthy people n. *hindittimengra* ER *xindo* 'lousy, shitty, bad'

find v. *lasta, latch, latcht* ER *lač-* 'find'

find v. *rod* ER *rod-* 'search'

finger n. *gushtra, vallashti, vonnish, wangisha, wunnishki* ER *angušt* 'finger'

fingers n. *fangasti, vangus, vawngasti, vongasta, wangesto, wangisto, wongust* ER *angušt* 'finger'

fingers n. *vastrus* ER *vast* 'hand, arm'

finish v. *kaer* ER *ker-* 'make, do'

fire n. *og, yag, yal, yeg, yog* ER *jag* 'fire'

fire oven n. *bov* ER *bov* 'oven'

fish n. *matcha, matchi, matchki, matcho, matchu* ER *mačho* 'fish'

fisherman n. *matchigera* ER *goro; mačho* 'man'; 'fish'

fisherman n. *matchkamush* ER *murš; mačho* 'man'; 'fish'

five num. *panch, pandj, pansh, pawnch, pendj, pengi, ponch, punch* ER *pandž* 'five'

five hundred num. *posh miya* ER *paš; mija* 'half'; 'thousand'

five pounds n. *panch bar, ponch bar* ER *bar; pandž* 'stone, rock'; 'five'

flea n. *jub, juv, juvli, juvva* ER *džuv* 'louse'

flour n. *vara, varo, varra, varro, vorro* ER *varo* 'flour'

flower n. *lulu, lullaga* ER *luludži* 'flower'

flower n. *roodji, rowzho, rowzo, rudjes, rusheni, rushli, rushna, rushnas, rushni, ruzha, urridjus* ER *ruža* 'rose'

food n. *gobbin, habben, hobben, hobbin, obben, obbin, ovven* ER *xaben* 'food'

food n. *skran* Cant *skran* 'food'

food n. *vikkels, vittels, wikkels* English *victuals* 'food' fool n. *dennolu, diddelo, didla, dimbero, din, dindelo, dindla, dindlo, dingero, dingla, dinglo, dinla, dinlai, dinli, dinlo, dinnilla* ER *dinilo* 'fool'

fool n. *doylem* ER *dinilo;* Yiddish *goylem* 'fool'

fool n. *div, divvi, divya* ER *divjo* 'wild'

fool n. *gagga* English slang *gaga* 'crazy'

foot n. *paeri, perri, piri, piro* ER *piro* 'foot'

foot n. *pirro* ER *piro* 'foot'

foreign language n. *waffatemjib* ER *vaver; čhib; them* 'other'; 'tongue, language'; 'country, land'

foreigner n. *duvver-tan mush* ER *murš; than; vaver* 'man'; 'place'; 'other'

foreigner n. *ravvatam* ER *them; vaver* 'country, land'; 'other'

foreigner n. *temeskamush, temeskimush* ER *murš; them* 'man'; 'country, land'

foreigner n. *waffatamengra* ER *vaver* 'other'

foreigner n. *wovvatemmush* ER *murš; them; vaver* 'man'; 'country, land'; 'other'

foreigners n. *wavvertemfowki* English *folk; them; vaver* 'people'; 'country, land'; 'other'

forest n. *vesh* ER *veš* 'wood, forest'

forest keeper n. *veshengra* ER *veš* 'wood, forest'

forester n. *yoggamengra* ER *jag* 'fire'

forget v. *bisharo, bista* ER *bistar-* 'forget'

forgive v. *fawdel* ER *del* 'give (3sg.)'

fork n. *possamengri, possimengrey, pursamengri, pusramangera, pussimangro, pussimengri* ER *phus* 'straw'

fork n. *trushel* ER *trušul* 'cross, trident'

fork n. *trushni* ER *trušul* 'cross, trident'

fortune-teller n. *dukka* ER *dokrapen, dorikeripe, doricaripe, dorikiriben* 'fortune-telling'

fortune-telling v. *dorrakin', dukkera, dukkerin', dukkering, dukrapen, durriking* ER *dokrapen, dorikeripe, dorikaripe, dorikiriben* 'fortune-telling'

fortune-telling v. *drabbalimos* ER *drab* 'medicine'

forty num. *shtada, shtardo, storanda* ER *štar; saranda* 'four'; 'forty'

four num. *doostar, shor, shtar, star, stor, stun* ER *štar* 'four'

fourteen num. *deshtastor, deshtushtar* ER *deštaštar* 'fourteen'

fox n. *mokkadi jukkel* ER *džukel; maxado* 'dog'; 'dirty, defiled'

fox n. *vesh jukkel, veshen jukkel, veshenjukkel, veshni jukkel* ER *džukel; veš* 'dog'; 'wood, forest'

friend n. *pal, palla* ER *phral* 'brother'

friend n. *tukla* ER *thukalo* 'friendly'

friendly adj. *tukla* ER *thukalo* 'friendly'

friends n. *tukla* ER *thukalo* 'friendly'

frighten v. *trash* ER *traš-* 'fear'

from prep. *arri, avrey, avri* ER *avri* 'out, outside'

frying pan n. *hotchamengra* ER *xač(ar)-* 'burn'

frying pan n. *saraskra, sastermengra* ER *sastri* 'iron'
frying pan n. *tattramengra, tattramengrey* ER *tato* 'warm, hot'
full adj. *paddo, pord, pordo, powdo* ER *pherdo* 'full'

gamekeeper n. *veshna* ER *veš* 'wood, forest'
gamekeeper n. *yog, yoggamengra, yoggengri* ER *jag* 'fire'
gamekeeper n. *yoggamush, yogmush* ER *murš; jag* 'man'; 'fire'
garden n. *barengro, bark* ER *bar* 'hedge, garden'
garden n. *yabtan* ER *than; jag* 'place'; 'fire'
gate n. *jigga* ER *jigger* Cant *jigger* 'door, gate'
gate n. *stigga* ER *stigga* Cant *jigger* 'gate, fence'
gate n. *wudder* ER *vudar* 'door'
gate-keeper n. *veshengra* ER *veš* 'wood, forest'
gathering n. *kongra* ER *khangeri* 'church'
gentleman n. *arai, herrai, rai, ria* ER *raj* 'gentleman, lord'
gentleman n. *rawni* ER *rani* 'lady'
get v. *jel* ER *džal* 'go (3sg.)'
get v. *kaer* ER *ker-* 'make, do'
get v. *lel* ER *lel* 'take (3sg.)'
ghost n. *ballamengra, bavvelingro* ER *balval* 'wind'
ghost n. *mulladi, muller, mullerdi* ER *mulo* 'dead'
gift n. *delliben* ER *del* 'give (3sg.)'
girl n. *bitti rakli* ER *bitti; rakli* 'little'; 'girl'
girl n. *chai, chi* ER *čhaj* 'girl'
girl n. *chavingra, chavvi* ER *čhavo* 'boy'
girl n. *juklo, juvel, juvvel* ER *džuvel* 'woman'
girl n. *monnishna, monnishni* ER *manušni* 'woman'
girl n. *rakli, rakya, rokli, rukki* ER *rakli* 'girl'
give v. *del, jel* ER *del* 'give (3sg.)'
give v. *kur* ER *ker-; kur-* 'make, do'; 'beat (up)'
glass n. *dikking-glass* ER *dikh-* 'see'
glass n. *dikkingkorro* ER *dikh-; khoro* 'see'; 'jug'
glass n. *ebs, ev, evya* ER *xev* 'hole'
glass n. *gleyta* ER *glayzer* Cant *glayzer* 'glass window'
glass n. *korro, korru* ER *khoro* 'jug'
glass n. *vassel* ER *vast* 'hand, arm'
glasses n. *vatermengris* Sinti *vater-* German *warten* 'watch, look'
glasses n. *yokking, yokkingras* ER *jakh* 'eye'
go v. *atch* ER *ač h-* 'stay'
go v. *draw, ja, jah, jaw* ER *dža-* 'go'
go v. *jal, jel, jella, jello* ER *džal* 'go (3sg.)'
go v. *jas, jassa* ER *džas* 'go (2sg.)'
go v. *jav, jov, jovva* ER *džav* 'go (1sg.)'
go v. *nash* ER *naš-* 'run (away), escape'

go v. *prasta* ER *prast-* 'run'
go v. *vel* ER *vel* 'come'
go away v. *nash avri* ER *avri; naš-* 'out, outside'; 'escape'
go back v. *av popli* ER *av-; palpale* 'come'; 'back, backwards'
go back v. *jah popli* ER *dža-; palpale* 'go'; 'back, backwards'
go out v. *avral* ER *avral* 'outside'
go out v. *avri* ER *avri* 'out, outside'
go outside v. *jas avri* ER *avri; džas* 'out, outside'; 'go (2sg.)'
go outside v. *jaw* ER *dža-* 'go'
goat n. *tudbukla* ER *bakro; thud* 'sheep'; 'milk'
goat (f.) n. *busni* ER *buzni* 'goat'
goat (m.) n. *busno* ER *buzno* 'goat'
God n. *daivla, davvilla, devel, devial, devla, devvel, dovvel, duvadi, duval, duvel,*
   duvla, duvlas, duvvel, duvvol, ma duvvalo, miduvvel ER *devel* 'God'
God n. *dibbel* ER *devel* 'God'
God n. *devvelessa* ER *devlesa* 'God (instr.) '
gold n. *sonakai, sonnakai, sonnaki, sonnokai, sonnokoi, suhaki, sunakai,*
   sunnakai, sunnather, sunnikai, zollakai ER *sonakaj* 'gold'
gold n. *vongus* ER *vangar* 'coal'
goldfinch n. *sonna cherkla, sunnakiski chiriklo* ER *čirikli; sonakaj* 'bird'; 'gold'
good adj. *chusti, chusto, koshko, kosko, kosliko, kushga, kushka, kushki,*
   kushti, kushto ER *kuč* 'dear'
good adj. *latcha, latchi, latcho* ER *lačho* 'good'
good adj. *mishto* ER *mišto* 'good, well'
good n. *kosko* ER *kuč* 'dear'
good day n. *latchi divvus* ER *dives; lačho* 'day'; 'good'
good looking adj. *kushti dikkin'* ER *kuč; dikh-* 'dear'; 'see'
good looking adj. *rinkna* ER *rankano* 'beautiful'
good luck n. *kushti bok, kushti buk* ER *baxt; kuč* 'luck'; 'expensive'
goodbye excl. *devvel* ER *devel* 'God'
goose n. *papna, pappen, pappin, pappinengri* ER *papin* 'goose, duck'
grandfather n. *dai* ER *daj* 'mother'
grandfather n. *phurodad, pura dad, purradad, purri dad* ER *dad; phuridaj*
   'father'; 'grandmother'
grandfather n. *puri dai, puro dai* ER *phuridaj* 'grandmother'
grandfather n. *purra dad* ER *dad; phuridaj* 'father'; 'grandmother'
grandmother n. *daieskra dai, mai* ER *daj* 'mother'
grandmother n. *pawra dai, puri mai, purno dai, puro mai, purri dai* ER *phuridaj*
   'grandmother'
grapes n. *mulleskras* ER *mol* 'wine'
grass n. *char, chor* ER *čar* 'grass'
grass n. *kas* ER *khas* 'hay'
grass n. *poov, puv* ER *phuv* 'ground, earth'
grave n. *mullev* ER *xev; mulo* 'hole'; 'dead'

graze v. *puv* ER *phuv* 'ground, earth'

great adj. *baro, barra, bori, boro, borro, burri* ER *baro* 'big'

greedy adj. *bokra* ER *bokh* 'hunger'

greedy man n. *jungalo mush* ER *murš; džungalo* 'man'; 'ugly'

green adj. *zellano, zennelo* ER *zeleno, zelano* 'green'

grey adj. *pawno* ER *parno* 'white'

ground n. *pul, pur, puv* ER *phuv* 'ground, earth'

guard v. *rik* ER *rakh-* 'guard'

guard v. *vater* Sinti *vater-* German *warten* 'to watch/look'

gun n. *jog, yog, yogga, yoggamengri, yogger, yoggi, yoggimengri, yoggingri, yoggramangi, yokka, yukka* ER *jag* 'fire'

gun n. *pushka, pussika* ER *puška* 'gun'

gun n. *squirter* English *squirt* 'squirt'

Gypsies n. *chavvi* ER *čhavo* 'boy'

Gypsies n. *rom* ER *Rom* 'autonym, man, husband'

Gypsies n. *Romanes* ER *romanes* 'in the Gypsy way, the Gypsy language'

Gypsies n. *romnis, Rumnis* ER *romani* 'Gypsy'

Gypsy n. *Romanachil, Romanichal, Romanichel, Rumnichal, rumnichel* ER *čalado; romani* 'family'; 'Gypsy (adj.)'

Gypsy n. *Romani, Romani, Rummani, Rumni* ER *romani* 'Gypsy'

Gypsy boy n. *chavvi* ER *čhavo* 'boy'

Gypsy child n. *javvi* ER *čhavo* 'boy'

Gypsy child n. *jor* ER *čhoro* 'poor'

Gypsy child n. *Romanichal tikna* ER *tikno; čalado; romani* 'small'; 'family'; 'Gypsy'

Gypsy girl n. *juvli* ER *džuvel* 'woman'

Gypsy girl n. *rakli* ER *rakli* 'girl'

Gypsy language n. *Romanes* ER *romanes* 'In the Gypsy way, the Gypsy language'

Gypsy man n. *Romanichal mush* ER *murš; čalado; romani* 'man'; 'family'; 'Gypsy'

Gypsy man n. *Romani rai* ER *raj; romani* 'gentleman, lord'; 'Gypsy'

Gypsy who is a different type to the speaker n. *diddikai* ER *akaj; dikh-* 'here'; 'see'

Gypsy woman n. *juvvel* ER *džuvel* 'woman'

Gypsy woman n. *Romanichal rakli* ER *rakli; čalado; romani* 'girl'; 'family'; 'Gypsy'

hair n. *bael, bal, ballo, bel, val* ER *bal* 'hair'

hair n. *shurra, shurri* ER *šero* 'head'

half n. *pash, posh* ER *paš* 'half'

half a shilling n. *posh-ora* ER *xajera, xajri, xajro, hal'ris; paš* 'penny'; 'half'

half blood Gypsy n. *diddikai* ER *akaj; dikh-* 'here'; 'see'

half blood Gypsy n. *poshrats* ER *rat; paš* 'blood'; 'half'

half bred adj. *poshrat* ER *rat; paš* 'blood'; 'half'

half crown n. *ponch kronna* ER *paš; kuruna, korona* 'half'; 'crown'

half penny n. *pawsh-ora, posh-aera, posh-eraw, posh-eru, posh-ora, push-aera*
   ER *xajera, xajri, xajro, hal'ris; paš* 'penny'; 'half'

ham bones n. *kokollus* ER *kokalo* 'bone'

hand n. *duk* ER *dokrapen, dorikeripe, doricaripe, dorikiriben* 'fortune-telling'

hand n. *vas, vash, vast, vasta, vasti, was, wast* ER *vast* 'hand, arm'

hand reading v. *dukkering* ER *dokrapen, dorikeripe, doricaripe, dorikiriben*
   'fortune-telling'

handbag n. *gunna* ER *gono* 'bag, sack'

handcuffs n. *vastamengras* ER *vast* 'hand, arm'

handkerchief n. *dikla, diklo* ER *diklo* '(hand)kerchief, shawl'

handkerchief n. *mendik* ER *diklo; men* '(hand)kerchief, shawl'; 'neck'

hands n. *fams* ER *fams, fambles* Cant *fams, fambles* 'hands'

handsome adj. *rinkana, rinkini* ER *rankano* 'beautiful'

happy adj. *sala* ER *sal(a)* 'laugh (3sg.)'

happy adj. *sav* ER *sav* 'laugh (1sg.)'

hare n. *kannengra, kannengro, kanningo, kanningra, kannivoro, konengro* ER
   kan 'ear'

harness n. *grai izers* ER *graj; idža, id'a* 'horse'; 'clothes'

hat n. *kaerdi, kaydi, staddi, staddia, staerda, stardi, studdi* ER *stadi(k)* 'hat'

haunted adj. *mullerdi* ER *mulo* 'dead'

have v. *lel* ER *lel* 'take (3sg.)'

hawking v. *mongipen* ER *mangipen* 'begging'

hay n. *kas, kaz, kussi* ER *khas* 'hay'

hay n. *pus* ER *phus* 'straw'

he pr. *leski* ER *leske* 'he (dat.)'

he pr. *lesti* ER *leste* 'he (loc.)'

he pr. *yo, yor, yov* ER *jov* 'he'

head n. *cherro, serro, sharro, sharrus, sherra, sherro, shira, shirro, shurra,*
   shurro ER *šero* 'head'

headache n. *dook shaera* ER *šero; dukh* 'head'; 'pain'

headstone n. *sherrabar* ER *bar; šero* 'stone, rock'; 'head'

health n. *sasto, sastov* ER *sasto* 'healthy'

healthy adj. *kushti* ER *kuč* 'dear'

hear v. *shoon, shum, shun, shurn* ER *šun-* 'hear'

hear v. *shunta* ER *šun-; -tar* 'hear (imp.)'

heart n. *si, zi* ER *(o)zi* 'heart/soul'

heat n. *tatta, tattapen, tattu* ER *tato* 'warm, hot'

heaven n. *chaerus, cherro* ER *čeri* 'sky'

heaven n. *cherribim* ER *čeri;* English *cherubim* 'sky'; 'angels'

heaven n. *preyatem* ER *upre; them* 'up, on'; 'country'

heavy adj. *piro, poro* ER *pharo* 'heavy'

hedge n. *bar, baw, bor* ER *bar* 'hedge, garden'

hedge n. *rukka* ER *rukh* 'tree'

hedgehog n. *gotchi witchi, hotcha, hotchawitcha, hotchi, hotchi witchi, hotchiwitchi, kotcha wudjus, otchi, otchi witchi, otchi-pog, otchipig, otchipigs, otchri, utchi* ER *xač(ar)-; určos* 'burn'; 'urchin'

hedgehog n. *nigli, niglo* Sinti *niglo* German *Igel* 'hedgehog'

hedgehog n. *otch* ER *xačardo* 'burnt'

hell n. *bengratem* ER *beng; them* 'devil'; 'country, land'

hen n. *akanni, kani* ER *kaxni* 'hen'

her pr. *lesti* ER *leste* 'he (loc.)'

here adv. *adai, adoi* ER *adaj, odoj* 'here, there'

here adv. *adri* ER *andre* 'in'

here adv. *akai, akoi, kai, koi* ER *akaj* 'here'

here adv. *ginna, kanna* ER *akana* 'now'

hid v. *atched* ER *ačh-* 'stay'

hide v. *garra, garrav, gavva, gurav* ER *garav-* 'hide'

him pr. *duvva* ER *(o)dova* 'that'

him pr. *les, los* ER *les* 'he (obl.)'

him pr. *lesti* ER *leste* 'he (loc.)'

his pr. *lesti's* ER *leste* 'he (loc.)'

hit v. *del, delled* ER *del* 'give (3sg.)'

hit v. *mor* ER *mar-* 'hit'

hit v. *pagger, pogger* ER *phager-* 'break'

hold v. *lel* ER *lel* 'take (3sg.)'

hold v. *tul* ER *thil-* 'hold'

hole n. *ev, hev* ER *xev* 'hole'

home n. *kan* ER *ken* Cant *ken* 'house'

homosexual n. *mofradaik* English *hermaphrodite*

homosexual n. *pash rat* ER *rat; paš* 'blood'; 'half'

honey n. *gudla, gudli, gudlo* ER *gudlo* 'sweet, sugar'

honey bee n. *gudlapishun* ER *gudlo; pišom* 'sweet, sugar'; 'flea'

horse n. *grah, grai, grey* ER *graj* 'horse'

horse dealer n. *graiengra* ER *graj* 'horse'

horseshoe n. *grai's chokki, grai's choxa* ER *tirax, graj* 'shoe'; 'horse'

horseshoe n. *petla, pettalo* ER *petalo* 'horseshoe'

hot adj. *hotchi, otchi* ER *xačar-* 'burn'

hot adj. *taito, tatra, tatro, tatta, tattel, tatti, tatto* ER *tato* 'warm, hot'

hour n. *chaerus* ER *čiros* 'time'

hour n. *ora* ER *ora* 'hour'

house n. *gur, kaer, kar, kir, korri* ER *kher* 'house'

house n. *ken, kenna* ER *ken* Cant *ken* 'house'

house n. *tam, tan* ER *than* 'place'

house-bred adj. *gawdja-bred* ER *gadžo* 'non-Gypsy '

housedweller n. *gawdja, gawdji* ER *gadžo* 'non-Gypsy '

how inter. *sa, sar, sarra, shar, so* ER *sar* 'how'

how are you? phrase *sar tutti* ER *tute; sar* 'you (loc.)'; 'how'

how are you? phrase *sarshin, sason, sassan, sha han, sha shan, shaw shan, sashin* ER *san; sar* 'to be (2sg.)'; 'how'

how do you do phrase *sashin* ER *san; sar* 'to be (2sg.)'; 'how'

how much inter. *so booty* ER *but; so* 'much, many'; 'what'

how much? inter. phrase *sar kizzi* ER *sar; kici* 'how'; 'much/many'

hunchback n. *paldumor* ER *dumo; pale* 'back'; 'back, backwards'; 'again'

hundred num. *shel* ER *šel* 'hundred'

hunger n. *boklipen, buk* ER *bokh* 'hunger'

hungry adj. *bokka, buk* ER *bokh* 'hunger'

hungry adj. *bokkalo, bokkoli, boklo, boktalo, booklo, bukelo, bukkalo, bukla, buklo, buklu* ER *bokhalo* 'hungry'

hungry adj. *buktamulla* ER *bokh; mulo* 'hunger'; 'dead'

hungry adj. *skrannin'* ER *skran* Cant *skran* 'food'

hurry up v. *jel on* ER *džal* 'go (3sg.)'

hurt adj. *mullered* ER *mulo* 'dead'

husband n. *rom, rowm, rum* ER *rom* 'autonym, man, husband'

I pr. *ma, mai, me, mei, mey, mi* ER *me* 'I'

I pr. *manda, mandi, mandi's, mandis* ER *mande* 'I (loc.)'

I am v. *shium, shom, showm* ER *som* 'I am'

ice n. *gib* ER *iv* 'snow'

idiot n. *dendla, dinla, dinlo* ER *dinilo* 'fool'

ill adj. *gammi* English slang *gammy* 'injured, painful, infected'

ill adj. *naffalo, nafla, nafli, naflo, naflu, nashfelo, nashval, nasvalo* ER *nasvalo* 'sick'; 'ill'

ill adj. *waffadi, waffati* ER *basavo, vasavo, wafedo* etc. 'bad'

in prep. *abri* ER *avri* 'out, outside'

in prep. *adrav, adrey, adri, adrin, drey* ER *andre* 'in'

in front of prep. *adrey* ER *andre* 'in'

in the middle prep. *maskra* ER *maškar* 'middle'

in-laws n. *stiffa* Sinti *štif* German *stief* 'step- (relation by marriage)'

insect n. *pish, pishun* ER *pišom* 'flea'

inside adv. *adrin* ER *andre* 'in'

Irish people n. *fowkidelallipani* ER *pani; lolo;* English *folk* 'water'; 'red'; 'people'

Irish people n. *intramengras* ER *xindo* 'lousy, shitty, bad'

Irish person n. *hingermenga, ingrittamengra* ER *xindo* 'lousy, shitty, bad '

iron n. *mullok* ER *molivi* 'lead'

iron n. *sashtah, sasner, saster, sasti, susta, trast, trasta* ER *sastri* 'iron'

is v. *si* ER *si* 'to be (3sg.)'

is not v. *nai* ER *na* 'no, not'

jacket n. *chukka* ER *coxa* 'skirt'

Jesus n. *shadai* ER *shaday* Hebrew 'the protector, the Lord' jewel n. *sonnakai* ER *sonakaj* 'gold'

Jews n. *shinafowki* ER *čhin-;* English *folk* 'cut'; 'people'

jockey n. *kistagaera* ER *goro; klis-* 'gawdja who intermarried with Gypsies'; 'ride'

jumper n. *ganzi* Shelta *ganzi* 'frock'

kettle n. *kekavvi, kekkari, kekkavi, kekkordi, kekkorvia, kekkova, kekovvi, kikkova, kikovvi, kukavi, kukkavi* ER *kakavi* 'kettle'

kettle iron n. *kukkavi saster* ER *kakavi* 'kettle'

kettle prop n. *kekkavisast* ER *kakavi; sastri* 'kettle'; 'iron'

kettle prop n. *kikovvi kosh* ER *kašt; kakavi* 'wood'; 'kettle'

key n. *klerrin, klessin, klism, klitsen, kludjen* ER *klisin* 'key'

keys n. *klissems* ER *klisin* 'key'

kill v. *del, delli* ER *del* 'give (3sg.)'

kill v. *mar, mor, mori, mur* ER *mar-* 'hit'

kill v. *muller* ER *mulo* 'dead'

killed v. *mored* ER *mar-* 'hit'

killed v. *mullered* ER *mulo* 'dead'

killing v. *morin', moring* ER *mer-* 'die'

king n. *kina* Sinti *kinego* German *König* 'king'

king n. *grallis, kallis, krallis, krellis* ER *kralis* 'king'

king n. *rai* ER *raj* 'gentleman, lord'

kiss n. *chum, chumas, chumma, chummaben* ER *čumi* 'kiss'

kiss n. *moi* ER *muj* 'face, mouth'

kiss v. *chummer* ER *čumer-* 'kiss'

knee n. *changa, chong* ER *čang* 'knee'

knees n. *chongus, kon* ER *čang* 'knee'

knickers n. *rokkemries* ER *raxami, rexami* 'coat'

knife n. *charri, chori, chuddi, churi, churri, shurri* ER *čhuri* 'knife'

knife n. *chiv, chivvi, chivvimengri, chivvomengro* ER *čhin-* 'cut'

know v. *jan, jun, juns* ER *džan-* 'know'

know v. *jannav* ER *džanav* 'know (1sg.)'

know v. *jannes, jenes* ER *džanes* 'know (2sg.)'

know v. *jin, jins* ER *džin-* 'know'

know 1sg. v. *jinnav* ER *džinav* 'know (1sg.)'

knows v. *jinnel* ER *džinel* 'know (3sg.)'

know(s) v. *juns* ER *džan-* 'know'

lace n. *tav* ER *thav* 'thread'

ladies' underwear n. *rokrawnis* ER *rani; raxami, rexami* 'lady'; 'coat'

lady n. *arawna, raienna, ranni, rawni, roienna* ER *rani* 'lady'

lady n. *rakli* ER *rakli* 'girl'

lake n. *pani* ER *pani* 'water'

landlord n. *gaera* ER *goro* 'man'

landlord n. *kitchema mosh* ER *murš; kirčima* 'man'; 'pub'
language n. *jib* ER *čhib* 'tongue, language'
language n. *rokker, rokkerbun, rokkerpen* ER *raker-* 'speak'
laugh n. *sav, savva* ER *sav* 'laugh (1sg.)'
laugh v. *sav, savvapan* ER *sav* 'laugh (1sg.)'
lawyer n. *pukkamengri* ER *phuker-* 'speak'
lead n. *mollis, mollus, mulliven, mullivin* ER *molivi* 'lead'
leaf n. *papatri, patrin, petra* ER *patrin* 'leaf'
leave v. *mok, muk* ER *muk-* 'let, allow'
left adj. *banglo, bango, bongo* ER *bango* 'crooked'
left handed man n. *bangla mush* ER *murš; bango* 'man'; 'crooked'
leg n. *aera, erra, herri, herro, herroi, kerra* ER *heroj* 'leg'
legs n. *hollivas* ER *holova* 'trousers'
legs n. *kashtas* ER *kašt* 'wood'
legs n. *perrias, piris* ER *piro* 'foot'
lesbian n. *chor* ER *čhoro* 'poor'
let v. *muk* ER *muk-* 'let, allow'
letter n. *chinnamangri, chinnamengra* ER *čhin-* 'cut'
letter n. *lil* ER *lil* 'letter, book'
liar n. *ukraben* ER *xoxavipen* 'lie'
lice n. *joov, juval, juvlas, juvli, juvri, juvs, juvvas* ER *džuv* 'louse'
lie n. *okkapen, okkipen, okraben, okrapen, oxanno, ukrabens* ER *xoxavipen*
   'lie'
lie v. *okki* ER *xox-* 'lie'
lie down v. *sutti* ER *suto* 'sleeping, asleep'
life n. *jiaben, jiddo* ER *dživiben* 'life'
life n. *merriben, merripen* ER *mer-* 'die'
light n. *dood, dud, duddi* ER *dud* 'light'
light n. *eb* ER *xev* 'hole'
like v. *kam, kom, kum* ER *kam-* 'love, want'
listen v. *ark* English *hark* 'listen'
listen v. *shun* ER *šun-* 'hear'
little adj. *betto, bitta, bitti, bitto* Cant *bitti* French *petit* 'little'
little adj. *chitchi* ER *či(či)* 'nothing'
little adj. *tanna, tardi, tawni* ER *terno* 'young'
little girl n. *tikna* ER *tikno* 'small'
live v. *beshenus* ER *beš-* 'sit'
live v. *jib, jiv, jivva* ER *dživ-* 'live'
liver n. *bukka, bukko, bukku, buko* ER *buko* 'liver'
lock n. *klism, klisma, klissem, klissen* ER *klisin* 'key'
lock n. *pallo, pandalo* ER *phandlo* 'closed, shut'
locked up adj. *lelled* ER *lel* 'take (3sg.)'
locksmith n. *klissemengri* ER *klisin* 'key'
long adj. *bori* ER *baro* 'big'

long adj. *durra* ER *dur* 'far'
long adj. *longo* English *long* 'long'
long road n. *durra drom* ER *drom; dur* 'way, road'; 'far'
look v. *atch* ER *ačh-* 'stay'
look v. *deek, dik, dikkai* ER *dikh-* 'see'
look v. *vater* Sinti *vater-* German *warten* 'to watch/look'
look v. *yag* ER *jakh* 'eye'
looking-glass n. *vatering-evya* ER *xev; vaxtr-* 'hole'; 'to watch/look'
lord n. *rai, raia, ria* ER *raj* 'gentleman, lord'
lord n. *Romani rai* ER *raj; romani* 'gentleman, lord'; 'Gypsy'
lost adj. *latched, latchedd* ER *lač-* 'find'
lots adj. *dorsus, dosta, dowstis* ER *dosta* 'enough'
louse n. *ju, jub, juv, juvva* ER *džuv* 'louse'
lousy adj. *juvli, juvvari, shuvvalen* ER *džuvalo* 'lousy'
lousy (has lice) adj. *juvri* ER *džuvalo* 'lousy'
love n. *kam, kom, kommorto, kum* ER *kam-* 'love, want'
love v. *kom* ER *kam-* 'love, want'
lovely adj. *komli* ER *kam-* 'love, want'
luck n. *bok, buk, bokt* ER *baxt* 'luck'
luck n. *boktalo* ER *baxtalo* 'lucky'
lucky adj. *baktalo, boklo, boktalo* ER *baxtalo* 'lucky'
lucky adj. *kushti bok* ER *baxt; kuč* 'luck'; 'dear'
lullaby n. *suttajinni* ER *suto; gili* 'sleeping, asleep'; 'song'
lunatic asylum n. *dindla kaer* ER *kher; dinilo* 'house'; 'fool'
lying v. *dukkering* ER *dokrapen, dorikeripe, doricaripe, dorikiriben* 'fortune-telling'

mad adj. *dinalo, dindla, dingla, dinglo, dinla, dinlo, dinnila, dinnilla* ER *dinilo* 'fool'
mad adj. *divvi, divvius, divvo, divya* ER *divjo* 'wild'
mad person n. *dindla* ER *dinilo* 'fool'
mad-house n. *divya tan* ER *than; divjo* 'place'; 'wild'
mad-man n. *divya* ER *divjo* 'wild'
magistrate n. *borapukkamengri* ER *baro; phuker-* 'big'; 'speak'
magpie n. *kala pawni cherkla, kula porna cherkla, porno-kawla cherkli* ER *kalo; čirikli; parno* 'black'; 'bird'; 'white'
make v. *kaer, kel, kerra, kia* ER *ker-* 'make, do'
male n. *mush* ER *murš* 'man'
man n. *chavvi* ER *čhavo* 'boy'
man n. *chor, chuvno* ER *čhoro* 'poor'
man n. *gadji, gawdja, gawdjan, gawdjo, goidji* ER *gadžo* 'non-Gypsy'
man n. *gaer, gaera, gaeri, gaero, giri* ER *goro* 'man'
man n. *mush, musha* ER *murš* 'man'
man n. *rai* ER *raj* 'gentleman, lord'

man n. *rakla, rakli* ER *raklo* 'boy'

man n. *rom, rommi, rowm* ER *Rom* 'autonym, Gypsy man, husband'

man in authority n. *muskra, muskro* ER *mujeskero* 'policeman'

man who speaks different languages n. *lavvengremush* ER *lav; murš* 'word'; 'man'

Manchester n. *bawlagav* ER *gav; baro* 'village'; 'big'

Manchester n. *panigav* ER *gav; pani* 'village'; 'water'

many adj. *boot, butti* ER *but* 'much, many'

many adj. *dosta, dostus, dowstis, dusta* ER *dosta* 'enough'

mare n. *gras, grasni, grasseni, gris, rashni* ER *grasni* 'mare'

market n. *farro, forra, forras* ER *foro(s)* 'town, fair'; 'market'

married adj. *rommered, rummered* ER *romer-* 'marry'

marry v. *rommer, rummer, rummi* ER *romer-* 'marry'

match n. *yogkosh* ER *kašt; jag* 'wood'; 'fire'

mate n. *pal* ER *phral* 'brother'

me pr. *man* ER *man* 'I (obl.)'

me pr. *mandi* ER *mande* 'I (loc.)'

meal n. *habben, obben* ER *xaben* 'food'

meat n. *bollo mas* ER *balo; mas* 'pig'; 'meat'

meat n. *mas* ER *mas* 'meat'

medicine n. *drab, drabba* ER *drab* 'medicine'

mental institute n. *divya kaer* ER *kher; divjo* 'house'; 'wild'

metal n. *saiesta, saster* ER *sastri* 'iron'

midday n. *paladivvus* ER *dives; pala(l)* 'day'; 'behind'

mile n. *maia, miu, miya* ER *mija, maja* 'mile'

milk n. *dood, tood, tud, tut, twud, zud* ER *thud* 'milk'

milkman n. *tuddamengra* ER *thud* 'milk'

miller n. *poramengra, pornomeskro* ER *parno* 'white'

miller n. *varramengra* ER *varo* 'flour '

mind n. *zi* ER *(o)zi* 'heart, soul'

mine pr. *mandi's* ER *mande* 'I (loc.)'

mirror n. *dikkamengri* ER *dikh-* 'see'

mirror n. *dikkin' evya* ER *dikh-; xev* 'see'; 'hole'

mirror n. *evya* ER *xev* 'hole'

Monday n. *tuvvin' day, tuvvin' divvus* ER *thov-* 'wash'

money n. *larvo, lauwi, lovva, lovvo, lowvi, luv, luvva, luvvay, luvverd, luvvi, luvvo, luvvu* ER *love* 'money'

money n. *poshas, poshus* ER *paš* 'half'

money n. *posh-ora* ER *xajera, xajri, xajro, hal'ris; paš* 'penny'; 'half'

money n. *vonga, wonga* ER *vangar* 'coal'

money belt n. *kissi* ER *kisi* 'purse'

monkey n. *jot, jotto* ER *jotto* Cant *jotto* 'monkey'

monkey n. *pogarus, poggaera, poggaerus, poggarus, puggaera, puggasar, puggus* ER *phager* 'to break'; 'train or tame an animal' monkey n. *rukkamengra* ER *rukh* 'tree'

moon n. *choon, chownus, chun, kongi, tyoon* ER *čhon* 'moon'

more adj. *boot* ER *but* 'much, many'

more adj. *burrader* ER *bareder* 'bigger'

more adj. *dosta* ER *dosta* 'enough'

morning n. *divvus* ER *dives* 'day'

morning n. *sala, sawla, sawlo, sora, sowla* ER *tesarla, tajsarla, tehara, teharin* 'morning'

mother n. *dai, daia, daiev, dia, mai* ER *daj* 'mother'

mother n. *mammus* ER *mammus* Cant *mammus* 'mother'

mother-in-law n. *sassori* ER *sasuj* 'mother-in-law'

mother-in-law n. *stiffa mammas* Sinti *štif* German *stief* 'step- (relation by marriage)'; Cant *mammus* 'mother'

motor n. *kista, kistra* ER *klisto* 'riding'

motor n. *skreev* ER *skreev* Cant *skreev* 'car'

mouth n. *mai, meu, mo, moi, mowi, mui, mutti, muwi, myer* ER *muj* 'face, mouth'

much adj. *boot* ER *but* 'much, many'

much adj. *dosta, dusta* ER *dosta* 'enough'

my pr. *ma, mai, mi* ER *my* 'my'

my pr. *mandi, mandi's* ER *mande* 'I (loc.)'

my pr. *miro, mirra, mirri, mirro* ER *miro* 'my'

myself pr. *kukkeri, kukkeru, kukri, me kukkero, mikukkeri, mikukkeroo* ER *korkořo* 'alone'

naked adj. *nanga, nango* ER *nango* 'naked'

name n. *lab, lav* ER *lav* 'word'

name n. *nav* ER *nav* 'name'

narrow adj. *tang* ER *tang(o), tanko* 'narrow, tight, constricted'

naughty adj. *abeng* ER *beng* 'devil'

near adj. *pasha, posha* ER *paša(l)* 'nearby'

neck n. *dumma* ER *dumo* 'back'

neck n. *men, nen* ER *men* 'neck'

neck-tie n. *menkangushi* ER *angrusti; men* 'ring'; 'neck'

neck-tie n. *pengushi* ER *angrusti; phand-* 'ring'; 'tie'

needle n. *sivva, sivvimengri, soov, thuv* ER *siv-* 'sew'

nephew n. *palleska* ER *phral* 'brother'

new adj. *navvo, nevvi, nevvo, nevya* ER *nevo* 'new'

next to prep. *pasha* ER *paša(l)* 'nearby'

niece n. *penneski* ER *phen* 'sister'

night n. *divvus* ER *dives* 'day'

night n. *raddi, radi, rai, rat, rati, ratti, vatchi* ER *rati* 'night'

nine num. *enga, enna, ennia, enya, hina, ina* ER *enja* 'nine'

nineteen num. *deshtaenna, deshtuindya* ER *deštaenja* 'nineteen' ninety num. *endo* ER *enja* 'nine'

nits n. *jubli* ER *džuv* 'louse'

no interj. *chitchi, chitti* ER *či(či)* 'nothing'

no interj. *kek, kekka* ER *kek* 'not'

no interj. *nai, ni, norredo* ER *na* 'no, not'

no interj. *niks, niksi, nistis* ER *niks* Cant *niks* 'no, nothing, not'

none adj. *chitchi* ER *či(či)* 'nothing'

non-Gypsies n. *gadjos, gawdja, gawdjas, gawdjos* ER *gadžo* 'non-Gypsy'

non-Gypsy n. *gadji, gadjo, gadjos, gawdja, gawdjas, gawdji, gawdjo, gawdjos, godja, godji, godjo* ER *gadžo* 'non-Gypsy'

non-Gypsy n. *gaeri* ER *goro* 'man'

non-Gypsy n. *kollia* ER *xalo* 'non-Gypsy'

non-Gypsy n. *mumpa* ER *mumper* Cant *mumper* 'beggar'

non-Gypsy n. *mumpafowki* English *folk* 'people'*;* Cant *mumper* 'beggar'

non-Gypsy n. *rakla* ER *rakli* 'girl'

non-Gypsy n. *rakli* ER *raklo* 'boy'

non-Gypsy boy n. *raklo* ER *raklo* 'boy'

non-Gypsy girl n. *chavvi* ER *čhavo* 'boy'

non-Gypsy girl n. *gadji* ER *gadžo* 'non-Gypsy'

non-Gypsy man n. *gadjo, gawdjo* ER *gadžo* 'non-Gypsy'

non-Gypsy man n. *gaera* ER *goro* 'man'

non-Gypsy 'pretender' n. *waido* English slang *wide-o* 'pretender'

non-Gypsy traveller n. *mumpa, mumpas* ER *mumper* Cant *mumper* 'beggar'

non-Gypsy woman n. *gaeri* ER *gori* 'woman'

non-Gypsy woman n. *gawdji* ER *gadži* 'non-Gypsy woman'

non-Gypsy woman n. *juvvel* ER *džuvel* 'woman'

non-Gypsy woman n. *monnishin* ER *manušni* 'woman'

non-Gypsy woman n. *rakli* ER *rakli* 'girl'

nose n. *nak, nog, nok, nokka* ER *nakh* 'nose'

not adv. *kek* ER *kek* 'not'

not adv. *na, nai, ni, nor* ER *na* 'no, not'

nothing n. *cheetchi, chi, chitch, chitchi, chitti, chutchi* ER *či(či)* 'nothing'

nothing n. *kaerka, kek* ER *kek* 'not'

nothing n. *niks, niksi, niksis, niksus* Cant *niks, niksis* 'no, nothing, not'

now adv. *akonnaw, kanna, kon, konnaw* ER *akana* 'now'

now adv. *kanna adrey* ER *andre; akana* 'in'; 'now'

now adv. *karrisig* ER *akana; sigo* 'now'; 'soon'

nut n. *akkar* ER *akhor* 'nut'

official adj. *gavmush* ER *gav; murš* 'village'; 'man'

official document n. *chinnamengra* ER *čhin-* 'cut, write'

old adj. *parro, pora, pori, poro, porri, pura, purna, purno, purra, purri, purro* ER *phuro* 'old'

old Gypsies n. *purra ratti* ER *phuro; rat* 'old'; 'blood'

old man n. *purri mush* ER *murš; phuro* 'man'; 'old'
old people n. *purra fowki* English *folk;* ER *phuro* 'people'; 'old'
old woman n. *purri rakli* ER *rakli; phuroi* 'girl'; 'old'
on prep. *adrey, drey* ER *andre* 'in'
one num. *yak, yeg, yek* ER *jekh* 'one'
one hour n. *yekora* ER *jekh; ora* 'one'; 'hour'
one hundred num. *shel* ER *šel* 'hundred'
one thousand num. *yek meel* ER *jekh; mil* 'one'; 'thousand'
onion n. *poramar, punnim, purrum* ER *purum* 'onion'
open v. *puter, utra, utta* ER *puter-* 'open'
orange n. *shuliki* ER *šuklo* 'sour'
other adj. *duvva* ER *(o)dova* 'that'
other adj. *waiver, wavver, wavvo, weyver, wuvver* ER *vaver* 'other'
other adj. *woffa* ER *vaver* 'other'
out prep. *arey, avrey, avri* ER *avri* 'out, outside'
outside adj. *avrey, avri* ER *avri* 'out, outside'
outside n. *jel out* ER *džal; out* 'go (3sg.)'; 'out'
over prep. *adrey* ER *andre* 'in'
over the country prep. *preyatem* ER *upre; them* 'up, on'; 'country, land'
own adj. *kukkeri* ER *korkořo* 'alone'

pain n. *dook, duk* ER *dukh* 'pain'
palm n. *duk* ER *dokrapen, dorikeripe, doricaripe, dorikiriben* 'fortune-telling'
pants n. *rokkunyas* ER *raxami, rexami* 'coat'
paper n. *lil* ER *lil* 'letter, book'
paper n. *pappa, pappairis* ER *papiro* 'paper'
pawn shop n. *simmerin' tan* ER *than; simado, simadi, simagi* 'place'; 'pawned,
    pawn'
pay v. *pessa, pesta, presta* ER *ples-* German *Preis* 'price, pay'
pear n. *ambrol, ambrul, andel* ER *ambrol* 'pear'
peg n. *koshna* ER *kašt* 'wood'
peg maker n. *waido* English slang *wide-o* 'pretender'
penis n. *kor, kori, korri, kuri* ER *kar* 'penis'
penny n. *heyro, hora, horro, ora* ER *xajera, xajri, xajro, hal'ris* 'penny'
penny n. *posh-bar* ER *bar; paš* 'stone, rock'; 'half'
penny n. *posh-ora* ER *xajera, xajri, xajro, hal'ris; paš* 'penny'; 'half'
penny n. *yek-ora* ER *xajera, xajri, xajro, hal'ris; (j)ekh* 'penny'; 'one'
people n. *fowki, fowkis* English *folk* 'people'
pepper n. *dantimengra* ER *dand* 'tooth'
perfume n. *funken* English *funky* 'smelly'
person n. *chal* ER *čalado* 'family'
person n. *lesti* ER *leste* 'he (loc.)'
pheasant n. *borrikanni* ER *kaxni; baro* 'hen'; 'big'
pheasant n. *divya kani* ER *kaxni; divjo* 'hen'; 'wild'

pheasant n. *kanni* ER *kaxni* 'hen'

pheasant n. *veshni kanni* ER *kaxni; veš* 'hen'; 'wood, forest'

picture n. *parranitch* ER *paramiči, paramisi* 'story'

pig n. *ballo, balo, bawla, bawlo, bawra, bollo* ER *balo* 'pig'

pig n. *bollo mas* ER *balo; mas* 'pig'; 'meat'

pig n. *gruffi, grufna* ER *guruvni* 'cow'

pipe n. *swagla, swaglas, swegli, swigla* German *Schwegel* 'pipe, flute'

pitchfork n. *possamengri, pussimengro* ER *phus* 'straw'

place n. *tam, tem* ER *them* 'country, land'

place n. *tan* ER *than* 'place'

plate n. *char, charo, charra, cherrah, cherro, chorro, chowr* ER *čaro* 'bowl, plate'

play v. *bosh* ER *bašav-* 'to play an instrument'

play v. *kal, kel* ER *khel-* 'dance, play'

plenty adj. *adosta, dosta, dosti, dowsa, duksta, dukstras, dusta, dusti* ER *dosta* 'enough'

plough n. *povvestachuddi* ER *phuv; čhud-* 'ground, earth'; 'throw, scatter, sow'

pocket n. *portsi, powtsi, putchdi, putchni, putsi, putta* ER *poski, posita* 'pocket'

poison n. *drab, drav* ER *drab* 'medicine'

police n. *bawlos* ER *balo* 'pig'

police n. *gavver* ER *gav* 'village', or *garav-* 'to hide'

police n. *muskero, muskers, muskra, muskras, muskros, muzgrowvs* ER *mujeskero* 'policeman'

policeman n. *bawlo* ER *balo* 'pig'

policeman n. *gavvamush* ER *murš; gav* or *garav-;* 'man'; 'village' or 'to hide'

policeman n. *mengra, mengris, mingra, mingras, mingri, proskamangra* ER *prastimangero* 'runner, policeman'

policeman n. *muskramush* ER *murš; mujeskero* 'man'; 'policeman'

policeman n. *plastamengra, plastamengro, prasta, prastamengra, prastamengri, prastamengro, prastamingra, prostamingra* ER *prast-* 'run'

pond n. *pani* ER *pani* 'water'

poor adj. *chor, chorda, chorikeni, chorokoni, chorvano, churkenus, churri, churro, chuvvani* ER *čhoro* 'poor'

poor man n. *chor* ER *čhoro* 'poor'

posh adj. *rawni* ER *rani* 'lady'

posh person n. *rai* ER *raj* 'gentleman, lord'

posterior n. *jaer, jeer* Cant jeer 'bottom (anatomy)'

pot n. *koro, kurra* ER *khoro* 'jug'

pot n. *pawru, piri, pirri* ER *piri* 'pot, pan'

potato n. *povvengra, povvengro, povvingra, puvengra, puvvengra, puvvengri, puvvengro, puvvingra* ER *phuv* 'ground, earth'

pound n. *baer* ER *bar* 'stone, rock'

pound (money) n. *bar* ER *bar* 'stone, rock'

pregnant adj. *bawro, bora, bori, bowro* ER *baro* 'big'

pregnant adj. *komborri, kamborri, kambri* ER *kamni* 'pregnant'

pretty adj. *arinkina, rinkeni, rinkni* ER *rankano* 'beautiful'

priest n. *rashai, rashi, rushai* ER *rašaj* 'priest'

prison n. *distarabin, staeripen, staerpen, staraben, starapen, stardi, stariben, staripen, starrapan, starriben, starripen, sterriben, sterripen, stirripen* ER *staripen* 'prison'

prostitute n. *lubni, luveni, luvni, luvvani* ER *lubni* 'prostitute'

pub n. *kaera* ER *kher* 'house'

pub n. *ketchema, kitchem, kitchema, kitchemo, kitchima, kitchna, kitchum* ER *kirčima* 'pub'

pub n. *piva* ER *piv* 'drink (1sg.)'

pudding n. *goi, gui* ER *goj* 'sausage'

purse n. *putsi* ER *poski, posita* 'pocket'

put v. *chiv* ER *čhiv-* 'put'

put v. *lel* ER *lel* 'take (3sg.)'

put v. *tuv* ER *thov-* 'put'

putting the horses in the field v. *puvvin' the grais* ER *phuv; graj* 'ground, earth'; 'horse'

quarrel n. *chingerpen* ER *čhingeripen* 'quarrel, shout'

quarrel v. *chinger* ER *čhinger-* 'quarrel, shout'

queen n. *rawni* ER *rani* 'lady'

quick adj. *seggo, sigo* ER *sigo* 'soon'

quiet! interj. *ark* English *hark* 'listen'

rabbit n. *kannengro* ER *kan* 'ear'

rabbit n. *shoshi, shusha, shushi, shusho, sushi* ER *šošoj* 'hare'

racehorse n. *rat grai* ER *graj; rat* 'horse'; 'blood'

rag n. *misli* ER *mesali* 'towel, scarf'

rain n. *bisha, bishen, bishin, bishno, breshin, brish, brishendo, brishiben, brishin, brishindo, brishno, brishum, briskeno, mishum* ER *brišind* 'rain'

rain n. *pani, panni* ER *pani* 'water'

rainbow n. *duvla's pani* ER *pani; devel* 'water'; 'God'

ram n. *bukro* ER *bakro* 'sheep'

rat n. *muski* ER *kermuso* 'mouse, rat'

read v. *gin* ER *gin-* 'count'

real adj. *tatcho* ER *čačo* 'right, true'

real Gypsy n. *tatcha romani chal* ER *čačo; čalado; romani* 'right, true'; 'family'; 'Gypsy (adj.)'

receipt n. *lil* ER *lil* 'letter, book'

red adj. *alullo, lal, lalla, lalli, lalo, lol, lolla, lolli, lollo, lullo, ral* ER *lolo* 'red'

red rose n. *lolla rushli* ER *lolo; ruža* 'red'; 'rose'

respect n. *patch* ER *pača-* 'believe'

ribs n. *kokollus* ER *kokalo* 'bone'
rich adj. *barvelo, bavla, bavvalo* ER *barvalo* 'rich'
rich adj. *dusta luvva* ER *dosta; love* 'enough'; 'money'
rich lady n. *rawni* ER *rani* 'lady'
rich man n. *rai* ER *raj* 'gentleman, lord'
rich widow n. *pivvali rawni* ER *rani; phivli* 'lady'; 'widow'
ride v. *kis, kisda, kista, kistan, kistas* ER *klisto* 'riding'
right (direction) n. *tatchi* ER *čačo* 'right, true'
ring n. *fawni* Shelta *fawni* 'ring'
ring n. *grawn* Shelta *grawni* 'ring'
ring n. *vangasti, vangustri, vawnustri, vokkishna, vong, vonga, vongasha,
    vongashi, vongista, vongrushni, vongusha, vongusti, vongustri, vonnishin,
    wangustri, wongesta, wongushi* ER *vangrusti* 'ring'
river n. *pan, pani* ER *pani* 'water'
road n. *drom, drum* ER *drom* 'way, road'
road n. *puv* ER *phuv* 'ground, earth'
roast v. *pek* ER *pek-* 'roast, bake'
rob v. *luer* ER *lurr-, lur-* 'rob'
rods n. *ranyes, ronyes* ER *ran(ik)* 'stick', 'twig', 'branch'
Romani gentleman n. *Romani rai* ER *raj; romani* 'gentleman, lord'; 'Gypsy
    (adj.)'
Romani language n. *Romanes, Romanis, Rommanes, romnes, romnis,
    Rumanes, Rumnus* ER *romanes* 'in the Gypsy way, the Gypsy language'
Romani language n. *Romani* ER *romani* 'Gypsy (adj.)'
Romani language n. *Romani jib* ER *čhib; romani* 'tongue, language'; 'Gypsy
    (adj.)'
rose n. *lulludji* ER *luludži* 'flower'
rose n. *rushli* ER *ruža* 'rose'
rough Traveller n. *diddikoi* ER *akaj; dikh-* 'here'; 'see'
rubbish n. *rammel* ER English slang *rammel* 'rubbish'
rug n. *dikla* ER *diklo* '(hand)kerchief, shawl'
run v. *jel* ER *džal* 'go (3sg.)'
run v. *jes* ER *džas* 'go (2sg.)'
run v. *nash* ER *naš-* 'run (away), escape'
run v. *prast, prasta, prastem, prasti* ER *prast-* 'run'
run away v. *nash* ER *naš-* 'run (away), escape'

sack n. *gonno, gunna* ER *gono* 'bag, sack'
sad adj. *ruv* ER *rov-* 'cry'
sailor n. *barringro, berramengra, berrengro, berromeskro* ER *bero* 'ship, boat'
sailor n. *paningramush* ER *murš; pani* 'man'; 'water'
salt n. *lon, lonna, loon, lown, lub, lun* ER *lon* 'salt'
Saturday n. *kinning divvus* ER *dives; kin-* 'day'; 'buy'
sausage n. *goi* ER *goj* 'sausage'

say v. *pen, penner* ER *phen-* 'say'
say v. *pukker* ER *phuker-* 'tell'
say v. *putch* ER *phuč-* 'ask'
say v. *rokker* ER *raker-* 'speak'
scared adj. *trashed* ER *traš-* 'frighten'
scarf n. *dikla, diklo* ER *diklo* '(hand)kerchief, shawl'
scarf n. *stardi* ER *stadi(k)* 'hat'
school n. *kaer* ER *kher* 'house'
school n. *kongli, kongri, konli* ER *khangeri* 'church'
school boy n. *konligaera* ER *goro; khangeri* 'man'; 'church'
school master n. *kongri mush* ER *murš; khangeri* 'man'; 'church'
school teacher n. *kongligaera* ER *goro; khangeri* 'non-Gypsy who intermarried with Gypsies'; 'church'
scolded adj. *chingered* ER *čhinger-* 'quarrel, shout'
Scottish people n. *apreyatempo* ER *apre; them* 'on'; 'country, land'
scrap n. *saiesta* ER *sastri* 'iron'
scream v. *chinger* ER *čhinger-* 'quarrel, shout'
sea n. *bori lun pani, lon bori pani* ER *pani; barol-i; lon* 'water'; 'big'; 'salt'
sea n. *derria, derrian, dorrian, dowyav, durria* ER *dorjav, derjav* 'sea, river'
sea n. *pani* ER *pani* 'water'
see v. *deek, dik, dikki, dikkon* ER *dikh-* 'see'
see v. *dikkes* ER *dikhes* 'see (2sg.)'
see v. *dikhav* ER *dikhav* 'see (1sg.)'
see v. *vater, wart* Sinti *vater-* German *warten* 'to watch/look'
self n. *kokkeri, kokkeru, kukkeri, kukkero, kukra, kukri, pukkero* ER *korkořo* 'alone'
sell v. *bik, bikka, bikken, bikkin, biknas* ER *bikin-* 'sell'
send v. *bitch* ER *bič̌h-* 'send'
seven num. *afta, eft, efta, ekka, hefta* ER *efta* 'seven'
seventeen num. *deshtahefta, deshtueft* ER *deštaefta* 'seventeen'
seventy num. *defredesh* ER *deš; efta* 'ten'; 'seven'
seventy num. *efta, efto* ER *efta* 'seven'
shame n. *patch* ER *pača-* 'believe'
shameful adj. *ladjed, ladjful* ER *ladž-* 'be ashamed'
she pr. *lakki* ER *lake* 'she (dat.)'
she pr. *latti* ER *late* 'she (loc.)'
she pr. *linga* ER *lenge* 'they (dat.)'
she pr. *lesti* ER *leste* 'he (loc.)'
she pr. *yoi* ER *joj* 'she'
sheep n. *bakra, bakral, batchiko, bawkaro, bawkero, bawkra, bokkasha, bokkencha, bokkenshi, bokkero, bokkishna, bokkoro, bokra, bokro, okri* ER *bakro* 'sheep'
sheep n. *bawla* ER *balo* 'pig'
sheepskin n. *bokramutsi* ER *bakro; morti* 'sheep'; 'leather'

shepherd n. *bawkaingru, bawkoringro, bokkorengro, bokramengra, bokromangro* ER *bakro* 'sheep'

shepherd n. *bokra mush* ER *bakro; murš* 'sheep'; 'man'

shilling n. *kalor, kulla* ER *xajera, xajri, xajro, hal'ris* 'penny'

ship n. *baera, baero, barro, berringeri, biero, birro* ER *bero* 'ship, boat'

shirt n. *gad, gat, yad* ER *gad* 'shirt'

shit n. *hin* ER *xind-* 'defecate'

shit-house n. *pani-kenna* ER *pani; ken* 'water'; 'house'

shitty adj. *hinditti* ER *xindo* 'lousy, shitty, bad'

shoes n. *chakka, chakkan, chawan, chihor, chirris, chittaws, chittiows, choka, chokka, chokkas, chokkis, chuddias, churrias, churrios, churris* ER *tirax* 'shoe'

shop n. *buddika, budika, burrika, burruko* French *boutique* 'shop'

short adj. *bitti* Cant *bitti* French *petit* 'little'

shoulders n. *pikkus* ER *phiko* 'shoulder'

show v. *sikker* ER *sikar-* 'show, teach'

showman n. *sikkamangi, sikkamengra* ER *sikar-* 'show, teach'

shut v. *pander, panner* ER *phandar-* 'close, lock'

sick adj. *lish* ER *liš* 'shock'

sick adj. *naffala, nafli, nassalo* ER *nasvalo* 'sick, ill'

sickness n. *naffilisolli, naflipen* ER *nasvalo* 'sick, ill'

side n. *rig* ER *rig* 'side'

sign n. *kosh* ER *kašt* 'wood'

sign n. *patrin* ER *patrin* 'leaf'

sign-post n. *drom* ER *drom* 'way, road'

sign-post n. *kosh pukker me the drom, kosh pukker the drum, kosh pukkered the drum, kosh pukkers the drom* ER *kašt; drom; phuker-* 'wood'; 'way, road'; 'tell'

sign-post n. *pogger the drom* ER *drom; phuker-* 'way, road'; 'tell'

sign-post n. *pukkering kosh* ER *kašt; phuker-* 'wood'; 'tell'

sign-post n. *sikkering kosh* ER *kašt; sikar-* 'wood'; 'show, teach'

silver adj. *grupakano* ER *rupikano* 'silver (adj.)'

silver n. *grup, roop, rup, rut* ER *rup* 'silver'

silver n. *rupaka, rupna, ruppeni* ER *rupikano* 'silver (adj.)'

sing v. *charn* French *chanter* 'sing'

sing v. *gil, giv, givellan, givvella, givvi, jil* ER *gil(av)-* 'sing'

sing v. *kel* ER *khel-* 'dance, play'

singer n. *chanta* French *chanter* 'sing'

singer n. *gilli, gillier* ER *gili* 'song'

sister n. *pan, pen, pey* ER *phen* 'sister'

sister n. *rakla* ER *rakli* 'girl'

sister-in-law n. *stiffa pen* ER *phen* 'sister'; Sinti *štif* German *stief)* 'step- (relation by marriage)'

sit v. *atch* ER *ačh-* 'stay'

sit v. *besh* ER *beš-* 'sit'

sit down v. *besh aley, besh teley, tallabesh* ER *tele; beš-* 'down'; 'sit'

six num. *chov, sharn, shik, sho, shob, shor, shov, showv* ER *šov* 'six'

sixpence n. *shik-ori, shokkora, shook-hari, showheyra, shu-hora, shuk ori, shuk-ora* ER *šov; xajera, xajri, xajro, hal'ris* 'six'; 'penny'

sixteen num. *deshdeduitrin* ER *thaj; duj; deš; trin* 'and'; 'two'; 'ten'; 'three'

sixty num. *shobda, shobdo* ER *šovardeš* 'sixty'

sky n. *cherribim* ER *čeri* 'sky'; English *cherubim* 'angels'

slap v. *del* ER *del* 'give (3sg.)'

sleep v. *lutherun* ER *lod-* 'to settle, to be unloaded, to lodge'

sleep v. *savvano, sov, sovva* ER *sov-* 'sleep'

sleep v. *sotto, sutri, sutti, sutto, sutty* ER *suto* 'sleeping, asleep'

sleep v. *wudrus* ER *vodros* 'bed'

slutty adj. *chikla* ER *čhikelo* 'dirty'

small adj. *biddi, bitta, bitti* Cant *bitti* French *petit* 'little'

small adj. *tikna, tikno, trikni* ER *tikno* 'small'

smell n. *foi, foil, fowgal* Sinti *fojl-* German *faul* 'rot'

smell n. *kanda, kander* ER *khan(d)-* 'smell'

smell n. *sum, sung* ER *sung* 'smell'

smell v. *foi* Sinti *fojl-* German *faul* 'rot'

smell v. *kan* ER *khan(d)-* 'smell'

smith n. *pettelengra, pettulemengri* ER *petalo* 'horseshoe'

smoke n. *toof, tuv* ER *thuv* 'smoke'

smoke v. *huvvi, thu, tow, towf, tud, tuv, tuvla, tuvna, tuvva* ER *thuv[(j)ar]-* 'smoke '

snake n. *sap, sep* ER *sap* 'snake'

snow n. *biffi, deev, eef, eev, gib, giv, iv, wiv* ER *iv* 'snow'

soap n. *saffen, sapna, sapnus, sappenus, sappin, soppernis, sopponus* ER *sapuj, sapuni, saponi* 'soap'

socks n. *olliva, ollivas* ER *holova* 'trousers'

soft adj. *kuvvelo* ER *kovlo* 'soft'

soil n. *chik* ER *čhik* 'mud, dirt, earth'

soldier n. *koramengra, koramongra, korimingra, kuramengra, kuramungeri, kurramangero* ER *kur-* 'beat up'

something n. *chommani, chumni* ER *čomoni* 'something'

son n. *chav, chavvo* ER *čhavo* 'boy '

song n. *dilli, gilli, gillia, gilliben, jilli* ER *gili* 'song'

soul n. *ji* ER *dži* 'soul, heart, belly'

soup n. *bruv* dialectal English *brov* 'broth (soup)'

soup n. *zimmin, zimmins, zinni, zumi* ER *zumi* 'soup'

sour adj. *shukelo, shuklo, shutlo* ER *šuklo* 'sour'

sovereign n. *posh-ora* ER *xajera, xajri, xajro, hal'ris; paš* 'penny'; 'half'

sovereign n. *sonnakai-ora* ER *xajera, xajri, xajro, hal'ris; sonakaj* 'penny'; 'gold'

speak v. *pukker* ER *phuker-* 'tell'
speak v. *rakkerin', rokker* ER *raker-* 'speak'
spoon n. *oiya, rai, roi, rowi* ER *řoj* 'spoon'
squirrel n. *rukkamengri* ER *rukh* 'tree'
stable n. *stannia* ER *stanja* 'barn, stable'
stairs n. *porras, puddis, purrases, purruses* ER *podo* 'floor'
stallion n. *palengo, pellengro* ER *pelengro grai* 'stallion'
stars n. *duddis* ER *dud* 'light'
starving v. *bukt to mulla* ER *bokh; mulo* 'hunger'; 'dead'
stay v. adj., *atch, atchi* ER *ačh-* 'stay'
stay v. *besh* ER *beš-* 'sit'
steal v. *chor, chowa, kowr* ER *čor-* 'steal'
steal v. *law, luer* ER *lurr-, lur-* 'rob'
stick n. *kosh, kosht, koshti* ER *kašt* 'wood'
stick n. *pukking kosh* ER *kašt; phuk(er)-* 'wood'; 'tell'
stink v. *kan, kander* ER *khan(d)-* 'smell'
stitched up adj. *ladjed up* ER *ladž-* 'be ashamed'
stomach n. *paer, por, pur* ER *peř* 'belly, stomach'
stone n. *baer, bar* ER *bar* 'stone, rock'
stop v. *atch, hatch* ER *ačh-* 'stay'
stop v. *kek, kekka* ER *kek* 'not'
stop v. *stawl* English *stall* 'stall'
stopping place n. *atchin' tan, atching tam* ER *ačh-; than* 'stay'; 'place'
storm n. *boot brishin* ER *brišind; but* 'rain'; 'much, many'
story n. *parranitch* ER *paramiči, paramisi* 'story'
story-teller n. *parrameshengra* ER *paramiči, paramisi* 'story'
stove n. *bor* ER *bov* 'oven'
straw n. *kaz* ER *khas* 'hay'
straw n. *poos, pul, pus* ER *phus* 'straw'
stuff n. *kuvva* ER *kova* 'thing'
stupid adj. *dindla, dingla, dinglo, dinla, dinlo, dinnilla* ER *dinilo* 'fool'
stupid adj. *divvi* ER *divjo* 'wild'
stupidity n. *divya* ER *divjo* 'wild'
sugar n. *dudli, googlo, gudla, gudlam, gudli, gudlo, gudlu, gugli* ER *gudlo*
  'sweet, sugar'
sugar n. *kukki* ER *cukro* 'sugar'
summer n. *lenna, lilai, lillai, linnai, maili, neel, nyli* ER *nilaj* 'summer'
summer n. *tattabeen, tatto* ER *tato* 'warm, hot'
sun n. *kam, kan, tam* ER *kham* 'sun'
Sunday n. *devla divvus* ER *devel; dives* 'God'; 'day'
Sunday n. *kamdivvus* ER *dives; kham-* 'day'; 'sun'
Sunday n. *kawkey, kawko, kuku, kurkeni divvus* ER *kurko* 'week, Sunday'
Sunday n. *mas divvus, masdivvus* ER *mas; dives* 'meat'; 'day'
swap v. *boot* ER *buti* 'work'

swear v. *chinger* ER *čhinger-* 'quarrel, shout'

swear v. *lab, larv* ER *lav* 'word'

swear v. *sovellahol, sovvekon, sovvoxollo, sullavolla, suvvalo, suvvalol, suvvalolla* ER *sovexer-, sovaho-* 'swear (an oath)'

swear v. *sovvol* ER *sovel* 'swear (3sg.)'

swear v. *suv* ER *sov-* 'sleep'

sweet adj. *gudla, gudli, gudlo, guli* ER *gudlo* 'sweet, sugar'

table n. *bresh* ER *beš-* 'sit'

table n. *messala, mishelli, missali, mistali* ER *misali* 'table'

take v. *jel* ER *džal* 'go (3sg.)'

take v. *lel* ER *lel* 'take (3sg.)'

take off v. *randja* ER *randž-* 'dress, undress'

talk v. *pukker* ER *phuker-* 'tell'

talk v. *rokker, rokkerpen* ER *raker-* 'speak'

tall adj. *bori* ER *baro* 'big'

tall adj. *lang* German *lang* 'long'

tall adj. *tang* ER *tang(o), tanko* 'narrow, tight, constricted'

tart n. *luvli* ER *lubni* 'prostitute'

tea n. *chai, chaiyo, chaiyo's, char* ER *čajo* 'tea'

tea n. *kudli* ER *gudlo* 'sweet, sugar'

tea n. *livni* ER *lovina* 'beer'

tea n. *mangra, mangri, mungri, muttramongra* ER *muterimangeri* 'tea'

tea n. *mot, mukkerangri, mutramengri, mutrimongri, mutsimengri, muttamengri, muttermangri, muttermengri, muttramangeri, muttrimangri* ER *muter* 'urine'

tea n. *piamengra, piamengri, pimengri, pimmesti, pium* ER *pi-* 'drink'

teach v. *sikker* ER *sik(ar)-* 'show, teach'

teacher n. *konligirra* ER *goro; khangeri* 'man'; 'church'

teeth n. *dan, danda, dandras, dandrus, dandus, danno, danyas, denna* ER *danda* 'teeth'

telephone n. *rokkermengri* ER *raker-* 'speak'

telescope n. *dur dikkinengri, dur dikkiningri* ER *dikh-; dur* 'see'; 'far'

television n. *dikkalowmas, dikkelomus* ER *dikh-* 'see'

tell v. *mang* ER *mang-* 'beg, ask, demand'

tell v. *pen, penni* ER *phen-* 'say'

tell v. *pukker* ER *phuker-* 'tell'

tell v. *putch* ER *phuč-* 'ask'

tell v. *rokker* ER *raker-* 'speak'

tell fortunes v. *dukker, durrik, durruk* ER *dokrapen, dorikeripe, doricaripe, dorikiriben* 'fortune-telling'

tell off v. *chinger* ER *čhinger-* 'quarrel, shout'

temperature n. *pobbor* ER *phabar-* 'burn'

ten num. *desh* ER *deš* 'ten'

ten pounds n. *desh bar* ER *bar; deš* 'stone, rock'; 'ten'

tent n. *benda* ER *berand* 'tent pole'

tent n. *selta* Sinti *celta* German *Zelt* 'tent'

tent n. *tarn* ER *than* 'place'

thank you id. *parrakro* ER *pariker-* 'thank'

thank you id. *parrakrotut* ER *pariker-; tut* 'thank'; 'you (obl.)'

thanks id. *paks, parrako, parrakro* ER *pariker-* 'thank'

that dem. *dobba, dovva, dovvai, dovvo, duvva, duvya, odovvi* ER *(o)dova* 'that'

that dem. *guvva, keda, kuvva* ER *(o)kova* 'that'

them pr. *lendi* ER *lende* 'they (loc.)'

there dem. *adai, adoi, adowi, adui* ER *adaj, odoj* 'here, there'

there dem. *akai, akoi* ER *akaj* 'here'

there dem. *adrey, drey* ER *andre* 'in'

there dem. *arri* ER *avri* 'out, outside'

these dem. *duvva* ER *(o)dova* 'that'

these dem. *woffa* ER *vaver* 'other'

they pr. *lendi* ER *lende* 'they (loc.)'

they pr. *lengi* ER *lenge* 'they (dat.)'

they pr. *lesti* ER *leste* 'he (loc.)'

thief n. *chor, chora, choramengra, surramongra* ER *čor, čor-* 'thief, steal'

thin adj. *tang* ER *tang(o), tanko* 'narrow, tight, constricted'

thing n. *duvva* ER *(o)dova* 'that'

thing n. *kavva, kovva, kowva, kuvva* ER *(o)kova* 'that'

things n. *kovvas, kuvvas* ER *(o)kova* 'that'

think v. *pench* French *penser* 'think'

thirsty adj. *trisno, troshalo, trushalo, trushillo, trushlo, trushna* ER *trušalo* 'thirsty'

thirsty adj. *trush* ER *truš* 'thirst'

thirteen num. *deshdetrin, deshtatrin, deshtutrin* ER *deštatrin* 'thirteen'

thirty num. *trerndo, trianda, trinda* ER *tr(i)anda* 'thirty'

this dem. *adella* ER *adala* 'these'

this dem. *adrey* ER *andre* 'in'

this dem. *dovva, dubba, duvva* ER *(o)dova* 'that'

this dem. *woffa, wovva* ER *vaver* 'other'

this country people n. *wovvatemfoki* English *folk;* ER *them; vaver* 'people'; 'country, land'; 'other'

this morning n. *tesala* ER *tesarla, tajsarla, tehara, teharin* 'morning'

this thing n. *wovva kovva* ER *(o)kova; vaver* 'that'; 'other'

thousand num. *desh shel* ER *deš; šel* 'ten'; 'hundred'

thousand num. *meel* French *mille* 'thousand'

thousand num. *miya* ER *mija* 'thousand'

three num. *trien, trin* ER *trin* 'three'

three pence n. *treen-haera, trin-ora* ER *xajera, xajri, xajro, hal'ris; trin* 'penny'; 'three' throat n. *jib* ER *čhib* 'tongue, language'

throat n. *kurla* ER *kerlo, kurlo* 'throat'

through prep. *adrey* ER *andre* 'in'

throw v. *bitcha* ER *bičhar-* 'send'

time n. *chaero, chaeros, chaerus, chellus, cherris, chiris, chiro, chiros, chirrus, chirus, churnus, shaerus* ER *čiros* 'time'

tired adj. *kino* ER *khino* 'tired'

to prep. *ketti, ki* ER *ka, ke, ki* 'to, at'

to me pr. *mangey* ER *mange* 'I (dat.)'

tobacco n. *tivvalo, tugla, tuvla, tuvvelo* ER *thuvalo* 'tobacco'

tobacco n. *tuv* ER *thuv* 'smoke'

today n. *devvus, divvus, kedivvus* ER *dives* 'day'

today n. *tedivvus, todivvus* ER *dives* 'day'; English *to-* > 'to'

toddler n. *bitti chavvi* ER *čhavo* 'boy'; Cant *bitti* French *petit* 'little'

toilet n. *mutter-tan, mutterin' tan, muttertam, muttertan* ER *than; muter* 'place'; 'urine'

toilet n. *pani-kenna* ER *pani; ken* 'water'; 'house'

tom cat n. *matchko* ER *mačka* 'cat'

tomorrow n. *kallako, kollako, kolliko* ER *kaliko(s)* 'yesterday'

tomorrow n. *sowla, tehala, tesawlo* ER *tesarla, tajsarla, tehara, teharin* 'morning'

tomorrow n. *wavver divvus* ER *dives; vaver* 'day'; 'other'

tomorrow morning n. *tesala* ER *tesarla, tajsarla, tehara, teharin* 'morning'

tongue n. *chib, chiv, jib, sheeb* ER *čhib* 'tongue, language'

tonight n. *arati, rati* ER *rati* 'night'

tonight n. *terati, torati* ER *rati; to* 'night'; 'to'

too much adv. *butti* ER *but* 'much, many'

town n. *farro, foro, forros* ER *foro(s)* 'town, fair'; 'market'

town n. *gab, gav* ER *gav* 'village'

town n. *tan* ER *than* 'place'

town n. *tem* ER *them* 'country, land'

trailer n. *varda* ER *vordon* 'cart, wagon'

train n. *saster grai* ER *graj; sastri* 'horse'; 'iron'

tramp n. *chor* ER *čhoro* 'poor'

traveller n. *pirramanga* ER *phir-* 'walk'

traveller n. *waido* English slang *wide-o* 'pretender'

travellers n. *fowki* English *folk* 'people'

tree n. *kosh* ER *kašt* 'wood'

tree n. *rokka, rook, ruk, rukka* ER *rukh* 'tree'

trouble n. *chinger* ER *čhinger-* 'quarrel, shout'

trouble n. *mitchipen, mizhipen* ER *midžax, mižax* 'bad, wicked, wrong'

trousers n. *browg, browgs* English *brogue* 'trousers'

trousers n. *gads* ER *gad* 'shirt'

trousers n. *rammias, ranyas, rohunis, rokkengras, rokkenyas, rokkernis, rokkumas, rokkunya, rokkunyas, rorhunnis, runis* ER *raxami, rexami* 'coat'

trousers n. *strides* English *strides* 'trousers'

truth n. *chutchi, tatchapen, tatchapi, tatchipen, tatchipens, tatrapen, tetchapan* ER *čačo* 'right, true'

turnip n. *kanafni, kanarfri, kannafia, kannarfni, kannawvo, krafni* ER *karfiol* 'cauliflower'

twelve num. *deshdedu, deshtadui, deshtudui* ER *deštaduj* 'twelve'

twenty num. *beesh, besh, bis, bish* ER *biš* 'twenty'

twenty-one num. *beeshtuyek* ER *bišthajekh* 'twenty-one'

twenty-two num. *beeshtudui* ER *bištaduj* 'twenty-two'

twig n. *kosh* ER *kašt* 'wood'

twins n. *dui tiknas* ER *duj; tikno* 'two'; 'small'

two num. *du, dui, dun* ER *duj* 'two'

two pence n. *dui ora* ER *duj; xajera, xajri, xajro, hal'ris* 'two'; 'penny'

two shillings n. *dui kalor, dui kalor* ER *duj; xajera, xajri, xajro, hal'ris* 'two'; 'penny'

ugly adj. *jungalo* ER *džungalo* 'ugly'

ugly adj. *yugli, yuglo* English *ugly* 'ugly'

uncle n. *kakko, kawk, kawko, kok, kokko, kokkodus, kokkol* ER *kako* 'uncle'

unclean adj. *mokkadi* ER *maxado* 'dirty, defiled'

under prep. *tiley* ER *tele* 'down'

underpants n. *rokkunyas* ER *raxami, rexami* 'coat'

understand v. *jun, jin* ER *džin-* 'know'

undress v. *randja* ER *randž-* 'dress, undress'

undressed v. *rango* ER *nango* 'naked'

unlucky adj. *bokki, borka* ER *baxt* 'luck'

up prep. *aprey, apreya* ER *apre* 'on'

up prep. *deprey, oprey, prey, upra, uprey* ER *upre* 'up, on'

upon prep. *pria* ER *upre* 'up, on'

urinate v. *mutter* ER *muter-* 'urinate'

urinate v. *muttri* ER *muter* 'urine'

urine n. *mutter* ER *muter* 'urine'

urine n. *pani* ER *pani* 'water'

vagina n. *mindj* ER *mindž* 'vagina'

venereal disease n. *otchaben, otchraben* ER *xačariben* 'burn, burning'

very adv. *boot* ER *but* 'much, many'

very old adj. *purrana* ER *phurano* 'old'

very soft adj. *nesh* ER *nasvalo* 'sick'; 'ill'

village n. *bitti gav* ER *gav* 'village'; Cant *bitti* French *petit* 'little'

village n. *gab, gal, gav* ER *gav* 'village'

village n. *tan* ER *than* 'place'
vinegar n. *tattamengri* ER *tato* 'warm, hot'
violent people n. *kura fowkis* English *folk;* ER *kur-* 'people'; 'beat (up)'
violin n. *bosh, boshamungeri, mashumangri* ER *bašav-* 'to play an instrument'
violin player n. *boshengra* ER *bašav-* 'to play an instrument'

wagon n. *vadon, varda, vardo* ER *vordon* 'cart, wagon'
waistcoat n. *baiengri, bangaeri, bangori, ben, bengori, bengri, bennengro, biengri* ER *baj* 'sleeve'
walk v. *pia, pieri, pir, pirro* ER *phir-* 'walk'
walk v. *pirriv, pirruv* ER *phirav* 'walk (1sg.)'
walking v. *piering, pirreno* ER *phir-* 'walk'
walking stick n. *vasti kosh* ER *kašt; vast* 'wood'; 'hand, arm'
want v. *kom* ER *kam-* 'love, want'
war n. *chingamos, chingerpen* ER *čhinger-* 'quarrel, shout'
warm adj. *kaermul* ER *ker-; mol* 'make, do'; 'wine'
wash v. *tov, towv, tuv* ER *thov-* 'wash'
wash v. *tovval* ER *thovel* 'wash (3sg.)'
wash v. *tovvav, towamma* ER *thovav* 'wash (1sg.)'
watch v. *vater, water* Sinti *vater-* German *warten* 'to watch/look'
water n. *pali, pani, panni* ER *pani* 'water'
way n. *droom, drum* ER *drom* 'way, road'
we pr. *wovva* ER *vaver* 'other'
weak adj. *nesh* ER *nasvalo* 'sick'; 'ill'
week n. *kawkey, kawko, kruki, krukki, kurikus* ER *kurko* 'week, Sunday'
week n. *shov divvus, shuv divvus* ER *dives; šov* 'day'; 'six'
weigh up v. *vater* Sinti *vater-* German *warten* 'to watch/look'
well adj. *bisto, mishta, mishti, mishto, misto* ER *mišto* 'good, well'
well dressed adj. *kushti rudded* ER *kuč; urado* 'dear'; 'dressed (adj.)'
Welsh adj. *lavveen* ER *lav* 'word'
Welsh Gypsies n. *lavvingro* ER *lav* 'word'
Welsh people n. *lavna foki* ER *lav* 'word'; English *folk* 'people'
went v. *jalled, jel, jelled* ER *džal* 'go (3sg.)'
what pr. *ko, koin* ER *kon* 'who'
what pr. *saw, so, sor* ER *so* 'what'
wheat n. *giv* ER *giv* 'wheat'
where inter. *kai* ER *kaj* 'where, which'
whiskey n. *tatta mul* ER *čačo; mol* 'right, true'; 'wine'
whiskey n. *tattapani, tattipani* ER *pani; tato* 'water'; 'warm, hot'
white adj. *parna, parno, pawli, pawni, pawno, porna, porno* ER *parno* 'white'
who inter. *kon, kun* ER *kon* 'who'
who inter. *savvo* ER *savo* 'what, who, which'
whore n. *privilli juvvel* ER *džuvli; phivli* 'woman'; 'widow'
wide adj. *bori* ER *baro* 'big'

widower n. *pivli* ER *phivli* 'widow'
wife n. *bori* ER *bori* 'bride, daughter-in-law'
wife n. *rommadi* ER *romardi* 'married (adj.)'
wife n. *romni, rummi* ER *romni* 'Romani woman, wife'
wild adj. *divya* ER *divjo* 'wild'
wind n. *barval, bavval, bavvalo, bevval* ER *balval* 'wind'
windmill n. *bavvalpoggermengri* ER *balval; phager-* 'wind'; 'break'
window n. *dikkinev, dikkinevs* ER *dikh-; xev* 'see'; 'hole'
window n. *duddev* ER *xev; dud* 'hole'; 'light'
window n. *ebs, ev, evya, hev, kow* ER *xev* 'hole'
window n. *gleyta* ER *glayzer* Cant 'glass window'
window n. *yusa* ER *užo* 'clean (adj.)'
windy adj. *bavlo* ER *balval* 'wind'
windy adj. *boot bavvelo* ER *balval; but* 'wind'; 'much, many'
wine n. *mol, mool, mor, mowl, mul* ER *mol* 'wine'
wine n. *peev* ER *piv* 'drink (1sg.)'
winter n. *iven, ivent, ven, vend, wen* ER *ivend* 'winter'
winter n. *shillalo, shillo* ER *šilelo* 'cold'
witch n. *bad bokri* ER *baxt* 'luck'
witch n. *chivvia, chovvikanon, chowvahawn, chuvvionni* ER *čovexani* 'witch'
witch n. *muller* ER *mulo* 'dead'
with God n. *develessa* ER *develesa* 'God (instr.)'
with me pr. *mansa* ER *mansa* 'I (instr.)'
without prep. *chitchi* ER *či(či)* 'nothing'
wizard n. *chuvvionna* ER *čovexani* 'witch'
woman n. *byuwa* English slang *buer* 'woman '
woman n. *duvvel, juvel, juvvel* ER *džuvel* 'woman'
woman n. *filli* English slang *filly* 'woman/girl'
woman n. *mannashi, mannishi, monnasha, monnisha, monnishi, monnishin,*
   monnishna, monnishni, monnush, munnishi, mushi ER *manušni* 'woman'
woman n. *rakli* ER *rakli* 'girl '
woman n. *rawni* ER *rani* 'lady'
woman n. *rommi, romni* ER *romni* 'Romani woman, wife'
woman who looks like a man n. *mush-rakli* ER *murš; rakli* 'man'; 'girl'
wood n. *hasht, kash, kosh, kosht* ER *kašt* 'wood'
wood n. *vesh, vesht, wesh* ER *veš* 'wood, forest'
wood n. *yog* ER *jag* 'fire'
word n. *lab, lav* ER *lav* 'word'
work n. *buti, butsi, butti* ER *buti* 'work'
work n. *mongi* ER *mang-* 'beg, ask, demand'
work n. *shafraben* ER *šafreben* 'work'
worm n. *chik chani* ER *čhik; čermo, kermo, kirmo* 'mud, dirt, earth';
   'worm'
write v. *chinnamengri* ER *čhin-* 'cut'

write v. *gin* ER *gin-* 'count'
wrong adj. *banglo* ER *bango* 'crooked'
wrong adj. *bango* ER *bango* 'crooked'
wrong adj. *fashna* Sinti *falš* German *falsch* 'wrong'
wrong adj. *nash* ER *nasvalo* 'sick'; 'ill'

year n. *besh, besht, baersh, bersh* ER *beš-* 'sit'
yellow adj. *gelbera, gelbi* ER *galbeno* 'yellow'
yes n. *auli, auwaley, ava, avaley, avali, avva, awal, awwa, hauley, onaula, ovva*
    ER *ava, aua* 'yes'
yesterday n. *arati* ER *rati* 'night'
yesterday n. *kolliko* ER *kaliko(s)* 'yesterday'
yesterday n. *wavver divvus* ER *dives; vaver* 'day'; 'other'
Yorkshire n. *guiallameskrapen* ER *goj; xal* 'sausage'; 'eat (3sg.)'
you pr. *toot, tot, tut* ER *tut* 'you (obl.)'
you pr. *totti, tuti, tutti* ER *tute* 'you (loc.)'
you pr. *tu* ER *tu* 'you'
you say v. *pennes* ER *phenes* 'say (2sg.)'
young adj. *tarna, tarno, torno* ER *terno* 'young'
yourself pr. *kukkeri, kukri, yer kukra* ER *korkořo* 'alone'

Appendix II Predecessor expressions by origin

1 Romani predecessor expressions

ačh-	'stay'
adala	'these'
akaj	'here'
akana	'now'
akhor	'nut'
ambrol	'pear'
andre	'in'
anglal	'in front, before'
angrusti	'ring'
angušt	'finger'
apre	'on'
av-	'come'
ava, aua	'yes'
avri, avral	'out, outside'
baj	'sleeve'
bakro	'sheep'
bal	'hair'
balevas	'bacon'
balo	'pig'
balval	'wind'
bango	'crooked'
bar	'hedge, garden'
bar	'stone, rock'
barba	'beard'
bareder	'bigger'
baro	'big'
barvalo	'rich'
bašav-	'to play an instrument'
basavo, etc.	'bad'

bašno	'cockerel'
baxt	'luck'
baxtalo	'lucky'
beng	'devil'
berand	'tent pole'
bero	'ship, boat'
beš-	'sit'
bibaxt	'without luck'
bibi	'aunt'
bičh(ar)-	'send'
bikin-	'sell'
bilačho	'bad'
biš	'twenty'
bištaduj	'twenty-two'
bistar-	'forget'
bišthajekh	'twenty-one'
bobo	'bean'
bokh	'hunger'
bokhalo	'hungry'
bold-	'baptise'
bori	'bride, daughter-in-law'
bov	'oven'
brek	'breast'
brišind	'rain'
buko	'liver'
bul	'buttocks, bottom'
but	'much, many'
buti	'work'
buzno	'goat'
čačo	'right, true'
čajo	'tea'
čalado	'family'
čang	'knee'
čar	'grass'
čaro	'bowl, plate'
čeri	'sky'
čhaj	'girl'
čhavo	'boy'
čhib	'tongue, language'
čhik	'mud, dirt, earth'
čhikelo	'dirty'
čhin-	'cut'
čhinger-	'quarrel, shout'

čhiv-	'put'
čhon	'moon'
čhoro	'poor'
čhuri	'knife'
či(či)	'nothing'
čirikli	'bird'
čiros	'time'
čomoni	'something'
čor	'thief'
čor-	'steal'
čovexani	'witch'
coxa	'skirt'
cukro	'sugar'
čumer-	'kiss'
čumi	'kiss'
dad	'father'
daj	'mother'
dand	'tooth'
dandar-	'bite'
dar	'fear'
del	'give (3sg.)'
deš	'ten'
deštaduj	'twelve'
deštaefta	'seventeen'
deštaenja	'nineteen'
deštajekh	'eleven'
deštajoxto	'eighteen'
deštapandž	'fifteen'
deštaštar	'fourteen'
deštatrin	'thirteen'
devel	'God'
devlesa	'God (instr.)'
dikh-	'see'
diklo	'(hand)kerchief, shawl'
dinilo	'fool'
dives	'day'
divjo	'wild'
dokrapen, etc.	'fortune-telling'
dorjav, derjav	'sea, river'
dosta	'enough'
drab	'medicine'
drom	'way, road'
dud	'light'

duj	'two'
dukh	'pain'
dumo	'back'
dur	'far'
dža-	'go'
džan-	'know'
dži	'soul, heart, belly'
džin-	'know'
dživ-	'live'
džukel	'dog'
džungado	'awake'
džungalo	'ugly'
džuv	'louse'
džuvel	'woman'
efta	'seven'
enja	'nine'
foro(s)	'town, fair, market'
ful	'excrement'
gad	'shirt'
gadžo	'non-Gypsy'
garav-	'hide'
gav	'village'
gil(av)-	'sing'
gili	'song'
giv	'wheat'
godi	'mind, brain'
goj	'sausage'
gono	'bag, sack'
goro	'man'
graj	'horse'
grasni	'mare'
gudlo	'sweet, sugar'
guruv	'bull'
guruvni	'cow'
heroj	'leg'
holova	'trousers'
idža	'clothes'
iv	'snow'
ivend	'winter'

jag	'fire'
jakh	'eye'
jaro	'egg'
jekh	'one'
joj	'she'
jov	'he'
ka, ke, ki	'to, at'
kaj	'where, which'
kakaraška	'magpie'
kakavi	'kettle'
kako	'uncle'
Kalderaš	'coppersmiths, kettle-makers (name of group)'
kaliko(s)	'yesterday'
kalo	'black'
kam-	'love, want'
kamni	'pregnant'
kan	'ear'
kangli	'comb'
kapa	'blanket'
kar	'penis'
karfin	'nail'
karfiol	'cauliflower'
kašt	'wood'
kaxni	'hen'
kek	'not'
ker-	'make, do'
kerlo	'throat'
kermuso	'mouse, rat'
kham	'sun'
khan(d)-	'smell'
khangeri	'church'
khas	'hay'
khel-	'dance, play'
kher	'house'
khil	'butter'
khino	'tired'
khoro	'jug'
khos-	'wipe'
kici	'how many'
kin-	'buy'
kiral	'cheese'
kirčima	'pub'

kisi	'purse'
klisin	'key'
klisto	'riding'
kokalo	'bone'
kon	'who'
korkořo	'alone'
kořo	'blind'
košnica	'basket'
kova	'thing'
kovlo	'soft'
kralis	'king'
kuč	'dear'
kur-	'beat up'
kurko	'week, Sunday'
lač-	'find'
lačho	'good'
ladž-	'be ashamed'
lake	'she (dat.)'
late	'she (loc.)'
lav	'word'
lel	'take (3sg.)'
lende	'they (loc.)'
lenge	'they (dat.)'
les	'he (obl.)'
leske	'he (dat.)'
liger-, irigr-, igar-	'carry'
lil	'letter, book'
liš	'shock'
lod-	'to settle, to be unloaded, to lodge'
lolo	'red'
lon	'salt'
lošano	'glad, joyful'
love	'money'
lovina	'beer'
lubni	'prostitute'
luludži	'flower'
lurr-, lur-	'rob'
ma	'not, don't'
mačho	'fish'
mačka	'cat'
man	'I (obl.)'
mande	'I (loc.)'

mang-	'beg, ask, demand'
mange	'I (dat.)'
mangipen	'begging'
mansa	'I (instr.)'
manušni	'woman'
mar-	'hit'
mařikli	'cake'
maro	'bread'
mas	'meat'
maškar	'middle'
mato	'drunk'
maxado	'dirty, defiled'
me	'I'
men	'neck'
mer-	'die'
mesali	'towel, scarf'
midžax	'bad, wicked, wrong'
mija	'thousand'
mindž	'vagina'
miro	'my'
misali	'table'
mišto	'good, well'
mol	'wine'
molivi	'lead'
momeli	'candle'
moxto	'box, chest'
muj	'face, mouth'
mujeskero	'policeman'
muk-	'let, allow'
mulo	'dead'
murš	'man'
musi	'arm'
muter	'urine'
muter-	'urinate'
na	'no, not'
nakh	'nose'
nango	'naked'
naš-	'run (away), escape'
našar-	'lose'
nasvalo	'sick, ill'
nav	'name'
nevo	'new'
nilaj	'summer'

odova	'that'
ora	'hour'
oxto	'eight'
pača-	'believe'
pala(l)	'behind'
pale	'back, backwards, again'
palpale	'back, backwards'
pandž	'five'
pani	'water'
papin	'goose, duck'
papiro	'paper'
paramiči	'story'
pariker-	'thank'
parno	'white'
paš	'half'
paša(l)	'nearby'
patrin	'leaf'
pek-	'roast, bake'
pelengro grai	'stallion'
peř	'belly, stomach'
per-	'fall'
perdal	'through, across, over'
petalo	'horseshoe'
phabaj	'apple'
phabar-	'burn'
phager-	'break'
phandar-	'close, lock'
pharo	'heavy'
phen	'sister'
phen-	'say'
pherdo	'full'
phiko	'shoulder'
phir-	'walk'
phivli	'widow'
phral	'brother'
phuč-	'ask'
phuker-	'tell'
phurano	'old'
phurd	'bridge'
phurd-	'blow'
phuridaj	'grandmother'
phuro	'old'
phus	'straw'

phuv	'ground, earth'
pi-	'drink'
piben, pi-	'drink'
piri	'pot, pan'
piro	'foot'
pišom	'flea'
podo	'floor'
por	'feather'
poski, posita	'pocket'
poxtan	'linen'
prast(er)-	'run'
praxo-	'bury'
purum	'onion'
puška	'gun'
puter-	'open'
raca, reca, reč(k)a	'duck'
raj	'gentleman, lord'
raker-	'speak'
rakh-	'guard'
rakli	'girl'
raklo	'boy'
ran(ik)	'stick, twig, branch'
randž-	'dress, undress'
rani	'lady'
rankano	'beautiful'
rašaj	'priest'
rat	'blood'
ratavel	'bleed (3sg.)'
rati	'night'
raxami, rexami	'coat'
rig	'side'
rod-	'search'
řoj	'spoon'
rom	'autonym, man, husband'
romanes	'in the Gypsy way, the Gypsy language'
romani	'Gypsy'
romardi	'married'
romer-	'marry'
romni	'Romani woman, wife'
rov-	'cry'
rukh	'tree'
rup	'silver'

rupikano	'silver (adj.)'
rušto	'angry'
ruža	'rose'
sa	'all'
san	'to be (2sg.)'
sap	'snake'
sapuj, sapuni, saponi	'soap'
sar	'how'
saranda	'forty'
sasto	'healthy'
sastri	'iron'
sastro	'father-in-law'
sasuj	'mother-in-law'
sav	'laugh (1sg.)'
savo	'what, who, which'
šax	'cabbage'
šel	'hundred'
šero	'head'
si	'to be (3sg.)'
sigo	'fast, soon'
sik(ar)-	'show, teach'
šil	'cold'
siv-	'sew'
skamin	'chair'
sme(n)tana	'cream'
so	'what'
som	'I am'
sonakaj	'gold'
šošoj	'hare'
šov	'six'
sov-	'sleep'
šovardeš	'sixty'
sovel	'swear (3sg.)'
sovexer-, sovaho-	'swear (an oath)'
stadi(k)	'hat'
stanja	'barn, stable'
štar	'four'
staripen	'prison'
šukar	'beautiful'
šuklo	'sour'
šun-	'hear'
sung	'smell'
suto	'sleeping, asleep'

taj	'and'
tajsarla	'morning'
tamlo	'dark'
tang(o), tanko	'narrow, tight, constricted'
tasarla	'morning'
tato	'warm, hot'
tele	'down'
terno	'young'
than	'place'
thav	'thread'
them	'country, land'
thil-	'hold'
thov-	'put'
thov-	'wash'
thud	'milk'
thukalo	'friendly'
thulo	'thick, fat'
thuv	'smoke'
thuv[(j)ar]-	'smoke'
thuvalo	'tobacco'
tikno	'small'
tirax	'shoe, boot'
tover	'axe'
traš-	'frighten, fear'
trianda	'thirty'
trin	'three'
trupo	'body'
truš	'thirst'
trušalo	'thirsty'
trušul	'cross, trident'
tu	'you'
tut	'you (obl.)'
tute	'you (loc.)'
upre	'up, on'
urado	'dressed (adj.)'
užo	'clean'
valgora, agora	'fair, market'
valin	'glass, glass (material), bottle, window'
vangar	'coal'
vangrusti	'ring'
varo	'flour'
vast	'hand, arm'

vaver	'other'
vel	'come'
veri, veriga	'chain'
veš	'wood, forest'
vodros	'bed'
vordon	'cart, wagon'
vraker-	'speak'
vudar	'door'

xaben	'food'
xač(ar)-	'burn'
xajera, xajri, xajro, hal'ris, paš	'penny, half'
xal	'eat (3sg.)'
xalo	'non-Gypsy'
xev	'hole'
xind-	'defecate'
xindo	'lousy, shitty, bad'
xoli	'anger'
xox-	'lie'
xoxavipen	'lie'

zeleno, zelano	'green'
zi	'heart, soul'
zumi	'soup'

2 English expressions

babby	'baby'
bastard	'bastard'
brogue	'trousers'
brov	'broth (soup)'
buer	'woman'
cherubim	'angels'
chubby	'chubby'
churn	'churn'
filly	'woman/girl'
folk	'people'
funky	'smelly'
gaga	'crazy'
gammy	'injured, painful, infected'
hark	'listen'
hermaphrodite	'hermaphrodite'
long	'long'

rammel	'rubbish'
smother	'smother'
squirt	'squirt'
stall	'stall'
strides	'trousers'
ugly	'ugly'
victuals	'food'
wide-o	'pretender'

3 Shelta and Cant expressions

bitti (Cant)	'little'
daddus (Cant)	'father'
fams, fambles (Cant)	'hands'
fawni (Shelta)	'ring'
ganzi (Shelta)	'frock'
glayzer (Cant)	'glass window'
grawni (Shelta)	'ring'
jeer (Cant)	'bottom (anatomy)'
jigger (Cant)	'door, gate'
jotto (Cant)	'monkey'
kasum (Cant)	'cheese'
ken (Cant)	'house'
mammus (Cant)	'mother'
mumper (Cant)	'beggar'
niks (Cant)	'no, nothing, not'
skran (Cant)	'food'
skreev (Cant)	'car'
stigga (Cant)	'gate, fence'

4 Other sources

bitti (French *petit*)	'little'
boutique (French)	'shop'
celta (German *Zelt*)	'tent'
chanter (French)	'sing'
falš (German *falsch*)	'wrong'
fojl- (German *faul*)	'rot'
goylem (Yiddish)	'fool'
granša (French *grange*)	'stable'
kinego (German *König*)	'king'
lang (German)	'long'

mille (French)	'thousand'
niglo (Sinte, German *Igel*)	'hedgehog'
penser (French)	'think'
ples- (German *Preis*)	'pay'
schwegel (German)	'pipe, flute'
šifa (German *Schiff*)	'ship'
štif (German *stief*)	'step- (relation by marriage)'
vater- (German *warten*)	'watch, look'

References

A. R. S. A. 1888. A Spanish Gypsy vocabulary. *JGLS* 1: 177–8.

Ackerley, F. G. 1929. Basque Romani. *JGLS*, third series, 8: 50–94.

Acton, T. ed. 2000. *Scholarship and the Gypsy struggle: commitment in Romani studies.* Hatfield: University of Hertfordshire Press.

Acton, T. and Davies, G. 1979. Educational policy and language use among English Romanies and Irish Travellers (Tinkers) in England and Wales. *International Journal of the Sociology of Language* 19: 91–110.

Acton, T. and Kenrick, D. eds. 1984. *Romani rokkeripen to-divvus.* London: Romanestan.

Althaus, H. P., Wiegand, H. E. and Henne, H. eds. 1980. *Lexikon der germanistischen Linguistik.* Tübingen: Niemeyer.

Ambrosch, G., Halwachs, D. and Schrammel, B., eds. 2005. *General and applied Romani linguistics.* Munich: Lincom Europa.

Arends, J., Muysken, P. and Smith, N. eds. 1995. *Pidgins and creoles: an introduction.* Amsterdam: Benjamins.

Auer, P. 1984. *Bilingual conversation.* Amsterdam: Benjamins.

Avé-Lallemant, F. C. B. 1858–62. *Das deutsche Gaunertum.* Leipzig, Munich and Berlin: Müller Buchdruckerei.

Baker, P. 2002. *Polari: the lost language of gay men.* London: Routledge.

Bakker, P. 1991. Basque Romani: a preliminary grammatical sketch of a mixed language. In: Bakker and Cortiade (1991: 56–90).

Bakker, P. 1995. Notes on the genesis of Caló and other Iberian Para-Romani varieties. In: Matras (1995: 125–50).

Bakker, P. 1997. *A language of our own: the genesis of Michif, the mixed Cree–French language of the Canadian Métis.* New York: Oxford University Press.

Bakker, P. 1998. Para-Romani language versus secret languages: differences in origin, structure, and use. In: Matras (1999b: 69–96).

Bakker, P. 1999. The Northern branch of Romani: mixed and non-mixed varieties. In: Halwachs and Menz (1999: 172–209).

Bakker, P. 2000. The genesis of Angloromani. In: Acton (2000: 14–31).

Bakker, P. 2001. Romani and Turkish. In: Igla and Stolz (2001: 303–27).

Bakker, P. 2002. An early vocabulary of British Romani (1616): a linguistic analysis. *Romani Studies*, fifth series, 12 (2): 75–101.

Bakker, P. and Cortiade, M. eds. 1991. *In the margin of Romani: Gypsy languages in contact.* Amsterdam: Institute for General Linguistics.

Bakker, P. and Matras, Y. 1997. Introduction. In: Matras et al. (1997: vii–xxx).

Bakker, P. and Mous, M. 1994a. Introduction. In: Bakker and Mous (1999b: 1–11).

Bakker, P. and Mous, M. eds. 1994b. *Mixed languages: 15 case studies in language intertwining.* Amsterdam: IFOTT.

Bakker, P. and Muysken, P. 1995. Mixed languages and language intertwining. In: Arends et al. (1995: 41–52).

Bakker, P. and van der Voort, H. 1991. Para-Romani languages: an overview and some speculations on their genesis. In: Bakker and Cortiade (1991: 16–44).

Barthelemy, A. 1979. English Romany word book (extraits). *Etudes Tsiganes* 25 (2/3): 2–4.

Baudrimont, A. 1862. Vocabulaire de la langue des bohémiens habitant le pays basque français. *Actes de l'Académie Impériale des Sciences, Belles-Lettres et Arts de Bordeaux*, third series, 24: 81–112.

Binchy, A. 1993. The status and functions of Shelta. PhD thesis, University of Oxford.

Binchy, A. 1994. Travellers' language: a sociolinguistic perspective. In: McCann et al. (1999: 134–54).

Binchy, A. 2002. Travellers' use of Shelta. In: Kirk and Ó Baoill (2002: 11–17).

Boretzky, N. 1983. *Kreolsprachen, Substrate und Sprachwandel.* Wiesbaden: Harrassowitz.

Boretzky, N. 1985. Sind Zigeunersprachen Kreols? In: Boretzky et al. (1985: 43–70).

Boretzky, N. 1992. Romanisch-zigeunerischen Interferenz (zum Caló). In: Erfurt et al. (1992: 11–37).

Boretzky, N. 1998. Der Romani-Wortschatz in den Romani-Misch-Dialekten (Pararomani). In: Matras (1998b: 97–132).

Boretzky, N. 2007. The differentiation of the Romani dialects. *Sprachtypologie und Universalienforschung* 60: 314–36.

Boretzky, N. and Igla, B. 1994. Romani mixed dialects. In: Bakker and Mous, (1999b: 35–68).

Boretzky, N. and Igla, B. 2004. *Kommentierter Dialektatlas des Romani.* Wiesbaden: Harrassowitz.

Boretzky, N., Enninger, W. and Stolz, T. eds. 1985. *Akten des 1. Essener Kolloquiums über Kreolsprachen und Sprachkontakt.* Bochum: Brockmeyer.

Bright, R. 1818. *Travels from Vienna through Lower Hungary, with some remarks on the state of Vienna during the Congress, in the year 1814.* Edinburgh: Constable.

Buckler, S. 2007. *Fire in the dark: telling Gypsiness in North East England.* New York and Oxford: Berghahn.

Burridge, K. and Allen, K. 1998. The X-phemistic value of Romani in non-standard speech. In: Matras (1998b: 29–49).

Cortiade, M. 1991. Romani versus Para-Romani. In: Bakker and Cortiade (1991: 1–15).

Coughlan, T. 2001. *Now shoon the romano gillie: traditional verse in the high and low speech of the Gypsies of Britain.* Cardiff: University of Wales Press.

Croft, W. 2003. Mixed languages and acts of identity: an evolutionary approach. In: Matras and Bakker (2003: 41–72).

Crofton, H. 1907. Borde's Egipt Speche. *JGLS*, third series, 1 (2): 157–68.

Dawson, R. 2002. *The dialect of Derbyshire's traditional Travellers.* Self-published.

Dawson, R. 2006. *Rokkering, clacking and cracking: aspects of Romany and Traveller vocabulary.* Self-published.

De Goeje, M. J. 1903. *Mémoire sur les migrations des tsiganes à travers l'Asie*. Leiden: Brill.

De Luna, J. C. 1951. *Gitanos de la Bética*. Madrid: Efesa.

Derrington, C. and Kendall, S. 2004. *Gypsy Traveller students in secondary schools*. Stoke on Trent: Trentham Books.

Douglas, S. 2002. Travellers' Cant in Scotland. In: Kirk and Ó Baoill (2002: 125–37).

Eckert, P. 2008. Variation and the indexical field. *Journal of Sociolinguistics* 12: 453–76.

Efing, C. 2005. *Das Lützenhardter Jenisch*. Wiesbaden: Harrassowitz.

Ehrenborg, H. 1928. Djôs Per Andersson's vocabulary. *JGLS*, third series, 7: 11–30.

Elšík, V. 2000. Romani nominal paradigms: their structure, diversity, and development. In: Elšík and Matras (2000: 9–30).

Elšík, V., and Matras, Y. eds. 2000. *Grammatical relations in Romani: the noun phrase*. Amsterdam: Benjamins.

Elšík, V. and Matras, Y. 2006. *Markedness and language change: the Romani sample*. Berlin: Mouton.

Engebrigtsen, A. 2007. *Exploring Gypsiness: power, exchange and interdependence in a Transylvanian village*. New York and Oxford: Berghahn.

Erfurt, J., Jessing, B. and Perl, M. eds. 1992. *Prinzipien des Sprachwandels, I: Vorbereitung. Beiträge zum Leipziger Symposion Prinzipien des Sprachwandels 1991 an der Universität Leipzig*. Bochum: Brockmeyer.

Eriksen, T. H. 2007. Creolisation in anthropological theory and in Mauritius. In: Stewart, C., ed. *Creolization: history, ethnography, theory*. Walnut Creek, CA: Left Coast Press, 153–77.

Etzler, A. 1944. *Zigenarna och deras avkomlingar i Sverige*. Uppsala: Almqvist och Wiksell.

Evans, I. H. N. 1929. Gleanings from English Gypsies. *JGLS*, new series, 8 (3): 140–2.

Evans, S. 1999. *Stopping places: a Gypsy history of South London and Kent*. Hatfield: University of Hertfordshire Press.

Fowkes, R. A. 1977. Onomastic sophistication of the Gypsies of Wales. *Names* 25 (2): 78–87.

Francis, H. J. 1955. No. 747 , being the autobiography of a gypsy. Part II: vocabulary. *JGLS* 34: 83–108.

Friedman, V. A. and Dankoff, R. 1991. The earliest known text in Balkan (Rumelian) Romani: a passage from Evliya Celebis SeyÇhat-nÇme. *JGLS*, fifth series, 1: 1–20.

Gay-y-Blasco, P. 1999. *Gypsies in Madrid: sex, gender and the performance of identity*. Oxford: Berg.

Gay-y-Blasco, P. 2000. The politics of evangelism: hierarchy, masculinity and religious conversion among Gitanos. *Romani Studies* 10: 1–22.

Gilliat-Smith, B. J. 1915. A report on the Gypsy tribes of North East Bulgaria. *JGLS*, new series, 9: 1–54, 65–109.

Gmelch, G. and Gmelch, S. B. 1987. Commercial nomadism: occupation and mobility among Travellers in England and Wales. In: Rao (1987: 133–53).

Goffman, E. 1983. Felicity's condition. *American Journal of Sociology* 89: 1–53.

Golovko, E. V. 2003. Language contact and group identity: the role of 'folk' linguistic engineering. In: Matras and Bakker (2003: 177–207).

Golovko, E. V. and Vakhtin, N. 1990. Aleut in contact: the CIA enigma. *Acta Linguistica Hafniensia* 22: 97–125.

Gotti, M. 1999. *The language of thieves and vagabonds: 17th and 18th century Canting lexicography in England.* Tübingen: Niemeyer.

Grant, A. P. 1998. Romani words in non-standard British English and the development of Angloromani. In: Matras (1998b: 165–91).

Graur, A. 1934. Les mots tsiganes en roumain. *Bulletin Linguistique Romane* 2: 108–200.

Grellmann, H. M. 1783 [1787]. *Historischer Versuch über die Zigeuner, betreffend die Lebensart und Verfassung, Sitten und Schicksale dieses Volkes seit seiner Erscheinung in Europa und dessen Ursprung.* Göttingen: Dietrich.

Grenoble, L. A. and Whaley, L. J., eds. 1998. *Endangered languages: language loss and community response.* Cambridge: Cambridge University Press.

Griffiths, J. and Yates, D. E. 1934. Sanderson's vocabulary, part 4: Rommano-English vocabulary. *JGLS*, third series, 13: 8–14.

Groome, F. H. 1928. Groome's letters to Smart and Crofton. *JGLS*, third series, 7: 54–78.

Grosvenor, Lady Arthur. 1908. Whiter's Lingua Cinguariana. *JGLS*, new series, 2: 161–79.

Grosvenor, Lady Arthur. 1910. A pilgrim's progress. *JGLS*, new series, 3: 204–24.

Gumperz, J. 1981. *Discourse strategies.* Cambridge: Cambridge University Press.

Halwachs, D. W. and Menz, F. eds. 1999. *Die Sprache der Roma: Perspektiven der Romani-Forschung in Österreich im interdisziplinären und internationalen Kontext.* Klagenfurt: Drava.

Hancock, I. F. 1970. Is Anglo-Romanes a creole? *JGLS*, third series, 49: 41–4.

Hancock, I. F. 1984. Romani and Angloromani. In: Trudgill (1984: 367–83).

Hancock, I. F. 1992. The social and linguistic development of Scandoromani. In: Jahr (1992: 37–52).

Hancock, I. F. 2002. *We are the Romani people.* Hatfield: University of Hertfordshire Press.

Hancock, I. F. 2008. Mind the doors! The contribution of linguistics. Paper presented at the international conference 'All Change! Recent debates over the history and origin of the Roma/Gypsies/Travellers', University of Greenwich, June.

Hannerz, U. 1992. *Cultural complexity.* New York: Columbia University Press.

Hayward, J. 2003. *Gypsy Jib: a Romany dictionary.* Wenhaston: Holm Oak.

Helm, J. ed. 1967. *Essays on the verbal and visual arts.* Seattle: University of Washington Press.

Helzle-Drehwald, B. 2004. *Der Gitanismo im spanischen Argot.* Geneva: Librairie Droz.

Highfield, A. and Valdman, A. eds. 1981. *Historicity and variation in Creole studies.* Ann Arbor: Karoma.

Holm, J. 2000. *An introduction to pidgins and creoles.* Cambridge: Cambridge University Press.

Hopper, P. J. 1991. On some principles of grammaticization. In: Traugott and Heine (1991: 17–36).

Hopper, P. J. and Traugott, E. C. 2003. *Grammaticalization.* Cambridge: Cambridge University Press.

Horvath, J, and Wexler, P. eds. 1997. *Relexification in creole and non-creole languages, with special attention to Haitian Creole, Modern Hebrew, Romani, and Rumanian.* Wiesbaden: Harrassowitz.

Igla, B. and Stolz, T. eds. 2001. *Was ich noch sagen wollte: Festschrift für Norbert Boretzky.* Munich: Akademie.

Iversen, R. 1944. *Secret languages in Norway, 1: the Romany language in Norway.* Norsk Videnskaps-Akademi, II Filosofisk-Historisk Klasse 1944, part 3. Oslo: Norsk Videnskaps-Akademi.

Jahr, E. H. ed. 1992. *Language contact: theoretical and empirical studies.* Berlin: Mouton de Gruyter.

Jiménez, A. 1853. *Vocabulario del dialecto Jitano.* Seville: Imprenta del Conciliador.

Johansson, R. 1977. *Svensk Rommani.* Acta Academiae Regiae Gustavi Adolphi, 55. Uppsala: Lundquist.

Juilland, A. 1952a. Le vocabulaire argotique roumain d'origins tsigane. In: Juilland, (1952b: 151–81).

Juilland, A. ed. 1952b. *Cahiers Sextil Pușcariu I.* Rome: Dacia.

Karttunen, L. 1974. Presupposition and linguistic context. *Theoretical Linguistics* 1: 181–94.

Keenan, E. L. 1998. Two kinds of presupposition in natural language. In: Kasher, A., ed. *Pragmatics: critical concepts.* London: Routledge, 8–15.

Keesing, R. M. 1988. *Melanesian Pidgin and the Oceanic substrate.* Stanford: Stanford University Press.

Kenrick, D. 1979. Romani English. *International Journal of the Sociology of Language* 19: 79–88.

Kenrick, D. and Clark, C. 1999. *Moving on: the Gypsies and Travellers of Britain.* Hatfield: University of Hertfordshire Press.

Kirk, J. and Ó Baoill, D. P. eds. 2002. *Travellers and their language.* Belfast: Queen's University Belfast/Cló Ollscoil na Banríona.

Kluge, F. 1901. *Rotwelsch: Quellen und Wortschatz der Gaunersprache und der verwandten Geheimsprachen.* Strasburg: Karl Trübner.

Kluyver, A. 1910. Un glossaire tsigane du seizième siècle. *JGLS*, new series, 4: 131–42.

Kochanowski, V. 1994. *Parlons tsigane: histoire, culture et langue du peuple tsigane.* Paris: L'Harmattan.

Kotsinas, U. 1996. *Stockholm-slang: folkligt språk från 80-tal till 80-tal.* Stockholm: Norstedts.

Kouwenberg, S. and LaCharité, D. 2004. Echoes of Africa: reduplication in Caribbean Creole and Niger-Congo languages. *Journal of Pidgin and Creole Languages* 19: 285–331.

Kyuchukov, H. and Bakker, P. 1999. A note on Romani words in the gay slang of Istanbul. *Grazer Linguistische Studien* 51: 95–8.

Labov, W. 1981. Speech actions and reactions in personal narrative. In: Tannen (1981: 217–47).

Labov, W. and Waletzky, J. 1967. Narrative analysis. In: Helm (1967: 12–44).

Ladefoged, J. 1998. Romani elements in non-standard Scandinavian varieties. In: Matras (1998b: 133–61).

Ladstätter, O. and Tietze, A. 1994. *Die Abdal (Äynu) in Xinjiang.* Vienna: Verlag der Österreichischen Akademie der Wissenschaften.

Lefebvre, C. 1998. *Creole genesis and the acquisition of grammar: the case of Haitian Creole*. Cambridge: Cambridge University Press.

Leigh, K. 1998. Romani elements in present-day Caló. In: Matras (1998b: 243–82).

Lemon, A. 2000. *Between two fires: Gypsy performance and Romani memory from Pushkin to post-socialism*. Durham, NC: Duke University Press.

Leschber, C. 1995. Romani lexical items in colloquial Rumanian. In: Matras (1995: 151–76).

Levinson, S. C. 1983. *Pragmatics*. Cambridge: Cambridge University Press.

Lewis, G. 1950–5. The secret language of the Geygeli Yürüks. In: Velidi, Z. ed. 214–226.

Lindell, L. and Thorbjörnsson-Djerf, K. 2008. *Ordbok over svensk romani*. Stockholm: Podium.

Löffelad, P. and Ruoff, A. eds. 1997. *Syntax und Stilistik der Alltagssprache*. Tübingen: Niemeyer.

Marsden, W. 1785. Observations on the language of the people commonly called Gypsies. *Archeologica* 7: 382–6.

Marsh, A. R. N. 2008. 'No promised land': history, historiography and the origins of the Gypsies. PhD thesis, University of Greenwich.

Matras, Y. 1991. Zur Rekonstruktion des jüdisch-deutschen Wortschatzes in den Mundarten ehemaliger 'Judendörfer' in Südwestdeutschland. *Zeitschrift für Dialektologie und Linguistik* 58 (3): 267–93.

Matras, Y. ed. 1995. *Romani in contact: the history, structure and sociology of a language*. Amsterdam: Benjamins.

Matras, Y. 1997. Zur stilistischen Funktion der Sondersprache Lekoudesch in südwest-deutschen Erzählungen. [The stylistic function of the special language Lekoudesch in narratives in southwest German dialect]. In: Löffelad and Ruoff (1997: 97–106).

Matras, Y. 1998a. Deixis and deictic oppositions in discourse: evidence from Romani. *Journal of Pragmatics* 29 (4): 393–428.

Matras, Y. ed. 1998b. *The Romani element in non-standard speech*. Wiesbaden: Harrassowitz.

Matras, Y. 1999a. The speech of the Polska Roma: some highlighted features and their implications for Romani dialectology. *JGLS*, fifth series 9: 1–28.

Matras, Y. 1999b. Johann Rüdiger and the study of Romani in 18th century Germany. *JGLS*, fifth series 9: 89–116.

Matras, Y. 1999c. The state of present-day Domari in Jerusalem. *Mediterranean Language Review* 11: 1–58.

Matras, Y. 2002. *Romani: a linguistic introduction*. Cambridge. Cambridge University Press.

Matras, Y. 2003. Mixed languages: re-examining the structural prototype. In: Matras, Y. and Bakker (2003: 151–75).

Matras, Y. 2004. Romacilikanes: the Romani dialect of Parakalamos. *Romani Studies* 14: 59–109.

Matras, Y. 2005. The classification of Romani dialects: a geographic-historical per-spective. In: Ambrosch et al. (2005: 7–26).

Matras, Y. 2009. *Language contact*. Cambridge: Cambridge University Press.

Matras, Y. and Bakker, P. eds. 2003. *The mixed language debate: theoretical and empirical advances*. Berlin: Mouton de Gruyter.

Matras, Y., Bakker, P. and Kyuchukov, H. eds. 1997. *The typology and dialectology of Romani.* Amsterdam: Benjamins.

Matras, Y., Gardner, H., Jones, C. and Schulman, V. 2007. Angloromani: a different kind of language? *Anthropological Linguistics* 49 (2): 142–64.

McCann, M., Ó Síocháin, S. and Ruane, J. eds. 1994. *Irish Travellers: culture and ethnicity.* Belfast: Queen's University Belfast.

McConvell, P. and Meakins, F. 2005. Gurindji Kriol: a mixed language emerges from code-switching. *Australian Journal of Linguistics* 25: 9–30.

McGowan, A. 1996. *The Winchester Confessions 1615–1616.* South Chailley: Romany and Traveler Family History Society.

McLane, M. 1977. The Caló of Guadix: a surviving Romany lexicon. *Anthropological Linguistics* 19: 303–19.

McWhorter, J. H. 2000. *The missing Spanish creoles: recovering the birth of plantation contact languages.* Berkeley: University of California Press.

McWhorter, J. H. 2005. *Defining creole.* Oxford: Oxford University Press.

Meakins, F. 2007. Case marking in contact: the development and function of case morphology in Gurindji Kriol, an Australian mixed language. PhD dissertation, University of Melbourne.

Miklosich, F. 1872–80. *Über die Mundarten und Wanderungen der Zigeuner Europas X–XII.* Vienna: Karl Gerold's Sohn.

Miklosich, F. 1874–8. *Beiträge zur Kenntnis der Zigeunermundarten. I–IV.* Vienna: Karl Gerold's Sohn.

Miskow, J. and Brøndal, V. 1923. Sigøjnersprog i Danmark. *Danske studier* 20: 97–145.

Möhn, D. 1980. Sondersprachen. In: Althaus et al. (1980: 384–90).

Mous, M. 2003a. *The making of a mixed language: the case of Ma'a/Mbugu.* Amsterdam: Benjamins.

Mous, M. 2003b. The linguistic properties of lexical manipulation and its relevance for Ma'á. In: Matras and Bakker (2003: 209–35).

Muysken, P. 1981. Halfway between Quechua and Spanish: the case for relexification. In: Highfield and Valdman (1981: 52–78).

Muysken, P. 1997. Media Lengua. In: Thomason (1997b: 365–426).

Muysken, P. 2000. *Bilingual speech.* Cambridge: Cambridge University Press.

Myers-Scotton, C. 1998. A way to dusty death: the Matrix Language turnover hypothesis. In: Grenoble and Whaley (1998: 289–316).

Nahir, M. 1998. Micro language planning and the revival of Hebrew: a schematic framework. *Language in Society* 27: 335–57.

N. A. [no author]. 1912. Roberts's vocabulary. *JGLS*, new series, 5: 177, 92.

N. A. [no author]. 1925. Irvine's vocabulary. *JGLS*, third series, 4: 115–39.

N. A. [no author]. 1929. Anglo-Romani gleanings: from East Anglian Gypsies. *JGLS*, third series, 8: 105–34.

Ó Baoill, D. 1994. Travellers' Cant: language or register. In: McCann et al. (1994: 155–69).

O'Shannessy, C. 2005. Light Walpiri: a new language. *Australian Journal of Linguistics* 25: 31–57.

Okely, J. 1983. *The Traveller Gypsies.* Cambridge: Cambridge University Press.

Pistor, J. 1998. Berwick-upon-Tweed: Romani words in an English dialect. In: Matras (1998b: 231–42).

Pott, A. 1844–5. *Die Zigeuner in Europa und Asien: ethnographisch-linguistische Untersuchung vornehmlich ihrer Herkunft und Sprache.* Halle: Heynemann.

Prideaux, W. F. 1910. Major-General John Staples Harriott. *JGLS*, new series, 4: 1–20.

Quindalé, F. [= Francisco de Sales Mayo]. 1867. *El gitanismo.* Madrid: V. Suarez.

Rao, A. ed. 1987. *The other nomads: peripatetic minorities in cross-cultural perspective.* Cologne: Böhlau.

Rijkhoff, J. 1998. Bystander deixis. In: Matras (1998b: 51–67).

Román, M. 1995. El dialecto Gitano–Espanol, Calo: Análisis semántico del léxico conservado en la provincia de Valladolid. *Neuphilologische Mitteilungen* 96: 437–51.

Ruch, M. 1986. Zur Wissenschaftsgeschichte der deutschsprachigen 'Zigeuner-forschung' von den Anfängen bis 1900. PhD dissertation, Universität Freiburg.

Rüdiger, J. C. C. 1782 [reprint 1990]. *Von der Sprache und Herkunft der Zigeuner aus Indien.* In: *Neuester Zuwachs der teutschen, fremden und allgemeinen Sprachkunde in eigenen Aufsätzen, 1. Stück.* Leipzig, 37–84. Hamburg: Buske.

Russell, A. 1916. Bright's Anglo-Romani vocabulary. *JGLS*, new series, 9: 165–85.

Sampson, J. 1911. Jacob Bryant: being an analysis of his Angloromani vocabulary, with a discussion of the place and date of collection and an attempt to show that Bryant, not Rüdiger, was the earliest discoverer of the Indian origin of the Gypsies. *JGLS*, new series, 4: 162–94.

Sampson, J. 1923. On the origin and early migrations of the Gypsies. *JGLS*, third series, 2: 156–69.

Sampson, J. 1926a. Samuel Fox's *The dialect of the Derbyshire Gypsies. JGLS*, third series, 5: 62–94.

Sampson, J. 1926b [reprint 1968]. *The dialect of the Gypsies of Wales, being the older form of British Romani preserved in the speech of the clan of Abram Wood.* Oxford: Clarendon Press.

Sampson, J. 1930. An East Anglian Romani vocabulary of 1798. *JGLS*, third series, 9: 97–147.

Scott Macfie, R. A. and Winstedt, E. O. 1939. Goddard Johnson's vocabulary. *JGLS*, third series, 18: 1–18, 70–109.

Sechidou, I. 2000. A Greek variety of a mixed romani dialect. Paper presented at the Fifth International Conference on Romani Linguistics, Sofia, 14–17 September.

Siewert, K. ed. 1996. *Sondersprachenforschung: Rotwelschdialekte.* Wiesbaden: Harrassowitz.

Simson, W. 1866. *A history of the Gipsies: with specimens of the Gipsy language.* London: Sampson, Low, Son and Marston.

Smart, B. C. 1862. *The dialect of the English Gypsies: appendix to the Transactions of the Philological Society,* 3–87.

Smart, B. C. and Crofton, H. T. 1875. *The dialect of the English Gypsies.* London: Asher.

Smart, H. and Crofton, B. T. 1913. *English Gypsy vocabulary, or index to the principal words and roots in the Gypsy vocabulary and its appendix.* London: Gypsy and Folk-Lore Club.

Smith, N. 1995. An annotated list of creoles, pidgins, and mixed languages. In: Arends et al. (1995: 331–74).

Sobell, R. 1999. Chavva talk: young people's Romani slang in Hexham. BA dissertation, University of Manchester.

Spears, A. K. and Winford, D. eds. 1997. *The structure and status of pidgins and creoles*. Amsterdam: Benjamins.

Stewart, M. 1995. *The time of the Gypsies*. Boulder, CO: Westview Press.

Tannen, D. ed. 1981. *Analyzing discourse: text and talk*. Georgetown University Round Table on languages and linguistics. Washington, DC: Georgetown University Press.

Thomason, S. G. 1995. Language mixture: ordinary processes, extraordinary results. In: Silva-Corvalán, C., ed. *Spanish in four continents: studies in language contact and bilingualism*. Washington, DC: Georgetown University Press, 15–33.

Thomason, S. G. 1997a. A typology of contact languages. In: Spears Winford (1997: 71–88).

Thomason, S. G. ed. 1997b. *Contact languages*. Amsterdam: Benjamins.

Thomason, S. G. 1999. Speakers' choices in language change. *Studies in the Linguistic Sciences* 29: 19–43.

Thomason, S. G. 2001. *Language contact: an introduction*. Edinburgh: Edinburgh University Press.

Thomason, S. G. and Kaufman, T. 1988. *Language contact, creolization, and genetic linguistics*. Berkely: University of California Press.

Tipler, D. 1957. Specimens of modern Welsh Romani. *JGLS*, third series, 36: 9–24.

Torrione, M. 1987. *Diccionario caló-castellano de don Luis Usoz y Rio: un manuscrito del siglo XIX*. Perpignan: Université de Perpignan, Publications du Centre de Recherches Ibériques et Latino-Américaines, 1.

Traugott, E. C. and Heine, B. eds. 1991. *Approaches to grammaticalization, I*. Amsterdam: Benjamins.

Trudgill, P. ed. 1984. *Language in the British Isles*. Cambridge: Cambridge University Press.

Turner, R. L. 1926. The position of Romani in Indo-Aryan. *JGLS*, third series, 5: 145–89.

Turner, R. L. 1932. So-called prothetic V- and Y- in European Romani. *JGLS*, third series, 11: 115–20.

Vakhtin, N. 1998. Copper Island Aleut: a case of language 'resurrection'. In: Grenoble and Whaley (1998: 317–27).

van den Eijnde, A. 1991. Romani vocabulary in Swedish slang. In: Bakker and Cortiade (1991: 185–192).

Velidi, Z. ed. 1950–5. *Symbolae in Honorem Z. V. Togan*. Istanbul: Maarif Basimevi.

Ward, H. G. 1936. Romani words in Swedish slang. *JGLS*, third series, 15: 78–85.

Wexler, P. 1997. The case for the relexification hypothesis in Romani. In: Horvath and Wexler (1997: 100–61).

Willems, W. 1997. *In search of the true Gypsy: from enlightenment to final solution*. London: Frank Cass.

Williams, P. 1991. Le miracle et la nécessité: à propos du developpement du Pentecotisme chez les Tsiganes. *Archives de Sciences Sociales des Religions* 73: 81–98.

Windolph, W. 1998. *Nerother Jenisch*.Wiesbaden: Harrassowitz.

Winstedt, E. O. 1915. The Norwood Gypsies and their vocabulary. *JGLS*, new series, 9: 129–65.

Winstedt, E. O. 1948. Anglo-Romani gleanings from the northern counties. *JGLS*, third series, 27: 83–110.

Winstedt, E. O. 1949. Anglo-Romani gleanings from the northern counties. *JGLS*, third series, 28: 50–61.

Wolf, S. A. 1985. *Wörterbuch des Rotwelschen: Deutsche Gaunersprache.* Hamburg: Buske.

Author Index

Subject Index

Note: page numbers in *italics* denote tables or figures

Abdal peripatetics, 23, 39
ablative, 68, *72, 73*n3, 83
Aboriginal languages, 17–18, 27
abstract terms, 14, 36, 70, 83, 110
adjectives
  agreement, 74, 91–2, 118
  borrowed, 75
  comparatives, 46, 65, 75
  demonstrative, 112–13
  inflection, *74*
  superlatives, 46
Adriatic coast, 44, 48, 51, 52
adverbial clauses, 37
adverbial expressions, 69
adverbs, 35, 111, 112, 170
affixes, 22, 35–6, 45; *see also* prefixes; suffixes
affrication, 32, 50, *66*, 77, 85
Afghanistan, 38
Africa, North, 22
Africa, West, 15, 16
agentive derivation, 63, 104, 107, *108, 109*,
  125
agglutination, 34, 68
aktionsart, 46, 104
Albania, 49, 63
Aleut, 18, 19, 27, 130
anaphora, 113, 120
Anatolia, 35, 38, 39, 42
Angloromani, xi, xii, 1, 3
  authentic reconstruction effect, 97
  camouflage function, 139–40
  as code, xiv, 96, 139, 150
  as community language, 152–3, 164
  compounding, 62, 106–7, *108, 109*, 176–7
  conversational use, 131, 133, 141–2, 151–2
  as creole, 13
  data corpus, 95–9
  documentation of, 96n1, 130–1
  emblematic function, 174
  emotive content, 96, 134–5, 173, 175
  grammaticalisation, 175
  identity, 173
  and inflected Romani, 90, 157, 168–9

insiders/outsiders, 89, 96, 173
intertwined, 17, 150–1
lexicon, xi–xii, xiii, 86, *87*, 97–9, 102–3,
  122–9, 141–3, 145
as mixed language, 18–19, 111, 130–3,
  174–5
morphosyntax, 119–22
narration, 141–9
numerals, 103, 116, *117*, 123
old/new dialects, 59–60, 93
online dictionary, xiv
phonology, 99–102
Romani-derived insertions, 9, 11, 19–20,
  25–6, 93
as speech-act device, 133–42
as superstrate, 15
taboo topics, 137–8
and Welsh Romani, 86, 89–90
word choice, 135
word forms, *101–2*, 102–19
see also British Romani
Anglo-Romani (Sampson), 10
Angloromani speakers, 125, 133–4, 149–57
anti-Gypsy persecution, 41
Appleby fair, 134, 153–4
Arabic, 5, 8, 22
archaisms, 23, 53, 77, 88, 153, 168
Arli-type dialect, 49
Armenian, 35, 39
arrested matrix language turnover, 27
Asia, Central, 38, 39
aspectual constructions, 46, 120, 170; *see also*
  aktionsart
aspiration, 35, *66*, 67, 102, 156
associative-figurative derivation, 22, 104, 106,
  110
Atlantic creoles, 15
Australia, xii, 17–18, 27
Austria, 24, 48, 49, 52
Austria-Ukraine, 53
authentic reconstruction effect, 97
auxiliary verbs, 76, 92, 94, 120, 170–1
Äynu peripatetics, 23